Ben Ó Ceallaigh
Neoliberalism and Language Shift

Contributions to the Sociology of Language

Edited by
Ofelia García
Francis M. Hult

Founding editor
Joshua A. Fishman

Volume 115

Ben Ó Ceallaigh

Neoliberalism and Language Shift

—

Lessons from the Republic of Ireland Post-2008

ISBN 978-3-11-128149-0
e-ISBN (PDF) 978-3-11-076890-9
e-ISBN (EPUB) 978-3-11-076892-3
ISSN 1861-0676

Library of Congress Control Number: 2022938845

Bibliographic information published by the Deutsche Nationalbibliothek
The Deutsche Nationalbibliothek lists this publication in the Deutsche Nationalbibliografie;
detailed bibliographic data are available on the internet at http://dnb.dnb.de.

© 2023 Walter de Gruyter GmbH, Berlin/Boston
This volume is text- and page-identical with the hardback published in 2023.
Cover image: sculpies/shutterstock
Typesetting: Integra Software Services Pvt. Ltd.
Printing and binding: CPI books GmbH, Leck

www.degruyter.com

Contents

List of figures —— IX

List of tables —— XI

Abbreviations —— XIII

Part 1: Foundations

1   **Introduction** —— 3
1.1   Language loss and macro-level social change —— 3
1.2   Book structure —— 5
1.3   Methodology —— 8
1.3.1   My personal background in the Gaeltacht —— 8
1.3.2   Methodological overview: Changing conceptions of LPP —— 9
1.3.3   Research sites and participants —— 11
1.3.4   Analysis of policy documents and quantitative data —— 16

2   **Irish, Ireland, neoliberalism: Some background** —— 18
2.1   Introduction —— 18
2.2   Irish-English language shift: A historical overview —— 18
2.3   Early state policy and the institutionalisation of the Gaeltacht —— 21
2.4   State withdrawal from the revitalisation project —— 24
2.5   Language policy during the Celtic Tiger —— 30
2.6   Neoliberalism: The emergence of a global hegemony —— 33
2.7   The Great Recession —— 37
2.8   Economic development in the Republic of Ireland – peaks and troughs over recent decades —— 38

Part 2: Overt and covert Irish-language policy post-2008

3   **Official Irish-language policy post-2008** —— 43
3.1   Introduction —— 43
3.2   *An Bord Snip Nua:* The special group on public service numbers and expenditure programmes —— 44

3.3	The *20-year strategy for the Irish Language 2010–2030* —— 47
3.4	The *Gaeltacht Act 2012* —— 50
3.5	Conclusion —— 60

4 **Irish-language institutions: Covert policy and state retrenchment —— 62**
4.1	Introduction —— 62
4.2	Údarás na Gaeltachta —— 63
4.3	The department of state responsible for the Gaeltacht —— 69
4.4	Foras na Gaeilge's New Funding Model —— 71
4.5	Controversy surrounding the publication of the *Nuashonrú ar an Staidéar Cuimsitheach Teangeolaíoch ar úsáid na Gaeilge sa Ghaeltacht: 2006–2011* —— 75
4.6	Conclusion —— 77

5 **Austerity and Irish-language media —— 79**
5.1	Introduction —— 79
5.2	Raidió na Gaeltachta —— 79
5.3	TG4 —— 83
5.4	Print media —— 89
5.5	Conclusion —— 93

6 **Neoliberalism and language policy in public and private spheres: Structural impediments —— 95**
6.1	Introduction —— 95
6.2	New Public Management: Irish in the public service —— 95
6.3	Policy making under austerity —— 106
6.4	Neoliberalism and the formation of social attitudes —— 110
6.5	Conclusion —— 112

Part 3: Neoliberalism and the Gaeltacht – an ethnographic study

7 **Quantitative background to Part 3 —— 117**
7.1	Introduction —— 117
7.2	Quantitative background —— 118
7.2.1	Demographic change 2006–2016 —— 118
7.2.2	Irish-speaking demographics 2006–2016 —— 120
7.2.3	Social class in the Gaeltacht —— 122

8	**Effects of the post-2008 crisis on the Gaeltacht labour market —— 125**
8.1	Construction —— 125
8.2	Deindustrialisation —— 127
8.3	The hospitality industry —— 131
8.4	Criticisms of the Foreign Direct Investment model —— 133
8.5	Further implications of the decline in employment opportunities —— 140
8.5.1	Summer work for students —— 140
8.5.2	Community pride —— 141
8.6	Conclusion —— 142

9	**Migration —— 144**
9.1	Introduction —— 144
9.2	Out-migration —— 144
9.2.1	Education and out-migration —— 150
9.3	In-migration —— 152
9.4	Conclusion —— 155

10	**Tourism and the Gaeltacht post-2008: Uneasy bedfellows —— 158**
10.1	Introduction —— 158
10.2	Tourism in Galway —— 161
10.3	Tourism in Donegal —— 164
10.4	Linguistic tourism —— 167
10.4.1	Summer language schools —— 167
10.5	The linguistic landscape – shifting terrain —— 171
10.6	Conclusion —— 175

11	**Community responses to austerity —— 177**
11.1	Introduction: Organised opposition to state policies —— 177
11.2	Guth na Gaeltachta —— 179
11.3	Dearg le Fearg —— 183
11.4	Reform of island transport links —— 187
11.4.1	The Oileáin Árann air service —— 187
11.4.2	The Toraigh ferry service —— 190
11.5	"Corporate Social Responsibility" and the Gaeltacht – fighting neoliberalism with neoliberalism? —— 191
11.6	Conclusion —— 193

12 Cuts to other community projects — 195
- 12.1 Community co-operatives — 195
- 12.2 Pléaráca — 198
- 12.3 Conclusion — 202

13 Further observations on language use — 204
- 13.1 Introduction — 204
- 13.2 Language practices of young people: A family vignette — 205
- 13.3 Additional explanations of language shift — 208
  - 13.3.1 Information and communications technology — 208
  - 13.3.2 Irish-language competence of young people — 213
  - 13.3.3 Reconstruction of youth identities — 215
- 13.4 Conclusion — 217

Part 4: Conclusion

14 Summary and conclusion — 223
- 14.1 Introduction — 223
- 14.2 Summary of findings — 223
- 14.3 International comparisons: Scottish Gaelic and Welsh — 229
- 14.4 The loss of the Gaeltacht and the threat of further recessions — 232
- 14.5 The Covid pandemic — 233
- 14.6 Conclusion: Language revitalisation in a time of crises — 236

Bibliography — 239

Index — 285

List of figures

Figure 1 Map of Ireland and the Gaeltacht —— 12
Figure 2 "English must be spoken at all times" – memo sent to staff in a factory in the Donegal Gaeltacht, 2021 —— 136
Figure 3 *"Ár nEisimircigh Ionúin"* – the emigrants' corner in a Donegal pub —— 147
Figure 4 A hotel in Galway, photographed first in 2015 and then again in 2016 —— 171
Figure 5 A restaurant in Galway, bilingual in 2012 but English only in 2014 —— 172
Figure 6 An official sign modified to include English —— 174

List of tables

Table 1 Comparison of enterprise promotion agencies' budgets 2008–2015 —— **63**
Table 2 Population change in the Galway Gaeltacht 2006–2016 —— **120**
Table 3 Population change in the Donegal Gaeltacht 2006–2016 —— **120**
Table 4 Daily speakers of Irish in the Gaeltacht 2006–2016 —— **121**
Table 5 Daily speakers of Irish on a national level 2006–2016 —— **121**

Abbreviations

FnaG	Foras na Gaeilge, the all-Ireland Irish-language promotion and funding body
IDA	Industrial Development Agency, the body responsible for attracting Foreign Direct Investment to the Republic of Ireland
IMF	International Monetary Fund
LPP	Language Planning and Policy
NPM	New Public Management
RnaG	Raidió na Gaeltachta, the only Irish-language radio station which is broadcast nationally on FM
RTÉ	Raidió Telefís Éireann, the state broadcaster
TG4	The television station which broadcasts mostly through Irish
ÚnaG	Údarás na Gaeltachta, the Gaeltacht development authority

Part 1: **Foundations**

1 Introduction

1.1 Language loss and macro-level social change

As many authors working in the area of language loss and endangerment have observed, the majority of the roughly 7,000 languages currently spoken are destined to be extinct by the end of the present century. Figures show that language shift has accelerated in recent decades and that the "terminal speakers" of more than half the world's languages are already alive (Harrison 2007).

In attempting to explain this enormous, unprecedented rate of loss, it has often been observed that language shift is an epiphenomenon of macro-level social change (e.g., Nettle and Romaine 2001; Mufwene 2017). With the early years of the 21st century being marked by "fundamental social transformation perhaps unmatched since industrialization" (Putnam and Goss 2002: 14), it is unsurprising that we face such an immense reduction in global linguistic diversity.

Endeavouring to get closer to the root of what drives such developments, statements linking language loss to economic forces are commonplace in Language Planning and Policy (LPP) literature. Grenoble and Whaley, for instance, state that economics "may be the single strongest force influencing the fate of endangered languages" (1998: 52) and Romaine, drawing on Ó Riagáin (1997), similarly notes that

> the power of state language policies to produce intended outcomes is severely constrained by a variety of social, political and economic structures which sociolinguists have typically not addressed, even though their consequences are profound and of far more importance than language policies.[1]   (Romaine 2006: 456)

Despite the frequency of comments about economic forces driving language shift, as Romaine notes, there have been very few attempts made at explaining how precisely this process occurs. In light of the immediacy of the challenges facing those committed to the maintenance of linguistic diversity, it is, however, appropriate that a detailed understanding of this fundamental link be developed. This book takes some steps towards filling this gap in our knowledge.

---

[1] Statements linking language minoritisation to economic forces can also be found in the following works, amongst many others: Baker 2011: 62; Crystal 2014: 175–176; Edwards 1984: 304; Euromosaic 1996: 7–11; Harbert 2011; Kaplan and Baldauf 1997: 280; McColl Millar 2005: 26; Nettle and Romaine 2000: 126–147; O'Rourke and Pujolar 2013: 54; Phillipson 2008; Skutnabb-Kangas 2000: 436–476; Tabouret-Keller 1968: 113; UNESCO n.d.; Williams 1991: 4.

In order to move beyond the high level of abstraction seen in much of the LPP literature which refers to economic factors, the consequences of the global economic crisis that began in 2008 for the Irish language, particularly in its heartland communities – collectively known as the "Gaeltacht" – are explored. A case study is thereby provided in how macro-level developments in the global economy can precipitate significant social – and sociolinguistic – change in endangered language communities. With the post-2008 "Great Recession" (Roche, O'Connell and Prothero 2017) ultimately being a crisis of neoliberalism – the present phase of capitalism – the analysis of neoliberal theory and policies makes up a key part of this work. This recession was the second most severe crisis in the history of industrial capitalism (Tooze 2018) and, as will be seen, it was particularly severe in the Republic of Ireland, where its consequences continue to shape society today. While Grin (1999) has discussed the implications of both regulated and deregulated market contexts for minoritised languages, this study documents a period of transition between these two poles, from a relatively heavily regulated language policy regime to a much more deregulated, neoliberal one in the years since 2008.

Through examining the interaction between macro- and micro-level developments, I offer a contribution to the study of social causality and the effects of economic structures on minoritised language communities and language revitalisation policy. In doing so, I demonstrate that even in a country in which the state is ostensibly committed to language revitalisation, language policies can be decisively shaped by macro-economic forces.

Although the concept of language shift has been problematised by some scholars (e.g., Heller and Duchêne 2007: 3), this work follows Potowski's definition of it being "the replacement of one language by another as the primary means of communication and socialization within a community" (2013: 321). By better understanding the causes of language shift, it is hoped that the path to reversing this process will become more evident (cf. Fishman 1991: 39), both for Irish and other threatened languages.

Despite having undergone centuries of minoritisation, Irish is constitutionally the first official language of the Republic of Ireland, the state which comprises some three-quarters of the landmass of the island of Ireland. This contrasts with the political situation in Northern Ireland (a contested term which refers to the north east of the island, which is still part of the United Kingdom), where the language is in a weaker position (Muller 2010; Walsh 2021: 336). This work focuses on the Republic of Ireland, being as that is where all of the official Gaeltacht is located and where the effects of the 2008 crash on language policy are most evident. Unless otherwise noted, figures given for speaker numbers, funding etc. refer to the Republic.

Constitutional primacy notwithstanding, Irish is categorised as "definitely endangered" by UNESCO (2018). According to the 2016 census, just 1.6% of the population speak Irish daily outside the education system – 73,803 out of a population of 4,757,956 (Central Statistics Office 2017a: 8, 66). After the foundation of the state in 1922, Irish enjoyed a level of institutional protection much greater than other similarly sized minoritised languages (see section 2.3). This support was particularly important for Gaeltacht communities, which are overwhelmingly located in poorer, peripheral areas. As will be demonstrated, however, the austerity measures which followed 2008 saw the strength of this support greatly weakened. Indeed, capital expenditure on Irish by 2017 was less than one seventh of what it had been in 2008 (see 4.2), despite the economy having returned to rapid growth by then.

1.2 Book structure

This book is divided into four parts. The first, "Foundations", consists of Chapters 1 and 2. This introductory chapter will proceed to outline the methodology used in this study – a combination of policy analysis, ethnographic participant observation, semi-structured interviews and reference to previously extant statistical data. Chapter 2 offers a brief history of Irish-English language shift and revitalisation measures pre-2008. It also discusses the nature of neoliberalism, recent developments in the economy of the Republic of Ireland and the socioeconomic consequences of the 2008 crash for the country.

In Part 2, consisting of Chapters 3 to 6, I discuss overt and covert Irish-language policy post-2008, drawing on concepts which are popular in public policy and political economy literature, but which have not been widely adopted by scholars in the field of LPP. The extreme rationalisation of the Irish-language sector during this time is detailed and many examples are given of the vastly disproportionate budgetary cuts language promotion schemes received. I argue that these cuts are reflective of neoliberalism's antipathy towards both redistributive economic policies and social planning, particularly with regards to "culturalist" endeavours such as minoritised language promotion, which are seen to be of little or no value to the interests of international capitalism.

As well as further examining the wider socio-political context in which language policy reforms were introduced, Chapter 3 considers the content and implementation of key policies such as the *20-Year Strategy for the Irish Language 2010–2030* and the *Gaeltacht Act 2012*. I contend that these amount to a withdrawal from the language revitalisation project on a scale not hitherto seen, with the 2008 crisis having punctuated the previous policy equilibrium and allowed for widespread rationalisation of Irish LPP. As such, these policies present an archetypal example of the type of state reform that is characteristic of neoliberalism. I continue this discussion in Chapters 4 and 5. Chapter 4 examines "covert" language policy by referring to the impact of austerity on various Irish-language promotion institutions such as *Údarás na Gaeltachta*, the Gaeltacht development organisation, and all-island funding body *Foras na Gaeilge*. In a similar vein, the effects of the cuts to Irish-language media funding are discussed in Chapter 5. I explain how reduced budgets resulted in both less new material being available in Irish and smaller audiences engaging with much of the material that was produced.

Chapter 6 elaborates on the idea that neoliberalism is in fundamental contradiction with many of the requirements of language revitalisation. I begin by arguing that "New Public Management" reforms in the Irish civil service were responsible for the failure of many language schemes in the wake of 2008, with the worsening of employment conditions for public servants leaving them with little time to focus on language promotion. This structural account serves as a counterpoint to the individualist explanations for the failure of Irish-language policies which are often heard in both popular and academic discourse, whereby the ineffective nature of language policies is seen to reflect the antipathy of "anti-Irish" public servants, rather than broader forces not related to language. I then explore some further ways in which neoliberalism limits the avenues open to policy makers and how economic instability can generate understandings of the world which are not conducive to valuing post-material causes such as language revitalisation. By opposing both social planning and policies for progressive wealth redistribution, neoliberalism conflicts with what are typically fundamental requirements of language revitalisation.

Part 3 of the book presents the findings of my ethnographic fieldwork, serving to illustrate the meso- and micro-level consequences of the macro-level policy developments previously discussed. The fieldwork for this study took place in the mid- and north-west of Ireland, in counties Galway and Donegal, which are home to the strongest remaining Irish-speaking areas – although even there the language was under severe pressure before the 2008 crash, as discussed in the following chapter.

Chapter 7 introduces Part 3 of the book by offering an overview of relevant census data from before and after 2008. In order the contextualise my ethnographic data, I look at demographic change, numbers of Irish speakers and issues related to social class and economic deprivation. Chapter 8 then proceeds to examine disruptions to the Gaeltacht labour market, particularly the sharp increase in unemployment and its consequences for the social vitality of the Gaeltacht. Chapter 9 follows with an examination of the widespread emigration that resulted from this increased unemployment, and the deleterious social and sociolinguistic implications thereof. The fraught nature of the tourist industry in the Gaeltacht and the anglicisation of the linguistic landscape during my fieldwork – itself seemingly a response to wider economic challenges – are discussed in Chapter 10.

Of course, Gaeltacht residents, like communities elsewhere, did not just acquiesce to their fate during the worst years of austerity. In Chapter 11 I detail community responses to the crisis, including various protest movements and, more unusually, attempts to overcome reduced state support via recourse to "corporate social responsibility" programmes. I also look at how the state reacted to resistance movements and, indeed, how it successfully suppressed the most significant of them.

Chapter 12 presents two case studies which are representative of wider patterns, examining the effects of austerity for some particularly important community institutions. Cuts to the funding of community development co-operatives and the closure of the *Pléaráca* arts and culture group are explored, with emphasis on the consequences of these disruptions for community and Irish-language vitality, as well as the way in which the state targeted publicly-funded groups which were seen to oppose it.

In Chapter 13 I examine some further factors which contributed to the 11.2% decrease in the number of daily Irish speakers in the Gaeltacht which was recorded in the 2016 census, including the increased use of information technology, reduced Irish-language competency of younger speakers and the breakdown of Irish as a distinctive identity marker. I also include some additional observations on the extent to which language shift was visible during my fieldwork and explore how these various issues relate to economic forces.

Part 4 concludes the book with a summary of my findings and some more general comments on the nature of language loss in a time of numerous intersectional political and environmental crises. While the long-term effects of the Covid pandemic and its attendant economic disruption remain unknown at the time of writing, I discuss some of the potential consequences, and give some examples of neoliberal austerity negatively affecting nearby minoritised language communities in Scotland and Wales.

1.3 Methodology

1.3.1 My personal background in the Gaeltacht

Although from the west of Ireland, I am not from the Gaeltacht and did not grow up speaking Irish. I am what has come to be known as a "new speaker" of the language (O'Rourke and Walsh 2020). Driven by a personal conviction regarding anti-colonial politics, I undertook to learn Irish to a high level of competence as a young adult and now use it regularly in my personal and professional life. I was able to reach fluency through receiving significant linguistic input both inside and outside of an institutional context. Key to my progress with the language, however, were the years I spent living in a Gaeltacht community called Mionloch in Galway. While this is one of the weakest Gaeltacht areas, during my time in Mionloch I was fortunate to live with a middle-aged native Irish speaker, Padhraic, who became a close friend. Padhraic has an above-average interest in the language and frequently attends language-focused and cultural events throughout the country, maintaining friendships with people throughout the Gaeltacht. I therefore had the opportunity to travel to various areas in the Gaeltacht and to develop a familiarity with communities where Irish is relatively strong. While living in Mionloch I did a Master's degree in Language Planning and Policy in *Acadamh na hOllscolaíochta Gaeilge,* the division of the National University of Ireland, Galway which runs third-level courses through the medium of Irish. This was a valuable experience which helped me make connections that would later become useful during the research of the PhD which this book is based on. Being involved with grassroots language activism prior to and during this study also helped me familiarise myself with the issues and communities which I discuss in this work. During my fieldwork, several people I met when studying in the Acadamh or through activist groups served as "key informants", people who helped with issues of access and clarification when needed (Bryman 2008: 409). While certainly not giving me the in-depth understanding of a Gaeltacht native, these years of experience nevertheless greatly facilitated my research, making it far easier for me to recruit informants, understand contexts, and, hopefully, to interpret data with a greater degree of insight than would otherwise have been the case. As McCarty reminds us, "sometimes the best research context is not far away or "exotic," but is one we already know something about" (2015: 84), something which I hope is true of this study.

1.3.2 Methodological overview: Changing conceptions of LPP

As stated above, this study adopted an ethnographic approach to data collection. While not having been traditionally favoured in LPP research, the use of ethnography has become increasingly popular over the last several decades as the discipline has distanced itself from the more "technocratic" measures that were associated with earlier scholarship (Hult and Johnson 2015: 1; King and Rombow 2012: 404–405). This move away from the traditional approach to LPP led to the emergence of two major developments in the field. Initially, what has been termed "critical language policy" was developed by scholars such as Tollefson (1991, 2006), who sought to emphasise the differential power relations that are ever present in matters of LPP. This research paradigm "eschews apolitical LPP approaches", instead cultivating the understanding that language policies "often create and sustain various forms of social inequality, and ... promote the interests of dominant social groups" (Johnson 2013: 40). It also seeks to increase democratic input into policy making in order to help reduce inequality and ensure the maintenance of minority languages (Johnson 2013: 40; Tollefson 2006).

While certainly a welcome improvement on previous research, more recently the critical approach to LPP has itself been challenged for being overly deterministic and not fully capturing the processes involved in language planning (Johnson 2013: 42), thereby leading to the development of the ethnography of LPP paradigm. This methodology attempts to combine an awareness of both the macro and micro "layers" of LPP, while remaining "committed to issues of social justice, particularly pertaining to the rights of Indigenous and minority language speakers" (Johnson 2013: 45). As Tusting and Maybin describe, the ethnography of LPP approach is particularly suitable for demonstrating links between different sociological levels "in the contexts of late modernity and globalisation" (2007: 576).

In exploring the effects of such macro-level developments, recent LPP work has also placed an increased emphasis on the tension between structure and agency (Hornberger and Johnson 2011: 279), a trend which I follow by detailing how neoliberal structures have restricted agency in the Irish case since 2008. Similar to literature such as Johnson (2010), I discuss the ways in which top-down language policy can disenfranchise linguistic minorities, but also how this is contested from the bottom up. In doing so, I offer an example of how LPP scholars can "bridge from micro-level ethnography to macro-level LPP (and back) in systematic and principled ways", something which has been seen as a "key challenge" facing the discipline at this juncture (Hornberger and Johnson 2011: 283; see also Hult 2010: 7; Ricento 2000: 208–209).

Although various scholars, including Ricento (2015) and Del Percio, Flubacher and Duchêne (2017), have made notable efforts towards integrating a political economic perspective with discussions of LPP, this research has typically focused on issues such as the spread of English as a global language, rather than interrogating how political economy effects the vitality of already minoritised languages. In building on this literature, however, this study endeavours to help address the "blind spot" in the field identified by Block, Gray and Holborow (2012: 1; also Block 2018a) and avoid the trend seen in much LPP scholarship to let "capitalism off the hook" (Block 2018b: 580).

An overemphasis on top-down language policies has led to another oversight in LPP research which recent work has attempted to overcome by decentring the role of the state in language issues (Moriarty 2015: 5). While I welcome this trend and personally have no allegiance to the state as a political construct (indeed, I find Graeber's (2004: 9, 2018: 270) cynicism regarding "policy" as conventionally understood very refreshing), with this being a book about neoliberalism, state action necessarily looms large throughout the discussion. Resistance to state policies, is, however, also a topic I discuss at length. In doing so, I follow Hornberger's advice regarding the need to consider "ideology, ecology, and agency" (2006: 34; also Spolsky 2004: 187), as well as foregrounding an awareness of "whose interests and whose values are being served when language plans and policies are proposed, implemented, or evaluated" (Ricento 2006: 6), something ethnography is perhaps uniquely well placed to do (McCarty 2011).

In contrast to the approach once favoured by anthropologists, however, it must be noted that current understandings of ethnography no longer see this methodology solely as an exercise in participant observation. It is now appreciated that the analysis of other relevant data, such as texts (in my case budgets, policy documents, etc.) and quantitative data can greatly contribute to the "thickness" of an ethnography (Bryman 2008: 402; Ortner 2010: 219). In line with this trend towards adopting an "expansive" approach to ethnographic production, I made much use of already available data in order to support the findings that emerged from my fieldwork. The analysis of relevant policy material is presented in Part 2 of this work, while ethnographic findings buttressed with reference to previously extant quantitative data are presented in Part 3.

In applying the ethnography of LPP approach, I have also aspired to follow Lin's (2015: 21) call for researchers to be aware of, articulate and challenge how their own personal backgrounds and the ideological assumptions of their discipline influence their interpretation of data and creation of knowledge. This requires not only reflexivity around issues of researcher positionality, but also regarding how a study will affect those who are being researched. This "critical research paradigm" asks how ethical research can best be done in an unjust world in order to empower subordinated groups and inhibit the reproduction of dominating institutions or practices. The adoption of such a stance is, as Lin puts it, "very important if LPP research is to contribute to promoting social justice and challenging unequal relations of power" (2015: 30). It is hoped that the use of such an approach helps ensure that while there will be inherent biases in this research (as there inevitably are in the social sciences), they have been duly acknowledged and addressed as is required by an ethical approach to ethnography.

1.3.3 Research sites and participants

With this project aiming to gain a detailed understanding of how macro-level processes of economic disruption play out at meso- and micro-levels, it was important that my methodology allowed me to conceptualise the research subject in the most holistic terms possible, while also allowing insight into the destabilisation of social relations under globalisation. Thankfully, this is something ethnography can excel at, as shown by Gille and Ó Riain (2002) and Nic Craith and Hill (2015). Although counterfactuals are notoriously hard to construct in the social sciences, and it is impossible to conclusively "prove" the impact of an event such as the Great Recession on any community or its language practices (we can never, of course, know how things would have proceeded in the Gaeltacht if the global economy had *not* crashed in late 2008), ethnography offers a useful tool for attempting to examine such phenomena. Through ethnographic inference and comparing my data with pre-cash patterns and projections, the effects of the post-2008 disruption can be explored in the most complete way we can hope for.

Over eight months were spent conducting fieldwork in the Gaeltacht for this project, primarily during the summers of 2015 and 2016, although additional, shorter visits took place at different times of year up to the end of 2018 – something which was important for gaining an insight into the nature of the "off season" in communities that are often heavily dependent on tourism. The writing of much of this text was conducted while once again living in a strongly-Irish speaking community.

During my fieldwork I lived in communities in both the Conamara area of west Galway and also in north-west Donegal (figure 1). Although there are also Gaeltacht areas in Munster, the southern province of Ireland, an examination of these districts was beyond the scope of this project. As Galway and Donegal contain the largest "category A" Gaeltacht areas, where census returns state that over two-thirds of the population speak Irish outside the education system on a daily basis (Ó Giollagáin and Charlton 2015a), it was felt that these would provide greater opportunities for addressing the research topic. Furthermore, the southern and eastern parts of the country are significantly better off socio-economically than the west and north, which are categorised differently in European Union development typologies (Ó hAoláin 2002: 31). All of my research sites were classed as category A areas, although ethical restrictions regarding anonymity prevent me from naming them directly. While census data must be approached cautiously when it comes to questions about language (Ó hIfearnáin 2022: 111–112), based on such data from 2011, research published in 2015 concluded that category A areas comprised just 13.5% of the official Gaeltacht – 21 of the 155 electoral divisions therein. 26 electoral divisions (16.8%) were classed category B (44–66% daily speakers), and 108 – 69.7% – were classified as category C, where less than 44% of the population speak Irish daily (Ó Giollagáin and Charlton 2015a: 7).

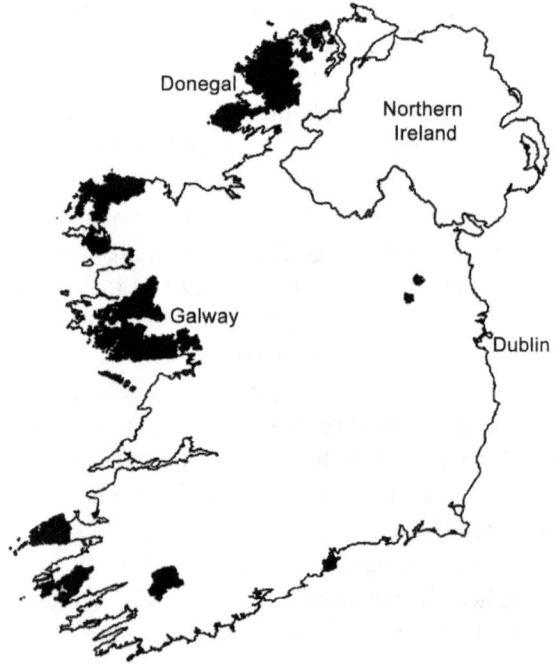

Figure 1: Map of Ireland. Official Gaeltacht areas are shaded in black.

While the focus of my research is relatively standard ethnographic fare – involving rural, often isolated communities in the west of Ireland notable for a unique linguistic trait – the multi-sited nature of my study sees it diverge from more orthodox ethnographies. Where ethnographers traditionally locate themselves in a single community, often with a relatively clear delineation of its boundaries, I did not focus on one single "bounded" community for the duration of my fieldwork, making this more a work of comparative ethnography. Focusing on communities in both Galway and Donegal was partly a response to the varied locations of my existing contacts, no significant majority of which were located in any one area, but also in deference to Marcus' (1998) contention that the study of an increasingly globalised world is best accomplished through the use of multisited ethnography. Such an approach allowed for a wider view of the interplay between language and neoliberal economics than would have been obtained by focusing solely on one community, and the comparison between the two main Gaeltacht areas of Galway and Donegal is informative. With the Donegal Gaeltacht being in a significantly more peripheral location than most of Galway, the spatially differentiated consequences of the economic crisis were particularly apparent in my research.

As is common practice in ethnography, I spent much time during my fieldwork involved in the day-to-day life of the community – at least in so far as an outside researcher can be – attending public meetings, festivals, sporting matches, protests etc. Throughout this time, I took anonymised fieldnotes detailing events that were telling with regard to the socioeconomic vitality of these areas and the use of Irish in the community. Linguistic landscape data (Gorter 2006) were also documented during these periods. This research was augmented through 52 semi-structured interviews.

When setting out on this study, I used the network of contacts that I had built up over the years as a pool from which to locate potential interviewees. Having been fortunate enough to have already visited strongly Irish-speaking Gaeltacht areas on many occasions, I had a reasonable understanding of the social terrain I intended to traverse. Nonetheless, as ethnographers inevitably are, I was ultimately reliant on acquaintances who acted as gatekeepers, facilitating access and offering guidance as required.

These "key informants" were mostly people I knew from my time living in the Gaeltacht and being a student of the Acadamh, and were typically involved in community development projects of various types. Further to being "local power brokers" (Fetterman 1989: 12), they were mostly individuals who had previously shown an interest in my research and expressed a desire to assist me where possible. Making the most of such generosity, I was able to gain access to situations which would likely otherwise be out of bounds for a researcher (Bryman 2008: 407–408).

Working with these key informants, I then employed the "snowball", friend-of-a-friend method to recruit informants who were not previously known to me. At the end of each interview, participants were asked if they could recommend anyone else who might be interested in talking to me about the same sort of issues, which almost all were happy to do.

As is typical for ethnography, rather than attempting to obtain a totally random or proportional sample, I applied a process of "judgemental" or "purposeful" sampling (Fetterman 1989: 43; Crang and Cook 2007: 12). This approach relies on the judgment of the ethnographer to ensure the appropriateness of a sample and attempts to capitalise on "natural opportunities, convenience and also luck" (Crang and Cook 2007: 12), rather than making pretensions to total randomness. Unlike pure convenience sampling (where a sample is studied simply because it happens to be available to the researcher), judgemental sampling is conducted with specific goals in mind, allowing the researcher to follow up on certain cohorts or individuals who are particularly pertinent to the research project. This method seeks to confirm the relevance of informants to the target information and thus ensures that those most capable of providing useful and valid data are not lost to the randomness that defines many other sampling methods (Bryman 2008: 415).

Key to the effective use of purposeful sampling for a project such as this, of course, is ensuring that a wide variety of informants of different backgrounds with varying roles in the community are sought out. An effort was therefore made to include not only well-known and vocal "community leaders" amongst my interviewees, but also the less outspoken but equally relevant individuals who make up the bulk of any community (Crang and Cook 2007: 18). While this does not totally nullify sampling bias, it is hoped that my efforts in this regard obtained a representative range of community opinions, thereby adding to the validity of the data. After conducting 52 interviews, it was clear that I had achieved theoretical saturation, having heard the dominant discourses relating to the research topic that are prevalent in the Gaeltacht repeated many times.

The recorded interviews were later transcribed, providing a corpus of some 375,000 words which were then coded and analysed thematically. While attempting to balance the representation of dialectal features with standard conventions for writing Irish, interviews were transcribed to give as accurate a reflection as possible of what interviewees said, non-standard grammatical features and profanities included. As such, the interview extracts used throughout often include instances of words not being mutated as standard usage might expect. Furthermore, irregular verbs are often regularised or other non-standard conjugations used, and there is a large amount of code-mixing and outright switching to English, as is typical of colloquial Gaeltacht speech (Ní Ghearáin 2018). All such features were transcribed as uttered, with non-standard spellings being used to convey dialectal pronunciation where deemed appropriate, broadly following the practices of Ó Curnáin (2007) and Ó Laoire (2002) regarding Galway and Donegal

Irish respectively. As codeswitching was unmarked by my informants it has not been indicated in transcription. Such codeswitching aside, all but two interviews were conducted in Irish – the remaining two were with learners who preferred to be interviewed in English. In quotes from interviews, unspaced ellipses, "...", are used to indicate an unfinished statement, while square bracketed, spaced ellipses, "[. . .]", denote that a section of the informant's speech has been removed from the extract for reasons of brevity, anonymity, or clarity. All identifying features in extracts have been removed and the name initials that begin longer quotes reference pseudonyms used during coding. Translations of interview extracts and other Irish-language materials quoted in the text are my own.

23 of my interviewees were from Galway and 26 from Donegal, with the remaining three being employees of language promotion bodies based in Dublin. Despite my best efforts to gain a more even gender mix, just fifteen of these informants were female. This is the result of several issues. Primarily, due to the patriarchal nature of Irish society (O'Connor 2008; Irish Times 2020a), those involved in economic development and other areas of key importance to this study, including business owners, executives in development agencies, local politicians and community activists, are all much more likely to be male. Sadly, females were noticeably more reluctant to discuss their opinions on record, even when anonymity was ensured, although several agreed to less formal interviews which were not recorded. Embedded as my own gender identity inevitably was in this research (Lumsden 2009: 497), such a dynamic was unfortunately almost inevitable, especially considering the limited time available to me for conducting this study. As has often been noted in commentary on gender dynamics in ethnography, it is typically easier for men to gain access to other men during fieldwork, while it is "almost a truism in the methodological literature of interview research" that women will find it easier to achieve rapport with a wider range of informants (Warren and Hackney 2000: 6). Indeed, it is partly for this reason – regrettable as it is – that "[b]oth in sociology and in anthropology, fieldwork has been associated with women and quantitative work with men" (Warren and Hackney 2000: 42; see also Kelly et al. 1994: 34). One approach sometimes adopted to help overcome this trend in the field is the use of mixed gender pairs or teams of researchers (Warren and Hackney 2000: 29–30). Ideally, a second, female researcher would have been employed in order to alleviate this bias, but such a solution was beyond the scope of possibility for this project.

16 of my informants were in the "young adult" category, aged 18–34. Six were employees of Údarás na Gaeltachta. Two were politicians (one local, one national). Two were owners of large businesses which employed in excess of 30 people each. At least eleven were rearing children under the age of 18, many others had adult children. As is typical for the Gaeltacht, many of my informants

worked in sectors that are dependent on state support. The gender imbalance notwithstanding, these 52 informants covered a wide range of social classes and backgrounds, with interviewees being chosen to ensure I spoke to people from various socioeconomic positions, including skilled and unskilled workers, as well as those who owned large businesses and the unemployed.

As this methodology adopts a non-probability sample, it must be understood that its findings cannot be automatically generalised to the whole population. As with any ethnography, it is nonetheless expected that the patterns observed offer a certain amount of resonance with other cases. As Hult and Johnson note, although "[v]ariability across contexts is taken for granted", in cases where the ethnographer takes care to provide sufficient detail about their particular context "it should be possible for the reader familiar with another local context to sort out what findings might or might not transfer" (2015: 17). I hope that the data presented here allow for such fruitful comparison.

1.3.4 Analysis of policy documents and quantitative data

As noted, in addition to my fieldwork data, a key part of this work analyses language policy decisions made since 2008. As well as providing an important insight into the effects of the economic crisis and the austerity measures that ensued, this analysis, along with existent quantitative data on the Gaeltacht, helped me triangulate and corroborate much of the information I obtained through interviews and participant observation.

Fortunately, there is a vast amount of sociolinguistic literature pertaining to Irish, and much of this focuses on the Gaeltacht. Indeed, as the next chapter describes, Irish is the object of one of the longest ongoing revitalisation efforts in the world, now counting well in excess of 125 years. Additionally, it has a significant amount of legal and institutional provision. This support extends to the legal delineation of the Gaeltacht as an area with a unique linguistic heritage and which has been privileged with supports not available to areas of similar socioeconomic standing outside its borders. As this involves state provision, there is a large amount of pertinent documentation and legislation which was most amenable to analysis for this study. State budgets and memoranda post-2008, for instance, were very instructive in the way they have addressed issues of funding for the Gaeltacht. While public spending in almost all sectors was reduced after the economic crash, Chapter 4 shows cuts to funding for Gaeltacht-based institutions to have been more severe than for similar non-Gaeltacht bodies. The analysis of such differential rates of budgetary contraction comprises a key part of my argument in relation to neoliberalism's antipathy towards language revitalisation efforts and accords with many of the ethnographic findings presented in Part 3 of this book.

As well as quantitative works such as that by Ó Giollagáin et al. (2007a), the detailed information pertaining to language use, employment, migration and so on that is available in the records of the Central Statistics Office was also immensely useful. This provided a statistical overview of the demography of specific Gaeltacht areas, allowing me to explore, for instance, migration patterns to and from the Gaeltacht, employment and labour force participation rates, commuting trends, rates of educational attainment and other markers of socioeconomic prosperity or deprivation. Relevant Central Statistics Office data are presented in Chapter 7 at the beginning of Part 3 to help contextualise the ethnographic findings which make up the bulk of that section, and to offer a diachronic overview of economic and social change in the Gaeltacht before, during and after the Great Recession.

2 Irish, Ireland, neoliberalism: Some background

2.1 Introduction

As described in Chapter 1, despite being the first official language of a developed European nation state, Irish is spoken daily outside the education system by just 1.6% of the population in the Republic of Ireland, and survives as a community language in only a handful of peripheral communities. This chapter discusses how what was once the language of the whole of Ireland was reduced to this minoritised state, as well as the considerable efforts made to reverse this process which began in the 19th century. The foundation of the Irish Free State in 1922 saw these efforts significantly intensified, when a pioneering programme of language revitalisation was undertaken. While state policies were defective in many ways and met with only limited success, as will be seen, they were nonetheless key to preventing the total loss of Irish as a spoken vernacular during the 20th century. In order to contextualise what follows in Parts 2 and 3 of this work, this chapter will discuss how different phases of the revival effort proceeded and how they were conditioned by developments in the Irish economy pre-2008. An overview of economic development in the Republic in recent decades is also presented, as is a discussion of the neoliberal ideology which has been the dominant economic hegemony globally for some four decades now, and which is fundamentally opposed to many of the requirements of language revitalisation programmes. The crash of this model in 2008 is discussed, along with the severe effects of the crisis for the country.

2.2 Irish-English language shift: A historical overview

Similar to many minoritised languages, the roots of the Irish language's marginalisation lie in colonial conquest. While the Anglo-Normans took control of much of the island following an invasion in 1169, they were assimilated into Irish-speaking society relatively quickly. With the exception of some anglicised settlements, primarily near Dublin, Irish consequently remained dominant across the island throughout the Middle Ages (Doyle 2015: 11–18).

It was only in the wake of the Tudor conquest which concluded with the final destruction of the native Gaelic political order in the early 17th century that widespread shift towards English began, with urban centres and the upper classes adopting the language first (Ó Murchú 1970: 25–26). In addition to military oppression and the exiling of the Gaelic aristocracy, the indigenous population were subjugated by the plantations which occurred throughout this period and the decades that followed, whereby the most fertile land was confiscated and given to English speakers who settled in Ireland in their thousands. Although a rebellion in 1641 saw some initial success, it was ultimately suppressed during the brutal Cromwellian conquest, with the population being reduced by a staggering 50% between 1641–1651 (Curtis 1993: 28; Mac Ionnrachtaigh 2013: 25). The Penal Laws (enacted 1695–1704) institutionalised yet further marginalisation of the Irish-speaking, Catholic majority. Further to restricting the operations of the Catholic church, these laws prevented Catholics from voting, running for office, practicing law, buying land, bearing arms and owning either horses or property worth more the £5 (Doyle 2015: 81–82).

This destruction of Irish political autonomy sparked a concomitant loss of cultural sovereignty, with an unstable Irish-English diglossic situation emerging in which English was definitively established as the language of power. The Catholic church's adoption of English as the language of instruction in the Maynooth seminary (founded 1795) was a further blow to Irish-language vitality, with the religion that was to become so central to Irish identity being largely associated with English from this point on (see Wolf 2014, however, for examples of the clergy using Irish throughout the 1800s). The establishment of the English-medium-only national school system in 1831 was a further factor detrimental to Irish, with nationalist revolutionary Pádraig Mac Piarais (Patrick Pearse) famously describing it as "the murder machine" due to its anglicising effects (Pearse 1976 [1912]). These various forces combined thus began a steady westward retreat for the Irish language, the final stages of which are being played out in the present day.

In light of these assimilatory dynamics, by the time Ireland was formally incorporated into the British state under the Acts of Union in 1801, Irish was already spoken by only a minority of the population (Fitzgerald 1984). As Wall describes, it had "ceased to be the language habitually spoken in the homes of all those who had already achieved success in the world, or who aspired to improve or even maintain their position politically, socially or economically" (1969: 82). Nonetheless, the Irish-speaking minority was a sizeable one. Ó hIfearnáin estimates that out of a population of 5.4 million at the beginning of the 19th century, some 2.4 million were Irish speakers (2010: 541). While numerous, these speakers were amongst the poorest sections of Irish society and overwhelmingly concentrated in peripheral areas, typically in the west of the country, where the introduction of the potato allowed the population to grow rapidly throughout the 1700s. Irish speakers therefore suffered disproportionately during the Great Hunger of 1845–1850, when the combined effects of starvation and emigration saw the population of the island fall by some 20–25%, equal to roughly two and a half million people (Ó Murchú 1970: 28). This period initiated an enduring pattern of mass emigration, with the population continuing to decline until the 1960s, when it began to slowly increase. This widespread out-migration caused English to be seen as a key skill necessary for emigrating (McMahon 2008: 15), thereby destroying what little prestige the language had maintained and prompting an extremely rapid process of language shift in the latter half of the 19th century.

The 1851 census, conducted in the immediate wake of the Great Hunger, was the first to include a question on language ability. It recorded some 1,524,286 Irish speakers (29%), including 319,602 monoglots (Fitzgerald 1984: 140), although methodological issues mean this may have been an underestimate (Ó hIfearnáin 2010: 542). As might be expected, areas with a high concentration of monoglots in 1851 closely correspond to districts where Irish has survived to this day. By 1891, however, the census registered only 680,000 Irish speakers, and, of these, a mere 3.5% were under 10 years of age (Hindley 1990: 15). As Ó Cuív summarises, so rapid was language shift throughout the 19th century that by 1891 99% of the population could speak English and 85% could not speak Irish (1969: 128). Of those who were Irish speakers at the close of the 19th century, over 80% lived in counties which are home to Gaeltacht areas in the present day (Ó Neachtain 2014: 373), with the exception of Meath, where a small "neo-Gaeltacht" was established in the 1930s, when grassroots agitation saw some Gaeltacht people granted more fertile land by the state as a poverty alleviation measure.

In response to the widespread disruption of the era, political nationalism took on a renewed vigour throughout the country from 1798 on, with groups such as Young Ireland and the Irish Republican Brotherhood organising failed rebellions throughout the 19th century. Although these organisations and other important movements such as the Land League and the campaign for Catholic Emancipation operated overwhelmingly through English, in the last quarter of the century cultural nationalism emerged as a significant ideological force in Irish society. Taking influence from a mixture of romanticism, Darwinism and fin de siècle thinking (Ó Conchubhair 2009), those involved in this "Gaelic revival" saw Irish as the key marker which indexed Irish identity. While a number of language-focused scholarly and antiquarian organisations were established in the early 1800s, The Society for the Preservation of the Irish Language (founded 1876) was the first organisation which specifically aimed for the restoration of Irish as the nation's vernacular (Ó Murchú 2001). This society was succeeded in 1893 by Conradh na Gaeilge [The Gaelic League], which quickly grew into a mass movement, ultimately serving a key role in the ideological development of many of those involved in the struggle for independence (Garvin 1987: 80). Within twenty years membership had grown to 100,000 and some 950 branches had been founded (McMahon 2008: 87–88).

As well as organising night classes, immersion courses for teachers and publishing propaganda and educational materials, the League achieved several important political goals, particularly regarding the use of Irish in the education system. As part of their policy of "killing Home Rule with kindness" (Jackson 2010: 147), in 1900 the British authorities permitted the teaching of Irish as an optional subject in schools, and competency in the language became compulsory for admission to the National University of Ireland in 1913 (Ó hÉallaithe 2004: 161). Despite those involved in the League being predominantly middle-class urbanites, the importance of maintaining Irish-speaking communities came to be widely accepted amongst revitalisation advocates (e.g., Bergin 1911: 8). Indeed, it was during this period that the term "Gaeltacht" first came to prominence as a way of denoting such areas, with "Galltacht" occasionally being used to refer to the rest of the country (Ó Torna 2005). Echoing romanticist understandings of the pre-industrial peasantry, Gaeltacht communities were seen as untarnished by colonial influence or the homogenising effects of contemporary society, a resource which could be drawn upon to support revitalisation efforts throughout the country (Doyle 2015: 193–200). This understanding would be of key importance to early language policy after the Free State was founded in 1922, and continues to hold some currency to this day.

2.3 Early state policy and the institutionalisation of the Gaeltacht

Shortly after its establishment following the partition of the island, the Irish Free State set about implementing an extensive programme of language revitalisation. This "megapolicy" (Ó Buachalla 1994) rested on four main pillars, namely (i) using the education system to spread knowledge of Irish in areas where it had died out; (ii) encouraging the use of Irish in the civil service and institutions of public administration; (iii) elaboration and standardisation of the language, including the "domain recapture" of higher registers that had been lost during the process of language shift; and (iv) maintenance of communities where Irish remained a vernacular, which were seen as "the repository of the linguistic elixir of Irish nationhood" (Ó Tuathaigh 1990: 11; Ó Riagáin 1997: 15–19).

Although evidence suggests that the political elite of the newly founded state never believed these measures would truly reinstate Irish as the nation's vernacular, but at best hoped for a bilingual society (Ó Tuathaigh 2011: 82), these early policies were adopted with a vigour that has not since been matched. Despite the economic situation of the country being dire during these early years, such was the influence of revivalist ideology on Free State leaders that they were willing to commit resources to revitalisation measures in a way that has not occurred since the end of the nationalist and protectionist phases of Irish political development in the 1960s (Watson 2016).

In order to provide an empirical basis for the formulation of Gaeltacht policy, a Gaeltacht Commission was established in 1925 with the goals of deciding what percentage of speakers would warrant an area being officially classified as Irish-speaking, as well as making recommendations regarding maintaining the use of Irish in such communities (Coimisiún na Gaeltachta 1926: 1). The commission's report proposed that those areas in which Irish was spoken by over 80% of the population be recognised as fíor-Ghaeltachtaí [true-Gaeltachts], while those where between 25–79% were Irish speakers would be deemed breac-Ghaeltachtaí [speckled-Gaeltachts]. These categories contained 168,279 and 307,907 people respectively (Ó Riagáin 1997: 18), although the number of these who were competent or regular Irish speakers was almost certainly overstated (Ó Cuív 1951: 29). While 18% of the population were returned as Irish speakers in the 1926 census, Ó Riagáin estimates that by this stage only 3% of the population lived in Irish-dominant communities (1997: 271). Further to the vast majority of Irish speakers living in areas where the language was already moribund and of very low prestige, the concentration of the language in areas of widespread underdevelopment meant that Gaeltacht life was "characterized by extensive out-migration, depopulation and deprivation" (Ó Riagáin 1997: 17; see also 7.2.3). The challenging economic situation of the Gaeltacht continued to be a major impediment to language maintenance throughout the 20th century and, as this work will describe, continues to be of great significance to the present day.

Amongst the proposals made by the 1926 commission were recommendations for incentivising and spreading the use of Irish in Gaeltacht schools, including offering additional training and wages to teachers and third-level scholarships to Gaeltacht residents, with the hope that many would become teachers themselves. The recruitment of native Irish speakers to the civil service, army and police force was recommended, as was giving greater remuneration to public servants stationed in the Gaeltacht. It was additionally stated that no non-Irish speaker should be employed by the state in the Gaeltacht, a proposal yet to be implemented, as section 3.4 describes.

The commission also made proposals regarding the economic development of the Gaeltacht in the hope of reducing population loss via emigration. These included land redistribution and agricultural aids such as state-funded vets and plant nurseries; grants for the improvement of housing; the resettlement of communities as "large homogenous groups" to more productive land elsewhere in the country; development of the fishing industry via the building of ports and processing factories; and supporting the homespun cloth industry.

As Ó Tuathaigh notes, however, a fundamental problem with implementing such policies was that the state "did not have a coherent policy of economic investment and social planning within the context of overall community development" at this time (1990: 5). Furthermore, prefiguring the post-2008 developments that this book focuses on, financial constraints were a major stumbling block which impeded the acceptance of many of these proposals (Mac Giolla Chríost 2008: 77), with Lee arguing that the commission was "duly sabotaged" as a result (1989: 135). Key proposals were rejected by the Department of Finance – despite its then head, Earnán de Blaghd (Ernest Blythe), being a committed Gaelic League member – seemingly for fear that non-Gaeltacht areas would demand similar provision, something Blythe believed state finances could not support (Lee 1989: 135, 192). Overall, only 14 of 82 recommendations contained in the white paper published in response to the commission were ever implemented (Uí Chollatáin 2016: 192). Early attempts at maintaining the Gaeltacht ultimately thus amounted to little more than "preservation through neglect and seclusion" (Watson 2016: 66), with Ó Tuathaigh describing those schemes that were implemented as being merely "plugs in a shattering dyke" (1990: 5).

Despite this, some innovative measures were instigated in the early years of the state, chief amongst them perhaps being *Scéim Labhairt na Gaeilge* [the Irish-speaking scheme], established in 1934. Under this scheme, described by Ó Broithe as one of the most important LPP initiatives the state ever implemented (2012: 238), an annual grant was given to Gaeltacht parents whose children passed an Irish-competency exam designed to test whether Irish was spoken to them at home. Further to the monetary incentive and the valorisation of what had been for several hundred years a deeply stigmatised language, this scheme provided an important insight into rates of intergenerational transmission in the Gaeltacht (Ó Broithe 2012: 239–240). As Chapter 3 describes, however, this initiative was one of many discontinued under post-2008 austerity measures.

Significant progress was also made regarding the position of the language in the education system. Irish-medium teacher training colleges were established, Irish was made a compulsory subject in all schools and the percentage of schools teaching entirely or partially through Irish reached 55% by 1940 (Fishman 1991: 138), with all Gaeltacht schools being entirely Irish-medium. Irish competency was also made compulsory for new recruits to the civil service.

Nonetheless, in the decades following the foundation of the state the Gaeltacht continued to atrophy. With the hoped-for national revitalisation failing to materialise and language shift continuing apace, in 1956 a specific state department for the

Gaeltacht was established and the borders of the Gaeltacht were redrawn, with the fíor-/breac-Ghaeltacht distinction being abolished and most Breac-Ghaeltacht areas losing their Gaeltacht status entirely (Walsh 2012a: 181–182). The new borders more accurately reflected the true standing of the language than the heavily aspirational designations proposed in 1926, which included areas where Irish was spoken "regardless of the extent to which English may have an ascendancy in daily use" (Coimisiún na Gaeltachta 1926: 6–7). Under the new delineations, however, the "political Gaeltacht" continued to be larger than the "real Gaeltacht" (Lee 1989: 673). The first Gaeltacht minister, Patrick Lindsay, saw to it that the borders were defined in such a way as to maximise the flow of grant aid to residents in deeply impoverished – but only weakly Irish-speaking – areas of his constituency in north-west Mayo (Ó Giollagáin 2016: 99–100). With the official Gaeltacht nonetheless shrinking considerably as a result of this review, the non-contiguous nature of the remaining Irish-speaking territories became even more apparent, with Gaeltacht areas not corresponding to administrative districts such as county councils. This continues to provide a major managerial challenge – particularly in light of the country's lack of empowered local government institutions – with such disparate enclaves being deeply "unamenable to bureaucratic convenience or administrative economies" (Ó Tuathaigh 1990: 6).

In response to the mass emigration from the Gaeltacht that occurred throughout the 1950s (see 9.2), a more concerted approach to economic development was adopted towards the end of the decade. A Gaeltacht-specific development agency, Gaeltarra Éireann, was established in 1958 at a time when state economic policy was beginning to undergo a major re-orientation, as the following section describes. Although initially focused on the development of indigenous industry in much the same way the 1926 commission had proposed, Gaeltarra played a key role in modernising the economy of the Gaeltacht by attracting much needed inward investment and subsidising industry which would otherwise not have located in such areas. As noted below, however, this strategy itself presented distinct challenges for language maintenance.

2.4 State withdrawal from the revitalisation project

While including some commendable efforts at reinvigorating the flagging revitalisation process, the second half of the 20th century saw state commitment to Irish-language promotion wane considerably. At the request of Taoiseach (i.e., Prime Minister) Éamon de Valera, in 1958 *An Coimisiún um Athbheochan na Gaeilge* [The Commission for the Revival of Irish] was established to assess policies to date and offer advice regarding future measures. This commission's report was explicit in its opinion that funding for revitalisation efforts needed to be increased significantly: *"[i]s lánmhithid a aithint go soiléir go mbainfidh caiteachas mór le hathbheochan na Gaeilge, caiteachas nach féidir dul uaidh má tá uainn go mairfidh an teanga. Ní leor go mbeadh rún daingean againn an Ghaeilge a shábháil muna mbíonn rún eile, lán chomh daingean leis, againn an cúnamh airgid atá riachtanach chuige a chur ar fáil"* [It is high time to clearly acknowledge that the revival of Irish will involve significant expenditure, expenditure which cannot be avoided if we want the language to survive. It is not enough to intend to save Irish unless there is another intention, equally determined, to provide the financial assistance that this requires] (An Coimisiún um Athbheochan na Gaeilge 1963: 85).

The government white paper published in response to the report made no such promise of appropriate funding, however, instead couching many of its commitments in terms like "as far as practicable" (Ó Croidheáin 2006: 220; see also Chapter 6). Furthermore, this paper provided the first official acknowledgment that re-Gaelicisation was not a viable policy (Government of Ireland 1965: 10–12). In what can be seen as one of the first steps in the state's abandoning of its revitalisation goals, it instead acknowledged the importance of English and proposed the creation of a bilingual society as an official goal, conceding that *"[i]s mór is fiú an Béarla mar theanga idirnáisiúnta i gcúrsaí cumarsáide, trádála agus cuartaíochta agus mar mheán rannpháirtíochta i ngnóthaí ar fud an domhain"* [English is of great value as an international language in matters of communication, trade and tourism and as a medium of participation in affairs all over the world] (Government of Ireland 1965: 11). With the stage thus set for the beginning of state withdrawal from the language project, by 1968 the original commission claimed that "few of the recommendations of the white paper policy had been put into effect" (in Ó Huallacháin 1994: 152).

As well as the cynicism brought about by several decades of failure to revive the language, wider economic and political developments in Irish society at this time contributed to the lacklustre nature of this official response. As the state's first generation of leaders began to retire, by the mid-1960s and early 1970s a new cohort was coming to power. Many of this second generation of politicians were closely linked to business (Coakley 2012: 163) and intent on reforming what were seen as failed policies in both the economic and cultural spheres. The adoption in 1958 of the *Economic Development* plan written by Department of Finance official T. K. Whitaker "in close consultation with World Bank advisors" (Coakley 2012: 158) led to the end of protectionist policies under the modernising government of Seán Lemass (1959–1966; Bew and Paterson 1982: 118). In accordance with this shift, political support for ambitious – and often unpopular (Ó Riagáin 1997: 21) – language revitalisation measures began to diminish, as protectionism receded before a new policy of "openness" to cultural and market forces, "the new setting in which Irish identity would be refurbished and reconfigured" (Ó Tuathaigh 2008: 33).

The implementation of this new development policy by the state opened the door for the development of neoliberalism as the key economic paradigm in the Republic of Ireland over the following decades (Kirby 2010: 14–30). In accordance with the arguments that I will make throughout this text regarding the fundamental tension between such policies and language revitalisation, the withdrawal of state support for Irish at this juncture must be placed in the context of this move towards economic liberalisation, which made it all but inevitable that the state would begin to withdraw from this area (see sections 2.6; 6.3 and 7.1).

The period of "stagnation and retreat" (Ó Riagáin 1997: 19) in Irish-language policy that followed this economic re-orientation did indeed see a significant decline in institutional support for the language from the early 1970s onwards. This included the abolition of the language requirement for entrance to the civil service, the closing of Irish-medium teacher training institutions, the removal of the requirement to pass Irish to earn the Leaving Certificate on finishing secondary school, as well as a sharp decrease in numbers of Irish-medium schools outside the Gaeltacht (Ó Riagáin 1997: 19–25).

Although official language policy weakened considerably post-1965, it must be acknowledged that the reformed state economic programme did bestow considerable benefit on the Gaeltacht, compared with previous protectionist policies. The successful attraction of industry to the Gaeltacht for the first time saw employment opportunities increase and, following massive emigration in the 1950s, "the historic pattern of demographic decline was arrested and reversed between the mid-1960s and the late 1970s" (Ó Tuathaigh 1990: 9). Nonetheless, young adults continued to leave the Gaeltacht, although, for the first time, in-migration helped to compensate for some of this loss (Ó Tuathaigh 1990: 10). Furthermore, while conferring some benefits, the new economic model was far from the panacea many had hoped for: an important report published in 1975 still found cause to state that "[t]he main underlying problem of the Gaeltacht is the weakness of its economic base" (CILAR 1975: 347; see also An Coimisiún um Athbheochan na Gaeilge 1963: 181–220).

This period also saw those involved in the revitalisation effort begin to engage with language planning on a more scientific basis, taking lessons from the burgeoning field of sociolinguistics. The advisory group *Comhairle na Gaeilge*, established in 1969 as a result of the 1965 white paper (Government of Ireland 1965), published important works that situated Irish-language planning in the context of contemporary developments in the linguistic and social sciences (e.g.,

Ó Murchú 1970; CILAR 1975). While its founding was an extremely fraught process (Ó Huallacháin 1994: 170–187), the opening of *Institiúid Teangeolaíochta Éireann* [The Linguistics Institute of Ireland] in 1974 as a full-time research and policy unit was also an important development. The following year a nationwide language promotion body, *Bord na Gaeilge*, was established (since succeeded by *Foras na Gaeilge*, discussed in 4.4).

Additionally, a small Gaeltacht Civil Rights Movement based in Galway in the late 1960s and early 1970s successfully campaigned for the establishment of a Gaeltacht radio station (see 5.2) and a democratic authority for the Gaeltacht. *Údarás na Gaeltachta* (hereafter ÚnaG), was founded in 1979, replacing Gaeltarra Éireann as the Gaeltacht development organisation. Unlike Gaeltarra, the majority of the board of ÚnaG was elected by Gaeltacht residents every five years. The establishment of such a democratic body was a major achievement for grassroots campaigning at a time when the state was withdrawing support for many language revitalisation policies. While originally intended to have a significantly wider remit than its predecessor, such powers failed to be granted to – or demanded by – ÚnaG, meaning that it ultimately failed to live up to the aspirations of those who campaigned for it (Walsh 2011a: 299). As Chapter 4 describes, the ÚnaG election was abolished in 2012 as a cost-saving measure, and the institution's budget cut by almost 75% between 2008–2015.

While the "ethnic revival" of the 1960s and 70s saw significant gains by linguistic minorities in many parts of the world, in the Republic of Ireland developments were thus more modest, with progressive energies on the island focusing, particularly throughout the 1970s, on the war in the north (Fennell 1981a: 37). Consequently, there was relatively little grassroots resistance to the state's "de-institutionalization of the Irish language" (Mac Giolla Chríost 2005: 122). Such was the extent of state prevarication on language policy during this time that Joshua Fishman, writing to Irish-language scholar and activist Colmán Ó Huallacháin in 1971, claimed that

> What does disturb me . . . is the now quite apparent delaying tactics whereby recommendations are neither rejected nor implemented but simply surrounded by administrative silence and inaction. After four years of waiting I have come to the conclusion that I have been used not as a consultant but as an unwitting participant in a master plan to do nothing, i.e. nothing real or decisive . . . Policy has continued to be mere verbiage, being neither decisive no[r] informed. I have lately concluded that this then is *exactly* what the Irish government wants and my only regret it that it hasn't had the courage to say so to me, to you and to the public. (in Ó Huallacháin 1991: 133, original emphasis)

One striking illustration of this behaviour which is of particular relevance to this study, particularly Chapter 4, can be seen in a formerly confidential document written at the height of the recession of the 1980s. The document in question, which was released under the 30-year rule in December 2015, is an internal ministerial memorandum which details the Department of Education's decision to publish, but, due to budgetary constraints, not implement a far-reaching policy for reforming Gaeltacht education. Indeed, the then minister for finance noted the need to ensure "that expectations are not raised and interest groups given no encouragement to press for implementation" (in Delap 2015). It is, of course, notoriously difficult to measure what public policy scholars term the "second face of power" – the decision by elites *not* to act (Cairney 2012: 52; sections 4.2, 6.3 below; see Mills 2000 [1956] for explanation of the term "elites"). Nonetheless, such documents provide perhaps the most tangible proof of this concept that social scientists could hope for and clearly demonstrate the challenges Fishman and others faced in dealing with the Irish state.

This lack of concerted support unsurprisingly saw Irish-speaking areas continue to shrink, with language shift continuing unabated throughout the latter half of the 20th century. Those efforts that were made to resist this were in no way sufficient to counteract the major socioeconomic changes which began to take place in the country from the mid-1960s onwards and which spurred an increased turn towards English in the Gaeltacht. As Ó Riagáin describes, the transformation of traditional agrarian society and the integration of the Gaeltacht into the wider national and international economy at this time saw language shift begin even in areas that had previously been relatively stable linguistically. Increased rates of car ownership allowed those from remote areas to travel much more readily for employment located outside their communities. Shopping, recreation and pursuing education outside the Gaeltacht also became much more commonplace, thereby "intensif[ying] the frequency of interactions between Irish-speakers and English-speakers" (Ó Riagáin 2008: 57). Ó Riagáin's assessment thus sees the 1960s and 70s as the period when language shift began in heartland Gaeltacht areas, rather than being confined to the contraction of much more weakly Irish-speaking areas on the periphery of the Gaeltacht, as had previously been the case (2008: 57).

In accordance with this analysis, Ó Curnáin has described the linguistic implications of the Conamara Gaeltacht becoming increasingly integrated into wider patterns of socioeconomic organisation. Offering a typology which sees those born before the 1960s as being speakers of "traditional Irish", Ó Curnáin details the linguistic changes and reduced acquisition of younger speakers, defining those born between 1960–1990 as speakers of "non-traditional Irish" whose speech is marked by high levels of English-influenced idiom and morphological/phonological innovation (Ó Curnáin 2012a: 287). As discussed in Chapter 13, the most recent generations of Gaeltacht natives (born since 1990) are seen by Ó Curnáin to be speaking "reduced Irish", a variety notable for a high degree of influence from English and significant use of functional code switching (cf. Dorian 1977).

In light of all this, in 1981 Fennell, writing about recent developments where he lived in Maínis, Co. Galway – one of the strongest Irish-speaking communities – claimed that the shift to English had begun even there (Fennell 1981b). Seeing return migration as a key factor triggering this anglicisation (see 9.3), Fennell claimed that "[i]n the course of the 70s, in most parts of the (real) Gaeltacht, most parents of young children began to rear them in English" (1981b: 8). Assessing the strength of the language in the mid-1970s, he concluded that only about 1/3 of the population of the official Gaeltacht lived in communities where Irish was dominant, amounting to some 25,900 people spread across three main areas in counties Donegal, Galway and Kerry (1981b: 11).

These observations were later echoed by Hindley's oft-cited findings which presented a bleak picture of the level of Irish use in the Gaeltacht. While not published until some years later, Hindley's research throughout the 1970s and 1980s led him to very similar conclusions, namely that language shift was occurring rapidly in the strongest remaining Gaeltacht districts, with it thus being only a matter of time until even the most remote areas shifted to English, just as the rest of the country had done over the preceding centuries (Hindley 1990). Reflecting on this continuing contraction of the Gaeltacht and the generally weakened nature of state support for the language compared to the early decades of Free State efforts, in 1989 Lee thus concluded that "[p]olicy for about two decades has clearly been to let the language die by stealth" (1989: 673).

Adopting the terminology of public policy studies, language policy since the foundation of the state can therefore be broadly characterised as consisting of a period of "incrementalist" progression (Cairney 2012: 94–108) from 1922 until the mid-1960s. A large-scale re-evaluation of state priorities at this time, however, saw this equilibrium punctuated, with the beginning of a further incrementalist process of withdrawal which was to continue steadily – albeit with some important exceptions – over the following decades. The economic transformations of the time also saw the Gaeltacht integrated into the modern economy to a degree that had not previously occurred, with the erosion of the strongest remaining Gaeltacht areas consequently beginning in earnest from the 1960s onwards.

2.5 Language policy during the Celtic Tiger

Despite the overall trend following the pattern of withdrawal that had been underway since the 1960s, the Celtic Tiger period of the 1990s and early 2000s in which the Irish economy underwent a process of rapid growth (described in detail in 2.8) nonetheless saw several noteworthy and positive developments take place in Irish-language policy. The prosperity accompanying the boom allowed for some significant investments to be made in the sector, although relatively little was done to engage with the challenge of ongoing language shift in the Gaeltacht. Indeed, similar to the transformations of the 1960s and 70s, this era of socioeconomic change intensified language shift in core Gaeltacht areas, exacerbating an already precarious linguistic situation (cf. Ó Curnáin 2007: 59; 2012a).

Following the steady marginalisation of Irish over the preceding decades, at the beginning of the Celtic Tiger in 1993 the Department of the Gaeltacht had its remit significantly expanded, being renamed the Department of Arts, Culture and the Gaeltacht. While some were hopeful this would give the relevant minister more bargaining power at the cabinet table, it ultimately amounted to a substantial reduction of the importance of the Gaeltacht at government level. As a civil servant who has been in the department since the 1980s explained to me during an interview, this was a *"céim mhór chun cúil"* [major step backwards] which meant that there was no longer any state department which operated entirely through Irish.

The department's portfolio was expanded yet further in 1997 when it became the Department of Arts, Heritage, Gaeltacht and the Islands, a pattern of expansion which, as described in 4.3, has continued during the post-Celtic Tiger period.

A significant boon for the language, however, came in 1996 with the establishment of the Irish-language television station, TG4 (then TnaG/Telefís na Gaeilge). While this was a very positive development, it is notable that – as with the Gaeltacht radio station – it was brought about due to the sustained efforts of grassroots campaigners, rather than being an example of the ambitious top-down LPP measures that characterised earlier state policy (Watson 2003: 62–115). Nonetheless, this was a key development in making language-based employment available not only where the TG4 headquarters is based in Conamara in west Galway, but throughout the Gaeltacht, with independent production companies in many Gaeltacht areas working as contractors for the station (TG4 2016a: 22). It has also had a significant positive impact on the language's prestige nationally (Mac Donnacha 2008: 104). A detailed discussion of the effects of austerity measures on the station is provided in section 5.3.

In 2000, the Department of Arts, Heritage, Gaeltacht and the Islands undertook a review of the status of the Gaeltacht, which, it has been argued by Mac Donnacha (2014), was the belated official response to Hindley's controversial work (1990). Taking precedent from the initial Gaeltacht Commission in 1926, this "Second Gaeltacht Commission" reported in 2002 and made clear that the policy status quo was untenable if the state intended to maintain the Gaeltacht as a distinct linguistic community. One of its main recommendations which was implemented was the commissioning of a comprehensive study of the current status of Irish in the Gaeltacht (Coimisiún na Gaeltachta 2002: 17). This study, discussed below, ultimately demonstrated that "not only was Hindley's analysis accurate, but that he had been, if anything, slightly optimistic", as one of the report's main authors has since put it (Mac Donnacha 2014).

A further key recommendation of the second Gaeltacht commission was that a language act be implemented which would give legislative force to the constitutional status of Irish (Coimisiún na Gaeltachta 2002: 17). While the government had committed to such an act in 1998, this promise was followed by a period of typical equivocation and delay, until the process was spurred on by a case taken against the state by a private citizen in 2001 (Bohane 2005: 2). Two years later the *Official Languages Act 2003* finally came into being (Government of Ireland 2003).

While some commentators saw this Act as being too little, too late – "a last hurrah" in Ó Riagáin's words (2008: 65) – it was nonetheless generally welcomed by the Irish-speaking community as a positive development. It legislated for a variety of language rights and provisions, including regarding the use of Irish in the courts, in interactions with the state, in parliament, on road signs, etc. Notably, however, the Act prefixes many of these measures with the remarkable disclaimer "with the consent of the minister for finance" (Government of Ireland 2003: 12, 18, 20). Perhaps the most important provision made in the Act was to establish an independent language commissioner, An Coimisinéir Teanga, whose office monitors the implementation of the Act, particularly the requirement for public bodies to prepare language schemes detailing services that they will provide through Irish if requested to do so by the department responsible for the Gaeltacht. The relevant minister is required to give approval to such schemes in order for them to come into effect. The Act also requires that such schemes make provision for ensuring that Irish becomes the working language of state offices in the Gaeltacht and that all services are available in Irish therein, as originally proposed by the 1926 Gaeltacht Commission. As section 6.2 describes, however, the work of the Coimisinéir has been most challenging, with the Act being widely ignored, a tendency seemingly intensified as a result of extensive public sector rationalisation since 2008.

Another change of note during the Celtic Tiger period was the acceptance in 2005 of Irish as an official working language of the EU, with full translation provision to begin in 2007. This too was amongst the recommendations of the second Gaeltacht commission (Coimisiún na Gaeltachta 2002: 17) and had been the focus of a sustained campaign by activists over several years which culminated in a 5,000-strong march in Dublin in 2004. Despite this development being welcomed by language organisations, Irish was placed under "derogation" by the government and as such the EU was not required to provide the full range of translation services afforded to other official languages. In 2015, under pressure once again from language groups, it was announced that the government would endeavour to end this derogation status by the end of 2021 (OLRS 2016: 25) – a far from ambitious target, albeit one which was eventually met.

This period also saw the publication of the *Statement on the Irish Language 2006* (Government of Ireland 2006). With there having been no explicit elucidation of state ambitions for the language since the *White Paper on the Restoration of the Irish Language* (Government of Ireland 1965), the Statement was greatly anticipated. The appearance of this statement, a glossy full-colour document typical of government publications during the Celtic Tiger, strikingly contrasts with the black and white, pictureless *20-Year Strategy for the Irish Language* published in 2010. While short and making few new commitments, it reaffirmed state support for the preservation of the Gaeltacht and announced the intention to produce the *20-Year Strategy* for the language (Government of Ireland 2006: 4–6), the result of which is discussed in Chapter 3.

A year later, the *Comprehensive Linguistic Study of the Use of Irish in the Gaeltacht* (henceforth "*Comprehensive Linguistic Study*"; Ó Giollagáin et al. 2007a, 2007b) was published. This report, which marks the final important development regarding the language that took place before 2008, claimed that without drastic ameliorative action, based on current trends Irish would no longer be the dominant language in even the strongest Gaeltacht areas within 15–20 years (Ó Giollagáin et al. 2007b: 27).

Although the case of the Gaeltacht was repeatedly demonstrated to be worsening throughout this time, there were nonetheless several important macro-level policy developments during the Celtic Tiger. A new discourse about language rights that emerged during the period, and which culminated in the *Official Languages Act 2003*, brought a "fresh dynamism" to discussions (Mac Giolla Chríost 2005: 175–177, 190–191). In a significant change from previous understandings of the place of the language in Irish society, this, however, saw policy "increasingly framed in terms of minority rights rather than the discourse of the national language" (Walsh 2021: 329–330). While advancing the debate in some important ways, as scholars such as Ó Murchú (2002: 38) claimed at the time, this discursive shift ultimately meant that the language was being seen to an ever greater degree as an issue of private concern, of individual identity construction, rather than a social good deserving of the type of policy interventions seen in earlier periods of state language policy. As will be seen, this is in many ways what might be expected during an era of rapidly advancing neoliberalisation (see 2.6, 2.8). Nevertheless, it must be also noted that the affluence of the Celtic Tiger saw investment in important projects such as TG4, as well as ÚnaG receiving some €25.5 million in funding by 2008. This was to be short-lived, however, with the 2008 crash seeing a drastic change in the policy climate which engendered this progress. As the following sections describe, the 2008 crash was a crisis of neoliberalism, the dominant economic paradigm of our era.

2.6 Neoliberalism: The emergence of a global hegemony

Neoliberalism is the name most commonly given to the present phase of capitalism, one which replaced the Keynesian and social democratic consensus that dominated in the developed west for approximately 30 years post-WWII. Neoliberal ideology was originally theorised between the mid-1940s and 60s by economists such as Friedrich Hayek, Milton Friedman and other members of the Mont Pelerin Society, a group Hayek helped establish in 1947 to further his ideas via an international network of think tanks (Mirowski 2013: 44–47). Seeing attempts by states to regulate the market as being responsible for the totalitarianism of both Nazi Germany and the USSR, Hayek claimed that the redistribution of resources via welfare programmes and social planning was "the road to serfdom" (2006 [1944]) which must be avoided at all costs.

While often conflated with laissez-faire liberalism or free-market libertarianism, neoliberalism stands apart from such ideologies. Despite sharing with these theories an understanding of the market as being a "super information processor" capable of distributing resources with an efficiency that human planning can never hope to match (Mirowski and Nik-Khah 2017: 59), neoliberalism does not argue for a complete withdrawal of the state from the market as some related ideologies do. Indeed, Hayek himself claimed that "[p]robably nothing has done as much harm to the liberal cause as the wooden insistence of some liberals on certain rough rules of thumb, above all the principle of laissez-faire" (2006 [1944]: 18), and that

> it is the character rather than the volume of government activity that is important . . . a government that is comparatively inactive but does the wrong things may do much more to cripple the forces of a market economy than one that is more concerned with economic affairs but confines itself to actions which assist the spontaneous forces of the economy.
>
> (Hayek 2011 [1960]: 331)

As Mirowski thus summarises, "mature neoliberalism is not at all enamoured of the minimalist night-watchman state of the classical liberal tradition" (2013: 40). Instead, it envisions a utopia consisting of "the free economy and the strong state" (Gamble 1994), with such a state providing the legal and judicial structures required to both create and maintain the market. In contrast to neoclassical theories, neoliberalism therefore sees a role for significant state intervention in the market, but argues that economic intercessions should take place only in favour of capital, and that the state should not stray into other areas of social policy or governance (Hayek 2006 [1944]: 43–44, 98; Mirowski 2013). It was based on this distinction that Foucault (2008: 131) concluded that neoliberalism was not just old wine in new bottles, but instead marked a distinct phase in the development of capitalism.[2]

Neoliberalism contends that ensuring capitalist enterprises are as successful as possible will lead to the greatest aggregate benefit for all, as wealth "trickles down" from the top of the class structure to the bottom (Greider 1981). The pursuit of profit is therefore seen as an eminently moral act, with Milton Friedman famously declaring that "[t]he social responsibility of business is to increase profits" on this basis (2007 [1970]: 173).

Further to inevitably paving the way to totalitarianism, theorists associated with neoliberalism claim that state provision of welfare inhibits the entrepreneurial spirit naturally present in human beings, conceptualised as *homo economicus*, causing them to become lazy and dependent (Murray 1990). By limiting the maximisation of profit in this way, welfare states are seen to inevitably act against society's best interests. Neoliberalism thus explicitly rejects the notion of collective rights and is characterised by a strongly negative conception of liberty.

Such theoretical arguments notwithstanding, as Harvey (2005) has explained, neoliberal doctrine ultimately served to justify policy changes proposed by an

---

[2] As Chomsky (2012: 262) has pointed out, however, in practice the policies of pre-neoliberal capitalism often closely resembled those espoused by neoliberalism. While publicly advocating a market free from state interference, early capitalists depended enormously on state intervention to forcibly enclose commons, to remodel the economies of colonised areas, to create a "surplus population" which provided a cheap source of labour, etc. While philosophically distinct, neoliberalism can nonetheless certainly be seen as a continuation of centuries-old capitalist strategies of accumulation, albeit in an intensified form.

international capitalist class which, due to the confluence of a number of important factors, felt their position threatened. By the early 1970s, almost three decades of Keynesian and social democratic policies redistributing wealth downwards, the oil shock and the emergence of numerous anti-systemic movements across the world had combined to see the balance of power shift firmly away from capital. These and various other internal contradictions of Keynesianism (see Blyth 2016, drawing on Kalecki 1943) saw rates of profit falling globally, with the "stagflation" period of the early 1970s being the most severe economic crisis since the 1930s. Both stagflation and many of the forces depressing rates of profit were eventually overcome by the abandonment of Keynesianism in favour of neoliberal reforms, which were promoted as policy solutions by a capitalist class anxious to shift the balance of power away from labour (Harvey 2005: 19; Blyth 2016: 220).

This intensification of neoliberalism over the following years saw spending on a wide range of welfare programmes reduced in states across the developed west. While the concept of austerity only came to public prominence after 2008, scholars such as Pierson (2002) had long since claimed that neoliberal states entered a period of "permanent austerity" in the 1970s, when the growing costs of welfare programmes began to be tackled through retrenchment and the privatisation of various aspects of the public sector.

Although the implementation of neoliberalism on a global scale has been an uneven and contested process, it is fundamental to the process of globalisation which has occurred in recent decades (Gamble 2009: 67), and has become "a hegemonic discourse with pervasive effects on ways of thought and political economic practices to the point where it is now part of the common sense way we interpret, live in, and understand the world" (Harvey 2007: 22). As such it can be seen to fit Hall's notion of a "policy paradigm" so ingrained that it is taken for granted and enacted without question (Hall 1993: 279; see also Gramsci 1992).

It is the hegemonic aspect of neoliberalism at the individual level which has received most attention in LPP literature. As Urla (2020) explains, neoliberalism is now often understood as having moved beyond being just an economic model, to become an all-encompassing form of governmentality. As will be seen in Chapter 13, it affects even the way in which people construct their personal identities – with distinct implications for minoritised languages. Relatedly, various other authors in the field, including Heller, Pujolar and Duchêne (2014) and Heller and McElhinny (2017) have discussed neoliberalism and language commodification. While valuable, such discussions, however, have tended to remain focused on the micro-level, discussing consumers and products, rather than examining neoliberalism as the fundamental force conditioning how liberal democratic states make public policy in the 21st century – including language revitalisation policy. These studies consequently miss crucial ways in which neoliberal restructuring affects the fate of minoritised languages and diverge from the manner in which other branches of the social sciences tend to discuss neoliberalism (e.g., Springer, Birch and MacLeavy 2016; see Block 2018a, 2018b for discussion of this deficit in LPP literature).

In the context of this work's emphasis on the effects of the 2008 economic crisis, it is important to note that the political manipulation of crises has been a key strategy through which neoliberal goals have been furthered (Klein 2007). With the mass of the population otherwise occupied by the exigencies of daily life and the political elite generally desperate for solutions that appease international investors, crises often see the opening of a "policy window", allowing for the implementation of measures that would be politically unthinkable in times of relative stability. "Only a crisis – actual or perceived – produces real change", as Friedman put it (2002 [1962]: xiv).

Further to manipulating crises in order to ensure pro-market reforms, neoliberalism is also crisis-generating. While the cyclical move from boom to bust has long been accepted by economists as fundamental to capitalism's mechanics, this trend has been greatly intensified since the 1970s, with there having been hundreds of financial crises since then, compared to relatively few prior to this period of reform (D. Harvey 2012a: 4).

Despite claims about it being an efficient way to ensure a just distribution of resources, a vast body of research across the social sciences has documented how neoliberalism has ultimately served to create enormous levels of inequality which, in turn, have egregious social consequences (e.g., Picket and Wilkinson 2010; Piketty 2014). It has significantly contributed to the creation of deeply precarious living conditions for huge sections of the world's population and has led to a series of interconnected environmental catastrophes so severe that they present existential challenges regarding the very future of civilisation (Saad-Filho and Johnston 2006; Standing 2014; Verhaeghe 2014; Monbiot 2016).

As will be demonstrated throughout this book, neoliberalism also inherently conflicts with efforts to ensure the vitality of minoritised languages. Through opposing state intervention in areas which do not facilitate the needs of capital, the adoption of neoliberal policies has "profound implications for the orthodox understanding of language planning" (Williams and Morris 2000: 180). While not always explicitly framed in such terms, language revitalisation typically requires the redistribution of resources to marginalised groups (see 6.3). With neoliberalism conceiving the market as a moral as well as economic force, it argues against such redistributive "social justice" policies on the grounds that they require the redistribution of resources which the market has justly allocated, with such policies therefore being neither social nor just. It is thus in fundamental tension with many language revitalisation efforts. Parts 2 and 3 of this book explore in detail the implications of this tension after 2008 in the Republic of Ireland, which, as section 2.8 explains, is an extremely neoliberal country.

2.7 The Great Recession

The economic crash of 2008 marked the onset of the third generalised crisis of industrial capitalism in its 250-odd year history as a global economic force, seeing neoliberalism enter a period of transnational crisis (Gamble 2009: 10). Similar to the depression of the 1930s, the only other crisis of this scale in capitalism's history, the 2008 crash began in the United States, but quickly became an international phenomenon whose ramifications continue to be felt across much of the world well over a decade after it began. While the various economic crises that occurred post-2008 (e.g., the Eurozone crisis, at its height from approximately 2010–2015), have sometimes been interpreted as discrete events, I follow Tooze's (2018) understanding of these as being various aspects of the same phenomenon, and therefore typically use the term "crisis" in the singular when discussing developments since 2008.

The early tremors that foreshadowed what would become known as the "Great Recession" (Roche, O'Connell and Prothero 2017) were felt when the "credit crunch" began in late 2007, with the Bear Stearns investment bank announcing significant losses and a run on British high-street bank Northern Rock taking place, the first such run in Britain in over 100 years. It was in 2008, however, that the full magnitude of the coming disruptions started to become clear, as the insolvency of much of the financial sector and the collapse of Bear Stearns and Lehman Brothers quickly led to international crisis (Gamble 2009: 23).

As Gamble has explained, the roots of the Great Recession can be traced to the policies adopted in the 1970s as a way to overcome stagflation, with the solution to one crisis ultimately generating the next (2009: 10). While it was neoliberal economics which caused the 2008 crash (see Blyth 2013 and Bresser-Pereira 2010 for detailed discussion of this process), the Great Recession was peculiar in that it did not see capitalism adopt a new regime of accumulation in response to the crisis, as has historically occurred in response to such challenges, such as the move from Keynesianism to neoliberalism. Instead, neoliberal measures were intensified after the crash, which was used as an opportunity to further the programme of privatisation and restructuring to a degree not previously possible (Mirowski 2013). In accordance with neoliberalism's requirements for implementing pro-capital interventions, both nation-states and supra-national bodies such as the International Monetary Fund (IMF) and the World Bank enforced harsh programmes of austerity which saw an enormous transfer of wealth to the upper-classes. As the following section describes, the Republic of Ireland was one of the countries most severely affected by the recession, in no small part due to its having adopted neoliberal policies with particular vigour in the years preceding 2008.

The disastrous social consequences of austerity have been documented at length in a vast body of literature produced since the crash (e.g., Mendoza 2015; Varoufakis 2016; Cooper and Whyte 2017). Notably, however, there has been very little substantive discussion of the Great Recession in LPP literature.

2.8 Economic development in the Republic of Ireland – peaks and troughs over recent decades

As Britain's first colony, Ireland was chronically underdeveloped by the time three quarters of the island gained political independence in 1922 (Coakley 2012). With the legacy of centuries of colonialism being exceedingly difficult to overcome, the Irish Free State (as the Republic of Ireland was called until 1937) remained one of the most impoverished polities in Europe for most of the 20th century (Lee 1989: 664). In the late 20th and early 21st centuries, however, the Republic's economic fortunes were transformed, triggering a rapid period of "catch up" growth (Kirby 2010). This transformation became known as the "Celtic Tiger". Although this term was first used in 1994 (Kirby, Gibbons and Cronin 2002: 17–18), as McDonough (2010) has demonstrated, the roots of the phenomenon can be traced back to 1987, when several key policy changes were implemented.

The country's economy was rapidly neoliberalised during the Celtic Tiger, which saw widespread privatisation and extremely low levels of regulatory oversight in the financial services and corporate sectors, and the development of the country as a prototypical "competition state" which serves the needs of capital above those of its residents (Kirby and Murphy 2011). Based initially on the Foreign Direct Investment of international corporations – for whom the country operates as a tax haven (McCabe 2013: 168–170; IMF 2019) – the Celtic Tiger later saw the development of a property bubble, with house prices trebling between 1998–2008 (Gamble 2009: 3). In line with international trends, labour was greatly weakened during this period, as trade unions adopted a managerialist negotiating strategy known as "social partnership" which effectively brought an end to industrial action, defanging what had within recent memory been an active and militant trade union movement (McDonough 2010: 452; section 11.1).

Although the steep increase in the country's GDP at this time saw it heralded internationally as an exemplary case illustrating the virtues of neoliberal policy, Kirby has characterised this "economic success" as being a "social failure" (2010: 7), due to wealth being squandered and structural inequalities and exclusion in Irish society going largely unchallenged.

The recession which began in 2008, of course, brought an abrupt end to this high-growth period. Having thoroughly embraced the neoliberal model, the country suffered enormously when the crisis struck. As Blyth explains

> The combined result of the property-bubble collapse and the banking system implosion was "the largest compound decline in GNP of any industrialized country over the 2007-2010 period." Government debt increased by 320 percent to over 110 percent of GDP as the government spent some 70 billion euros to shore up the banking system. Meanwhile, unemployment rose to 14 percent by mid-2011 [from approximately 5% pre-crash], a figure that would have been higher had it not been for emigration. (Blyth 2013: 66)

Responding to pressure from both national and international elites, the Irish government implemented a harsh programme of austerity consisting of a drastic contraction in public spending combined with tax increases that were particularly regressive for those on lower and middle incomes. These measures were necessary to fund the bailing out of the banks, which, as noted above, was itself an excellent example of the sort of pro-capital intervention that neoliberalism favours. As Blyth observed, this bailout cost the country's inhabitants an enormous €70 billion, described by the IMF as "the costliest banking crisis in advanced economies since at least the Great Depression" (2012: 20). Indeed, so severe was the crisis that supervision of the Irish economy was ultimately taken over by the IMF, the European Central Bank and the European Commission, colloquially known as the "Troika", between 2010–2013. A 2016 IMF report observed that "[t]he extent and rapidity of Ireland's fiscal deterioration in the latter part of the 2000s was virtually unprecedented among post war industrial country experiences" (2016: 11).

The magnitude of this crisis saw the proportion of the population deemed to be suffering from deprivation almost double between 2007–2010 – increasing from 11.8% to 22.5% (NERI 2012: 75). By April 2013, the IMF calculated that a "staggering" 23% of the labour force was either un- or underemployed (2013: 26). As a result of this, some 610,000 people (of a population of 4.59 million) left the country between 2008–2015 (Glynn and O'Connell 2017: 299), averaging one departure every six minutes in the twelve months to April 2013 (Financial Times 2013). Following the international pattern described in the previous section, despite this crisis of the neoliberal model, the country after 2008 saw an "intensification of neoliberal policies" (Allen 2012: 425), rather than any kind of reversal or re-orientation of this dominant economic orthodoxy.

Notably, however, by 2016 the country's economy had emerged from the crisis, and by 2018 was growing at three times the Eurozone average. While the activity of corporations registered in the Republic for tax avoidance purposes but with no significant operations in the country significantly distorts these figures (Irish Times 2018a), by April 2018 unemployment had nonetheless fallen to 5.9%, just 0.1% above the rate a decade previously (Central Statistics Office 2018a).

Despite the Irish economy having moved from peak to trough and back again in recent years, the spatial distribution of the recovery has been very uneven, occurring mostly in the main population centres, particularly Dublin. As Taft explained in 2016 "[w]hether in the last four years or the last year, Dublin has generated approximately two-thirds of jobs . . . Outside Dublin, even though 70 percent of the total labour force resides there, only a third of jobs were generated" (Taft 2016a). The age-graded nature of the recovery was also marked, with youth unemployment remaining high by April 2018, at 12% (Central Statistics Office 2018b), a figure since exacerbated by Covid.

In 2017 the Pobal HP Deprivation Index concluded that the country as a whole had recovered from the recession by just two-fifths (Hasse and Pratschke 2017a: 8). Disposable incomes, too, remained well below their peak even after growth had returned (Taft 2016b). With chain migration continuing to entice people to emigrate, by 2017 more Irish people were still leaving the country than returning (Irish Times 2017). Projections have suggested that public expenditure per capita will not exceed 2008 levels until 2023, 15 years after the crash (Taft 2018). In light of this, many have referred to the post-2008 period as being "a lost decade" (Irish Independent 2018), with the scars of austerity running deep in Irish society. This is particularly true in much of the Gaeltacht, as this work will demonstrate.

As a result of the policies of recent decades, the Republic of Ireland has been consistently ranked as one of the most globalised countries in the world. Indeed, it was placed second on the 2017 index of globalisation, which collates a variety of economic, political and cultural data for all countries, including number of cross-border financial transactions, investment and revenue flows, capital restrictions, number of international treaties ratified and cross-border information flows (KOF 2017). Mufwene's assertion that "[t]he higher the local globalization index, the stronger the tendency toward monolingualism" (2016: 132) is thus most pertinent to the fate of Irish. Accordingly, Romaine has claimed that "Irish warrants our gaze for what it may tell us of the fate that globalization portends for the survival of the world's linguistic diversity" (2008: 13), an opportunity which I aim to exploit in this study.

Part 2: **Overt and covert Irish-language policy post-2008**

3 Official Irish-language policy post-2008

3.1 Introduction

The death of the Celtic Tiger described in the previous chapter had an enormous impact on all manner of public policy, including, as will be seen in this and the following chapters, language policy. Developing on Ó Riagáin's observation that "[t]he various dimensions of Irish language policy have been heavily conditioned by the way the Irish economy and, in turn, Irish society has developed since independence" (1996: 36), it will be demonstrated that the extremes of neoliberal reform associated with the death of the Celtic Tiger led to an acceleration of state withdrawal from Irish-language maintenance efforts. I argue that there is not only a correlative link here, but a causative one, with neoliberal ideology militating against language revitalisation efforts. Adopting a term favoured in public policy studies, I contend that developments in Irish LPP since 2008, and particularly during the worst years of economic crisis, amounted to a "punctuated equilibrium", a sudden reform of a policy which had previously been changing only incrementally (Cairney 2012: 172–99).

To demonstrate this, my discussion will focus initially on the report of *The Special Group on Public Service Numbers and Expenditure Programmes*, which was the main document that informed the state's programme of austerity and restructuring after 2008 (McCarthy et al. 2009a, 2009b). Although this report effectively provided a road map for the reform of state language policy, it has to date received only very limited attention in academic literature on Irish and the Gaeltacht. I will then go on to provide "policy vignettes" (Cairney 2012: 29) of "overt" language policies (Shohamy 2006), namely the *20-Year Strategy for the Irish Language 2010–2030* and the *Gaeltacht Act 2012* which were introduced while the Irish economy was under the direction of the IMF, the European Central Bank and the European Commission, known as the "Troika". Subsequent chapters will discuss various aspects of "covert language" policy, particularly through referencing the severe cuts Irish-language institutions received.

By way of political background for the discussion that follows, a number of points about the general political situation in the wake of the 2008 crash are worthy of mention. One must be the arrival of the Troika in December 2010, a development which entrenched the neoliberal character of the state's response to the crisis. It would seem, however, that to a large degree the Troika merely insisted on an approach the Irish elite were intent on implementing regardless, a topic I discuss in detail in 6.3.

Another point of note was the electoral defeat of the dominant Fianna Fáil party in the February 2011 election and their replacement with a Fine Gael-led government. Having long since been understood as a party with limited sympathy for the language (Ó hÉallaithe 2004: 169), Fine Gael's election manifesto in early 2011 – just two months after the launch of the *20-Year Strategy for the Irish Language* – proposed the abolition of Irish as a compulsory subject for the Leaving Certificate secondary school examination. Although this plan was ultimately withdrawn due to widespread public opposition, the Fine Gael-Labour coalition of 2011–2016 nonetheless presided over a period of significant disruption in language policy, although, notably, this amounted to a continuation of the policy trajectory adopted by the previous government. Despite often being characterised as significantly more neoliberal than the Fianna Fáil-Green coalition that governed up to 2011, the new coalition's policies did not differ significantly from their predecessors: "[w]ith the Troika MOU [Memorandum of Understanding] as a roadmap, the new government continued the path dependence that locks Ireland into the liberal model. While partisan politics had some impact, both crisis governments were dominated by centre to centre right parties and were largely consistent" (Murphy 2014: 140). While far from an exhaustive account, the following sections discuss the way in which this model shaped the most significant changes in overt Irish LPP for many decades, starting with an examination of the report which played a key role in forming the state's response to the crisis.

3.2 *An Bord Snip Nua:* The special group on public service numbers and expenditure programmes

With its claim that "differential schemes aimed at Gaeltacht areas are not justifiable" (McCarthy et al. 2009b: 41) the *Report of the Special Group on Public Service Numbers and Expenditure Programmes* was unambiguous about its view of the approach the state should take towards the Gaeltacht as a result of the crisis. The report – which, along with the Troika's Memorandum of Understanding (IMF 2010) was a key blueprint for the state's austerity policies – included drastic recommendations for cost savings relating to the Gaeltacht and a huge number of other areas financed by the public purse. As all the more language-specific policy developments discussed in later sections of this chapter occurred under this report's influence, it is important that it be addressed firstly.

The Special Group was convened by finance minister Brian Lenihan in late 2008 and reported in July 2009. Known popularly as *An Bord Snip Nua* [The New Snip Board] or the *McCarthy Report* after the group's chairman, Colm

McCarthy, the report proposed €5.3 billion in cutbacks, including 17,300 public sector job cuts – a reduction of 5% in staffing numbers. While this seemed drastic at the time, these proposals would come to seem mild compared to the cuts of over €20 billion and the reduction of almost 10% in public servant numbers that ultimately occurred (MacCarthaigh 2017: 149). As noted by Mercille and Murphy, McCarthy himself, an economist based in University College Dublin and a competent Irish speaker, "had previously recommended 'slash and burn' policies during the economic recession of the 1980s". He had been part of the original *Bord Snip* established in 1987 to address that decade's recession and has long since had a "reputation for espousing the virtues of laissez-faire economics and market discipline" (Mercille and Murphy 2015: 133). Despite social partnership having been in place for almost two decades by 2009 (see 2.8; 11.1), membership of the "special group" included no trade union or "third sector" voices, a decision which foreshadowed the state effectively ending social partnership unilaterally later that year.

Gaining impact and implementation that very few policy-focused academics ever achieve, McCarthy's proposals heavily influenced the 2010 budget, along with much of the emergency financial legislation that followed. Despite having such high-level impact, the recommendations of the board were deeply unpopular, with John McHale, professor of economics in the National University of Ireland, Galway, comparing them to the "shock therapy" applied after the collapse of the USSR (Indymedia.ie 2009). While complete data on the implementation of the report's recommendations is difficult to obtain, some eleven months after the report's release the minister for finance reported that 145 of 271 recommendations had been implemented in full or in part (Dáil Éireann 2010).

As noted, the report made proposals for a radical reform of state engagement with the Gaeltacht. It observed that the Department of Community, Regional and Gaeltacht Affairs' seemingly very progressive remit was "to promote and support the sustainable and inclusive development of communities, both urban and rural, including Gaeltacht and island communities, thereby fostering better regional balance and alleviating disadvantage, and to advance the use of the Irish language" (McCarthy et al. 2009b: 33).

Nonetheless, the report proceeded to recommend that the department "should be closed and its various functions either redistributed to other Government Departments, or discontinued as appropriate", due to it having "a relatively lower priority in terms of the existing pressures on the public finances" (McCarthy et al. 2009a: 37). This would allow for a saving of some €151.1 million, with it being proposed that those residual matters relating to the Irish language and culture which were not discontinued be assigned to the Department of Education and Science (McCarthy et al. 2009a: 37; 2009b: 36), and that Department of Community,

Regional and Gaeltacht Affairs' staff be laid off. While proposing an overall reduction of 9.4% in state expenditure, the functions performed by the Department of Community, Regional and Gaeltacht Affairs were to be cut at a significantly higher rate of 32%, the highest of any state department. Furthermore, within the department, the cuts recommended for Gaeltacht and islands expenditure amounted to 58% (Guth na Gaeltachta 2010), a figure significantly higher than that recommended for any other subsector. Although the department was not ultimately closed, as will be seen in section 4.3, it suffered severe cuts in a very short period which have not since been reversed.

Another suggestion with extremely significant implications for the Gaeltacht was the proposal to "[c]onsolidate all indigenous enterprise support and sector marketing functions in Enterprise Ireland . . . and rationalise the organisations losing functions as appropriate" (McCarthy et al. 2009a: 27). This was to include ÚnaG, thereby saving €6.9 million (McCarthy et al. 2009a: 36), with the group noting "the high cost per job created" by ÚnaG as one of the reasons for its decision (McCarthy et al. 2009b: 42). Although the functions of ÚnaG would reportedly have been maintained under the aegis of Enterprise Ireland, campaign groups insisted this approach was deeply unsuitable considering the unique needs of the Gaeltacht (Guth na Gaeltachta 2010). As with the Department of Community, Regional and Gaeltacht Affairs, while ÚnaG was not closed – most probably due to such a proposal not being politically viable at the time – it suffered a massive reduction to its budget over a very short period, severely curtailing the organisation's work (see 4.2).

Other cuts proposed – and ultimately implemented – included the discontinuation of Gaeltacht-specific schemes such as the housing grant for Gaeltacht residents and the grant paid to parents of Irish-speaking children, *Scéim Labhairt na Gaeilge*, both of which aimed "to incentivise inhabitants to remain in Gaeltacht areas" (McCarthy et al. 2009b: 41). The *Community and Recreational Schemes* which funded infrastructure such as community centres and sports pitches in Gaeltacht areas and the *Gaeltacht Improvement Schemes* which aided physical and economic development were also abolished.

An Bord Snip Nua's proposals to discontinue *Scéim na bhFoghlaimeoirí Gaeilge* [the Irish-learners' scheme] and close COGG (a policy and promotion agency focused on Irish-medium education) were successfully resisted, however. The proposal to abolish *Scéim na bhFoghlaimeoirí Gaeilge* in particular, which provides a subvention for those who host attendees at Irish-language summer colleges for teenagers, was the subject of a well-organised campaign which successfully saw it maintained, although reduced by 10% for the duration of the crisis, as described in 10.4.1. Chapter 11 offers a detailed discussion of resistance to austerity in a Gaeltacht context.

Further to those measures that focused directly on the Department of Community, Regional and Gaeltacht Affairs, many of the cuts proposed by An Bord Snip Nua for rural areas more generally were also of direct relevance to Gaeltacht communities. Cuts to county councils, the *Local Development Social Inclusion Programme* and the *Community Development Programme* all further reduced the support available to such areas, as too did the recommendation to close or amalgamate primary schools with fewer than 100 pupils. With almost all Gaeltacht schools being in rural locations, this proposal threatened the great majority of schools therein, although it was at least partly resisted due to a nationwide campaign by both parents' groups and teachers' unions (Save Our Small Schools 2012; see also section 11.5). Similarly, the proposed discontinuation of the *Rural Environmental Protection Scheme* and other similar supports to disadvantaged regions such as the *Rural Transport Scheme* created a deeply unstable environment in what were already often vulnerable, underprivileged areas.

While the *Comprehensive Linguistic Study* described above called for a large-scale programme of investment in the Gaeltacht in 2007, in 2009 An Bord Snip Nua advised the exact opposite – a drastic programme of cuts that amounted to a rapid intensification of the state's steady process of withdrawal from supporting the Gaeltacht, which was disproportionately affected by the cuts. As would be predicted by much academic literature on public policy, the neoliberal direction pursued by the state throughout the Celtic Tiger proved to be a path dependent one, meaning that "initial moves in one direction elicit[ed] further moves in that same direction . . . [with] the trajectory of change up to that point *constrain[ing]* the trajectory after that point" (Kay 2005: 553, original emphasis). In the tense post-2008 economic climate many further neoliberal measures were thus implemented, in both the public and private sectors.

Significantly, perhaps the most important example of community resistance to austerity in the context of this book, the *Guth na Gaeltachta* campaign, was set up with the specific aim of opposing the recommendations of An Bord Snip Nua, as section 11.2 explains.

3.3 The *20-year strategy for the Irish Language 2010–2030*

Emerging from a commitment made in the *Statement on the Irish Language 2006* (see 2.5), the *20-Year Strategy for the Irish Language 2010–2030* (henceforth "*Strategy*") was the most detailed exposition of state language policy since 1965 (Government of Ireland 1965; see 2.4). Although it was originally planned for the *Strategy* to be published in 2008, this process was delayed for several years due to difficulties recruiting suitable consultants (Ó Murchú 2008: 42).

Most unserendipitously, the Strategy's eventual launch in December 2010 took place during the same week that the Troika took control of state finances. In this context it is unsurprising that the *Strategy* contained only an extremely watered-down set of goals compared to the recommendations made in Ó Giollagáin et al. (2007a, 2007b), despite it claiming that the government "accepts the broad thrust of the Comprehensive Linguistic Study" (Government of Ireland 2010: 20). With the overarching goal of "creating a bilingual society", the *Strategy* aims to increase the visibility of Irish in public life, ensure the provision of services through Irish and increase the number of Irish-speaking families (Government of Ireland 2010: 3). Furthermore, it contains the aim of increasing to 250,000 the number of daily Irish speakers outside the education system by 2030 (Government of Ireland 2010: 9), a figure which would have required a seemingly impossible 6% annual increase. In the Gaeltacht, it aims for a 25% increase of daily speakers, leading to the widespread derision of these goals as being utterly unattainable (e.g., Ó hÉallaithe 2017a). Ó Giollagáin (2014a: 104–106) has provided an in-depth comparison between the recommendations of the *Comprehensive Linguistic Study* and the Strategy, and consequently they will not be detailed here.

It must be noted, however, that the historical precedents described in 2.3 and 2.4 and international literature on evidence-based policy making would make it seem extremely unlikely that the state would ever have implemented the full range of recommendations included in the *Comprehensive Linguistic Study* (or, indeed, the *Strategy* itself), even if the economic climate had not been so trying at the time of its introduction. Nonetheless, politicians at the highest level stated both at its launch in 2010 and over the following years that the crisis significantly impinged on the state's ability to implement the *Strategy* (Irish Independent 2010; Seanad Éireann 2017). While plausible, this may also be more a convenient excuse for a policy trajectory which the state would have pursued regardless. Similar to opinions espoused by Klein (2007), Mirowski (2013) and Krugman (2015) regarding the use of crises as opportunities to implement radical neoliberal policy reforms long since desired by elites, Ó Giollagáin sees the recession as providing an "effective camouflage for language policy insincerity" with the "inertia and inaction . . . plausibly depicted as an unfortunate off-shoot of negative economic circumstances rather than a lack of will and concern" (Ó Giollagáin 2014a: 114). Of course, the question here must then be *why* this "lack of will and concern" has emerged, something I attempt to answer in this and following chapters by contending that this is a product of the hegemonic dominance of the neoliberal paradigm which sees no place for significant state intervention in such an area. While not addressing this particular topic, there is nonetheless merit to Ó Giollagáin's observation that "[i]t is probably more realistic to depict the excuse of the economic recession for the general institutional lassitude as a carriage of convenience for a much-awaited exit strategy from ideological and policy commitments for which the elite no longer has any patience" (Ó Giollagáin 2014a: 114).

In this way, under the rubric of fiscal responsibility, the state has been able to accelerate the deregulation of language policy, just as the crisis "facilitated the rolling out of drastic reforms more rapidly and thoroughly than would otherwise have been possible" in a wide range of public policy (Mercille and Murphy 2015: 27). In doing so, the "deepening" of neoliberalism was promoted to a degree "that had not yet been seen and with a noted vigour on the part of political and economic elites" (Mercille and Murphy 2015: 27).

Despite the weak nature of its proposals, it is widely understood that the *Strategy* has not been implemented in any meaningful way since its launch in 2010 (Walsh 2014b; Tuairisc.ie 2017b). Walsh, having initially welcomed the *Strategy* as offering the best chance for positive development that was likely to be available to the Irish-speaking community (2011b), observed that by early 2014 the *Strategy* was *"geall le corpán"* [like a corpse] and that Irish was *"níos imeallaí ná riamh sa státseirbhís"* [more marginalised than ever in the civil service] (2014a; see also section 6.2). A clear illustration of this can be seen in the fact that the Department of the Taoiseach's report on how they had been implementing the *Strategy* in their own department, published at the quarter-way point of the policy in December 2015, contained just 163 words. It stated merely that the Taoiseach was the chairperson of the committee dedicated to the Strategy's implementation, that his department was in discussions with stakeholders to overcome the EU derogation described in 2.5 and that future language schemes for the department would specify roles requiring fluency in Irish, with no such positions existing at the time of its writing (Department of the Taoiseach 2015).

Furthermore, in 2014 the reviews of the strategy's progress provided by state departments, in which most stated they did not have any roles requiring Irish-language competency, were so similar to one another that it would seem certain that they were simply copied and pasted from one original report or a sample that was provided to them (Tuairisc.ie 2014a). This level of indifference clearly demonstrates why, during the initial consultations about the Strategy, many experts claimed that the role of monitoring the Strategy's implementation should be given to the Coimisinéir Teanga, rather than allowing the department responsible for the Gaeltacht to police itself. As with the vast majority of recommendations made during the public consultation on a draft of the *Strategy* in 2009, however, such sentiments went unheeded (Ó Giollagáin 2014b: 26). This non-implementation has meant, effectively, a continuation of the pre-*Strategy* policy status quo, but with much less funding now available for policy implementation (Ó Giollagáin 2014b: 35).

In a further blow to the Strategy's effectiveness, in July 2017 the Oireachtas committee chaired by the Taoiseach which oversaw the implementation of the *Strategy* was abolished. While they had been meeting far less frequently than other committees and the importance of the *Strategy* to their work had been greatly reduced since receiving the additional duty of overseeing arts policy in 2016 (Tuairisc.ie 2017c), this nonetheless further relegated the *Strategy* to insignificance. Jordan and Richardson's concept of "placebo policies" which aim to create the appearance of action on issues in which the state is fundamentally uninterested is brought to mind (1987: 233).

Unsurprisingly in this context, a 2018 report compiled for TG4 by Seosamh Mac Donnacha, one of the main authors of the *Comprehensive Linguistic Study*, concluded that none of the structures proposed in the *Strategy* were operational, with many of them never having been established (Tuairisc.ie 2018a).

Shortly after this damning report was issued, an action plan for the *Strategy* was published in July 2018 with the aim of progressing the functioning of the policy (Government of Ireland 2018a). This came a full year late, however, with the result that it was renamed the *Plean Gníomhaíochta 2018–2022* [Action Plan 2018–2022], instead of covering the five-year period 2017–2022 as intended (Dáil Éireann 2018a). While containing various re-affirmations and commitments to implement areas of the *Strategy* that had been largely ignored over the previous eight years, this document, as Ó Giollagáin (2018) describes, contains little that is sufficient to address the continuing erosion of the Gaeltacht that was predicted in 2007 by the *Comprehensive Linguistic Study*, with it amounting largely to a continuation of the policy trajectory pursued pre-2018. As would be expected based on the precedents discussed above, the years since the publication of this action plan have not seen any great increase in the level of diligence with which the *Strategy* is implemented.

3.4 The *Gaeltacht Act 2012*

While not discussed with anything like the same frequency as the *Strategy* by either Irish-language media or advocacy groups, the *Gaeltacht Act 2012* (hereafter "2012 Act") is arguably of far greater significance for the Gaeltacht, not least because it, unlike the Strategy, has been largely implemented since its enactment. As an update to both the original *Gaeltacht Act 1956* which established the current Gaeltacht boundaries and the *Údarás na Gaeltachta Act 1979*, the 2012 Act – which gives legislative effect to some of the goals of the *Strategy* – was the first significant piece of legislation focused on the Gaeltacht in over 30 years. The 2012 Act was deeply controversial at the time of its proposal, however, being criticised by both opposition parties and language promotion groups. Despite over 150 amendments being proposed while the bill was going through the Dáil, all of these were rejected by the Fine Gael-Labour coalition during the three hours allocated for their discussion, thereby prompting a walkout of the opposition, an uncommon occurrence in Irish politics (Irish Examiner 2012).

The language planning process laid out in the 2012 Act ostensibly aimed to redefine the Gaeltacht on the basis of Language Planning Areas. Based originally on recommendations contained in the *Comprehensive Linguistic Study* and accepted in the *Strategy* which aimed to redraw the Gaeltacht borders to more accurately reflect the reality of the use of Irish as a community language, under the 2012 Act the official Gaeltacht was divided into 26 Language Planning Areas by the Department of Arts, Heritage and the Gaeltacht (as it was titled until May 2016). Each of these areas is required by the 2012 Act to write a language plan and have it approved by the department in order to retain their Gaeltacht status. According to the guidelines issued by the department (Department of Culture, Heritage and the Gaeltacht 2019), these plans must analyse the current status of the language in the area, as well as community aspirations for its future (this includes doing primary research consisting of questionnaires, focus groups, etc.). Based on the findings of this research, proposals for improving the standing of Irish in the community are made, along with a timeline and costing for their implementation. Proposed actions are divided amongst the following categories: education, childcare, youth services, public and private sector services, the media, recreation and physical planning. While seemingly quite broad, the remit of these plans is overwhelmingly limited to linguacentric issues, rather than them being able to intervene in the most pressing issues facing most Gaeltacht communities, such as employment, housing and other matters discussed in Part 3. Proposals in plans usually consist of interventions such as classes and other schemes for adult learners, extracurricular supports for schools, bilingual signage on businesses, creating publicity materials, provision of free translation services, petitioning for state services to be provided through Irish, etc. Typically, 50–60% of the budget discussed below is devoted to implementing these actions, with the remainder financing the employment of a local language planning officer who oversees this work (Ní Dhoimhín and Ó Baoill 2016; Ó Ceallaigh 2020).

As described in 2.3, ever since the first Gaeltacht commission reported on the extent of Irish-speaking areas in 1926, the official borders of the Gaeltacht have been aspirational in their expansiveness. This exaggeration continues to be a source of frustration for some Gaeltacht activists (Ó hÉallaithe 2017a). While the 2012 Act could have led to a re-drawing of the borders, the reluctance of employees of organisations such as ÚnaG to formally remove Gaeltacht status from any area means that language plans (completion of which is the sole requirement for the retention of Gaeltacht status) were written in even the weakest category C areas in which language shift is effectively complete. Illustrating the scale of this reticence to concede any part of the official Gaeltacht – likely for fear that such a reduction would see budgets fall further – during my fieldwork an ÚnaG employee told me of the frustration of working with language planning committees who are incapable of conducting their affairs through Irish.

The role of co-ordinating the language planning process under the 2012 Act is placed on ÚnaG. With its well-documented history of promoting industrial development in such a way that it contributed to the anglicisation of the Gaeltacht (Walsh 2010), it was sensible that a more language-focused approach would be recommended for the organisation. In light of the cutbacks to ÚnaG discussed in the following chapter, however, the implementation of the language planning process has been problematic, and it has delegated much of these duties to local *ceanneagraíochtaí* [head organisations] (Walsh 2021: 317). These *ceanneagraíochtaí* are typically community co-operatives (see 12.1), which were warned that their funding would be cut further if they were unwilling to comply with this measure. As one co-op member explained:

> T: Tá [an roinn] ag rá le Údarás na Gaeltachta "caithfidh sibh é a chur i gcrích nó bainfidh muid an t-airgead díbh" agus tá Údarás na Gaeltachta tar éis a rá leis an bpobal, "caithfidh sibhse é a chur i gcrích nó bainfidh muid an t-airgead díbh". Agus tá mé lárnach sa gcóras sin mé féin, ar an receiving end, agus sin atá ag tarlú.

> [T: [The department] is saying to Údarás na Gaeltachta "you have to implement this or we'll cut your funding" and Údarás na Gaeltachta has said to the community "you have to implement this or we'll cut your funding". And I'm central to this process myself, on the receiving end, and that's what's happening.]

Of course, it could surely be added here that the department for the Gaeltacht was itself forced to make such threats as a result of cuts to its own budget from the Department of Finance, which in turn was under duress from the Troika, which was compelled to defend capitalism from its own contradictions after the 2008 crash. Regardless, though, the co-operatives, as predicted by Ó Giollagáin (2014a: 109), have in turn delegated these plans to voluntary community committees, often functioning without adequate resources or expertise. In effectively placing the language planning duties formerly conducted by various state institutions onto voluntary community groups, the procedures spelled out in the Act are strikingly neoliberal, bringing Williams' and Morris' observations on the "grass-rootism of neo-liberalism" to mind, with highly localised structures often charged with implementing major reforms (2000: 180). Through outsourcing language planning responsibilities to marginalised communities, the state, under the guise of democratising the language planning process, is effectively able to withdraw from a key part of its historic commitment to language revitalisation, a move eminently characteristic of neoliberalism's favouring of rationalisation and retrenchment (Mercille and Murphy 2015: 91). As Ó Giollagáin has observed, the 2012 Act seemingly "overestimates the capacity of local Gaeltacht communities to influence societal trends through local plans", while simultaneously underestimating ways in which targeted state intervention could help resist language shift (Ó Giollagáin 2014a: 111). Furthermore, the far-reaching changes instigated by both the 2012 Act and the *Strategy* were matched not with extra resources for their implementation, but rather with budgetary cuts of over 70% to the two institutions most key to their implementation, as Chapter 4 explains.

An employee of a language promotion organisation who I interviewed explained the provisions of the 2012 Act and the manner in which it was forced through by the government as being a response from a civil service which had been frustrated by language rights victories achieved in recent years:

> B: D'éirigh le pobal na Gaeilge buanna áiride a bhaint amach [. . .] Rudaí ar nós TG4, mar shampla, stádas na Gaeilge san Eoraip, [. . .] an Coimisinéir Teanga [. . .] Scanraigh sé an státseirbhís [. . .] go raibh orthu glacadh leis an rud seo, [a bheith] dáiríre faoin rud. Agus ba léir gur frithionsaí cuid dhó seo [Acht 2012] [. . .] Toradh nádúrtha é sin ar an ais-throid sin, bhí sé thar a bheith lag. Bhí sé dochreidte ó thaobh córas polaitiúil nach raibh siad sásta glacadh le oiread is leasú amháin.

> [B: The Irish-speaking community achieved certain victories [. . .] Things like TG4, for example, the status of Irish in Europe, [. . .] the language commissioner [. . .] That scared the civil service [. . .] that they had to accept this, be serious about it. And it was clear that some of [the 2012 Act] was a counter attack [. . .] That's the natural result of that counter attack, it was extremely weak. It was incredible with regard to the political system that they weren't even willing to accept even one amendment.]

Although there may well be some truth in this sentiment, it must also be remembered that the 2012 Act was introduced at a time when the country was still beholden to the Troika's structural adjustment programme, unemployment had risen from under 5% in early 2008 to nearly 15% in 2012 and the state had already spent €70 billion on bank bailouts (Murphy 2014: 135). As Hardiman and Regan noted at the time: "[a]ll budget decisions must be cleared with the Troika, fiscal performance is subject to quarterly reviews and Troika personnel are embedded in the core government departments" (2012: 9). Furthermore, the conditions of the Memorandum of Understanding between the state and the Troika "required a continued liberalisation of Ireland's political economy and increased marketisation of previously protected public spheres" (Murphy 2014: 134).

While, then, the unsuitability of the 2012 Act may be connected to the attitude of hostile elements within the civil service, it would seem more likely that the extraordinarily constrained economic circumstances facing the state by mid-2012 made it all but inevitable that the implementation of the 2012 Act would deliver a far from satisfactory outcome. The truth, of course, may well lie in a mixture of these elements, with the crisis both providing an excuse for and requiring an accelerated withdrawal of state support for the language. Either way, the enactment of the 2012 Act and the provisions it contains echoes Williams' and Morris' comment that neoliberalism means that language planning "can no longer be conceived of in terms of the modernist conception of state benevolence, acting on behalf of the language group within a general framework of democracy and rights" (2000: 180).

Despite Ó Giollagáin's description of the 2012 Act as "the half-hearted conviction of a reluctant duty" (Ó Giollagáin 2014a: 111) being fully justified, his analysis fails to give sufficient attention to the economic and political conditions of crisis in which it was produced and, like my interviewee above, places excessive weight on the machinations of "anti-Irish" public servants, a topic I discuss in detail in 6.2. Furthermore, in his account of the state's ignoring of the recommendations of the *Comprehensive Linguistic Study* in both the *Strategy* and the 2012 Act, Ó Giollagáin (2014a: 103–115) does not acknowledge the fact that such ignoring of expert advice is not at all an uncommon occurrence in public policy making, either in Ireland or internationally. As discussed in 4.5 below, evidence-based policy making is very often the exception rather than the rule. Rather than being necessarily reflective of a political class expressly opposed to Irish, it can plausibly be seen as a product of the bounded rationality and "satisficing" which policy makers and the elite inevitably face, whereby they can only hope to make reasonably satisfactory policy in the face of incomplete knowledge and resources, as well as the structural factors which constrain their actions (Cairney 2012: 95–98, 111–131).

Tellingly, the mark of neoliberal austerity measures is very visible in relation to the 2012 Act, with the Explanatory and Financial Memorandum attached to it stating "[i]t is estimated that Part 3 of the Bill [regarding the ÚnaG election – see 4.2] will result in savings of approximately €100,000 annually and up to €500,000 every five years. It is not expected that the remaining Parts of the Bill will result in any additional costs to the Exchequer" (Government of Ireland 2012: 44).

This note provides a striking counterpoint to the various public assurances from the government after the enactment of the 2012 Act that resources would be made available for the language planning process laid out therein, an issue discussed further below.

The implementation of the Act has also been a fraught process. Recruitment to the very committees so central to implementing the Act's provisions, for instance, was very difficult in many areas. This challenge could be expected, considering the falling rates of voluntarism in the developed west (Putnam 2000), the fact that Ireland has long since had an uncommonly weak culture of civic engagement (Mac Cormaic 2011: 21), and the manner in which the neoliberal period that began in the country in the late 1980s has seen voluntary participation atrophy further (Khoo 2006; Neville 2015). While there are no comparable studies of Ireland, Lim and Laurence (2015) have also demonstrated that the economic crisis reduced volunteering levels in the United States and the United Kingdom (see also 6.4; Clarke and Heath 2014). As such, this difficulty in recruiting volunteers was also very likely exacerbated by the material uncertainty brought about by the recession. As one of my interviewees stated *"Roimh an phleanáil teanga caithfidh díon a bheith os do chionn agus caithfidh jab a bheith agat!"* [Before language planning you need to have a roof over your head and you need to have a job!].

State policy explicitly predicated on community voluntarism in a time of economic turmoil thus requires substantial efforts towards encouraging participation, even more so than during less testing periods. Financial constraints, however, prevented a co-ordinated publicity campaign to promote community involvement and ownership (cornerstones of any language revitalisation project) being implemented for the process. Such a publicity scheme was all the more necessary in light of public cynicism following the limited success of previous language policies and the suppression of an important, voluntary Gaeltacht movement which aimed to resist austerity at the same time as the 2012 Act was being implemented (see 11.2). Unsurprisingly, then, the imposition of what is allegedly meant to be an empowering and participatory process in this fashion, with little attempt to explain why exactly it is important or what value it adds to communities, was ineffective in promoting much public enthusiasm.

Widespread disinterest in or cynicism towards official policies is, of course, not unique to language planning. The heavily voluntarist aspect of the *Gaeltacht Act 2012* is, however, somewhat peculiar from a public policy perspective. The fact that it is based on community participation but nonetheless saw next to no extra resources devoted to promoting such engagement is clearly indicative of the extent of state "rollback" from language promotion efforts in recent years.

A comparison with the resources afforded to publicising LPP measures during the Celtic Tiger highlights the degree to which the cuts have affected the functionality of Irish-language institutions. Writing before the 2008 crisis about the *Official Languages Act 2003*, Walsh and McLeod explained that "[t]he Department of Community, Rural and Gaeltacht Affairs ran language awareness campaigns in 2004 and 2005 but the total budget for these was a mere €500,000" (2008: 42). In comparison with the non-existence of *any* such campaign during a much more substantial policy reform, occurring at a critical point for the language's future, this "mere €500,000" seems very substantial indeed. It is, in fact, more than the total made available for the implementation of the language planning process in any single year between 2012–2016, and five times the annual budget that most Language Planning Areas receive for implementing their plans.

Despite the limited publicity around the issue, as of the time of writing the majority of Language Planning Areas have a voluntary committee of some description. I was often told, however, that these were small and have a handful of people doing much more than the lion's share of the work – typically people who are also involved in other community development projects. It is also notable that the age group perhaps most important for the success of this process, young adults, tends to be absent from such committees. This is likely a result of various other structural issues discussed throughout this study, many of which disproportionately affect younger people – including out-migration, precarious employment conditions, income inequality and the general decline in civic engagement these factors produce (Putnam 2000; Steger 2002; Paskov and Dewilde 2012).

In order to compensate for their own lack of expertise, many committees have used the funding made available for preparing their plans to procure the assistance of an outside consultant to assist with this work. It was, however, difficult or impossible for many communities to find a suitably qualified person for this position. The fact that ÚnaG was forced to end its programme of paying the fees for students who did the MA in language planning in the Acadamh in the National University of Ireland, Galway the same year as the 2012 Act was enacted was, of course, in no way conducive to the capacity building needed to effectively implement such a policy. In addition to there being a relatively small number of people with the requisite qualifications, the short-term, low-pay nature of the contracts offered did little to make this work appealing to those who are suitably qualified. This extract from an interview with an informant who moved county four times in two years pursuing temporary contracts writing several of these plans is informative in this regard:

A: *Éinne leis na cáilíochtaí céanna is a bhí agamsa [. . .] má bhí post fiú ann leath-réasúnta faighte ag na daoine sin ní raibh siad á thabhairt suas le goil ag obair ar phlean teanga. Tá tú ag caint ar chonradh gearr-thréimhseach, gan aon chinnteacht. Níl tú ag caint ar airgead an-mhaith [. . .] Agus tá sé an-uaigneach mar obair, sin an rud ba mhó a chur isteach ormsa [. . .] Is obair chrua atá ann [. . .] D'fhág sé rian ar mo shláinte fiú ann, an strus a bhaineann leis [. . .] I mo chonradh-sa [. . .] bhí sé curtha in iúl nach obair lán-aimseartha a bhí ann [ach] bhí sé lán-aimseartha agus tuilleadh. Bhí mé ag obair cúig lá sa tseachtain [agus] ag tarraingt ar an deireadh, seacht lá sa tseachtain. Bheinn ag éirí ag a seacht, goil ag obair, críochnú ag meán oíche [. . .] Mar gheall nach raibh an t-airgead chomh hiontach sin [. . .] bhí mé ag aistriú, bhí mé ag múineadh, ag déanamh jabanna beaga eile [freisin] [. . .] Níl sé inbhuanaithe ní dóigh liom do dhuine.*

[A: Anybody with the same qualifications as I had [. . .] if they had gotten an even half decent job, they weren't going to give it up to go working on a language plan. You're talking about a short-term contract, without any certainty. You're not talking about very good money [. . .] And it's very lonely work, that's the thing that affected me the most [. . .] It's difficult work [. . .] It left its mark on my health even, the stress connected with it [. . .] In my contract it said that it wasn't full-time work, but it was full-time and more. I was working five days a week [and] nearing the end, seven days a week. I'd be getting up at seven, going to work, finishing at midnight [. . .] Because the money wasn't that great [. . .] I was translating, I was teaching, doing other little jobs [as well] [. . .] It's not sustainable for a person I don't think.]

The emergence of such undesirable, "atypical" working conditions (which are, of course, becoming ever more typical) and the so-called "precariat" class under neoliberalism is well documented in socioeconomic literature, as are the extremely detrimental consequences of such conditions for workers' physical and mental health (Standing 2014; Sparke 2016). The outsourcing of positions formerly occupied by relatively well-paid public servants is also a key feature of the neoliberal New Public Management measures discussed in Chapter 6: "outsourcing support[s] a casualization and peripherization of labor that treat[s] certain jobs within the organization as temporary or "as needed", and allows for readier workforce control and reduced costs to the state" (Ward 2011: 208–209).

While the level of education required to work in this sector means such consultants would not be classed as members of the precariat, it does place them in the category of "emergent service workers" – an emergent class better off than the precariat primarily by virtue of their higher levels of social and cultural capital (Savage 2015: 169–175).

Indeed, during the final year of the PhD which this book is based on, I myself was employed as a consultant for two Language Planning Areas – one in Donegal, one in Galway. Although this work was obviously not part of the research for this study and included its own stipulations regarding anonymity and the ownership of the data collected for writing the plans, it did nonetheless provide me with much first-hand experience of this process which accords with the findings of the ethnographic work conducted specifically for this project.

Another issue often cited as being a key deficit of the implementation of the 2012 Act was the long-standing uncertainty surrounding the funding that would be made available for implementing language plans after they were prepared. While the first several plans were being written (the timing of this was staggered throughout different areas), the state refused to give any indication of what, if any, funding would be made available for their implementation – an issue which, of course, made it very difficult to propose concrete recommendations. While researching this chapter I had the opportunity to challenge the minister then responsible for the Gaeltacht, Seán Kyne, on this issue at a public meeting in Conamara. When asked if he was willing to confirm that adequate resources would indeed be made available for the plans' implementation he stated simply *"níl mé sásta aon rud a gheallúint, Ben"* [I'm not willing to promise anything, Ben].

Although arguably a politically sensible position to adopt, responses such as this certainly did not suggest that the state is fully supportive of these communities' efforts and did little to encourage people to devote their free time to the process.

This uncertainty also further indicates the lack of priority afforded to the maintenance of the Gaeltacht by the political class, who are typically able to express approximately the level of funding a new policy will receive. It is also unusual that the relevant minister was willing to approve plans (as the 2012 Act requires), but not approve the funding required for the implementation of the recommendations contained within them. As a consequence of this and other deficits of the process, on more than one occasion that I am aware of diligent members withdrew from committees because of their understandable dissatisfaction.

With the publication of the 2018 budget, it finally became clear that some funding – €100,000 per plan per annum – would be made available for the implementation phase of the process. Strikingly, however, this itself was taken from the budget previously used to fund repairs to Gaeltacht roads – a great number of which are of a poor standard (Tuairisc.ie 2016k; Dáil Éireann 2017). Such decisions represent an extremely flawed view of language revitalisation, an unhelpful dichotomy that implies there is no connection between language vitality and the provision of basic community infrastructure such as adequately surfaced roads.

Furthermore, this funding is significantly less than required for those Language Planning Areas that have many thousands of residents, being under half of that required based on the costings provided in the plan prepared in the Cois Fharraige area, for instance, which has a population of circa 6,500. The issue was a further cause of dissatisfaction, with Professor Dónall Ó Baoill – who co-wrote a plan in Donegal (Ní Dhoimhín and Ó Baoill 2016) – stating that such inadequate budgets ensure that the plans will fail (Tuairisc.ie 2017p).

In response to the announcement of this funding, two of the first three committees to launch their plans (Cois Fharraige and Gaoth Dobhair/Íochtar na Rosann) announced in late 2017 that they were refusing to accept the €100,000 offered, demanding instead the amounts requested, €250,000 and €150,000 respectively. The Cois Fharraige committee went as far as to announce its intention to disband if their requests went unanswered. A third committee in Corca Dhuibhne also later announced their intention to boycott this insufficient funding upon completing their plan (Tuairisc.ie 2017q, 2017r). These developments marked a considerable escalation of tensions between these communities and the state, and, in response, €50,000 extra was offered to the committees involved in the boycott (Tuairisc.ie, 2017s). After some debate on the matter, this offer eventually saw these committees concede, not least due to their desire to proceed with implementing their plans rather than being stuck in a deadlock with the state.

Despite the country officially having recovered from the post-2008 crisis by this time, funding for these plans – which are required by law under the 2012 Act – was still enormously difficult to secure, requiring boycotts to gain resources to implement state policy, a further striking illustration of the extent to which Gaeltacht funding has been rationalised, something discussed in more detail in the following chapter.

In addition to these difficulties regarding community participation and funding, it is also notable that the state has refused to commit to ensuring its own activities in the Gaeltacht are conducted through Irish, with experts consequently feeling the language planning process is unlikely to succeed (Tuairisc.ie 2017t). One example of many which illustrate this negligence occurred in November 2017, when the Department of Agriculture advertised a managerial position based in Ros a' Mhíl in Galway which did not include Irish-language competency as a requirement for employment (Tuairisc.ie 2017u), despite this area containing the only electoral division in the country where Irish remains the dominant language of communication for those aged under-18 (Ó Giollagáin and Charlton 2015a: 9).

As a result of the manner in which the state has implemented the 2012 Act, even those heavily involved in the language planning process frequently described it to me as a ploy to open the way for further state withdrawal from language revitalisation efforts. Indeed, one long-term employee of the very state department responsible for Gaeltacht policy explicitly suggested to me that the 2012 Act was a *"cleas"* [trick] to *"fáil réití' leis an chúram. Agus ansin má thiteann an tóin amach as an rud uilig [. . .] beidh siadsan ábalta a rá, bhuel, níl an locht orainne, thug muidinne an cúram sin do na pobail agus má lig siadsan dó [. . .]*

is ar na pobail atá an locht" [Get rid of the responsibility. And then if the whole thing collapses [. . .] they'll be able to say, well, it's not our fault, we gave that duty to the community and if they let it slide [. . .] it's the communities that are to blame].

While neoliberal policy conventions are clearly visible in much Irish-language policy produced in recent years, the language planning process laid out in the *Gaeltacht Act 2012* is perhaps one of the clearest examples that this sector provides of the neoliberal "rollback" of the state famously described by Peck and Tickell (2002). It is also deeply reminiscent of their observation that under neoliberalism "local institutions and actors [are] given responsibility without power, while international institutions and actors [gain] power without responsibility", a process which sees "a form of regulatory dumping" occur at the local level, "while macro-rule regimes [are] remade in regressive and marketized ways" (Peck and Tickell 2002: 386).

Although allegedly meant to be empowering, the 2012 Act has instead bred cynicism and disdain and done far less than required to foster the community support and participation necessary for language revitalisation, factors all the more crucial at a time when so much of the available evidence shows the Gaeltacht to be facing sociolinguistic crisis.

3.5 Conclusion

When speakers of many other minoritised languages hear that there is an official government strategy for promoting Irish, that there is extensive legal protection for the language and numerous state-funded bodies operating to help ensure its survival, they are often shocked, even jealous. Recent developments, however, belie the truth of the situation and show that things are not quite as progressive as they might initially seem.

By drawing attention to various rarely discussed aspects of recent Irish LPP, this chapter has attempted to illustrate how the generally incrementalist pattern of language policy change that prevailed pre-2008 was ruptured by the adoption of a significantly more neoliberal language policy regime in the years since the economic crash. This new regime has seen support for the language greatly reduced, something very apparent from an examination of official Irish-language policy published in the intervening years.

As has been seen, one key aspect of the policy context in which recent reforms were made was the publication of the infamous report of An Bord Snip Nua, which laid out a blueprint for state austerity measures and proposed many of the changes which have since been implemented with regards to

Irish-language policy. Although the most significant Irish LPP reforms for many decades occurred at a time when the IMF, the European Central Bank and the European Commission Troika had a veto over public policy, scholarship on Irish LPP has not addressed this fact in any detail, despite it surely being a crucial part of the explanation for the unsatisfactory nature of these policies. The *20-Year Strategy for the Irish Language 2010–2030* contains only vague, unattainable goals, and much expert opinion and many responses to a public consultation on a draft of the policy were ignored during its preparation. The parliamentary discussion on the deeply flawed bill that became the *Gaeltacht Act 2012* was so curtailed that opposition parties walked out in protest after the government rejected every proposed amendment – over 150 in total, many of which were initially suggested by language promotion groups.

Further to the content of these documents being inadequate to reverse or halt language shift in the Gaeltacht, their implementation has been even more problematic. The *Strategy* has been largely ignored since it was launched in the same week that the Troika took over supervision of the country's economy. Indeed, the parliamentary committee which was meant to oversee the *Strategy* was abolished in 2017 and many of the structures which were meant to facilitate its implementation have never been established.

Unlike the Strategy, the *Gaeltacht Act 2012* has largely been implemented since its introduction, although as has been seen, this implementation has too been the subject of much contention. With the Act amounting to a significant rationalisation of state support for language planning in the Gaeltacht, funding has been insufficient and, unsurprisingly, the process has been met with a large degree of cynicism from Gaeltacht communities. The limited budget that has been made available for the language planning process laid out in the Act (typically €100,000 per plan per annum) has itself been taken from the fund that existed to finance the repair of Gaeltacht roads, which are often in great need of maintenance. The additional funding that is being made available for a handful of Language Planning Areas (an extra €50,000 per year) was only secured due to voluntary committees undertaking a boycott against the process they were charged with implementing.

In addressing these matters, I have endeavoured to centre the wider economic context in which these developments occurred because, as Lowi (1964) famously noted, too many assessments of policy focus on specific policy makers rather than the environment in which they operate, a tendency as prominent in LPP as in other spheres. The approach is continued in the following chapter, where "covert" language policy is discussed in detail, with it being shown that, if anything, covert policy is of greater importance in the Republic of Ireland than the official, "overt" language policy developments discussed above.

4 Irish-language institutions: Covert policy and state retrenchment

4.1 Introduction

With the previous chapter having discussed the most significant reforms to official, "overt" Irish-language policy since 2008, this chapter and the two that follow examine developments regarding "covert" policy. Deferring to Shohamy's important observation that language policy "should not be observed only through declared policy statements", but also those policies unrelated to language that serve "to perpetuate language practices, often in covert and implicit ways" (Shohamy 2006: xvi), the manner in which Irish-language institutions were rationalised is explored. The discussion in this chapter will focus primarily on the disproportionately severe budget cuts both ÚnaG and the state department with responsibility for the Gaeltacht received, as well as the closure in 2014 of 13 of 19 national language promotion bodies and the controversy surrounding the publication of the update to the *Comprehensive Linguistic Study of the Use of Irish in the Gaeltacht* in 2015.

The fact that the education system receives little attention in either this or subsequent chapters may strike some readers as unusual. Educational matters are only discussed in relation to other topics, for instance regarding cuts to training and scholarships, as mentioned in the following section about ÚnaG (see also 3.4; 5.3), or the drop in attendance at summer language schools (10.4.1). There are a number of reasons why I have not focused on this topic more, as discussions of language revitalisation so often tend to do. On a simple practical level, doing this subject justice would require more space than a work of this length can offer. Furthermore, while schools can certainly be an important aspect of revitalisation efforts, it seems curious that despite it being almost axiomatic in language revitalisation literature that schools alone are insufficient for revitalising languages, they are the focus of an enormous amount of research in the field, while economic change, perhaps *the* central factor in processes of language loss and revitalisation (also all but axiomatic, as described in 1.1), receives little scholarly interest. As stated from the outset, the goal of this work is to try to rectify this deficit. While this in itself does not, of course, require educational issues be ignored, the nature of Irish-language education at first and second level does mean that it does not readily lend itself to the sort of discussion that is the focus of this work. Although the teaching of Irish as a compulsory subject in all schools is an important aspect of official language revitalisation policy, this is funded by the budget of the Department of Education and Skills and is not ordinarily understood as dedicated Irish-language spending. While austerity saw education budgets cut, these measures did not result in reductions in the level of provision for Irish. Indeed, in response to a long campaign, a new Gaeltacht education policy was introduced in 2016. Ní Chuaig (2018) offers an analysis of this new curriculum, which has also been significantly under-resourced since its implementation (Tuairirsc.ie 2017a) – a topic I return to in section 11.5 where I discuss some of the ways in which communities tried to compensate for the drastic cuts to ÚnaG and the other developments described in this chapter.

4.2 Údarás na Gaeltachta

Since its foundation in 1979, Údarás na Gaeltachta (ÚnaG), the Gaeltacht development authority, has successfully attracted a significant number of enterprises to the Gaeltacht, at least for the short term. Implementing a localised version of the national economic strategy, this has been primarily achieved through offering tax breaks and other incentives to companies who are willing to locate there. Although this approach has been widely critiqued as being unsuitable for Gaeltacht development (e.g., Walsh 2011a; section 8.4 below), the proposal by An Bord Snip Nua that ÚnaG be abolished outright caused much concern for Gaeltacht communities. While this abolition did not ultimately occur, the institution, as will be seen, was severely debilitated by the ensuing cuts.

Indeed, one of the most expedient ways of gaining an insight into covert language policy in the wake of the crash is through examining the differential treatment visited on ÚnaG compared to its non-Gaeltacht equivalents. As Table 1 shows, ÚnaG's budget was reduced much more significantly than that of either the Industrial Development Agency (IDA) or Enterprise Ireland, despite it performing the functions of these two organisations combined, albeit in a Gaeltacht-specific context.

Table 1: Comparison of enterprise promotion agencies' budgets 2008–2015 (Údarás na Gaeltachta 2009a: 9, 2016a: 11; Enterprise Ireland 2009: 48, 2016: 42; IDA 2010: 36, 2016: 33. See also Conradh na Gaeilge 2017: 10–11).

	Údarás na Gaeltachta	Enterprise Ireland	Industrial Development Agency
2008	€25.5 million	€56.4 million	€78.5 million
2015	€6.7 million	€52.7 million	€116 million
% Change 2008–2015	−73.7%	−6.6%	+47.8%

The ÚnaG budget was, in fact, even lower in 2014 than the figure given in Table 1 (falling to its lowest point, €5.7 million), but the contrast with the other two institutions for that year is not quite as striking (Conradh na Gaeilge 2017: 10–11).

State attitudes towards ÚnaG are all the more evident when one considers that these cuts were made to an agency whose main duty – like the IDA and Enterprise Ireland – is to create employment, a goal which each government of the post-crash period regularly claimed to be a priority. Furthermore, this reduction was implemented despite an independent report concluding in 2010 that the organisation required a minimum budget of €12 million per annum simply to retain those jobs then in the Gaeltacht, without any consideration for increasing this amount (Ó Clochartaigh 2013). Unsurprisingly, these cuts led to a significant fall in the numbers employed in ÚnaG client-companies during this period, as well as an enormous drop in the funding the organisation made available for training, which fell from €12,766,480 to €1,582,030 between 2008–2015 (Conradh na Gaeilge 2017: 10–11; Údarás na Gaeltachta 2009b: 3, 2016b: 3). Staff numbers in the agency itself also declined as a result of these measures and the related early retirement schemes and recruitment moratorium introduced to cut state spending in the public sector. These policies cost ÚnaG many of its most experienced staff and offered no option for a managed handover of their duties. While the organisation had 130 staff members in 2008, this had fallen to 79 ten years later (Oireachtas Éireann 2018a). A welcome rise in 2021 brought this number to 93, the first increase in over a decade (Tuairisc.ie 2021a).

In an interview with a now-retired senior member of ÚnaG who presided over the organisation through both the height of the boom and the worst depths of the recession, he explained the implications of this enormous budget reduction as such:

> S: Nuair a thoisigh mise amach bheadh buiséad caipitil de 26 milliún againn. Bhí na feidhmeannaigh ábalta dul amach agus iad muiníneach astu féin dá mba rud é gur chas siad le infheisteoir [. . .] [bhí] siad ábalta a bheith láidir faoi agus a rá 'is féidir linn cuidiú leat' [. . .] Nuair a thiteann an buiséad go sé nó ocht milliún d'airgead caipitil, b'fhéidir go mbeidh na feidhmeannaigh ag rá an rud céanna, ach [. . .] déarfaidh siadsan 'bhuel an bhfuil buiséad agat?'

> [S: When I started out, we'd have a capital budget of 26 million. The executives were able to go out and be confident in themselves that if they met an investor [. . .] they could be strong and say 'we can help you' [. . .] When the capital budget falls to six or eight million, maybe the executives will be saying the same thing but [. . .] they'll say 'well do you have a budget?']

This view was echoed by many of the current staff I spoke to during my fieldwork. One of the executives referred to in the above quote explained his view of the matter to me as follows:

> É: Tá lá na himeartha caillte againn, you're not a player anymore. Ní bhíonn daoine ag caint fúinn, ní bhíonn muid ag caint ar an raidió, síleann daoine go bhfuil an cath caillte againn. Tá baint aige sin uilig leis an ghearradh siar tubaisteach a tharla dúinn [. . .] An rud a deir siad faoi neoliberalism, reductive, reductivism [. . .] reductivity. Tá achan rud gearrtha anuas. Tá monatóireacht mhór déanta ar achan rud. Tá níos mó monatóireacht déanta ar achan rud anois mar tá na budgets chomh teannta.
>
> [É: You're not a player anymore. People don't talk about us, we aren't talking on the radio, people think we've lost the battle. That's all to do with the catastrophic cut backs we had [. . .] And the thing they say about neoliberalism, reductive, reductivism [. . .] reductivity. Everything is cut back. There's huge monitoring of everything. There's more monitoring of everything because the budgets are so tight.]

After reaching such lows, ÚnaG's budget was gradually increased until it reached some €10 million for 2020, although this amount continued to be derided as being far from adequate to meet their needs (Tuairisc.ie 2019a). Significantly, as part of its commitment to "strengthening Ireland's rural fabric", the *National Development Plan 2018–2027*, launched in February 2018, stated that €178 million would be invested in the Gaeltacht, including an "incremental increase in the annual capital allocation to €12 million" for ÚnaG (Government of Ireland 2018b: 50). No deadline was provided for the fulfilment of this commitment, which, even if implemented as proposed, will see funding for ÚnaG at less than 50% of the 2008 figure come 2027 (Tuairisc.ie 2018b). Furthermore, research commissioned by the civil society campaign group *Teacht Aniar* demonstrated that during the four-year period between 2005–2009 capital expenditure on the Gaeltacht and islands was €299 million, vastly more than the €178 million which is promised for the nine-year period from 2018–2027. Even based on the assumption that this proposed investment is made in full, expenditure on Irish by 2028 will still be significantly less than it was in 2008. Indeed, this €178 million amounts to only slightly more than *half* of what was spent on this sector between 2006–2016, the cutbacks of this time notwithstanding (Byrne 2018: 10).

Another ÚnaG employee who I interviewed in 2016, talked at length about the *"titim thubaisteach"* [catastrophic fall] in employment in ÚnaG's industrial site in Donegal. He told me that there were almost 900 fewer jobs in the estate than there had been during the height of the Celtic Tiger, with the total having fallen from some 1,300 positions to 430, part-time and short-term contracts included. This same interviewee told me that the crash had seen the end of an era, the end of manufacturing in the area, and that the industries now supported on the estate are largely small-scale, local start-ups, as opposed to the industrial plants that had once employed hundreds each. He also commented on the tendency of large international companies to simply relocate overseas during challenging economic periods: *"Sin an rud atá tábhachtach, d'aistrigh siad. Cionn is go dtiocfadh leo 20 oibrí a fháil san Ind ar son pá oibrí amháin anseo"* [That's the important thing, they moved. Because you can get 20 workers in India for the pay one worker here gets].

While their inability to retain such companies long-term is a criticism frequently levelled at ÚnaG, this point goes to the heart of globalised neoliberalism. Such fluidity of capital is a defining trait of this paradigm, and one which is, clearly, almost impossible for a small enterprise promotion agency based on this model to resist while operating in some of the most remote parts of Ireland – particularly so in wake of a budget cut of almost 75%. The Foreign Direct Investment model based on attracting footloose international capital is clearly, however, deeply inappropriate for the Gaeltacht, as the many abandoned, dilapidated factories scattered across the Gaeltacht attest. Chapter 8 discusses this issue further.

In light of the various cuts detailed above, a letter from the trade union *Unite* to the management of ÚnaG in summer 2016 claimed that the relationship between staff and management was "at an all-time low" and "on the brink of collapse" (Tuairisc.ie 2016a). While interviewing a long-term employee of ÚnaG shortly after this story broke publicly in the media, he explained the situation to me as being even worse than was reported, describing morale in the organisation as having become *"iontach olc"* [extremely bad] over the preceding three or four years. When asked why exactly this was, he responded as follows:

> É: Rationalisation [. . .] Tá an tríú cuid den fhoireann [imithe], nuair a imíonn daoine cuireann siad cosc duin' neacht eile a fháil. I bhfad níos mó oibre a dhéanamh le níos lú daoine. Daoine ag an bharr, [. . .] tá an dúshlán acusan agus tá siad ar an chúigiú cuid den budget a bhí deich mbliana ó shin. Tá siad ar 30% níos lú foirne, tá an foireann atá fágtha aosta. Níl duine ar bith úr ag teacht isteach. Thit siad amach leis an cheardchumann. Tá siad seo ag iarraidh na rudaí seo a bhrú ar aghaidh gan pairtnéireacht ar bith, gan a ghoil i gcomhairle. Dhá vóta muiníne caillte ag an bhainistíocht le 70% le dhá mhí [. . .] Tá an bainistíocht ag brú, ag bulaíocht ar dhaoine.

> [É: Rationalisation [. . .] A third of the staff are gone, when someone leaves we're not allowed to recruit someone new. Much more work to do with less people. People at the top [. . .] have the challenge and they're on a fifth of the budget they were ten years ago. They have 30% less staff, the staff they have are old. No one new is coming in. They fell out with the trade union. They want to push these things through without any partnership, without any consultation. The management have lost two votes of confidence by 70% in the last two months [. . .] The management are pressuring, bullying people.]

Similar to the rest of the public sector (see 6.2), then, it is clear that ÚnaG was deeply affected by austerity measures, which certainly did not help them to ensure the "preservation and extension" of Irish in the Gaeltacht as their remit requires. Despite the reduction in the resources available to them, however, responsibility for the language planning process required by the *Gaeltacht Act 2012* was delegated to ÚnaG by the state department responsible for the Gaeltacht, as discussed in the previous chapter.

Further to these challenges, under the *Gaeltacht Act 2012*, the election for the board of ÚnaG was abolished, despite the institution having originally been established as a result of the Gaeltacht Civil Rights campaign aiming specifically for the creation of a democratic local government institution in the Gaeltacht. Partly undertaken in accordance with the Fine Gael-Labour coalition's *Public Service Reform Plan* (Department of Public Expenditure and Reform 2011), it was noted that this reform would save some €500,000 every five years (Irish Times 2011a; section 3.4).

Prior to 2012, three of the 20 members of this board were appointed by the minister responsible for the Gaeltacht, while the remaining 17 were elected by Gaeltacht residents (Walsh 2011a: 300). In line with the *Gaeltacht Act 2012*, the board is now composed of twelve political appointees selected both by county councils which contain Gaeltacht communities within their jurisdictions and the relevant minister (Government of Ireland 2012: 26–29).

While ostensibly a democratic forum, it is important to note that there was widespread dissatisfaction with the pre-2012 electoral process for the board. I was often told during interviews that the restructuring made little difference, with much of the population being indifferent to the internal workings of the organisation. Nonetheless, some of my interviewees had much more impassioned opinions on the matter. The Galway woman cited in the next extract, for instance, strongly felt that while it had been perhaps excessively clientelist, the loss of the election was a severe blow to Gaeltacht communities:

G: Is cuimhneach liom fadó toghchán an Údaráis agus [. . .] bhíodh an oiread caint air! [. . .] Is mó suím, caithfidh mé a rá, a bhíodh i dtoghchán an Údaráis ná sa toghchán náisiúnta [. . .] [Ba é stocaireacht ar bhaill an bhoird] an chaoi a bhfuair tú go leor rudaí déanta. Now ceart nó [contráilte], níl's a'm – sin an chaoi ar oibrigh sé. Yeah 'sé an feall nach bhfuil sé ann níos mó.

[G: I remember long ago the Údarás election and [. . .] there'd be so much talk about it! [. . .] There was more interest, I have to say, in the Údarás election than in the national election [. . .] [Lobbying elected board members was] how you got things done. Now right or [wrong], I dunno – that's how it worked. Yeah, it's terrible it doesn't exist anymore.]

Relatedly, an informant in Donegal strongly felt that those now being appointed to the board were "timeservers". Although his opinions were somewhat strident, they echoed sentiments I heard many times:

> M: An bhfeiceann tú cró na gcearc thíos ansin? [. . .] Na daoine atá siad ag ceapadh ar bhord Údarás na Gaeltachta, ní chuirfinn i mbun an fuckin cró cearc sin iad [. . .] Ní thig leotha áit a fháil ar chomhairle contae. Seasann siad don chomhairle contae agus teipeann orthu. So [. . .] deir na páirtithe 'cuirfidh muid suas thú le ceapadh go bord bainistíochta Údarás na Gaeltachta, you're so fuckin shite at everything else'.

> [M: Do you see that hen house down there? [. . .] I wouldn't put the people they're appointing to the board of Údarás na Gaeltachta in charge of that fuckin hen house [. . .] They can't get a place on the County Council. They stand for that and they fail. So [. . .] the parties say 'we'll put you up for appointment to the management board of Údarás na Gaeltachta, you're so fuckin shite at everything else'.]

While the board undoubtedly contains many hardworking and diligent individuals, one former member who I interviewed did, memorably, boast to me that he had little interest in the general business of the organisation and would pay attention in meetings only when informed that his local area was to be discussed.

The pre-2012 electoral process was not without its flaws, but its discontinuation has certainly not improved the standing of ÚnaG in the communities it serves. As Ó Neachtain has argued, the lack of political autonomy afforded to the Gaeltacht is "a serious handicap in terms of the linguistic community's authority and capacity to plan and implement programs which might more effectively contribute to the language community's survival and sustainable development" (2014: 367–368).

Although a blow to Gaeltacht democracy, however imperfect it may have been, this type of decision is not unique to the Gaeltacht. As Murphy noted, "further centralisation of power has been a key institutional strategy of both crisis governments", with many "key decisions and legislative changes hav[ing] bypassed parliamentary processes" (2014: 138) in the wake of the crash. Indeed, Bachrach and Baratz's famous conception of the "second face of power" (discussed further in 2.4 and 6.3) notes the appointment of supporters of the status quo to boards as a key way in which the powerful can set agendas and prevent public discussion of certain issues (Bachrach and Baratz 1970: 54–59, 70; see also Hay 2002: 175).

As Mercille and Murphy explain, such withdrawal of the state from areas in which it previously intervened significantly is entirely in accordance with the neoliberal project of privatisation and restructuring (2015: 91). When one considers Williams' contention "that political autonomy and economic autarchy [are] the twin pre-conditions . . . of successful language regeneration" (1991: 3), the removal of both the election for the ÚnaG board and the large majority of the organisation's budget, government policy towards the institution in recent years cannot but be seen as deeply damaging to the vitality of the Gaeltacht as a whole. These challenges notwithstanding, it is worthy of note that by 2017, there was a welcome growth in employment created by ÚnaG, with indications that the growth the national economy has been experiencing since 2016 was beginning to reach the Gaeltacht. Although this growth was modest in most areas (in Galway, for instance, the net gain was only one job), the 103 jobs created in Donegal were a welcome reprieve from the difficulties suffered in that county in recent years (Údarás na Gaeltachta 2017). Furthermore, such was the level of dissatisfaction with the abolition of the election that it saw a concerted community campaign aimed at having it re-instated, ultimately leading to the relevant minister announcing in 2021 that he would look into re-establishing a modified election process in the coming years – a significant victory for the campaigners' efforts, assuming it does eventually occur (Tuairisc.ie 2021b).

4.3 The department of state responsible for the Gaeltacht

The department of state responsible for the Gaeltacht was founded in 1956 under the same act that gave legal definition to the current Gaeltacht boundaries. As described in 2.5, it was known simply as the Department of the Gaeltacht until 1993. A designated minister was therefore able to represent Gaeltacht concerns at the cabinet table, giving the Gaeltacht significant representation in internal government debate. In 1993 it had its remit extended and became the Department of Arts, Culture and the Gaeltacht. While this title has gone through many permutations since then, with its rebranding as the Department of Arts, Heritage, Regional, Rural and Gaeltacht affairs in May 2016 it seemed that the Gaeltacht aspect of the portfolio was becoming ever more marginal. Indeed, in June 2017 a cabinet reshuffle proposed removing the word Gaeltacht from the title entirely, replacing it with a "Department of Culture", although this plan was not ultimately implemented, becoming instead the Department of Culture, Heritage and the Gaeltacht. Nonetheless, the Irish-speaking community's continued tendency to refer to the "Department of the Gaeltacht" is more of a throwback than a reality, with the Gaeltacht often appearing at the end of a long list of largely unrelated briefs. Indeed, as one opposition politician claimed after the 2016 reshuffle, it is in many ways a "Frankenstein department" covering the "bean an tí [women who host Irish-learners on summer courses], ballet, bogs, and broadband" (Irish Times 2016a) – a sentiment equally appropriate in light of its rebranding in 2020 as the Department of Tourism, Culture, Arts, Gaeltacht, Sport and Media.

While the continued existence of a department with "Gaeltacht" somewhere in the title perhaps obscures this fact, post-2008 developments concerning the department arguably amounted to an implementation in all but name of those proposals made by An Bord Snip Nua which aimed to abolish the then Department of Community, Rural and Gaeltacht Affairs. As the previous chapter detailed, An Bord Snip Nua recommended this abolition with the aim of saving some €151.1 million. The department responsible for the Gaeltacht was the only department whose outright closure was recommended.

Following the spirit of An Bord Snip Nua's recommendations, if not the letter, a government plan in 2010 proposed to reduce the department's budget from €105 million to €30 million between 2010–2016 (Department of Finance 2010: 101). Unlike the great majority of government plans and policies that concern the Gaeltacht which languish unimplemented for years, this one was executed in a significantly shorter timescale than that which was proposed: a minister of state in the department stated in 2016 that they lost 70% of their budget in just three years, 2008–2011 (Irish Times 2016b; see also Ó Murchú 2014: 210). This is a huge reduction by any standards and one which has not been restored. Although the 2018 budget saw the department receive €2.5 million extra to spend on Irish and the Gaeltacht, this was just half of the additional €5 million that their pre-budget submission to the Department of Finance claimed was necessary to meet its minimum requirements (Tuairisc.ie 2018c). In light of the fact that, as the previous section explained, total capital expenditure on the Gaeltacht and islands by 2017 was over seven times lower than in 2008, the insufficient nature of this increase could be expected.

Like many sectors facing neoliberal restructuring, the expanded remit of the department saw it left with a greater workload but much less funding, especially after having been given the additional remits of "Regional and Rural" affairs in 2016 (changed to "Sport and Media" in 2020). As a result of the disproportionate cuts the Gaeltacht sub-sector faced within the department, as someone working therein told me, it is now probably the smallest division of the smallest state department. Indeed, this informant went on to claim that there is now only one civil service office which operates entirely through Irish, although this office, in Donegal, has only three staff members.

This interviewee also told me that since the cutbacks removed their budget for community development work, this same office now conducts work largely unrelated to the Gaeltacht. Their standing in the community reflects this – when I asked for directions none of the employees in the factories directly adjacent to their office were able to tell me where I would find *"Roinn na Gaeltachta"* [the Department of the Gaeltacht], as it is still colloquially known.

Much of the infrastructural work which was formerly carried out by the department before the cuts involved schemes which were historically used to incentivise the use of Irish and retain the population of the Gaeltacht. While sometimes problematic in its implementation, one such support mechanism, the support scheme for parents of Irish-speaking children – *Scéim Labhairt na Gaeilge* – was nonetheless an extremely important policy intervention prior to it being abolished (Ó Broithe 2012).

As might be expected, then, when the abolition of this scheme was first proposed various groups campaigned in opposition. Despite these efforts, however, there was an outright refusal on the part of the state to negotiate such matters, and these cuts were implemented in disregard of both expert recommendation and community will, in a manner reminiscent of the debate on the 2012 Act (see 3.4) and the rationalisation of the voluntary sector discussed in the following section.

The crisis that began in 2008 and the punctuated equilibrium thereby created thus clearly opened a policy window which allowed reform of the department to take place at a very rapid pace, recalling the processes described by Klein (2007) or Mirowski (2013; see also 2.6; 3.3). While not closed outright, it would nonetheless seem that the core aim of the An Bord Snip Nua proposals was largely implemented, with Gaeltacht affairs becoming ever more marginal within the state apparatus.

4.4 Foras na Gaeilge's New Funding Model

Foras na Gaeilge (henceforth "FnaG") was founded in 1999 under the Good Friday Agreement which ended the violent conflict in the North of Ireland. It operates under the aegis of An Foras Teanga, which also supervises The Ulster-Scots Agency, receiving 75% of its funding from the southern state and 25% from the north. Its all-island jurisdiction sees it function primarily as a funding agency, distributing grants to various voluntary Irish-language organisations and community projects. Despite not receiving the significant increases in its budget that comparable institutions such as The Arts Council got during the Celtic Tiger, FnaG saw its funding (most of which is used to promote the language outside the Gaeltacht) peak at €20,125,000 in 2007, from which point it began to decline (Conradh na Gaeilge 2017: 8–9). The organisation's budget for 2018 was €14,532,000, 28% below its 2007 level, having received no increase at any time over this period. When inflation is taken into account, FnaG's budget for 2018 was 38% below the 2007 figure (Conradh na Gaeilge 2017: 8–9).

In December 2009, FnaG was directed by the North-South Ministerial Council (which has ultimate oversight of FnaG's work) to undertake a major reorganisation of the 19 language promotion organisations which received their "core" funding from the agency. The stated purpose for this restructuring was to eliminate duplication of efforts amongst these groups and reduce overheads. Although rationalisation of this nature might well have taken place regardless of the 2008 crash, budgetary contraction certainly expediated this process. As FnaG's 2008 annual report states: "[t]he change in economic circumstances worldwide was the most significant event during the year. It reminded us all of the importance of careful spending to ensure value for money. This gave rise to the review of corefunded organisations, although it was not the main reason for it" (Foras Teanga 2009: 8).

As discussed in 3.2 and 6.2, in accordance with the recommendations of An Bord Snip Nua, rationalisation was taking place at this time across all manner of public bodies and so-called "third sector" organisations, not just within the Irish-language sector.

FnaG initially proposed two possible methods of retrenchment. One would have seen language promotion activities contracted out via short-term tenders to organisations which did not receive any core funding from the agency. The other option proposed to maintain core funding, but make it available to a much smaller number of organisations (Ó Murchú 2014: 239).

FnaG ultimately decided to pursue the latter of these two proposals, seemingly seeing this as the least unpopular option. It was duly announced that this so-called "New Funding Model" would see 13 of the 19 core-funded organisations disbanded and their functions merged with those of the remaining six organisations. The *20-Year Strategy* discussed in Chapter 3 reaffirmed this course of action, committing to "a radical re-organisation of State-funded language organisations" – one of the few goals that have been implemented since the Strategy's introduction (Government of Ireland 2010: 25).

This proposal to close the majority of core-funded organisations was strongly opposed by both the sector and the vast majority of submissions to a brief public consultation process (Ó Murchú 2014: 239–240). In opposing the New Funding Model, core-funded organisations insisted that they were already collaborating on efforts to increase effectiveness and ensure there was no duplication of efforts. FnaG dismissed these efforts, however, as an employee of one of the core-funded organisations told me:

> T: *Just dhiúltaigh Foras na Gaeilge plé leis [na hiarrachtaí] sin. I ndáiríre bhí olc orthu go rabhamar ag plé leis sin, mar [. . .] bhí plean ag an bhForas, bhí siad ag iarraidh an rud seo a chur tríd, my way or the highway [. . .] Dá mba rud é go raibh tusa i mbun comhlachta [. . .] agus go raibh ort athrú ollmhór a dhéanamh, ní ghabhfadh tú ina mbun ar an gcaoi a rinne Foras na Gaeilge é [. . .] Ní raibh aon risk assessment de shaghas éigean, de shaghas ar bith déanta.*

[T: Foras na Gaeilge just refused to engage with [these efforts]. Really they were annoyed we were engaging with that, as [. . .] the Foras had a plan, they wanted to put it through, my way or the highway [. . .] If you were in charge of a company [. . .] and you had to make a huge change, you wouldn't go about it in the way Foras na Gaeilge did [. . .] There was no risk assessment of any description done.]

FnaG's refusal to engage with the sector's own proposals for reform, as well as their disregard for a great many other attempts by the sector to challenge the process, created a very fraught relationship between the agency and the core-funded sector. While space does not permit a full discussion of these developments, Ó Murchú (2014: 237–296) offers an exhaustive account of the affair. Notably, however, the voluntary sector claimed that they had "been consistently frustrated in every attempt [they] made to engage with the process" (Ó Murchú 2014: 248) and that "none of their arguments at meetings nor [. . .] the documentation they provided [were] taken seriously or fed in any way into [FnaG's] deliberations" (Ó Murchú 2014: 242). Such was the level of dissatisfaction that fifteen of the nineteen organisations eventually took to boycotting meetings with FnaG, stating that effective negotiation was being made impossible by, amongst other issues, FnaG's refusal to make pertinent documentation available before such meetings. The process nonetheless proceeded, with FnaG repeatedly citing the need to implement the directions of the North-South Ministerial Council. FnaG's board of directors – themselves paid appointees of the north and south governments – approved various contentious proposals despite the absence of productive discussion with key stakeholders (Ó Murchú 2014: 239). As an employee of FnaG itself told me *"Má deireanns an roinn [rialtais] caithfidh tú seo a dhéanamh, caithfear é a dhéanamh"* [If the [government] department says you have to do this, you have to do it].

Relations between FnaG and the sector ultimately became so strained that by 2011 the North-South Ministerial Council was calling for professional mediation to occur between the two sides (Ó Murchú 2014: 249).

In February 2012 the Irish media published an open letter by academics in the LPP field (both in Ireland and elsewhere) regarding the New Funding Model, claiming that the proposal was "completely at odds with international language planning principles" and destined to "prove detrimental to the development of Irish across the country". The letter was also publicised as a public petition which gathered some 2,000 signatures within a few months (Activism. com 2012; Ó Murchú 2014: 254).

The contentious nature of the proposed model and the energy spent lobbying against it also, of course, meant that affected organisations had less time to perform their main duties regarding the promotion of the language. As one of my interviewees, a former employee of one of these organisations, said:

> D: Rinneamar ana-obair ansin nuair a bhí sé sin ag dul ar aghaidh, chuireamar litreacha agus rinneamar teagmháil le gach uile TD [. . .] Rinne sé dochar d'obair [na heagraíochta] [. . .] Bhíomar ag caitheamh céatadán mhaith dár gcuid ama ag socrú rudaí mar sin in áit ag díriú ar obair óige [. . .] Bhí go leor deacrachtaí agus chruthaigh sé teannas i measc na grúpaí, bhí sé ar nós an seanmhana cineál 'divide and conquer'.

> [D: We did huge work then when that was taking place, we sent letters and got in contact with every TD ['Teachta Dála' – member of parliament] [. . .] It damaged [the organisation's] work [. . .] We were spending a big percentage of our time sorting out things like that instead of focusing on youth work [. . .] There were lots of difficulties and it created tension between groups, it was like the old mantra, kind of 'divide and conquer'.]

Several other interviewees who were involved in the process (including a disgruntled employee of FnaG itself) echoed this sentiment, feeling that these organisations expended an enormous amount of energy attempting to agree a compromise solution, only to find that FnaG was intent on implementing the New Funding Model regardless of the wishes of either the voluntary organisations or of the Irish-speaking community more generally.

Eventually, in January 2014 the six "lead organisations" FnaG would continue to fund were announced, namely *Gaelscoileanna, Gael Linn, Conradh na Gaeilge, Glór na nGael, Cumann na bhFiann* and *An tOireachtas*, with the remainder being disbanded come June of that year. While surely grateful to remain employed, even those employees whose organisations were maintained felt the process had been deeply flawed and showed a disregard for democratic procedure, language planning and management principles alike. Largely as a result of this vexed situation, the FnaG employee I interviewed told me that *"níl meas mada ag aon duine ar Fhoras na Gaeilge"* [nobody has an ounce of respect for Foras na Gaeilge].

Political lobbying and online petitions of the sort described above notwithstanding, fear of being disbanded and the divide and rule tactics inherent in this rationalisation process seemingly prevented the sort of collective action that could have rendered the new funding proposals inoperable. With such action not forthcoming, the majority of the main Irish-language promotion organisations ceased to exist from June 2014.

While the organisations that were retained initially saw their budgets increased (although they have since largely stagnated), this drawn-out and divisive rationalisation process was clearly far from conducive to language revitalisation, the stated aim of both FnaG and the sector it had aggravated so severely. The lack of consultation and refusal to engage with alternative proposals which characterised the affair is again reminiscent of the democratic deficit discussed above with regard to the *Gaeltacht Act 2012*, the abolition of the ÚnaG election or the many other schemes that were discontinued or reduced. Chapter 11 offers further examples of such disregard for popular will, and section 6.2 discusses broader implications of the rationalisation of public sector bodies for language revitalisation efforts.

4.5 Controversy surrounding the publication of the *Nuashonrú ar an Staidéar Cuimsitheach Teangeolaíoch ar úsáid na Gaeilge sa Ghaeltacht: 2006–2011*

The covert aspects of government policy are tellingly illustrated by the controversy surrounding the *Nuashonrú ar an Staidéar Cuimsitheach Teangeolaíoch ar úsáid na Gaeilge sa Ghaeltacht: 2006–2011* [Update to the Comprehensive Linguistic Study of the use of Irish in the Gaeltacht: 2006–2011] (henceforth *"Nuashonrú"*; Ó Giollagáin and Charlton 2015a). In 2013 ÚnaG commissioned an update of the original *Comprehensive Linguistic Study* (Ó Giollagáin et al. 2007a), with the aim of providing an analytic basis for the language planning process laid out in the *Gaeltacht Act 2012*. The *Comprehensive Linguistic Study* was based on the results of the 2002 census and data from the 2003/4 *Scéim Labhairt na Gaeilge* [the Irish-speaking scheme, see 2.3], as well as specially commissioned questionnaires and focus groups. The *Nuashonrú* referenced more recent census figures from 2006 and 2011, as well as data from *Scéim Labhairt na Gaeilge* in corresponding years. It concluded that the prognosis presented in the *Comprehensive Linguistic Study* had been overly optimistic and that language shift was proceeding at an even faster rate than the 2007 study had predicted (Ó Giollagáin & Charlton 2015a: 2). While the report does not reference the economic crisis, in light of the findings presented in this work, such a faster-than-expected rate of language shift post-2008 is unsurprising. Commenting on current language policy, it claimed that *"[i]s ionann cloí le cleachtais reatha agus glacadh go praiticiúil le próiseas an dul i léig mionteanga sa Ghaeltacht"* [adhering to current practice means accepting in practical terms the decline of the minority language in the Gaeltacht] (Ó Giollagáin and Charlton 2015a: 11).

Although the authors submitted the completed report in April 2014, publication was delayed as a result of both the state department responsible for the Gaeltacht and subsequently ÚnaG objecting to the inclusion of recommendations from the authors in the report (Tuairisc.ie 2015a). ÚnaG requested two further re-writings of the text, before deciding it was unwilling to publish it while it included the authors' recommendations.

After several months of deadlock, a compromise was eventually reached in May 2015 whereby the main body of the report was published by ÚnaG (Ó Giollagáin and Charlton 2015a) and the authors' recommendations were made available independently online (Ó Giollagáin and Charlton 2015b; subsequently published in Ó Giollagáin and Ó Curnáin 2016: 107–112). While the commissioning body were adamant that the authors were charged with producing a statistical analysis and that the inclusion of policy recommendations exceeded their remit, it must be remembered that, as noted in the recommendations themselves, modern liberal states are often reluctant to be connected to proposals that are not in accordance with the requirements of the market (Ó Giollagáin and Charlton 2015b: 9). As such ÚnaG's decision is not, perhaps, overly surprising. The whole affair does, however, echo Fishman's comments about a "master plan to do nothing" (see 2.4) and the covert policy agenda operating behind state rhetoric regarding the *20-Year Strategy* and similar policies.

One of the report's authors, Ó Giollagáin, has stated that he views the behaviour of both the department and ÚnaG as an attempt at censoring conclusions which conflict with their position (Tuairisc.ie 2017d). Such practices are far from unknown in Irish politics. A detailed report issued while the *Nuashonrú* controversy was ongoing described the various ways in which the state uses threats to funding and other surreptitious tactics to regulate those things "which are best left unsaid" and control the work of groups involved in advocacy and research which conflicts with official state narratives (Harvey 2014). The depth of the recent scandals in An Garda Síochána [the police force] have also shown such practices to exist across many levels of the public service (O'Toole 2017).

While it was the recommendations rather than the content of the report itself that were the main source of disputation, as an employee of the department responsible for the Gaeltacht asked me: *"Dá mbeadh tusa an tAire a bhí freagrach as cúrsaí Gaeltachta an mbeifeá ag iarraidh an t-eolas sin a scaipeadh?"* [If you were the minister responsible for Gaeltacht matters, would you be wanting to spread that information?].

It may well be the case that the minister then responsible for the Gaeltacht, Joe McHugh, or senior elements of the civil service hoped simply to delay the report's findings long enough for them to move departments (as McHugh did in 2016) and not have to deal with the fallout from the report's challenging findings, with the recommendations serving as a convenient excuse to postpone publication. Commenting on this, one of my interviewees from a language promotion group observed *"sin an rud faoin státseirbhís agus an rialtas go ginearálta, they play the long game"* [that's the thing about the civil service and the government generally, they play the long game].

Further to the delay to its publication, as noted by Ó Giollagáin (2017), the policy implications of the *Nuashonrú* have been ignored in the years since its publication. No changes have been made to existing policies as a result of its findings, nor have additional resources been made available for extant policies in light of the severe crisis it documented. While certainly creating the impression of a political elite ill-disposed to the language, as noted in 3.4, it is well established in the literature on public policy that states very commonly ignore expert advice about all manner of issues. Writing concomitantly to the *Nuashonrú's* publication – although about very different issues – two public policy academics noted that

> The use of research evidence in policy-making in Ireland has only ever been irregular and inconsistent. One explanation for this is that the barriers to change, to the proper implementation of research findings, are many and considerable. Some are even justifiable. Financial constraints, geographic considerations or social values may act as legitimate breaks [sic] on the application of new insights. But it is also clear that lobbying from vested interests and political favouritism present equally serious barriers to good practice.
>
> (Rouse and Duncan 2015)

Indeed, in 2013 a review of twenty years of reports on one of the greatest turmoils to have faced Irish society since independence, that of institutional child abuse, concluded that while many recommendations had been implemented, "recommendation fatigue" meant that their effect on "policy and practice" was far from optimal (Buckley and Nolan 2013). When an issue of such widespread concern as this struggles to produce the political action it deserves, it would seem inevitable that Irish-language policy recommendations would also be frequently neglected politically.

4.6 Conclusion

In 2018, as the *National Development Plan* was being launched to a backdrop of rapid economic expansion, Joe McHugh, then minister of state responsible for the Gaeltacht, announced that the "time of cuts" was over (Irish Times 2018c). As described in 4.2, however, this does not mean that those cuts implemented post-2008 will be reversed and, indeed, the proposals for Irish and the Gaeltacht included in the development plan will see expenditure on this area well below 2008 levels even decades after the crash. Even if the investments proposed in the *National Development Plan* for 2018–2027 are made in full, the budget of ÚnaG, for instance, will be just €12 million by 2027, compared to €25.5 million in 2008.

By highlighting such cuts, this chapter has attempted to draw attention to the importance of examining "covert" language policy (reflecting what states *do* rather than what they declare) in addition to the overt, official policies discussed in the previous chapter. While overt policies such as the *Gaeltacht Act 2012* and the *20-Year Strategy* are certainly of importance, in light of the degree to which the institutions charged with implementing them have had their functionality reduced, it would seem that covert policy is, if anything, more important than official policy in the Republic of Ireland.

When the duplicity that the budget cuts belie is considered, it is hard to not view the "end of the time of cuts" that was announced in 2018 as being too little, too late. This was perhaps best illustrated in the 2016 census results, which clearly demonstrated the extent of the damage done by the recession to the vitality of Irish, as 7.2.2 will explain. Showing little understanding of the severity of the decline demonstrated by the census, Seán Kyne, the minister of state for the Gaeltacht at the time of the results' publication in April 2017, told the Dáil that despite these figures the *20-Year Strategy* was succeeding and would still achieve its targets (Tuairisc.ie 2017k). While Part 3 of this book offers further detailed discussion of this decline and the social mechanisms which drove it, the remaining two chapters in Part 2 will first highlight other areas mentioned in the *Strategy*, but where its goals have again been relegated to insignificance in the face of a far-reaching programme of neoliberalisation. In addition to discussing how neoliberalism creates obstacles for language revitalisation at both the state and individual level, Chapter 6 will look at the use of Irish by civil and public service institutions (something the *Strategy* aimed to develop). In the following chapter, however, I draw attention to the degree to which Irish-language media have also been rationalised since 2008, resulting in decreased engagement with much of the content they produce.

5 Austerity and Irish-language media

5.1 Introduction

Although the extent to which having their own media outlets benefits minoritised languages is a source of debate (Cormack 2007; Fishman 1991: 374–375), grassroots campaigns between the 1960s-1990s consistently argued that Irish-language radio and television stations were necessary components of the revitalisation process. The campaigners' efforts eventually saw success – a radio station was established in 1972 and a television channel finally followed in 1996 (Watson 2003). Most of the Irish-language media provide employment which is located in the Gaeltacht and, in contrast to the majority of state-supported sectors situated therein, it is explicitly language-based. Accordingly, this sphere of economic activity holds particular relevance for Irish-language use in the language's core communities, even in an era in which the dominance of such "legacy media" is being challenged by web-based news and entertainment platforms.

As Watson recounts, the emergence of neoliberalism as the country's dominant economic paradigm has significantly influenced Irish-language media policy since the 1980s (2016: 73). Although Watson's research focuses on broadcast media, the effects of neoliberal reforms are also evident in print media in Irish, as I describe in 5.4. As with the institutions discussed in the previous chapter, budgetary re-allocation after 2008 saw Irish-language media become subject to market forces to an ever greater degree, with considerable effects in terms of audience numbers and scheduling for broadcasting in Irish, as well as the range of print media available in the language.

5.2 Raidió na Gaeltachta

While FnaG funds local radio stations in Dublin, Belfast and Galway city, the only Irish-medium radio station broadcast on FM across Ireland is, somewhat ironically, *Raidió na Gaeltachta* [Radio of the Gaeltacht; hereafter "RnaG"]. The station's national audience share is only 0.7%, but it has a high level of audience penetration within the Gaeltacht: the most recent survey publicly available showed that it enjoyed a 41% share of listenership in the Gaeltacht in 2009 (RTÉ 2009a; RTÉ 2018a: 37). Similar to Scotland's *Radio nan Gàidheal*, it is key for publicising Gaeltacht affairs (Dunbar 2003) and its importance to the Gaeltacht and the broader Irish-language community is widely accepted amongst

Irish speakers. Prior to the station's founding, Irish was frequently perceived by its native speakers as a purely localised code not associated with life outside their immediate area (Watson 2016: 69), but the establishment of RnaG is often understood as having been key to the "re-imagining" of the Gaeltacht as a unified community (cf. Anderson 1991), fostering a sense of shared ownership of the language.

The station operates under the auspices of the state broadcaster RTÉ [Raidió Teilifís Éireann] and has studios in the Gaeltacht areas of Galway, Donegal and Kerry, with its headquarters in Galway. As it would surely be very difficult to attract significant income via advertising to its small audience, the station does not broadcast commercial advertising and is funded solely by the licence fee. The secretary general of the Department of Communications, Energy and Natural Resources stated in 2013, however, that the combination of the recession and rapid technological change caused a steep increase in incidences of non-payment of the licence fee post-2008. Court cases brought for non-payment doubled between 2008–2013 (Oireachtas Éireann 2013a: 5–7) and have stayed at this elevated level (Irish Times 2018b). Such evasion is a significant source of RTÉ's financial difficulties (Indecon 2016: 146; Oireachtas Éireann 2017a: 14), with RnaG being affected accordingly.

Due to the decline in licence fee and advertising income for RTÉ as a whole, as well as cuts to direct state support, RTÉ's Irish-language budget was reduced by 29% between 2008–2012. With RnaG comprising the vast majority of RTÉ's Irish-language expenditure, it absorbed the bulk of this reduction. The station's funding fell from €15,063,000 in 2008 to €10,697,000 in 2012 (National Treasury Management Agency 2014: 61, 73). By 2017 the station's budget was €11,576,000 – still some 23% below the 2008 figure. Notably, RTÉ's overall budget for this time decreased by substantially less, by 8%, from €200,852,000 in 2008 to €186,068,000 in 2017 (RTÉ 2009b: 52; 2018: 126).

These cuts served to compound what were already unequal conditions for RnaG staff, who receive lower pay than their English-language counterparts in other branches of RTÉ. An employee of the station discussed this issue with me in 2016:

> P: Níl ciall ar bith leis [. . .] an méid ganntanas foirne atá ann agus an méid atá le déanamh againn [. . .] Tá mise ag obair ar chlár raidió laethúil agus tá mé ag léiriú agus ag láithriú liom féin [. . .] Dá mbeadh sin in RTÉ bheadh b'fhéidir seisear, seachtar ag obair ar an chlár [. . .] Tá [muid] ina saoránaigh den darna grád taobh istigh den eagraíocht [. . .] Tá muid ar tuarastal i bhfad níos ísle, i bhfad níos ísle [le béim] ná achan duine atá ag déanamh an obair chéanna in RTÉ [. . .] Tá siad i gcónaí ag caint air, ag rá gur chóir dúinn é a throid [. . .] iad a fuckin súe-áil like [. . .] But b'fhéidir bhí eagla ar dhaoine, bhí cúlú eacnamaíochta ann agus ní raibh tú ag iarraidh tabhairt le fios "ó sin an dream sin ag cuartú airgead".

[P: There's no sense to it [. . .] the huge lack of staff and the amount we have to do [. . .] I'm working on a daily radio programme and I'm presenting and producing by myself [. . .] If that was in RTÉ there'd be six, seven working on the programme [. . .] [We're] second class citizens within the organisation [. . .] We're on much lower pay, *much lower* [with emphasis] than everyone who does the same work in RTÉ [. . .] They're always talking about it, saying we should fight it [. . .] fuckin sue them like [. . .] But maybe people were scared, there was a recession and you didn't want people to think "oh that's that group looking for money".]

The National Union of Journalists drew attention to these unequal conditions in July 2017, at a time when the gender pay gap in RTÉ was being widely discussed in the media (NUJ 2017), although to no effect. Several submissions to the Joint Committee on the Future Funding of Public Service Broadcasting for their 2017 report also referred to this issue (Oireachtas Éireann 2017b: 122, 247) and in 2021 it was again raised at the Committee for Public Accounts, where it was noted that this effectively amounted to a punishment for working through Irish. It was also claimed by a committee member that RTÉ management were attempting to "block or fudge" and "fob-off" discussions of the matter by not providing the committee with requested documentation comparing remuneration in RnaG and the English-language stations run by RTÉ (Oireachtas Éireann 2021a).

Employment conditions which see those working in the Irish-language sector being paid less than people performing comparable work in other publicly funded organisations was something several other informants also addressed. As an interviewee with many years' experience working for Irish-language organisations told me:

D: De bharr go bhfuil tú ag obair leis an nGaeilge is léir go gcreidtear go bhfuil tú ag obair 'ar son na cúise' [. . .] Údaráisí, rialtais, daoine cumhachtacha, ní amharcann siad ar Ghaeilge agus obair forbairt pobail mar obair cheart [. . .] Ach is ceart go mbeadh, y'know, an pá agus an t-aitheantas féaráilte [. . .] Feictear sin go minic, aon rud a bhaineann le forbairt pobail, Gaeilge nó Béarla, glactar leis go dtarlóidh sé, in áit aitheantas a thabhairt. Like má íocann tú daoine faigheann tú – nó bheifeá ag ceapadh go bhfaigheann tú – daoine níos fearr agus go mbeidh rath níos fearr ar an obair atá ar siúl.

[D: Because you're working with Irish it's clear that people think you're doing it 'for the cause' [. . .] Authorities, governments, powerful people, they don't see Irish and community development as proper work [. . .] But y'know the pay and recognition should be fair [. . .] That's often the case, anything to do with community development, Irish or English, it's assumed it will happen, instead of giving acknowledgement. Like if you pay someone you get – or you'd assume you get – a better person and that the work will be more successful.]

Similarly, until 2016 those employed in ÚnaG were also paid significantly less than others in the public service who perform comparable work through English (Tuairisc.ie 2016b).

Figures made available in late 2017 showed daily listener numbers for RnaG had dropped by 40% since 2014, demonstrating the extent of the challenges faced by the station (Tuairisc.ie 2017e). While audience share had increased from 2005–2008, it then began to drop, with a National Treasury Management Agency report noting that this "may be attributable to the corresponding fall in opex [operational expenditure] during this period" (2014: 73). While it is difficult in the absence of detailed research on the matter to identify the exact causal factors behind this decrease, it would seem probable that it is at least partly the result of the budget cuts experienced by the station over the preceding years, just as the director of TG4 stated that that channel's declining viewership was a consequence of the cuts it received since 2008 (see following section).

Reflecting on the greater numbers of music programmes and repeats broadcast on the station in recent years, one of my interviewees claimed these developments made her reluctant to listen to it: *"Cheapfainnse ag an bpointe seo gur cur amú é RnaG [. . .] Níl na cláracha ann mar a bhí"* [I think at this point that RnaG is a waste of time [. . .] It doesn't have programmes like it used to].

The significant reduction in daily Irish speakers in the Gaeltacht that was demonstrated in the 2016 census is another factor possibly contributing to the station's declining listenership. With there being over 2,500 less daily speakers of Irish in the Gaeltacht in 2016 compared to 2011, as well as a drop in the number of daily speakers of Irish in the rest of the country, it is to be expected that there would also be a reduction in the numbers listening to the Gaeltacht radio station. Although the 40% decline in RnaG listeners is obviously much greater that the 11.2% decline in daily speakers in the Gaeltacht (see 7.2.2), this may partly reflect the fact that the station's listenership consists primarily of those in older age cohorts (Indecon 2017: 12). As the oldest of these listeners die off it seems plausible that they are not being replaced by younger listeners, who are less likely to be active Irish speakers (Ó Giollagáin and Charlton 2015a), more likely to have emigrated since 2008 (Chapter 9) and more likely to use online platforms for news and entertainment (Chapter 13).

Unfortunately, in October 2016 due to financial constraints RTÉ withdrew a call for tender for research which aimed to gain a better understanding of RnaG's listenership. This research would have aimed to address the lack of data about the channel's audience in the hope of allowing the station to provide improved services to listeners (Tuairisc.ie 2016c, 2016d). Such an insight is undoubtedly needed and was recommended by the parliamentary committee on the Irish language, the Gaeltacht and the Islands in their 2019 report on the challenges facing Irish-language broadcasting, which bluntly claimed that broadcasting in Irish is in a state of "crisis" (Oireachtas Éireann 2019: 16, 6). As of the time of writing, however, no such research has been undertaken.

Despite RnaG clearly being in need of increased investment, in light of its reduced budget and the ongoing challenges faced by traditional media, RTÉ began an organisation-wide rationalisation scheme in August 2017 that aimed to cut costs and reduce staff numbers by approximately 10%. Under this scheme, RnaG staff were offered the opportunity to apply for redundancy and early retirement packages, for which a significant number applied, including half of the staff in the Donegal studio (Tuairisc.ie 2017f). When the long-standing dissatisfaction with unequal working conditions experienced by those employed in the station are considered, it was perhaps predictable that such a large percentage would desire to leave the station. Seven RnaG presenters were ultimately granted these packages, all of whom had been employed for over the 18-year minimum required to ensure eligibility. This prompted significant scheduling challenges for the station and led to the shortening or discontinuation of some of its key chat and news programmes, these often being the programmes in which the most spoken Irish was to be heard (Tuairisc.ie 2018d).

In the wake of these developments, in 2021 a statement from station employees to the Future of Media Commission stated that staff numbers had decreased by 30–40% since 2008. It was also noted that the service was being eroded as a result of its "miniscule" funding (Future of Media Commission 2021a) – clearly a cause of much concern for a station that has long been credited with being of great benefit to the Gaeltacht and the wider Irish-language community.

5.3 TG4

Established in 1996 just as the Celtic Tiger was gaining momentum, TG4, the Irish-language television station, was perhaps the key victory secured by Irish-language campaigners during the boom period. The channel has more of a national focus than RnaG and, due to its presentation of Irish as contemporary and vital, it has often been seen to serve a significant status planning function for the language (O'Connell, Denvir and Walsh 2008). While having several vocal anti-Irish detractors in the media (Delap 2008: 158) and also receiving criticism from some Irish speakers who bemoan the excessive use of English in its programming (Mac Síomóin 2006: 3), the quality of its output is generally commended by both the Irish-speaking minority and the English-speaking majority. While having a very low percentage share, as discussed below, as of 2016 it had some 450,000 daily viewers, with a 92% weekly reach amongst Irish-language audiences (Oireachtas Éireann 2017c: 10; TG4 2018: 1).

As well as employing eighty people directly, primarily in the station's headquarters in Conamara, TG4 outsources much of its programming, spending €20 million annually on contracts with over 90 production companies who employ some 350 people in total (Crowe Horwath 2013: 148; TG4 n.d.). This investment has allowed for the growth of an independent production sector, much of which is based in the Gaeltacht, and, in some cases, reported to have been important for maintaining a community's use of Irish (TG4 2016a: 22; Tuairisc.ie 2017g).

One of my interviewees, who was himself involved in the campaign to have the station established, explained the beneficial social and linguistic consequences of the station in a way reminiscent of Strubell's "Catherine Wheel" model (2001: 79–281):

> S: Rinne sé sin difear an-mhór [. . .] Choinnigh sé ag obair san áit go leor daoine an-, an-, b'fhéidir, chruthaitheach, ealaíonta [. . .] Thug sé stádas áiride don teanga freisin i measc lucht gnó sa gceantar [. . .] B'fhéidir go mbíodh siad cineál diúltach ó thaobh na teanga, gur thosaigh siad ag smaoineamh, bhuel [. . .] tá stádas ag an nGaeilge anois, stádas na teilifíse agus cheapfainn go raibh sin tábhachtach ó thaobh íomhá na teanga sa nGaeltacht féin.

> [S: That made a huge difference [. . .] It kept a lot of people working in the area, people who are very, maybe very creative, artistic [. . .] It also gave a certain status to Irish amongst local business people [. . .] Maybe they used to be kind of negative about the language, they started thinking, well [. . .] Irish has status now, the status of television and I think that was important for the image of Irish in the Gaeltacht itself.]

State funding of the broadcaster increased significantly from €10 million in 2001 to €35.5 million in 2008 (Irish Times 2010; TG4 2009: 43), although this was subsequently reduced in line with the recommendations of An Bord Snip Nua (see 3.2) to reduce the exchequer subvention of TG4 by €10 million "at a minimum" (McCarthy et al. 2009b: 26). The cuts the station received, while significant, were nonetheless less than An Bord Snip Nua's proposal – a 2016 submission by TG4 to the Joint Committee on Communications, Climate Action and Environment noted that "funding ha[d] been reduced by over €3m per annum" between 2008–2015 (TG4, 2016b: 2), falling from €35,473,000 to €32,240,000 (TG4 2009: 42, 2016b: 30). When added, however, to "new levies and reductions in commercial income due to the downturn in the economy these have resulted in an almost €6m reduction in funds available for TG4's operations on an annual basis" (TG4 2016b: 2). This submission requested that the recommendations of various independent economic advisors be implemented and their budget increased "at the very least [to] €32.75m (TG4's current public funding for years 2011 to 2014 inclusive)". They also noted that "[t]he combination of the downturn and media market developments have resulted in TG4's advertising and sponsorship income declining by approximately 50% between 2008 and 2016" (TG4 2016b: 3–4; see also Ó Gairbhí 2017: 278–297).

While perhaps not giving due accord to the decline of legacy media that is occurring regardless of budgetary contraction, according to the channel's director inadequate funding was the primary cause of the fall in the channel's audience share from 3.2% in 2005 to 1.8% in 2016 (Oireachtas Éireann 2017c: 16–17). Similarly, an independent 2016 report stated that "an increase in funding is required if its audience share is not to continue on its downward trend" (Indecon 2016: ix). The Broadcasting Authority of Ireland also told the Oireachtas that the channel would be unable to deal with further cuts, it already being run on an extremely frugal basis (TG4 2016b: 4; see also Ó Gairbhí 2017: 285). In light of the aforementioned status-raising function of the channel, such a significant decline in viewership is surely unhelpful for the language's prestige both in the Gaeltacht and nationally. Despite numerous such appeals for the channel's budget to be increased to at least 2014 levels, by 2017 funding was €32.79 million, €147,000 below the 2014 figure, which itself was over €3 million less than the 2008 budget (TG4.ie 2018).

Under the *Broadcasting Act 2009* the Broadcasting Authority of Ireland (under whose direction TG4 is run) is required to "promote and stimulate the development of Irish language programming and broadcasting services" (Government of Ireland 2009: 33). Also included in this act is a requirement for the minister of communications to develop "broadcasting funding schemes" aiming, amongst other objectives, to "develop . . . programmes in the Irish language" (Government of Ireland 2009: 156–157). These schemes are to be funded by "an increase in the allocation of licence fee money from RTÉ to the Broadcasting Funding Scheme (from 5% to 7%), of which TG4 is a main beneficiary", in order to increase the quantity and quality of Irish-language broadcasting (Government of Ireland 2010: 27). Despite this positive legislative development, however, the 2008–2018 period saw the funding of this scheme become significantly more challenging. As explained in the previous section, the paying of licence fees dropped significantly after 2008, due to both the recession and the increasing turn away from traditional media.

Although the station continues to promote Irish in so far as it can, it would seem probable that its reduced budget and the consequent decline in ratings was responsible for some of the recent scheduling decisions which saw a decrease in the number of programmes directed at the station's "core" Irish-speaking viewers. Major changes were made to the station's schedule in 2017, with many programmes which had formats based primarily on interviewing native Irish speakers being discontinued. In their place there was an increase in programmes in which relatively little Irish is heard, such as those focusing on music like *Glór Tíre*, a talent show for up-and-coming singers from around the country, few of them Irish speakers. Sports coverage was also increased, it being seen as "a good attraction for non-Irish audiences and maintaining audience shares" (Indecon 2016: 30). The station also broadcasts a large number of repeats or imported filler programming such as English-language quiz or "reality" TV shows. Even before these scheduling changes took place, Indecon's 2016 review of TG4's funding noted that "[t]here has been a slight decrease in Irish language hours broadcast across 2013–2015", falling from 5,188 hours in 2013 to 4,956 (57% of its total broadcast hours) in 2015 (2016: 34). By 2019 this had fallen again to 4,484 hours – just 51% (Mediatique 2020: 53). Despite being well received by critics, some recent dramas have been notable for a high degree of bilingualism, perhaps imitating a Welsh model that aims to appeal to Welsh and non-Welsh speakers alike (Tuairisc.ie 2017h).

Despite the employment created by TG4 obviously being of great importance, much of this is itself problematic – not least due to a large amount of it being conducted through English, leading to the creation of the sort of "Potemkin village" that McLeod (2002: 68) warned against as being an unhelpful false illusion of language revitalisation. Several interviewees noted the tendency of those employed in TG4 to speak English at work, something not reported to be the case with RnaG or the print media discussed in the following section. While some of my informants claimed the station's employees lack sufficient ideological commitment to the language, it is often the case that those involved in the technical aspects of TG4's productions simply do not speak Irish, with many of these working for independent companies contracted by the station, including large numbers of camera operators (Ó Gairbhí 2017: 332–334). A direct employee of the station told me that it is for this reason that Irish is used only about 50% of the time on the set of one of the station's flagship shows. Indeed, during the research of this book I had numerous occasions to be on TG4 myself, and in all but one instance I was filmed by a camera operator unable to speak Irish, assisted by a reporter who talked to me in Irish before turning to the operator and repeating the substance of our conversation in English.

With this being a longstanding issue, before the crash ÚnaG part-funded a higher diploma in "broadcasting and television and radio journalism" taught by the Acadamh na hOllscolaíochta Gaeilge division of the National University of Ireland, Galway, aiming to rectify the lack of Irish-speaking workers with such skills. This course was delivered near the TG4 and RnaG headquarters in west Galway where work placements were available to students, but budgetary cuts have since led to ÚnaG discontinuing the paying of tuition fees for the course. Indeed, as noted in 4.2, grants provided by ÚnaG for training and education were reduced massively between 2008–2015, from €12,766,480 to €1,582,030 (Údarás na Gaeltachta 2009b: 3; 2016b: 3).

While the Acadamh continues to teach similar courses, they are now fully fee charging and include fewer opportunities for work experience than are thought necessary, developments which have surely not helped resolve this shortage of Irish-speaking staff in TG4 (Oireachtas Éireann 2017b: 143). Furthermore, between 2012–2018 full-time student numbers in the Acadamh's Gaeltacht centres fell by over 90%, from 248 to 20, with the 50% reduction in the institution's budget since 2008 and the abolition of the grant formerly paid to students studying in the Gaeltacht adding to the difficulties caused by the discontinuation of ÚnaG support (RTÉ 2018b).

Further to the obviously problematic issue of language use by both TG4 staff and the station's contractors, one of my interviewees, a man in his mid-20s who composes music used by TG4, told me of his frustration with the poor employment conditions he faces in the sector:

F: *Cúpla lá ó shin chuir mé isteach ar obair [. . .] Dúirt siad liom, bhuel, internship atá anseo, like comhlacht atá ag iarraidh stuif a dhéanamh do TG4. So gan mise a bheith in ann [tuarastal] mar is ceart a fháil bhí siad ag iarraidh bullshit a íoc domh, €20 extra ar an dól, right. Agus ní hé go bhfuil mise just mar amateur, tá mé literally, chuaigh mise chuig an ollscoil, NUI, the fuckin Acadamh in NUI agus chuir mé lear obair isteach ann. So fá choinne duine atá [cáilithe] tá siad ag ráit domh, y'know, 'fuck off'. Agus tá siadsan chun mo obair a úsáid chun fuckin lear airgead a dhéanamh!*

[F: A couple of days ago I applied for work [. . .] They said to me, well, this is an internship, like a company that wants to make stuff for TG4. So without me being able to get a proper [salary], they wanted to pay me bullshit, €20 extra on top of the dole, right. And it's not like I'm just an amateur, I literally, I went to university, NUI, the fuckin Acadamh in NUI and I put in loads of work. So for someone who's [qualified] they're saying to me, y'know, 'fuck off'. And they want to use my work to make a fuckin load of money!]

In light of the reduced income such companies receive from TG4 due to cuts to the station's budget, they – like so many other sectors – have adopted such internships as a way to lower overheads. The cuts have meant that TG4 pays these independent companies just 50% of the amount RTÉ pays its contractors, with employment in the sector falling accordingly (see consultation submissions from such contractors in Oireachtas Éireann 2017b: 70, 123, 161, 167, 247; also Olsberg SPI and Nordicity 2017: 64; Ó Gairbhí 2017: 329–331). As several other interviewees observed, frustration with employment conditions of this nature often prompts people to emigrate, or at least to seek employment in sectors unrelated to Irish (see also Glynn, Kelly and MacÉinrí 2013: 41–43; Oireachtas Éireann 2017b: 247).

Despite there being very little research on the effects of the 2008 crash on other linguistic minorities, it is of note that some of the few exceptions to this trend refer to cuts to stations comparable to TG4. The budget for the Basque broadcaster, EPiT, fell by €45 million between 2009–2019, having been at €175 million in 2009 (Culture, Welsh Language and Communications Committee 2019: 41). So too was funding for Catalonian broadcasting cut as a result of the economic crisis (Casado Del Río, Guimerà i Orts and Miguel De Bustos 2016), showing that TG4 and the Irish-language community are not by any means alone in this struggle which has become so prominent since 2008. I return to this issue in the final chapter where I discuss cuts to Scottish Gaelic and Welsh, including for their respective television stations.

For all TG4's continued popularity amongst many Irish speakers, the period since 2008 has clearly seen it face very significant challenges. As with Irish-medium radio and print media, not only has the station had to contend with the rapidly changing nature of media in the 21st century, but also with significant reductions to its budget. As the station's director told an Oireachtas committee in 2017: "*[n]í leor an leibhéal reatha maoinithe le gur féidir le TG4 dul i ngleic leis an margadh atá ag síor-fhorbairt agus athrú. Gan bonn il-bhliana faoin maoiniú, is doiligh pleanáil agus forbairt [a dhéanamh]*" [the current level of funding is not sufficient for TG4 to engage with a market that is constantly developing and changing. Without a multi-year basis for funding, it is difficult to plan and develop] (Oireachtas Éireann 2017d: 3).

He also noted that without significant investment over the next several years the station risks becoming lost in the "digital jungle", one of the 750+ channels available to the Irish public that attract less than 1% of viewers. Similar sentiments were expressed in the channel's 2018 strategy document, which noted that "the recession caused major damage, not just to TG4, but also to Ireland's creative economy" and that globalisation and the competition for audiences it brings has left the channel in great need of increased investment (TG4 2018: 2). One positive development was seen in July 2018 when the government announced that an additional €985,000 in funding was being made available for 2018. This increase in the overall budget was of limited effect, however, as RTÉ subsequently reduced its support for TG4 in both 2019 and 2020 (Tuairisc.ie 2021c). This occurred despite the Coimisinéir Teanga ruling in 2019 that RTÉ was completely failing to meet its statutory duty with regard to the creation of television programming in Irish, a duty which includes a requirement to provide one hour of programming to TG4 daily, which it does by producing TG4's news programme. RTÉ claimed this reduction was unavoidable, in large part a result of them having lost over €100 million in annual funding since 2008 (Coimisinéir Teanga 2019a: 16–19). As a result of these cuts, TG4's director claimed in a presentation to the Committee on the Irish language, the Gaeltacht and the Islands in 2021 that the station's news service was seriously deficient and that *"[n]íl dóthain acmhainní in iriseoireacht na Gaeilge agus sin tús agus deireadh an scéil"* [there are not enough resources in Irish-language journalism, that is the long and the short of the matter] (Tuairisc.ie 2021d; Oireachtas Éireann 2021b). As with RnaG, in light of the many benefits the station has provided the language, any further decline in TG4's status would surely be an enormous loss to Irish speakers both within and outwith the Gaeltacht.

5.4 Print media

Unusually for a minoritised language of its size, print media in Irish has a relatively well-established history, with the first Irish-language periodical, *An Gaodhal*, being printed monthly from 1881–1904 (Delap 2008: 153). Published bilingually by an Irish emigrant in New York, this publication was succeeded by more frequently published, all-Irish newspapers such as *Fáinne an Lae* and *An tÉireannach*, amongst many more. A highpoint for Irish-language print media was reached in the 1950s when *Inniu* was selling 20,000 copies a day (Foras na Gaeilge 2013: 1).

In spite of having had over a century for the market to mature, by 2008 all extant publications in Irish were in receipt of significant state support. In line with their wider process of rationalisation which saw them abolish 13 of 19 voluntary Irish-language organisations (see 4.4), FnaG also greatly reduced the amount of print media it funded. The extent to which these media were dependent on official subvention is clearly seen in the fact that all of those which did not secure alternative funding arrangements became defunct once their grants were discontinued.

In 2007, a daily paper called *Lá Nua* was founded as a successor to *Lá*, which had been in publication from 1984–2006. Although based primarily in Belfast, the paper also had an office in the Donegal Gaeltacht. It operated on a not-for-profit basis and was controlled by the *Preas an Phobail* co-operative (Ó Murchú 2008: 17). While partly financed by shareholder investors drawn primarily from Belfast's Irish-speaking community, the paper received the majority of its funding from FnaG. As with its predecessor (whose average daily sales reached 4,404 during the second half of 2003), five editions of *Lá Nua* were published each week, although by 2008 daily sales averaged only 1,500 copies, leading FnaG to withdraw funding for the paper in 2009 (Ó Murchú 2014: 464).

The case of *Foinse*, a Conamara-based weekly paper founded in 1996, is similar to that of *Lá Nua*. Sales reached approximately 8,000 copies a week by the year 2000, only for them to decline to 3,746 by the end of 2008 (Ó Murchú 2014: 464). As with *Lá Nua*, FnaG ceased funding *Foinse* in 2009. Further to the general trend towards falling newspaper reading in any language, such a steady decline in sales has also been observed with Welsh-language newspapers, as readers apparently no longer see the novelty in minority language newsprint and tire of supporting an enterprise *ar son na cúise* [for the cause] (Ó Murchú 2014: 464). Again, in the wake of the budget cuts that FnaG faced from 2008 onwards and with sales having fallen so significantly, it is unsurprising that the organisation ceased subsidising these papers. Although it must be acknowledged that such defunding may well have occurred regardless of the events of 2008, the economic climate certainly made it all the more likely. Despite losing its core funding, beginning in 2009 a shorter version of *Foinse* was published privately as a weekly supplement in the Irish Independent. The content of this iteration of the paper quickly came to focus on learners rather than fluent speakers, however, and the paper went online only in late-2013, before ceasing operations in 2015. The Irish Independent continues to publish a short weekly supplement in Irish, *Seachtain*, however, focusing primarily on the needs of learners and school students.

Having defunded both *Foinse* and *Lá Nua*, FnaG issued a call for tender in 2009 to establish a replacement publication under its *Scéim Nuachtán Seachtainiúil* [Weekly Newspaper Scheme]. It eventually opted to fund *Gaelscéal*, whose first issue was published in January 2010. Although the paper was widely commended for its coverage of national and international affairs, in addition to its analysis of Irish-language issues, its weekly sales never surpassed 1,500 copies, and had fallen to 1,300 by the time the paper's €400,000 annual subsidy was withdrawn in early 2013 (Ó Murchú 2014: 458). This decision to end Gaelscéal's funding was taken on the grounds that these low sales did not warrant such expenditure in light of *"an titim de 25% atá i ndiaidh teacht ar bhuiséad Foras [sic] na Gaeilge le cúig bliana anuas, mar aon le gearradh substaintiúil eile tuartha don bhliain seo chugainn"* [the 25% fall in Foras na Gaeilge's budget in the last five years, as well as another substantial cut predicted for next year] (Foras na Gaeilge 2013: 1–2).

Similar to the cases of RnaG and TG4 discussed in the previous sections, *Lá Nua*, *Foinse* and *Gaelscéal* all provided important language-based employment in the Gaeltacht, albeit on a smaller scale. While only employing low numbers of staff, *Foinse* and *Gaelscéal* each had their offices within ten miles of both the RnaG and TG4 headquarters, thereby contributing to maintaining the social density of Irish speakers and creating high prestige employment, both important ingredients for language maintenance in many communities.

The cuts to these newspapers were made despite an explicit commitment in the *20-Year Strategy* to encourage the growth of print media in Irish, albeit one which stipulated that print media will be supported on the basis of "reasonable and verifiable sales" (Government of Ireland 2010: 26). Such a sentiment accords with the rationalisation rhetoric so common in light of the economic crisis and wider neoliberal reform, running counter to economic intervention principles popular before the neoliberal era, whereby states readily supported loss-making public institutions due to the wider benefits they provided (Chomsky, in Bakan 2005 [2004]: 194; Chang 2007: 114).

In a further blow to the language's status in the print media, as well as its visibility on a national scale, the *Irish Times*, Ireland's main broadsheet and paper of record, reduced its Irish-language content from one full page weekly to a half page in July 2016. This decision was taken as part of a wider reorganisation of the paper whereby it reduced its total page content in an attempt to maintain profitability despite steadily declining circulation. The development was criticised by many in the Irish-language media, who observed that it halved the opportunities for Irish-language journalists to be employed by the paper, which is notable for the above-average rates of remuneration its writers receive (Tuairisc.ie 2016e).

A number of smaller-scale news services also ceased publication during this period. Among these were *Goitse* (which was published independent of state support in and for the Donegal Gaeltacht between 2009–2011), Foras na Gaeilge's monthly news bulletin *Saol* (which had been in existence for 25 years) and *Nuacht24*, a short-lived successor to *Lá Nua* in Belfast which was also self-financed (Ó Murchú 2014: 458). Various other print media and online news services previously funded by FnaG were also cut. Until June 2014 the periodicals *Feasta, An tUltach, An Timire, An Sagart* and *Nós* were all in receipt of funding, as were the news websites Gaelport.com, Saol.ie and Beo.ie. By 2015, however, cutbacks meant that FnaG was only supporting the monthly literary journal *Comhar*, the newly founded online news service Tuairisc.ie (discussed below) and the now online-only culture magazine *Nós*, which had previously been available both online and as a quarterly printed magazine (Ó Murchú 2014: 458). These cuts were made despite a 2011 report commissioned by FnaG extolling these publications and recommending they continue to be supported (Uí Chollatáin, Uí Fhaoláin and Lysaght 2011). Although *An tUltach* had its funding discontinued, organisations such as Conradh na Gaeilge and the Arts Council of Northern Ireland initially chose to finance it from their own internal budgets, being reluctant to see an end to a magazine which had been in publication since 1924. Nonetheless, in April 2018 *An tUltach* also ceased publication.

In mid-2018 the book publisher Cois Life announced it would close come 2019, citing amongst other reasons the decline in sales that the recession had seen (Cois Life 2018). Commenting on this news, the CEO of FnaG stated that funding for their Irish-language books scheme had fallen by over €700,000 between 2008–2017, from €1.8 million to €1.06 million (Tuairisc.ie 2018e), a development which exacerbated what was already a challenging publishing climate.

With traditional media in decline the world over due to the growth of the internet, it cannot be argued that the Great Recession is wholly responsible for the decline of print media in Irish. Similar to the cases of RnaG and TG4 discussed above, however, the coinciding of the crisis with the broader challenges faced by legacy media created a deeply unfavourable situation for Irish-language publications after 2008. The lack of disposable income experienced by the majority of the population during the recession made it all the less likely people would regularly buy such publications purely to support the language. When combined with the straitened budgetary circumstances FnaG have experienced since 2008, which required them to rationalise operations to a degree unlikely to have otherwise occurred, the fact that the period under examination saw such a large reduction in the range of print media available in Irish seems decidedly overdetermined.

Notably, the one Irish-language magazine which began publication in the years since 2008 and which remains in existence, *Mionlach*, explicitly eschews state or commercial funding. Since 2015 it has been published on a voluntary basis by activist group *Misneach* (mentioned in 11.1), and I, it must be stated, am on the editorial committee. The magazine has a print run comparable to that of *Comhar*, selling over 400 copies per issue.

Although the decrease in the availability of print media in Irish is notable, it has to a large degree been compensated for by the growth of vibrant online Irish-language media, all of which are provided free of charge. Gaelscéal has been succeeded by popular news service Tuairisc.ie, which attracted a very significant 250,000 users in 2016 after receiving a four-year long grant of €1.6 million (Foras Teanga 2017: 24). Nós continues to be widely read in its online form, attracting 128,000 readers in 2016 (Foras Teanga 2017: 24). There are also a number of smaller content providers such as Ulster-focused news site Meoneile.ie or portal site Peig.ie. These are certainly very positive developments that continue to provide language-based employment while reaching a far wider readership than the print publications discussed. Only one of these sites, Tuairisc.ie, however, has its office in the Gaeltacht and, unlike Gaelscéal, Foinse, etc., even this is located in an area where Irish is very weak, less than five miles from Galway city centre. It must also be noted that, as discussed in Chapter 13, the increased penetration of information technology into our daily lives is itself somewhat of a double-edged sword for minoritised languages, offering great opportunities, but also significant challenges.

In spite of their successes and an internal FnaG report recommending increased and longer-term funding, in 2019 a plan to further rationalise funding for *Comhar,* Nós.ie and Tuairisc.ie was announced (Daltún 2018; Tuairisc.ie 2019b). The funder proposed ceasing all support for Nós, halving funding for *Comhar*, ending its print edition and moving to an online-only format. While a €60,000 increase in funding for Tuairisc.ie was recommended, it was stated that its focus should be limited to Irish-language related matters, rather than being the general current affairs platform it currently is. Somewhat counterintuitively, FnaG also proposed establishing a new scheme of internships for journalism students, although commentators were quick to note that such a scheme would be preparing participants for jobs that no longer exist (Tuairisc.ie 2019b). Responses to a public consultation on these proposals, were, as might be expected, overwhelmingly negative (Foras na Gaeilge 2019). In response, FnaG announced they would continue the existent funding model temporarily. Come 2021, however, they reduced funding for *Comhar* by 33%, a substantial cut to an already tight budget. *Comhar* and Tuairisc.ie stated in a joint submission to the Future of Media Commission that this puts *Comhar's* future in a very precarious position, as it also does for the magazine's subsidiary projects such as the online academic journal *COMHARTaighde* and their book publishing scheme, *Cló Léann na Gaeilge* (Future of Media Commission 2021b). The submission also noted that funding of print/written media in Irish is currently €500,000, having been in excess of €800,000 before 2014, and that as with other Irish-language media outlets discussed above, Tuairisc.ie will require "significant additional resources in the years ahead" in order to fulfil its duties and remain relevant in a changing media landscape (Future of Media Commission 2021b).

5.5 Conclusion

While, as noted at the outset of this discussion, there is still debate in the academic literature regarding the degree to which media should be prioritised by those involved in language revitalisation, the evidence from Ireland would suggest that they can be a very important way to both create employment in the target language and increase its prestige. The media can, of course, also play an important role in both corpus and acquisition planning. Unfortunately, as with the institutions discussed in Chapter 4, Irish-language media organisations have been subjected to a programme of neoliberal rationalisation since 2008, having their funding repeatedly cut, and continuing to be threatened with further cuts as of the time of writing. Such withdrawal of state support is characteristic of the neoliberal reforms seen in so many areas of public policy all over the world in recent decades.

Although further research would be required to gain a complete understanding of the link between budgetary cutbacks and declining audience figures for both RnaG and TG4, staff at each station have repeatedly claimed that on their current budgets they cannot hope to maintain their audience figures, let alone increase them. In light of their important role in the maintenance of Irish, any further decline in the standing of these institutions would be immensely regrettable. Staff at the few print publications which were not closed outright since 2008 have also claimed that their position is deeply precarious in light of inadequate funding.

Confirming the perceptiveness of Shohamy's comments on the relevance of covert language policy (see 4.1), it is clear that covert state language policy regarding the media contradicts the official commitments made in the *20-Year Strategy,* as is the case with many of the issues discussed in the previous chapter. The data presented in this chapter therefore provide an important part of my analysis of how neoliberalism itself can operate as a form of covert language policy in the Gaeltacht and elsewhere in the state (see also Piller and Cho 2013: 23), a point which is elaborated on in the following chapter.

6 Neoliberalism and language policy in public and private spheres: Structural impediments

6.1 Introduction

While concentrating on the ways in which wider economic forces can affect language policy, much of the discussion in previous chapters has nonetheless focused on institutions specific to the Gaeltacht or Irish-language revitalisation more broadly, looking at policies such as the *Gaeltacht Act 2012*, cuts to ÚnaG or austerity and Irish-language media. This chapter begins to broaden the discussion by examining developments in areas not directly related to the Irish language, but which nonetheless have significant consequences for the efficacy of language revitalisation efforts.

I begin by examining the use of Irish in the public service and the neoliberal management structures that regulate this area. I argue that the major reforms to the public service that occurred as part of the state's response to the post-2008 economic crisis have negatively impacted the implementation of policies like the *Official Languages Act*. In doing so I provide a sociologically-informed structural account of the apparent antipathy of public servants towards the language, in opposition to the individualist explanations so often heard.

I then elaborate on my previous comments about neoliberalism fundamentally conflicting with language revitalisation, further exploring how this individualist hegemony rejects collective action and progressive wealth redistribution, key components of most revitalisation programmes. I conclude by exploring how neoliberalism's creation of widespread precarity is not conducive to people valuing "post-materialist" causes such as language revitalisation, with this economic system not only conditioning attitudes to language revitalisation at the state level, but also at the level of the individual – a key point missed in the discussions of language ideologies that are so common in sociolinguistics.

6.2 New Public Management: Irish in the public service

Despite having been one of the main foci of the early language revitalisation efforts of the Free State, the use of Irish in the public service has long since been a source of much contention. Senior public servants who had been employed in the British administration resisted attempts to Gaelicise their departments after independence (Ó hIfearnáin 2010: 547), leading Ernest Blythe, a Conradh na Gaeilge member and early Free State minister, to declare that "[i]f civil servants assemble . . . in great numbers in the Gaeltacht, they should be dispersed, if necessary, by machine guns" (in Kelly 2002: 105).

This tension exists to this day: a common discourse amongst the Irish-speaking community claims that a significant element within the public service is "opposed" to Irish. Such narratives feature frequently in both popular and academic commentary (Thejournal.ie 2013a; Ó Giollagáin 2014a: 102; Oireachtas Éireann 2020; Mac Cóil 2021). Indeed, the President of Ireland himself expressed concerns in 2016 that there was a *"fadhb chultúrtha éigean ag cur srian ar an gcóras"* [some cultural problem placing a restriction on the system] (Tuairisc.ie 2016f; see also Tuairisc.ie 2016g). This belief has been significantly strengthened by the reports and public declarations of both the current Coimisinéir Teanga and his predecessor. The first Coimisinéir, Seán Ó Cuirreáin, served from 2004 until 2014, when he unexpectedly resigned his position in protest at the widespread non-implementation of both the *20-Year Strategy* and the language schemes required of public bodies under the *Official Languages Act 2003*. While Ó Cuirreáin himself, as will be seen, offered a more nuanced analysis than is often assumed, his successor has also expressed similar frustrations on numerous occasions (e.g., Oireachtas Éireann 2016).

Several of my interviewees voiced such reservations, charging public servants with antipathy towards official language policies, as seen in the following representative quote:

A: *Cuid mhaith den am ní bhíonn na hAirí rialtais nó cibé polaiteoir atá i bhfeighil ar an réimse sin sásta dul i ngleic leis ná dul in éadán moltaí nó tuairimí an státseirbhís [. . .] Ó thaobh an státseirbhís [tá] an cultúr ann faoi láthair gur cineál inconvenience atá sa Ghaeilg.*

[A: A lot of the time government ministers or whatever politician is in charge of that area isn't willing to engage with or go against the recommendations or opinions of the civil service [. . .] With regard to the civil service there's the culture at the moment that Irish is a kind of an inconvenience.]

Given the historical evidence that shows civil service obstruction of language revitalisation measures was widespread in the Free State, there is likely an element of truth to these beliefs (Ó hIfearnáin 2010: 547–549). Here, however, I aim to propose an alternative explanation for the steady decrease in compliance post-2008 with the language schemes required of public bodies, detailed by the Coimisinéir Teanga in numerous reports (e.g., Coimisinéir Teanga 2012, 2014, 2015). In opposition to the individualist explanation so often heard in popular discourse, I believe that a strong case can be made that this marginalisation of Irish is to a significant degree a product of the neoliberal managerial reforms that began in the 1970s, gathered pace in the 1990s and have become even more widespread since the 2008 crash.

This common belief that large numbers of Machiavellian public servants are "anti-Irish" and therefore operate to render state language policy ineffective for their own ends is, I believe, an overly simplistic explanation, unlikely to be the main reason for the recent marginalisation of Irish in the public service. This is not least due to the fact that all available data suggests that the majority of the population are sympathetic towards Irish (e.g., Conradh na Gaeilge 2015) and there is no obvious reason why this would not be at least broadly replicated amongst public servants, much less why it would have become a significantly more severe problem in recent years. Although, as Ó hIfearnáin notes, it is easy to express pro-Irish sentiments when you are not required to act on them in any way (2010: 547), a senior member in the office of the Coimisinéir Teanga told me that they do not generally find such officials to have the anti-Irish views often ascribed to them:

> Údar: An bhfuil an státseirbhís chomh naimhdeach in aghaidh na Gaeilge is a shíleanns go leor de phobal na Gaeilge? Agus tú ag plé leofa an bhfaigheann tú an dearcadh sin?
>
> G: Ní fhaighim. Feictear dom go mbraitheann go leor [. . .] go bhfuil rudaí suntasacha eile le bheith ag plé leob seachas an cheist seo [. . .] Agus mise ag labhairt leob trasna an bhoird bíonn siad ag rá liom go bhfuil meas acub ar an nGaeilge, go bhfuil cion acub ar an nGaeilge, so ní fhéadfainn sin a bhréagnú, má tá duine ag rá liom go bhfuil meas acub ar an nGaeilge. But ó thaobh céard atá an státseirbhís goil a dhéanamh ar son na Gaeilge [. . .] Nuair a fheiceann muid na gealltanais atá á comhlíonadh, nó easpa gealltanais, [. . .] is ansin atá an laigeacht le feiceáil. Now cén fáth a bhfuil sé sin ag tarlú? Aríst I dunno. Y'know it's really, like it's really, it's ceist, I suppose, ceannaireachta really.
>
> [Author: Is the civil service as opposed to Irish as much of the Irish-speaking community thinks? When dealing with them is that the impression you get?
>
> G: It's not. It seems to me that many feel [. . .] that they have better things to do than be involved with this issue [. . .] When I'm sat across the table from them, they tell me they respect Irish, they like Irish. So I can't dispute that, if someone tells me they have respect for Irish. But in terms of what the civil service are going to do for Irish [. . .] When we see the commitments being fulfilled, or the lack of commitments, [. . .] that's when the weakness is to be seen. Now why is that happening? Again, I dunno. Y'know it's really, it's a question of, I suppose, leadership, really.]

It would appear clear from this experience, then, that the narrative of a large number of public administrators being opposed to Irish is indeed excessively simplistic, with them instead seemingly having at least the passive goodwill towards the language that is typical of the Irish population. As will be seen, however, in the absence of a suitably supportive workplace environment, this banal positivity is insufficient to see significant efforts made towards language promotion, with it being no surprise that this interviewee believed many public servants feel they simply have more pressing issues to handle.

As explained in 2.4, in 1974 the Fine Gael-Labour coalition government discontinued the Irish-language requirement for entry to the civil service. While factors such as the rise of the anti-compulsory Irish Language Freedom Movement surely contributed to this decision (Rowland 2016), it is also of note that this move was made the year after the Republic of Ireland joined the EEC and thereby came under the influence of international political and economic practices to a much greater degree than had previously been the case (Ó Tuathaigh 2008: 33). Furthermore, the early 1970s was a time of immense economic turmoil on a global scale, the stagflation crisis of this period being the first generalised crisis of capitalism to occur since the Great Depression (Gamble 2009: 6). As a result of this crisis and the neoliberal policies adopted to overcome it, by the late 1970s states all across the developed west were beginning to undertake fundamental reforms of their public services.

These "New Public Management" (NPM) reforms saw states endeavour to bring the logic of marketization and the practices of the private sector to bear on public sector institutions (Cairney 2012: 12). NPM drew in particular on the ideas of game theory and public choice theory which were cornerstones of neoliberal policy (Blyth 2013: 152–160), applying to the political sphere contrived economic models of self-centred individuals eternally attempting to maximise their personal benefit. With politicians perpetually compelled to maximise votes, public choice theorists claimed they would invariably implement unwise economic interventions in the hope of appeasing the electorate in the short term, with the inevitable result of generating inflation, which neoliberalism had sought to overcome (Cairney 2012: 152; Blyth 2013: 152–158). Similarly, without an appropriate incentive structure, public servants would continually seek to minimise their workloads and place personal benefit above public good, leading to the sort of inefficiencies that NPM aimed to address (Niskansen 1971).

NPM quickly gained popularity amongst policy makers, becoming "[o]ne of the key policy changes institutionalized across the Western world" in recent decades (Lynch 2012: 89). In this context, it is of little surprise that the Fianna Fáil government who won a landslide victory in 1977 did not see fit to reinstate the language requirement for civil service recruitment, despite having promised to do so should they regain power (Ó hÉallaithe 2004: 170). When combined with developments in public attitudes and the failure of the efforts of previous decades, the withdrawal of state commitment to Gaelicising the public service at this juncture appears to have been overdetermined by a confluence of factors both endogenous and exogenous to Irish society.

Ostensibly, the New Public Management model aims to increase the efficiency of the public sector. This is done through introducing challenging performance indicators designed to incentivise productivity (with continued employment often being dependent on meeting such targets), introducing "quasi-markets" or "market-type mechanisms" and interdepartmental competition to secure resources, reframing citizens as customers or "service users", and an increased reliance on outsourcing (Homburg, Pollitt and van Thiel 2007: 4–5; Cairney 2012: 158–159).

Despite its measures being promoted as a practical application of market logic, allowing for the "depoliticizing" of management practices, NPM is not simply a set of proposals for enhancing the efficiency of the increasingly large and complex bureaucracies that were required to manage capitalism under the post-war Keynesian compromise. Rather, as Lynch (2012: 89) points out, NPM is fundamentally a "management strategy for neoliberalism", being a key way in which neoliberal reforms have been enacted in "not just the political economy of states but the public institutions where people received services and worked" (Ward 2011: 206).

It is therefore unsurprising that a state which neoliberalised as thoroughly as the Republic of Ireland would have adopted NPM measures to a significant degree. An OECD report published on the eve of the crash in 2008 confirmed this to be the case, stating "Ireland has significantly advanced along a *"New Public Management"* continuum" (OECD 2008: 18, original emphasis). As will be shown, the reform measures implemented in the years following this pronouncement saw the state move yet further along this continuum, thereby creating, I believe, an environment inhospitable to the promotion of Irish in the public sector.

With "doing more with less" having been a central demand of NPM since its earliest years (Ward 2011: 207), this approach gained even greater prominence in the wake of the 2008 crash, with far-reaching reforms being implemented across the Irish public service. As MacCarthaigh explains:

> Adopting a 'never waste a crisis' approach . . . a wide range of reform measures . . . left no part of the public service unaffected . . . the 2011–16 period became one of unprecedented change for the Irish public service. The window of opportunity presented by the crisis was exploited by policy entrepreneurs from the political and administrative domains to implement major reform efforts in parallel. (MacCarthaigh 2017: 161)

Similarly, Boyle has argued that "[a]usterity has caused major change in the public service", with these measures amounting to "the biggest change to its public services since the foundation of the state" (2017: 226). As Hyndman and Lapsley (2016) and Randma-Liiv and Kickert (2017) describe, major public service reforms were also intensified elsewhere in Europe after 2008, particularly in those countries effected most severely by the crisis.

Guiding these reforms in the Republic of Ireland was the 2011 *Public Service Reform Plan*. This plan contained a host of targets aimed at reducing state expenditure, including a 12% reduction of public service staff numbers – by 37,500 to 282,500 by 2015 (MacCarthaigh 2017: 157). While this goal was not fully achieved, there was nonetheless a reduction of almost 10% during this period. As a senior member in the office of the Coimisinéir Teanga (which lost several employees due to such measures) told me when speaking about this time *"bhí gach duine hanging on for dear life really, ó thaobh foirne"* [everyone was hanging on for dear life really, with regard to staff] (see also 11.3).

One ÚnaG employee I interviewed explained that although they had significant impacts for Irish, these measures impacted the entire public service:

> É: *Baineann sé le achan earnáil [. . .] Cur chuige nua atá ilnáisiúnta [. . .] Fóireann sé do dhaoine atá i gceannas [. . .] Tá siad ábalta smacht níos fearr a choinneáil ar rudaí [. . .] leis an rud 'seo an méid atá agat le caitheamh don bhliain, seo an méid atá agat, caithfidh tú é a dhéanamh' [. . .] Ní shílim go mbaineann seo le Gaeilge amháin. Shíl mé sin go dtí gur thoisigh mé ag caint le daoine i rannóga rialtais eile [. . .] Rudaí céanna atá ann. Sílim gur sin rud a thiteann muid i gcónaí isteach ann, go bhfuil muid istigh sa súilín seo, bubble na Gaeilge, agus síleann muid go bhfuil achan rud [in ár n-aghaidh].*

> [É: It's happening in every sector [. . .] A new approach that's international [. . .] It suits those who are in charge [. . .] They're able to keep better control of things [. . .] with this thing that 'this is what you've got to spend for the year, this is all you have, you've got to do it' [. . .] I don't think it's only to do with Irish. I thought that until I started talking to people in other government departments [. . .] It's the same thing. I think that that's something we always fall into, that we're in this bubble, the Irish bubble, and we think that everything is [against us].]

Further intensifying the implementation of NPM measures, in 2013 the Department of Finance, on the basis of their negotiations with the Troika, oversaw the creation of a new system of measuring productivity. Under this system, all state departments are obliged to produce regular performance reports in order to improve "alignment of decisions on spending with policy outcomes" (MacCarthaigh 2017: 155). As a result of these and many other similar reforms, in comparison with other states between 2008–2014, Irish public service managers reported "a stronger deterioration with regard to the attractiveness of the public sector as an employer and staff motivation", as well as the trust of citizens in government (MacCarthaigh 2017: 161).

In the wake of such reforms, the Coimisinéir Teanga found that by 31 December 2016, of 113 public bodies with language schemes (see 2.5), 56 had let their scheme expire, with six expired for seven or more years (Coimisinéir

Teanga 2017b: 3). Following a notable peak in the number of schemes that were lapsed between 2011–2013 (Coimisinéir Teanga 2017a: 25), there was an increase in recent years in the number of schemes accepted by the relevant minister, as all schemes must be for them to have force under the *Official Languages Act 2003*. Despite this seemingly positive development, the Coimisinéir's office reported in 2017 that the majority of public bodies had reduced the provisions in their second and/or third schemes, with the usual response to an investigation into non-compliance with an aspect of a scheme simply being to remove the aggravating provision from subsequent iterations (Coimisinéir Teanga 2017b: 13). Consequently, although many public bodies have had their schemes accepted by the minister, they often contain very little of substance to provide for Irish speakers. When combined with the fact that Walsh (2011c; 2012b) reported that the original versions of these plans were themselves very weak, the extent to which this development rendered language revitalisation efforts in the public service almost worthless becomes apparent.

In light of the enormous NPM restructuring of public bodies, however, these developments could have been expected. Such widespread reforms and the overall worsening of employment conditions they entail can hardly be seen as conducive to implementing language schemes, which are never likely to be amongst the most pressing of issues in an assessment of any public body's duties. This is especially true due to the lack of powers available to the Coimisinéir Teanga to impose any significant penalties as a result of non-compliance. Given the fact that all Irish speakers can also speak English and that the *Official Languages Act* contains few clear, enforceable rights, the provision of Irish-language services is unlikely to ever be seen as anything more than a symbolic gesture of good will, liable to be removed when budgetary and human resource contractions so require.

Indeed, when faced with such heavy budgetary cuts and the compulsion to complete an ever greater range of duties, public bodies adopted a range of evasive tactics such as the common refrain that their language schemes will be implemented "in so far as resources allow" (in much the same way that the Act itself does – see 2.5). In the following extract a senior employee in the Coimisinéir's office discusses the Department of the Environment's language scheme:

> A: *Trí huaire déag bhí sé luaite go bhfuil sé ag brath ar acmhainní. Yeah. But tá sé sin ag tarlú go [go rialta] [. . .] B'fhéidir nach bhfuil sé chomh follasach anois, go bhfuiltear ag rá ag brath ar acmhainní, ach d'fhéadfadh sé a bheith curtha ar bhealach go bhfuil sé andeacair na gealltanais atá tugtha a bheith tomhaiste.*
>
> [A: Thirteen times it was mentioned that it was dependent on resources. Yeah. But that's happening [often] [. . .] Maybe it's not that transparent, that they say dependent on resources, but it could be put in a way that means it's very difficult to assess the commitments.]

Further examples of this tendency were given in the Coimisinéir's 2018 Oireachtas statement, where he stated that such was the extent of non-compliance and lack of worthwhile provisions contained in the schemes that his office was discontinuing monitoring their implementation, considering it to have become a waste of their limited resources (Oireachtas Éireann 2018b; Tuairisc.ie 2018f). Three years later, the Coimisinéir's *Monitoring Report 2020/2021* stated that the level of non-compliance with language schemes by county councils was so great that he was considering taking legal proceedings against a number of them (Coimisinéir Teanga 2021: 22–30).

This too, must be considered in its wider context, however. As has been well documented in public policy literature on governance in the Republic of Ireland, since 2008 the "local government level was . . . the hardest hit by employment cutbacks", experiencing a fall in staff numbers of 22% (Shannon 2016: 19; Boyle 2015: 15). IMF data reports that local government expenditure in the country declined by 32.6% between 2008–2015. The OECD give a figure of −56.9% for the same period, with the discrepancy being due to the differing ways in which each organisation defines this expenditure. Either way, these were the highest cuts in the EU (Turley, McNena and Robbins 2018: 7). Within the Republic of Ireland, it was "small rural county councils [that] endured the most austerity" (Turley, McNena and Robbins 2018: 1). Of course, such councils are more likely to contain Gaeltacht areas and, notably, many of the most seriously offending councils in the Coimisinéir's report could also be categorised thusly – small and rural. Furthermore, in late 2020 it was reported that so large were the budgetary deficits facing local authorities as a result of the Covid crisis (discussed in detail in 14.5) that they would be "forced to start cutting all services including housing maintenance, roads, lighting and parks services, community grants, festivals and arts" (Irish Times 2020b) – leaving it inevitable that Irish-language services would suffer too. Neither the Coimisinéir's reports nor any of the heated discussion thereof in Irish-language media made any reference to this important context.

One often-cited difficulty relating to the implementation of language schemes is the lack of Irish-speaking staff in the public service. As has repeatedly been stated by the Coimisinéir, the number of Irish speakers being recruited remains vastly inadequate to facilitate widespread implementation. Indeed, figures published by Tuairisc.ie in 2017 showed that just 15 of the 18,775 positions spread across 15 state departments have a specific Irish-language requirement – a minuscule 0.08% (Tuairisc.ie 2017i). Despite Seán Kyne, then minister of state responsible for the Gaeltacht, announcing that he intended to take steps to rectify this, less than a week later the position of secretary of his department, the most senior civil servant with responsibility for the Gaeltacht, was given to a woman unable to conduct her duties through Irish (Tuairisc.ie 2017i; 2017j). While the following years saw the number of positions with an Irish-language requirement increase, by 2019 the total proportion remained minute (84 out of 19,766), and the majority of these roles (67) were in the department responsible for the Gaeltacht (Coimisinéir Teanga 2019b: 11). In 2021 the Department of Public Expenditure and Reform reported that of 8,324 vacancies advertised in the civil service between January 1st 2018 and September 30th 2020, only 16 (0.2%) required a proficiency in Irish, with all of these being for very junior positions (Tuairisc.ie 2021e).

While often explained as resulting purely from a lack of political will, this issue of recruitment can also be read as a consequence of the NPM model. In the same way that the private sector (fully aware of the limited market value of minoritised languages) remains extremely unlikely to employ someone due to their being a minoritised language speaker, a public service governed by NPM is not likely to pay much heed to such matters. In the absence of an ambitious policy of affirmative action in favour of Irish, the NPM ideal of recruiting the "best" employees from either the public or private sector, nationally or internationally, means that the likelihood of a recruit being a competent Irish speaker is slim. The decision, for instance, by the board of directors of the National University of Ireland, Galway (ostensibly a bilingual university) to abolish the Irish-language requirement for the position of university president was made on the basis of such logic in 2016, with a similar decision being made with regard to administrative staff in 2021. The same year, the role of Vice President of Equality and Diversity was also determined to not require competence in Irish (Tuairisc.ie 2016h, 2021f, 2021g). Relatedly, it was in the wider context of civil service reform described above that the decision was made in October 2013 to discontinue the awarding of bonus points to those who completed the civil service entrance exams in Irish, a positive discrimination measure that had been introduced after the compulsory Irish exam was abolished in 1974 (Conradh na Gaeilge 2013).

With the programme for the "Government of National Recovery 2011–2016" committing to reviewing the *Official Languages Act 2003* to "ensure expenditure on the language is best targeted" (Government of Ireland 2011: 59), the department responsible for the Gaeltacht conducted a public consultation on amending the Act in 2014. Based on the submissions to this consultation, the draft heads of the *Official Languages (Amendment) Bill* were eventually released in 2017 and included a commitment to "the overall objectives of 20% of new recruits to the public service being Irish speakers", as well as "all public offices situated in Gaeltacht areas operating through the medium of Irish" (Government of Ireland 2017a: 15).

Although appearing to mark a major change of direction, the head of Irish-language policy in the department initially stated that this commitment would not be including a deadline or time frame for its implementation (Oireachtas Éireann 2018c). Both language promotion bodies and the Coimisinéir Teanga claimed that such a policy was all but meaningless without a delineated time frame, and was therefore surely set to be yet another failure (Coimisinéir Teanga 2018; Oireachtas Éireann 2018d). After repeated delays spanning multiple years (Tuairisc.ie 2019c), a new bill to update the legislation was brought forward in late 2019, and was eventually enacted in late 2021 during the writing of this volume. While still weaker than hoped by many, after much dissent from opposition parties, the Act was considerably strengthened, including through the addition of the ambitious time frame of ensuring that 20% of new recruits to the public service would be Irish speakers by 2030. So too, however, was a provision added which allows the relevant minister to extend this timeframe if necessary. Considering the extremely weak current position of the language in the public service, it seems very likely that such an extension will be required. Furthermore, while an improvement on the previous situation, without the structural issues I discuss here being addressed, even the reformed Act is unlikely to live up to the hopes that many have for it (see also 14.4).

Unlike other accounts about the status of Irish in the public sector, one well-informed interviewee, when I asked to what extent he felt the recession provided an excuse for the state to withdraw from Irish-language provision, expressed some awareness of the wider structural context in which public servants operate:

> S: Ní cuid den chúlú eacnamaíochta é sin, ach cuid den chúlú atá gá dhéanamh ag na státseirbhísigh agus ag an stát ó bheith freagrach as rudaí iad féin [. . .] Cheapfainn go bhfuil saghas meon nua tagtha isteach sa státseirbhís go bhfuil muid ag seasamh siar ó aon rud a dhéanamh nó aon cinneachaí a dhéanamh, fágfaidh muid é sin ag rialatóirí agus é sin, regulators. Ach tá muid sábhailte, so ní féidir aon cheisteanna crua a chur orainn sa Dáil, mar 'ó tá dream eile ag plé leis sin'.

> [S: That's not part of the recession, it's part of this rollback of civil servants and the state from being responsible for anything themselves [. . .] I think that there's a kind of new attitude now in the civil service that we're standing back from doing anything or making any decisions, we'll leave that to regulators. But we're safe, so you can't ask us any difficult questions in the Dáil because 'oh some other group is in charge of that'.]

While not explicitly naming it or appreciating the extent to which this process was accelerated by the recession, his statement is nonetheless perceptive and, indeed, fairly accurately describes the NPM approach. During the address to the parliamentary *Sub-committee on the 20-Year Strategy for the Irish Language* at which he announced his resignation, the first Coimisinéir Teanga made a similar allusion:

> Creidim go bhfuil an teanga á ruaigeadh ar leataobh go leanúnach chuig imeall na sochaí, agus áirím anseo cuid mhaith den riarachán poiblí. Ní chreidim ar chor ar bith gur ar an aicme pholaitiúil is mo atá an locht ina leith seo ach feictear dom, cé go bhfuil daoine sa státchóras a thacaíonn go láidir leis an Ghaeilge, go bhfuil fórsaí níos láidre agus níos forleithne fós ann ar cuma leo ann nó as dár dteanga náisiúnta (Oireachtas Éireann 2014).
>
> [I believe the language is being driven to the margins of society continually, and I include here much of the public administration. I don't believe at all that the blame for this is primarily on the political class, but it appears to me that although there are people in the civil service who strongly support Irish, there are stronger and more widespread forces that do not care whether our national language lives or dies (Oireachtas Éireann 2014).]

Despite not going any further to define what exactly was meant by *"fórsaí níos láidre agus níos forleithne"* [stronger and more widespread forces], this comment nonetheless clearly states that the issues faced by Irish are greater than just the apathy of public servants. In light of the evidence presented thus far, I believe it is clear that the neoliberal NPM paradigm is a key factor in this process. Explanations of the lack of adherence to the language schemes such as *"ní bhaineann sé sin leis an ngeilleagar, sin meon rialtais"* [that's not to do with the economy, that's the government's attitude], as one Irish-language activist put it to me, are, in my estimation, deficient. They fail to appreciate the extent to which an economic environment as challenging as the post-2008 one and the ideological hegemony that drives the Irish economy impact the organisational structures of the public service, and, therefore, the ability of the professional managerial class to implement language schemes and associated measures.

There is, of course, some amount of agency behind the sidelining of Irish in the public service, with at least some officials likely aware that their decisions to not implement language schemes – or to implement them only in part – are incompatible with the requirements of the Act (see Ó Flatharta, Sandberg and Williams 2014: 52 on the role of individual managers in implementing language policies). Nonetheless, this agency is clearly exercised under the restraints produced by NPM structures. Indeed, as one long-term civil servant told me *"feictear domhsa nach bhfuil ann ach pian sa tóin daofa"* [it appears to me that it's just a pain in the backside for them] – one more issue to be dealt with on top of an already excessive workload. While top-down minoritised language policy implementation would surely remain challenging under a different managerial paradigm (as the experience of the civil service before the 1970s demonstrates, see Ó Riagáin 1997: 18–19), NPM is most surely not an approach conducive to language revitalisation and constitutes an important structural obstacle which makes up part of the wider neoliberal paradigm that I further interrogate in the remainder of this chapter.

6.3 Policy making under austerity

As has been described, the impacts of the crisis and the ensuing policy reforms have significantly impacted the strength of Irish-language policy. While a number of these developments have already been documented in more detail than the length of this work permits (Ó Murchú 2014), there has as yet been no detailed attempt to situate them in the wider ideological context that drove the state's response to the crisis, that of neoliberalism.

The problematic nature of this ideology for those involved in language planning can be clearly seen in the fact that Hayek's *The Road to Serfdom*, a foundational text in the development of neoliberalism, consists almost entirely of a diatribe against economic (and, by extension, social) planning, with the author contending that "planning leads to dictatorship because dictatorship is the most effective instrument of coercion and, as such, essential if central planning on a large scale is to be possible" (2006: 74). Hayek reserves his greatest ire for those forms of economic planning which are redistributive in nature (2006: 36), a position which raises significant difficulties for the sort of revitalisation programmes that are typically required to reverse language shift. While slightly different from the dynamic often critiqued by neoliberals in which a wealthy minority has their wealth expropriated to support a larger, less well-off group, revitalisation projects aimed at strengthening the position of minority groups require significant investment, and almost by definition, the transfer of resources from dominant to minority groups. Furthermore, such redistributive efforts are likely to be required for the long-term. While there are, of course, some schemes that can be implemented at little cost, as Ó Riagáin notes, for language revitalisation policies to be successful "they will require large resources on a scale which has not been hitherto realised" and need to "affect all aspects of national life and will have to be sustained for decades, if not forever" (1997: 283).

If minoritised languages like Irish are understood as inherently social goods, as Grin (2006: 81) and Ó Flatharta, Sandberg and Williams (2014: 57) argue they should be, it becomes clear that they can only be effectively maintained through societal intervention. As Spolsky has pointed out, "[i]t is changes in society that affect linguistic diversity, so that it is social policy rather than language policy that is needed to maintain it" (2004: 8). Similar points have been made by a great many other prominent writers in the field (e.g., Cooper 1989: 1; Crystal

2000: 154; Fishman 1991; Romaine 2006: 456; Williams 2014: 243). Neoliberalism, however, is a firmly individualist ideology (cf. Thatcher's famous "there is no such thing as society" statement, itself based on Hayek 1988: 112–119) and is therefore contraindicated to the type of planning required for language revitalisation. As one of my interviewees – one of very few who explicitly mentioned neoliberalism – exclaimed:

> M: Sin an nualiobrálachas aríst – níl function ag an stát ach riar do lucht gnó. Níl dualgas sochaí ar an stát, agus tá an Ghaeltacht ina shochaí, agus is cuid de shochaí na tíre í an teanga. Ach [. . .] níl bocsa sa spreadsheet fá choinne seo, so níl baint acu leis.
>
> [M: That's neoliberalism again – the state has no function except as an administrator for business people. It has no duty towards society, and the Gaeltacht is a society, and the language is part of the country's society. But [. . .] there's no box in the spreadsheet for that, so they have nothing to do with it.]

This ideological bias, coupled with the fact that Irish is the preserve of a minority of regular speakers who had little experience of collective political mobilisation before the crash, and who were thus unlikely to mount significant resistance (see, however, Chapter 11), meant that language-related funding was disposed to receive very large cutbacks since 2008. Section 7.2.3 discusses the tendency of austerity to target the poorest most severely – an additional, major challenge in light of the class composition of much of the Gaeltacht.

In a telling example of the extent to which the language has been depoliticised in the Republic, despite the severity of the cuts to Irish-language provision, language advocacy groups and activists have been reluctant to make an explicit connection between neoliberal ideology and these decisions. Particularly amongst state-funded language groups there was almost no concerted opposition to austerity, although this was the case for campaign groups in many sectors which are fully or partly funded by the public purse (Harvey 2014; see also Chapter 11). Instead, similar to the discourses around the public service described in the previous section, the unambitious and underfunded language policy regime of recent years is widely understood to be the product of individual politicians' or specific parties' animosity to the language: *"Tá meon faoi leith [. . .] maidir leis an rialtas a bheith in aghaidh na Gaeilge"* [There's a specific attitude [. . .] with regard to the government being against Irish] as one informant told me, a statement typical of many others I heard.

As Ó Murchú has pointed out, however, *"[r]ómhinic sa tír seo cuirtear an locht ar dhaoine nuair is cirte é a chur ar chóras nó ar choinníollacha"* [too often in this country the blame is placed on people when it is more correct to place it on a system or conditions] (2002: 27). With neoliberalism being the consensus ideology amongst Irish elites (Murphy 2014: 139–140), the strength of language policy is not predominantly an issue of how much individual politicians like or dislike Irish, but rather of a hegemony that is inherently averse to public investment in such an area. Indeed, during a large part of the period described in this study, both the Taoiseach and the Tánaiste [Prime Minister and Deputy Prime Minister], were fluent Irish speakers, an uncommon occurrence (i.e., Enda Kenny and Eamon Gilmore, in office 2011–2017 and 2011–2015 respectively). Each was very willing to engage with Irish-language media and, seemingly, held positive sentiments towards the language. Such personal affiliation was clearly insufficient to prevent the severe cutting of Gaeltacht-focused schemes, however, with Irish coming low on the list of priorities for officials committed to restructuring measures in a time of crisis. As one of my informants, a lobbyist with considerable experience discussing Irish-language policy with politicians, told me when asked about the widely held belief that the current political elite are opposed to Irish:

> M: Léiríonn sé nach raibh an Ghaeilge-Gaeltacht mar thosaíocht [. . .] Ní hé go bhfuil naimhdeas ann, ag an gcuid is mó de pholaiteoirí in aghaidh na Gaeilge, ach nuair a bhí siad ag breathnú ar na fadhbanna a bhí acu le réiteach ní raibh an Ghaeilge-Gaeltacht mar chuid de sin.

> [M: It shows that Irish and the Gaeltacht were not priorities [. . .] It's not that there's animosity amongst most politicians against Irish, but when they were looking at the problems they had to solve Irish and the Gaeltacht were not part of that.]

Another activist commented that, similar to the reforms of ÚnaG described above being part of a wider policy of public service reform, cuts to language planning were not due to animosity to Irish per se: *"baineann sé le cinntí a ghlac an rialtas maidir le fiacha, seilbh a ghlacadh ar fiacha, nuair atá tú ag íoc ar ais an leibhéal fiacha is atá muid, gearrfar siar ar chuile rud"* [it's to do with decisions the government took regarding debt, to take ownership of debt, when you're paying back the level of debt that we are, everything is going to be cut]. Indeed, it is difficult to imagine a policy environment more inhospitable to Irish than that of the Great Recession, with massive cuts to state spending inevitably impacting a sector which survives in a "state-funded cocoon" (Wright 2016: 481).

As with the case of NPM, by emphasising the animosity of individual politicians or parties, popular non-structural assessments of language policy fail to accord adequate significance to the ideological paradigm which defines how states make social policy. This paradigm was promoted not just by the native political class post-2008, but by the Troika after they became involved in state finances in late 2010. While the depth of influence of such supranational constraints on policy is debatable, the role of the Troika during this time must be considered, not least due to their well-established reputations as institutions central to the propagation of neoliberalism internationally (Allen and O'Boyle 2013: 13–20). Notably, as several authors have observed (e.g., Murphy and Dukelow 2016: 322), there were many similarities between the state's *National Recovery Plan 2011–2014* and the *Memorandum of Understanding* agreed with the Troika. Although this memorandum required punitive austerity measures and the marketization of public spheres previously insulated from such measures (Mercille and Murphy 2015: 90–106), the extent to which the Irish elite were already committed to neoliberal ideology means that the Troika were largely "pushing an open door" (Dukelow 2015). Then finance minister Brian Lenihan repeatedly insisted that the policies enacted in 2010 were "ours alone" (BBC 2010), a fairly plausible statement considering the neoliberal policies his government had long since pursued and the path dependent nature of such fundamental policy trajectories. Although it is typically almost impossible to measure the extent to which policies are adopted as a result of coercion (Cairney 2012: 256), the Troika's influence seems most visible in the pace and intensity of austerity measures, as policymakers were "able to advance change without the domestic vetoes they might otherwise have expected" (Murphy and Dukelow 2016: 322).

With Irish elites anxious to be seen as compliant from the earliest days of the bailout programme, it is therefore unlikely the Troika would have even have had to mention the issue of reducing Gaeltacht funding. As Crenson explains in his influential work on agenda setting, the reputations of powerful institutions often guarantee a favourable outcome without them having to actively exercise power (1971: 125). The effective implementation of many of the language-related policies discussed in this chapter would thus have been kept off the agenda purely by virtue of the reputations of these institutions, the exigencies of the crisis and the anxiousness of the Irish elite to end the recession as quickly as possible via budgetary contraction. The contributions of Bachrach and Baratz (1963) and Lukes (1974) to the community power debate – a seminal discussion in political science in the 1960s and 70s about the nature of political power (Cairney 2012: 46–58) – are of great pertinence here. As these authors noted, the so-called "second face of power" (see also 2.4 and 4.2) is often exercised primarily to keep issues off the political agenda and away from public attention, a point which tallies with Dye's popular definition of public policy as "whatever governments chose to do or not do" (1972: 2). In the overall context of state expenditure, the amount spent on LPP was admittedly relatively small. Nonetheless, when the severity of the crisis and the presence of the Troika was combined with the requirements of small states under neoliberalism to compete with one another for Foreign Direct Investment, to keep existing investors happy and to not buck international trends (Cairney 2012: 11, 16; Block 2020 [1977]), programmes focused on language maintenance in peripheral communities like the Gaeltacht stood little chance in the wake of the 2008 crash.

6.4 Neoliberalism and the formation of social attitudes

A further important issue regarding minoritised language policy under neoliberalism relates to the ways in which social attitudes are conditioned by the economic environment in which we live. While the extent to which language policy attempts to form rather than merely respond to public attitudes has long since been debated (CILAR 1975: 289), there is little doubt that where significant public opposition to expenditure on the language exists, it is much less likely the political class will seek to dedicate resources to language revitalisation efforts. Neoliberal measures, however, decrease exactly the social solidarity which is required to ensure widespread public support for such expenditure.

As is well documented, neoliberalism and the Great Recession have led to massive, unprecedented levels of inequality (Piketty 2014). Commenting on data from before the crash, Judt explains that "[e]ven trust, the faith we have in our fellow citizens, corresponds negatively with differences in income: between 1983 and 2001, mistrustfulness increased markedly in the US, the UK and Ireland – three countries in which the dogma of unregulated individual self-interest was most assiduously applied to public policy" (2010: 20).

Even before 2008 wealth distribution in the Republic of Ireland was enormously unequal, with 1% of the population reported to own 34% of the wealth in 2007 (Bank of Ireland 2007: 12). The extent to which this has been exacerbated since then can be inferred from the *Irish Independent* report which found that the richest 300 people in the country doubled their wealth between 2010–2017, from €50 billion to €100 billion, giving them combined wealth significantly greater than that of the original bank bailout. The eleven richest people increased their wealth to have the same amount as the top 300 had in 2010, a roughly 27 times greater concentration of wealth amongst the super-rich during the most severe economic crisis in the state's history (Irish Independent 2017). The Covid pandemic has, of course, since aggravated this trend even further, as I discuss in the final chapter.

This inequality and its resultant decline in trust has considerable implications for social attitudes: "trusters tend to believe that everyone should be treated with respect and tolerance" (Pickett and Wilkinson 2010: 56). "Respect and tolerance" are, of course, fundamental prerequisites for the kind of pluralist society which is supportive of minoritised language rights. With its commitment to individualism and survival of the fittest competition, neoliberalism, then, quickly becomes "social Darwinism in an economic disguise" (Verhaeghe 2014: 119; see also Dorian 1999: 10–12 regarding the effects of social Darwinism on minoritised languages).

Relatedly, in polities with weak welfare provision, the population tends to be much more reluctant to accept radical policy changes (Chang 2016), a fact which also has obvious implications for the political viability of policies requiring widescale redistributive investment in the Gaeltacht. Conversely, the presence of a significant social safety net makes policies of investment in peripheral locations seem much less threatening. While such measures may not be universally supported, it is understood that they will not result in significant poverty or hardship for anyone, with state investment not being a zero-sum game consisting of an either/or Gaeltacht-Galltacht dichotomy whereby investment in the Gaeltacht likely means divestment from the Galltacht. Although the Irish welfare state was never as developed as others in western Europe (Walsh 2021: 331), the recession saw it significantly weakened in a short period (Mercille and Murphy 2015; Murphy and Dukelow 2016). In light of the perilous economic situation experienced by so much of the population in recent years and the hegemonic anti-collectivist sentiments that are fundamental to neoliberalism, it seems unlikely that there would be widespread acceptance of ambitious language revitalisation policies such as those proposed in the *Comprehensive Linguistic Study* (Ó Giollagáin et al. 2007b: 31–47), or by Ó Giollagáin and Ó Curnáin (2016: 59–68), thereby presenting a major challenge for those who espouse them.

Similarly, people living pay cheque to pay cheque – as a significant percentage of the population have been since 2008 (Irish Examiner 2013) – also have far less emotional energy and free time with which to be concerned about non-essential issues such as the fate of the Irish language. As Putnam (2000: 193) has explained, rather than radicalising people, the experience of unemployment more often leads the unemployed to become "passive and withdrawn, socially as well as politically", with trying economic circumstances forcing people to focus simply on personal survival (see also 13.2 and 13.3.3 regarding neoliberalism and the instrumental view of language).

While it is certainly true that the most ambitious revitalisation efforts in the Republic of Ireland were made while the country was still chronically impoverished, as described in Chapter 2, this was the product of a unique set of historical circumstances, not least the very significant influence romanticism and linguistic nationalism had on the early generations of Free State leaders. With such conditions not existing, most people are unlikely to be animated by such "post-materialist" causes. Inglehart (2018: 173–199) offers an important and detailed exploration of the decline of post-materialist values in recent years as a result of neoliberal precarity (see also 13.4; Connolly 1898).

An employee of ÚnaG in Donegal noted the effects of this very phenomenon with regards to concern for the language while we were discussing the local industrial estate:

> É: Chaill 950 [duine] jabanna anseo [. . .] but an rud a tharla faoin teanga, bhí sé iontach suimiúil because ghlac na postanna tús áite [. . .] Bhí cruinniú poiblí againn dhá bhliain ansin faoi fhostaíocht agus níl dóigh ar bith sa dá bhliain go raibh duine ar bith chun teanga a lua.

> [É: 950 [people] lost jobs here [. . .] but the thing that happened with regard to the language, it was very interesting because jobs took primacy [. . .] Two years we had public meetings about employment and there is no way in those two years that anyone was going to mention language.]

Similar to the constraints on policy makers at a macro-level, in times of economic distress, individuals and communities quite simply have more pressing issues facing them than language revitalisation. This material basis of ideology is a topic which has generally not been addressed in the considerable sociolinguistic literature on language ideologies.

By both affecting the conditions which give rise to public support for post-materialist issues and causing a move to a significantly more deregulated language policy regime since 2008, the neoliberal beliefs that dominate politics in the Republic of Ireland have therefore made the maintenance of Irish significantly more challenging. They have also caused widespread social disruption at the community level in the Gaeltacht, as Part 3 of this work will describe.

6.5 Conclusion

As demonstrated throughout this chapter, economic developments unrelated to language can have an immense impact on the efficacy of language policy. The problems surrounding the implementation of the *Official Languages Act* are common knowledge amongst many Irish speakers, but typical explanations for these issues invariably ignore the impact of wider forces. Although often maligned as being anti-Irish, public servants have had their work conditions drastically rationalised by New Public Management reforms in recent years, and it is unsurprising that they would have neglected all but the most essential of their duties. Despite its obvious significance for the implementation of top-down language policy, however, NPM has not to date been considered in detail in literature on "language management" (Spolsky 2009) or other aspects of LPP, either in Ireland or internationally. Notably, language management literature has largely failed to engage with the actual management strategies typically implemented by modern states.

Similarly, despite the severity of the cuts, as several well-informed interviewees noted, the political class have no particular animosity towards the language. Rather, the crisis period simply left them with bigger problems to deal with. This fact, when coupled with the dominance of neoliberalism, the paradigmatic ideological force of Irish politics, meant that the urgency of the linguistic crisis of the Gaeltacht was given insufficient support during the period under study. When coupled with Irish being the preserve of a dispersed minority and Gaeltacht communities generally being on the lower end of the Irish class scale (see 7.2.3), this made language revitalisation programmes easy targets for politicians making dramatic cuts across many sectors.

The discussion presented in this and the preceding chapters in Part 2 has, then, drawn attention to the significant impact of the Great Recession for Irish LPP. As Cairney has pointed out, however, all policy narratives are biased to view some indicators as more important than others, but this is not necessarily a disadvantage (2012: 29). While this present analysis offers but one of many possible readings of the recent language policy regime, analyses of this field have rarely engaged with wider politico-economic factors in detail, often falling into the trap of viewing "bilingual reproduction . . . as autonomous" (Ó Riagáin 1996: 35). Other studies of this period using alternative lenses of policy analysis would surely offer valuable insights not given here. In the timeframe in question, however, the impact of the economic crisis on social policy of all types simply cannot be ignored, with the spectre of austerity looming large over both the content and implementation of official policies. This assessment therefore offers a heuristic tool which allows us to gain a greater understanding of the intersection between macro-level economic forces and the policy decisions that can have such formative impacts on the vitality of minoritised language communities.

Similar to the economic transformations of the 1970s, the Great Recession and its long-lasting consequences represent an example of punctuated equilibrium in language policy, with drastic reforms being implemented in a very short period. The neoliberal ideology driving these reforms is fundamentally opposed to state involvement in social planning or wealth redistribution of the type necessary for language revitalisation and creates social conditions and attitudes which are inimical to such efforts. As noted in Chapter 1, the post-2008 period in the Republic of Ireland is of particular interest as it offers an example of state language policies shifting from being relatively heavily regulated to a much more neoliberal policy regime, an issue of concern in light of Grin's observations (1999: 179) about the inability of unregulated market forces to promote the survival of "lesser used languages".

Although ideological hegemonies such as that of neoliberalism are never monolithic, seamless or totally omnipotent, with people invariably finding ways to contest and renegotiate such forces, it is nonetheless imperative that an informed assessment of language policy in the 21st century takes account of the macro-level forces that shape all our lives. The second part of this book has highlighted fundamental tensions noted in a great deal of social science literature around agency and structure and the macro-micro dilemma of social causality, and as such can only hope to be but one part of a wider debate on these issues.

Important as this elucidation of some of the macro-level factors restricting revitalisation-focused language policies in a neoliberal society is, it is nonetheless of obvious importance that such theoretical discussion be accompanied by an understanding of the practical effects of this ideology on minoritised language communities. To this end, Part 3 will detail the ethnographic findings that emerged from more than eight months of participant observation and over 50 interviews. Taken in tandem with the descriptive policy analysis approach offered in Chapters 3 to 6, this offers a detailed exposition of how exactly neoliberalism has impacted the vitality of Irish in the Gaeltacht since the catastrophic collapse of 2008.

Part 3: **Neoliberalism and the Gaeltacht – an ethnographic study**

7 Quantitative background to Part 3

7.1 Introduction

As explained in Chapter 2, neoliberal theory contends that state intervention in social policy stifles the entrepreneurial impulses naturally present in homo economicus, thereby restricting profit maximisation, itself understood as an inherently moral act. Accordingly, the neoliberal era has seen a steady decrease in funding for a wide variety of welfare programmes, with economies worldwide being restructured to more closely serve the needs of capital (MacLeavy 2012: 251). In a world in which the nation-state is the primary unit of political organisation, however, state support is often very important for the maintenance of minoritised languages, thus leading to a fundamental tension between neoliberalism and minoritised language revitalisation.

Building on the policy analysis presented in Part 2, the ethnographic study presented in Part 3 will explore some of the key ways in which this tension played out in Gaeltacht communities in the years after 2008. The meso- and micro-level consequences of many of the macro-level reforms described in previous chapters will be explored, providing an insight into the practical consequences of neoliberal restructuring for a minoritised language community. While not necessarily the result of reformed Gaeltacht policy per se, other repercussions of the crisis such as transformed patterns of population mobility and the decline of important economic sectors will also be examined in relation to their implications for the social, economic and linguistic vitality of the Gaeltacht.

Given its immense significance, the full extent of the Great Recession's impact on the Gaeltacht cannot be covered in a book of this length. Rather than offering an encyclopaedic account of the innumerable ways in which austerity measures impinged on Gaeltacht life, I therefore present an overview of the most salient points that emerged from my research, particularly those that illustrate broader patterns likely to resonate in other contexts. After this chapter in which I offer an overview of quantitative data regarding changes in demographic and language use patterns in recent years, as well as the class composition of the Gaeltacht, the remainder of this work will be based on data gathered via participant observation and semi-structured interviews. While an effort has been made to address various issues discussed herein discretely, with the causes of language loss "generally [being] multiple and interrelated" (Mackey 2001: 68), there are inevitably numerous overlaps and interactions between the various topics discussed.

https://doi.org/10.1515/9783110768909-007

7.2 Quantitative background

The fact that the Republic's census of population took place in 2006, 2011 and 2016 allows for a convenient statistical analysis of the period on which this book focuses, although, unfortunately, this five-year schedule was disrupted in 2021 by the Covid pandemic. The 2006 census took place as the Celtic Tiger approached its zenith, before there was mainstream acknowledgement of such growth being unsustainable in the long-term. In 2011, by contrast, the country was suffering the full brunt of the second most severe crisis in the history of capitalism (Tooze 2018). The 2016 census took place at a sufficient remove from 2008 to provide a reasonably long-term assessment of the effects of the crash, at a time when the Irish national economy had returned to growth. As will be seen, however, this recovery was far less visible in Gaeltacht communities – particularly the more peripheral ones – than in the urban core. In order to help contextualise the ethnographic findings presented in the following chapters, I will first give a brief overview of some relevant trends visible in census data for the 2006–2016 period.

7.2.1 Demographic change 2006–2016

Although the state's population increased from 4,239,848 in 2006 to 4,588,252 in 2011 and 4,757,956 in 2016 (Haase and Pratschke 2017a: 10), this growth occurred primarily in the cities, particularly Dublin, which recovered relatively rapidly from the crash (Barry and Bergin 2017: 82). Although the recession was severe by 2011, large numbers of emigrants moved home during the 2006–2009 period, before the full extent of the challenges facing the country were apparent, with the lagged effects of the crisis therefore often being more clearly marked in the 2016 figures than those from 2011. For much of the country, the demographic impact of the crisis was seen primarily in a growth rate much lower than that experienced during the Celtic Tiger, with intercensal population growth falling to its lowest level for twenty years between 2011–2016 (Central Statistics Office 2017a: 8). County Galway exemplified this trend, with its population growing by 2.4% between 2011–2016, significantly less than the 10% increase between 2006–2011 or the 6.4% increase between 2002–2006. As will be shown to have been the case for many peripheral areas, County Donegal's population declined between 2011–2016, falling by 1.2%. While this may seem relatively slight, it too is in marked contrast to the growth of 9.4% between 2006–2011 or 4.2% from 2002–2006 (Haase and Pratschke 2017a: 10).

Prior to the crash, the Celtic Tiger period had seen a reversal of the widespread population loss which had occurred throughout the Gaeltacht for much of the 20th century. Between 2006–2011 there was a 5.2% increase in the population of the Gaeltacht over three years of age – from 91,862 to 96,628 (Central Statistics Office 2012a: 9). Although endogenous population growth is partly responsible for this increase (with families being more likely to have children during times of prosperity), much of it was due to in-migration, particularly the return of previously departed migrants and their families. The fact that some 1,197 residents of the Galway Gaeltacht had been living outside of Ireland a year before the 2006 census was conducted gives some indication of the extent of this phenomenon. By 2011 this number had fallen by over 50%, to 564, and increased only slightly (to 711) in 2016 (Central Statistics Office 2007a, 2012b, 2017b). Donegal saw a similar pattern – having 380 such in-migrants in 2006, 212 in 2011 and only marginally more, 240, five years later (Central Statistics Office 2007b, 2012c, 2017c).

Between 2011–2016, the total Gaeltacht population over three years of age fell marginally, by 0.6%, from 96,628 to 96,090 (Central Statistics Office 2017a: 69). This small reduction conceals considerable regional variation, however, with those areas nearest Galway city experiencing modest population growth during this time, while more distant areas suffered significant decline (Pobal.ie 2017). The extent of this disparate impact is perhaps best illustrated by reference to the islands, where, as Hindley observed, the "extremes of Gaeltacht 'deprivation'" (1990: 69) are most evident. Despite some exceptions such as Inis Oírr and Inis Meáin where the population increased slightly, most of the strongly Irish-speaking island communities saw significant population loss between 2011–2016, with decreases of 17.4% in Toraigh, 8.8% in Árainn Mhór (both in Donegal), 15.4% in Leitir Mealláin and 9.8% in Inis Mór, each of which are in Galway (Central Statistics Office 2017d). By contrast, Bearna/Cnoc na Cathrach, a peri-urban weak Gaeltacht area on the outskirts of Galway city, saw a small population increase between 2011–2016, from 11,164 to 11,696 (Department of Culture, Heritage and the Gaeltacht 2017). Such growth was itself partly the result of population movements from more rural areas (cf. O'Donoghue, Kilgarriff and Ryan 2017: 26).

While increases near the city meant that the population of the Galway Gaeltacht overall did not decline between 2006–2016, similar to the picture at a national and county level, its growth did slow significantly, as shown in Table 2. Donegal's Gaeltacht area, however, saw a 5.7% drop in population between 2011–2016 (Table 3). There was also a notable decrease in the 20–34 age group in the Gaeltacht in both Donegal and Galway during this time. In Galway this cohort numbered 10,972 in 2006, falling to 10,724 in 2011 and 9,339 in 2016 (–15% over

Table 2: Population change in the Galway Gaeltacht 2006–2016 (based on Central Statistics Office 2007a, 2012b, 2017b).

	Male	Female	Total	Total change	% Change
2006	22,524	22,528	45,052	–	–
2011	24,094	24,813	48,907	3,855	8.5%
2016	24,801	25,769	50,570	1,163	3.4%

ten years). In Donegal the same category fell from 3,805 in 2006 to 3,672 in 2011 and 2,833 in 2016 (−25.5% overall). As adults of this age are the most likely to form families and have children, such a decline is of particular concern for the continued domestic intergenerational language transmission that is so key to language maintenance.

Table 3: Population change in the Donegal Gaeltacht 2006–2016 (based on Central Statistics Office 2007b, 2012c, 2017c).

	Male	Female	Total	Total change	% Change
2006	12,165	11,618	23,783	–	–
2011	12,541	12,203	24,744	1,631	4.0%
2016	11,748	11,598	23,346	−1,398	−5.7%

7.2.2 Irish-speaking demographics 2006–2016

With the Gaeltacht having become ever more anglicised over the last several decades, by 2011 66,238 of 96,628 (68.5%) Gaeltacht residents claimed Irish-language ability. As with previous censuses, however, the number of daily speakers outside the education system was significantly lower, at 23,175 – just 24% (Central Statistics Office 2012d: CD964, CD965). Five years later, 63,664 (66.3% of the total Gaeltacht population) claimed the ability to speak Irish, with 20,586 (21.4%) speaking Irish daily outside the education system (Central Statistics Office 2017e: EA055). This represented a drop of 2,589 daily speakers (−11.2%) since 2011 – an alarmingly sharp decrease over such a short period. The dramatic nature of this decline becomes all the more apparent when contrasted with the 2006–2011 period, which saw a 1.4% increase in the same category (see Table 4).

Table 4: Daily speakers of Irish in the Gaeltacht 2006–2016 (based on Central Statistics Office 2007c: 87, 92; 2012d: CD964, CD965; 2017e: EA055).

	Speak Irish daily outside the education system	Speak Irish daily inside and outside the education system	Gaeltacht Total	% Change
2006	17,687	5,179	22,866	–
2011	17,955	5,220	23,175	1.4%
2016	16,199	4,387	20,586	–11.2%

As Table 5 shows, on a nationwide basis (including the Gaeltacht), between 2006–2011 the number of daily Irish speakers outside of the education system grew by 7%, from 72,148 to 77,185, before falling to 73,803 (–4.5%) between 2011–2016. The figures for the state outwith the Gaeltacht show a similar pattern – growth from 2006–2011 followed by decline from 2011–2016. Daily speakers outside of the education system increased from 49,282 in 2006 to 54,010 in 2011, but fell to 53,217 in 2016 (Central Statistics Office 2007c: 61, 6; 2012d: CD959, CD960; 2017e: EA055).

Table 5: Daily speakers of Irish on a national level 2006–2016 (based on Central Statistics Office 2007c: 61, 66; 2012d: CD959, CD960; 2017e: EA055).

	Speak Irish daily outside the education system	Speak Irish daily inside and outside the education system	State total	Total for areas outside the Gaeltacht
2006	53,471	18,677	72,148	49,282
2011	55,554	21,631	77,185	54,010
2016	53,162	20,641	73,803	53,217

As with population change, there are substantial regional differences in language use patterns in both the 2006–2011 and the 2011–2016 periods, with Donegal experiencing both slower growth during the years of prosperity and more severe impacts from the recession than Galway. 2006–2011 saw an increase of 5.2% in the number of daily Irish speakers outside the education system in the Galway Gaeltacht (10,394 to 10,932), while there was a decrease of 6.3% between 2011–2016 – from 10,932 to 10,243 (Central Statistics Office 2007a, 2012b, 2017b). In Donegal, the five-year period to 2011 also saw an increase in the number of daily Irish speakers, albeit a smaller one of 2.2% (7,012 to 7,166). 2011–2016, by contrast, saw a significant drop of 17.3% (1,237), to 5,929 (Central Statistics Office 2007b, 2012c, 2017c).

Following the historical pattern described in 2.4 of stronger Gaeltacht areas experiencing shift at a slower rate than weaker communities bordering the Galltacht, within category A areas the overall decline was less than the 11.2% drop experienced by the Gaeltacht in its entirety. Nonetheless, even in these strongest areas the decline was also pronounced: between 2011–2016 there was a loss of population of 3.4% and a decrease in daily speakers of Irish outside the education system of 8.4% in category A areas throughout the country (Ó hÉallaithe 2017b). Again, however, there is a wide range of variation between districts, with the Oileáin Árann, for instance, seeing an 11.4% fall in daily speakers, while An Cheathrú Rua (a comparatively well-developed town) was below the average, losing 5.3%. In the category A areas of north-west Donegal this trend was once more even greater – along with a population decrease of 6% there was a 14.5% reduction in the daily use of Irish outside the education system in these areas (Ó hÉallaithe 2017b). The greater contraction in the number of Irish speakers compared to the overall population decline is likely due to the death of elderly speakers who, as predicted by Ó Giollagáin et al. (2007a), are not being linguistically replaced by younger cohorts of daily Irish speakers, a long-term trend described in Chapter 2 (see also Chapter 13).

7.2.3 Social class in the Gaeltacht

The high levels of deprivation in communities that have retained Irish as a vernacular have long since been noted in commentary on the fate of the language. The fact that the Congested Districts Board (founded in 1891 as a relief effort for the most impoverished areas of rural Ireland) included under its remit almost all those areas that make up the official Gaeltacht today gives some indication of the long-standing nature of these difficulties (Hindley 1990: 28–29). Despite several decades of ameliorative efforts by this board, the terms of reference of the 1926 Gaeltacht Commission observed that widespread poverty persisted in the Gaeltacht, which presented "an economic problem of the greatest difficulty and complexity", and that "the language problem and the economic problem are in close relation to each other" (Coimisiún na Gaeltachta 1926: 3).

These high levels of impoverishment continued well after the founding of the Free State, leading novelist and socialist activist Máirtín Ó Cadhain to claim that the native Irish-speaking community comprised the most impoverished class in the country. Ó Cadhain consequently claimed that the language could not be saved without waging a class struggle aimed at alleviating the material deprivation of Gaeltacht residents (in Costigan and Ó Curraoin 1987: 326).

In contrast to an era when petty-bourgeois middle class individuals in the Gaeltacht (shopkeepers being an oft-cited example) were key in instigating language shift, the growth of Irish-language media and institutions such as ÚnaG helped with the development of a small but loyally Irish-speaking middle class in the Gaeltacht since the 1970s (Hindley 1990: 175–177, 219–220). It was with the exceptional economic growth of the Celtic Tiger that the Gaeltacht's history of impoverishment was most fully overcome, however, and by the year 2000 the Gaeltacht had near full employment (Walsh 2011a: 311). While more peripheral areas such as the island communities of Donegal continued to struggle with issues of structural unemployment even during the boom, this period undoubtedly saw a significant change in the Gaeltacht's economic fortunes. As observed by several researchers, however, the in-migration associated with this prosperity itself contributed to language shift in many cases (e.g., Ó hÉallaithe 2004: 174–176; see also 9.3).

As it did nationally, the 2008 crash saw a return to unemployment and emigration from the Gaeltacht – phenomena discussed at length in the following chapters. As may be expected, analysis of the 2016 census results showed that almost all the stronger Irish-speaking areas in Galway and Donegal were classed as disadvantaged areas, with the few exceptions all being within a half hour's drive of Galway city (Tuairisc.ie 2017l). Like the Scottish typology of "fragile areas" characterised by "population loss, low incomes, limited employment opportunities, poor infrastructure and remoteness" (Phillips 2017), the *Pobal HP Deprivation Index for Small Areas* combines various indices of deprivation such as unemployment, population loss, educational achievement and age dependency (Pobal.ie 2017). This index offers a valuable insight into the current extent of disadvantage in the Gaeltacht: based on the 2016 census results, the Abhainn Gabhla/Doire Iorrais area of west Galway, for instance, was 17% below the national average on this scale, and nearby areas such as Leitir Móir and Garmna were similarly disadvantaged (–16.9% and –16.5% respectively). Many of the "small areas" (subdivisions of larger electoral divisions) which are amongst the strongest of Irish-speaking communities suffer even higher levels of deprivation and are classed as "very disadvantaged", with Leitir Mealláin (21% below the national average) and Ros Muc (–26%) in Conamara providing particularly stark examples (Tuairisc.ie 2017l). The Donegal Gaeltacht also contains several equally deprived areas, including the only two full electoral divisions in the Gaeltacht classed as "very disadvantaged" (An Dúchoraidh and Árainn Mhór), although, as with Galway, several small areas within larger electoral divisions are also thus categorised, including strongly Irish-speaking Mín an Chladaigh (–26.5%)

(Pobal.ie 2017). The Donegal and Galway Gaeltacht areas contain five districts that appear on the Central Statistics Office's list of "unemployment blackspots" – the 79 electoral divisions (of 3,440 total) wherein the unemployment rate is at or above 27%. Indeed, Scainimh in west Galway and Mín an Chladaigh in north-west Donegal are included in the 15 electoral divisions with the highest unemployment rates in the country – the only two rural areas on a list of otherwise urban districts, most of which are in Limerick city (Central Statistics Office 2017f: 117).

Notably, almost all Gaeltacht areas in Munster were slightly above the national deprivation average (Tuairisc.ie 2017l), an indication of the differential socioeconomic status of the mid- and north-west compared to the south and east of the country which was described in Chapter 1.

While nowadays it would be incorrect to claim, as Ó Cadhain did in 1969, that native Irish speakers are the most impoverished group in Irish society, it is clear that much of the Gaeltacht retains a large number of inhabitants on the lower end of the class scale. In explaining the disproportionate rates of cutbacks suffered by Gaeltacht communities that were described in Part 2, it is worth recalling that it has been well documented both in Ireland and internationally that austerity primarily impacts the most disadvantaged sections of society (Bisset 2015: 175–177; Varoufakis 2016). The lower socioeconomic standing of a great many of the Gaeltacht's inhabitants and their dependence on state support thus left them susceptible to receiving severe cutbacks, a fact not hitherto addressed by Irish LPP literature published since the crash. Acknowledging this class bias of austerity and the inherently anti-neoliberal nature of language revitalisation measures (see 6.3) is therefore key to explaining many of the developments discussed in the following chapters and provides significantly greater explanatory power than those analyses of Irish LPP and the Gaeltacht that ignore such fundamental traits of Irish society.

8 Effects of the post-2008 crisis on the Gaeltacht labour market

As described in section 7.2.3, the Celtic Tiger period saw significant growth in the Gaeltacht economy. Between 2008–2012, however, the Republic of Ireland's workforce of two million suffered 300,000 job losses (O'Connell 2017: 232), with the Gaeltacht inevitably experiencing its share of this disruption. This chapter will discuss how labour market changes impacted the Gaeltacht, focusing on the main sectors in which significant shifts in employment patterns occurred, along with the numerous implications of these changes for community and language vitality.

8.1 Construction

As Harvey has explained, not only are property bubbles such as that which drove the latter years of the Celtic Tiger a recurrent feature in the history of capitalism, but they have become significantly more commonplace since neoliberal policies were widely adopted from the 1970s onwards (D. Harvey 2012b: 30–34). As such, the country's property bubble in the run up to 2008 provided an example of a much wider trend in global capitalism. By 2007, when the Celtic Tiger was at its height, more than 20% of male workers were employed in construction and the sector comprised an enormous 25% of GNP (Glynn, Kelly and Mac-Éinrí 2012: 38; O'Connell 2017: 239).

In late 2008 when the sub-prime mortgage crisis forced Irish banks (which had invested heavily in the credit default swap market) to withdraw credit from property developers in order to maintain the banking sector's liquidity, there were predictably grave consequences for the construction industry. By 2012 it had shrunk to make up less than 6% of GNP (Glynn, Kelly and MacÉinrí 2012: 38) and employment in the sector had declined enormously – "[falling] by 163,000 between 2007 and 2012, a contraction of over 60 per cent" (O'Connell 2017: 239).

With much of the Gaeltacht suffering from the type of educational inequality that militates against workers being employed in "white collar" positions, as well as there being a lack of employment for those who do attain higher level qualifications, many males from Gaeltacht areas found employment in construction pre-2008 and were thus hit hard by its collapse. This trend was visible throughout rural areas, where, between 2008–2014, "[u]nemployment increased by double the rate of cities, at about 200%, largely as a result of the collapse of the construction sector" (O'Donoghue 2014: 19). In line with other research on the matter (e.g., Glynn, Kelly and MacÉinrí 2013), the decline of construction was often cited during my interviews as a key reason for emigration (see also Chapter 9). A woman in her early 30s from Galway commented on this, seeing this sectoral contraction as causing the recession to affect men more severely than women:

> G: *Tá chuile dhuine san Astráil, na fir óga [. . .] Siod dream a bhí ag plé le siúinéireacht, ag obair ar shuíomhannaí tógála [. . .] Tá leath de mo rang, déarfainn, san Astráil, nó i Meiriceá, nó i gCeanada nó áit eicínt [. . .] Ní dóigh liom go raibh éifeacht chomh mór sin ag cúrsaí ar na mrá.*

> [G: Everyone is in Australia, the young men [. . .] This is the group who were working as carpenters, working on building sites [. . .] Half of my class, I'd say, are in Australia, or America, or Canada [. . .] I don't think things had as big an effect on women.]

The statistical evidence bears out this informant's instinct about male and female unemployment rates (although see Spillane 2015 for an account of the disparate impact of austerity on females). On a national scale, the male unemployment rate rose from 5.2% in 2007 to 16.6% in 2012, falling to 10.4% in 2015. While overall female labour market participation rates remain lower than for males, the rise in female unemployment, itself substantial, was less severe during this time – increasing from 3.9% to a high of 10.3% in 2013, before falling to 6.6% in 2015 (O'Connell 2017: 233). The decline of the manufacturing sector, discussed in the following section, also had a disproportionate effect on males, who were more likely to be employed therein, with females in the Republic of Ireland more often working in the service sector (Share, Tovey and Corcoran 2007: 176). Consequently, by 2012 "two in every three unemployed people were men and, among males, [long-term unemployment] accounted for 67 per cent of total unemployment, compared to 45 per cent of women" (O'Connell 2017: 234).

In light of the gendered patterns of language maintenance and shift that are often seen in minoritised language communities (Gal 1979: 167; Hill 1987: 121; also Labov 2001: 292), such a differential impact on males and attendant rate of emigration seems to have had implications for the vitality of Irish. Several of my informants who were apparently unaware of sociolinguistic principles commented on the greater propensity of males to speak Irish. "'*Siad na leaids sin is mó a labhródh Gaeilge*" [It's those lads most of all who'd speak Irish] as one young man, then a student in university, told me when talking about those males from his home village in Conamara who had not pursued third-level education. Although language shift can undoubtedly be driven by men in situations where factors such as the nature of the job market makes their integration into networks outside the local community more likely (Holmes 2013: 61), in the Gaeltacht males are often employed in domains which are more likely to preserve

Irish (section 13.2 below; also Eckert and McConnell-Ginet 2003: 283–828 for discussion of this phenomenon in various other contexts). While the difference is relatively slight, a comparison of the 2016 census figures to those from 2011 reports that the number of male daily speakers fell at a greater rate than the number for females during this time – falling 11.7% and 10.2% respectively (Central Statistics Office 2017e). Relatedly, Ó Giollagáin et al. have observed that in lower socioeconomic groups – who were most likely to be adversely affected by the recession – males were more likely to be daily speakers of Irish (2007: 132–133; also Ó Curnáin 2012b: 107).

8.2 Deindustrialisation

While not as dramatic as the collapse of the construction sector, Irish manufacturing industry was also seriously affected by the crash, with a 16.9% decrease in employment therein between 2007–2012, followed by a partial recovery of 4.7% from 2012–2015 (O'Connell 2017: 239).

As described in 4.2, the crisis saw ÚnaG lose approximately 75% of its budget, resulting in significant reductions in the amount of grant aid the agency was able to distribute. In 2008 ÚnaG funded 490 projects, but by 2015 this had fallen by almost three quarters, to 124. Their total expenditure on capital grants in 2008 was €13,944,440, which fell to €3,001,968 in 2015 (Údarás na Gaeltachta 2009: 3, 2016b: 3).

Unsurprisingly, the numbers employed in the "client companies" supported by the agency fell as a consequence of this reduced aid and the difficult international market, which led many of these companies to move overseas, following a wider, global pattern of capital relocation. As noted in section 4.2, this process is, of course, itself a result of the ability of capital to move to areas with lower wages and overheads, a phenomenon greatly facilitated in recent decades by the neoliberal policies of institutions such as the IMF, the World Trade Organisation and the World Bank (Parenti 2016).

An interviewee who works in the main ÚnaG-managed industrial estate in Donegal linked the estate's decline (from 1,300 jobs in 2008 to 425 by 2016) to a change in the makeup of the national economy, with manufacturing being replaced by the IT sector, which almost invariably locates in large cities, where they have access to a large pool of graduates, high quality internet connections, etc.

Another interviewee, a factory owner in Galway who employs approximately forty people within an hour's drive west of the city, challenged this narrative of the decline of manufacturing in Ireland as being "*seafóid*" [rubbish], however:

M: [Tá sé] ceart go leor rudaí a chur [thar sáile] [. . .] ach de réir a chéile [tiocfaidh] feabhas ar na háiteachaí sin agus [ardófar] na rátaí pá. Agus tá sé tarlaí'. Agus ansin [. . .] b'fhéidir nach bhfuil sé an oiread sin níos saoire ná rud a fháil déanta in Éirinn nó i Sasana ach go bhfuil an supply chain fada agus ní féidir brath air. Agus an rud eile atá tarlú ná an cineál digitisation den déantúsaíocht. Tá ceist scileannaí agus chuile shórt mar sin, agus automation [. . .] Déarfainn gur mó an bagairt é sin [ná postanna ag dul thar sáile].

[M: It's alright sending things [abroad] [. . .] but over time these places will improve and pay will rise. And it's happened. And then [. . .] maybe it's not that much cheaper than getting something made in Ireland or in England but that the supply chain is long and you can't depend on it. And the other thing that's happening is the kind of digitisation of manufacturing. There's a question of skills and everything like that, and automation [. . .] I'd say that's more of a threat [than jobs going overseas.]

While there may well be merit to this argument, especially in light of the disruption to international supply chains seen during the Covid pandemic, the 2008 crash nonetheless triggered a significant decline in the manufacturing sector, with overall employment in this field remaining well below pre-crash levels for many years, as described above. Furthermore, as Barry and Bergin detail, very little of the 2012–2015 growth in the sector occurred in peripheral areas such as the Gaeltacht (2017: 81).

Above all else, the peripherality of most of the Gaeltacht makes it unappealing to capitalists seeking a base for their operations. This same factory owner confirmed this, telling me that in his experience those areas in west Galway more than an hour's drive from the city are generally too remote to be viable locations for industrial development.

Despite these apprehensions, even the most remote parts of the Galway Gaeltacht that this interviewee felt unsuitable for economic development are less isolated than the Donegal Gaeltacht. As an ÚnaG executive in Donegal explained when I asked about the biggest challenge they faced when trying to attract investment:

É: Tá seo go hiomlán in éadan achan rud a deirim go poiblí ach, Tír Chonaill! [. . .] Iargúltacht. Jesus. Níl traein isteach sa chontae, tá muid scartha amach ón sé chontae eile le teorainn [. . .] Tá leathan bhanda millteanach tábhachtach fosta agus níl an tseirbhís cheart againn [. . .] Is míorúilt é go minic go bhfaigheann muid daoine isteach.

[É: This is completely against everything I say publicly, but Donegal! [. . .] Remoteness. Jesus. There's no train into the county, we're separated from the six counties by a border [. . .] Broadband is also extremely important and we don't have a proper service. It's often a miracle we get people to locate here.]

Similarly, a businessman from Galway told me that locating his business in the Gaeltacht is not an economically sensible thing to do, but instead reflective of his personal commitment to the area.

The challenges of Gaeltacht peripherality are exacerbated by EU regulations that prevent the state from offering higher rates of support to businesses located in remote locations (Ó Cuaig 2018a), an option which had been available to Gaeltarra Éireann, ÚnaG's predecessor, before the Republic joined the EEC in 1973. Gaeltarra, as a former employee of theirs who I interviewed told me, had made much use of this option, and were thus more effectively able to target economic interventions in remote areas with high rates of unemployment.

While the facts of geography are obviously immutable, economic development policy is not. Although globalisation has often been heralded as seeing the "death of distance" due to the capacity of technological innovations to minimise the challenges faced by remote areas, in the absence of policies and resources aimed at providing high-speed internet and transport links to such regions, this trend does little to overcome the core-periphery dichotomy which is so fundamental to the capitalist model (Wallerstein 2004).

As a Galway entrepreneur told me regarding this dearth of infrastructural provision in the Gaeltacht:

> B: Tá polasaithe éagsúla an rialtais go láidir ag tabhairt tacaíocht d'eacnamaíocht lárnach in áit eacnamaíocht réigiúnach nó imeallach. Bíodh sé go bhfuil siad á dhéanamh sin d'aon ghnó nó bíodh sé nach bhfuil's acu níos fearr nó píosa den dá rud. But tá sé ag tarlú agus níos measa atá sé ag fáil.

> [B: The various government policies are strongly supporting the central economy instead of the regional or peripheral economy. Whether that's being done intentionally or whether it's just that they know no better, or a bit of both. But it's happening and it's getting worse.]

The efforts of institutions such as ÚnaG notwithstanding, this tendency has certainly been aggravated by the policies pursued by the state in recent years. The lack of adequate internet provision in many rural areas, for instance, is itself a product of the privatisation drive of the last several decades. Having been state-owned since its founding in 1984, the national telecommunications provider Eircom was sold off in 1999, a move which the Irish Congress of Trade Unions termed "the biggest single economic mistake made by an Irish Government – until the disastrous blanket bank guarantee of September, 2008" (ICTU 2011: 1). Eircom has since been acquired by a French billionaire who has little incentive to invest in servicing the most remote communities, leaving much of the Gaeltacht to endure extremely slow internet which makes stimulating economic activity, industrial or otherwise, exceedingly challenging (Ó Cuaig 2018b). This poor connectivity also, I was told, disinclines third-level students to return home at weekends as they once did (cf. 8.3; 8.5.1). A 2016 report concluded that the Gaeltacht includes some of the worst areas in the country in terms of broadband provision (Tuairisc.ie 2016i). In light of the move from industrial manufacturing towards the "knowledge economy" discussed above, such infrastructural deficiencies and the profit motive militating against their resolution comprise a major challenge for Gaeltacht-based economic development.

The following extract, from an interviewee heavily involved in the private sector in the Gaeltacht, describes the impact of the crisis on smaller-scale businesses in rural areas more generally:

> B: Naoi gcinn as chuile deich gcomhlacht beag a dhún síos idir 2006 agus 2011 bhí siad lasmuigh de Bhleá Cliath [. . .] Daoine a chaill postannaí in san chúlú eacnamaíochta idir 2006-2011, thart ar 90% acub ní raibh oideachas tríú leibhéal acub [. . .] Tá 40% d'eacnamaíocht na hÉireann timpeall ar Bhleá Cliath [. . .] Agus cuireann sé as dom nuair a chloiseas tú na ESRI reports [faoin] méadú 26% ar an GDP, sin bullshit. Ach b'fhéidir méadú 4-5% ar an eacnamaíocht [. . .] But céard faoi Ghaoth Dobhair? Céard faoi Acaill? Céard faoi Ballina fiú atá níos mó ná sin? Fíor, fíor bheagán.

> [B: Nine out of every ten small companies that closed between 2006 and 2011 were outside of Dublin [. . .] People who lost jobs in the recession between 2006-2011, around 90% of them didn't have third-level education [. . .] 40% of Ireland's economy is based around Dublin [. . .] And it annoys me when you hear ESRI reports about the 26% increase in GDP, that's bullshit. But maybe a 4-5% increase in the economy [. . .] But what about Gaoth Dobhair? What about Acaill? What about Ballina even that's bigger than that? Very, very little.]

Further to the ideological bias towards privatisation, the state's relative neglect of rural development is reflective of a long-established structural feature of capitalism, with the centripetal tendencies and uneven development thereby produced having been well demonstrated (Scott 2007; Harvey 2008). Indeed, the suppression of rural life was central to the development of early industrial capitalism (Thompson 1991), with urbanisation offering a way for capitalists to overcome "the barriers to continuous capital circulation and expansion", therefore being a strategy for the absorption of surplus product, which in turn produces profit, the fundamental goal of capital (D. Harvey 2012b: 5–6). Indeed, in a succinct example of the mainstream economic argument *against* rural development, Crowley (2018) states that "development is actually best left unspread" and that "[g]rowing cities are critical for development", thereby illustrating the sort of position that the interviewee cited above found most objectionable (see also World Bank 2009). As seen in the following chapter, the tendency towards urbanisation in capitalist economies is a key factor driving out-migration from the Gaeltacht, along with the linguistic assimilation such migration typically entails (Harrison 2007: 14; Saarikivi and Marten 2012: 2). While ÚnaG endeavours to promote the economic development of the Gaeltacht, not only is it doing so in the face of budgetary cuts and a state economic policy that favours major population centres, but in its efforts it must also act against capitalism's fundamental tendency towards centralisation.

Although by 2017 job creation figures for ÚnaG were at their highest point since 2007, there was nonetheless much discussion around this time about the persistence of widespread structural unemployment in remote Gaeltacht areas (TG4 2017; Irish Times 2018d; Ó Catháin 2018). Furthermore, an ÚnaG spokesperson warned that Brexit – itself largely a reaction to the 2008 crash and decades of neoliberalism (Powell 2017) – "may well be one of the biggest challenges Gaeltacht companies will face in the years ahead" (Irish Times 2018e). The statement by ÚnaG's CEO that "nearly a quarter (24.5%) of Údarás na Gaeltachta client company exports, at a value of €154 million, are to the United Kingdom" and that "nearly 60% (€224m) of client companies' raw materials are imported through or from the UK" highlights the scale of this potential disruption (Connacht Tribune 2017), which has only been exacerbated by the Covid pandemic (section 14.5).

8.3 The hospitality industry

Many of my informants commented on the extent to which unemployment and the attendant drop in disposable income affected the social life of the communities I studied, particularly by reducing the vibrancy of local nightlife. Even before the crash, the frequenting of pubs in rural areas was in decline due to factors such as the smoking ban introduced in 2004, the increasingly stringent proscription of driving under the influence of alcohol and the high rates of tax on alcohol sold in pubs (Cabras and Mount 2015). Like Irish-language media, this sector's difficulties are therefore not entirely a consequence of the economic crisis, although the recession exacerbated their already challenging circumstances. Pub closures increased dramatically during the worst years of the crisis, with over 1,000 closing down nationally between 2007–2014, reaching a rate of one a day in 2011 (Irish Independent 2014; Thejournal.ie 2014). A Drinks Industry Group of Ireland submission to an Oireachtas committee in 2014 showed that the west of the country was hit much more severely by such closures than the area around the capital (DIGI 2014: 4). Large numbers of hotels also closed during the recession, including many built in rural areas due to their qualifying developers for tax breaks (Whelan 2013: 28). Many of these were taken over by the National Asset Management Agency ("NAMA", a state agency founded in 2009 to take bad loans from property developers). Citing the "commercial sensitivity" of the issue, NAMA refused to release data on the number of hotels it was closing (The Guardian 2011). A 2009 report for the Irish Hotels Federation, however, claimed that some 15,000 rooms needed to be removed from the market for the industry to remain viable (Bacon and associates 2009), although data as to what extent this eventually occurred are not publicly available.

These closures impacted many Gaeltacht communities, with the loss of such establishments being lamented by many of my informants, who often noted that the fate of these establishments was intimately linked to that of the construction and industrial sectors discussed above. Pubs in particular have long been central to the social life of rural areas where there are few other options for night-time socialising, and their loss was thus seen to have left a void in the social fabric of many communities. One area of the Donegal Gaeltacht saw five out of six hotels in the district closed by 2015, something many felt had a very negative impact on community vitality.

An employee of ÚnaG discussed the linguistic implications of such closures, telling me that *"Sin go háirithe infreastruchtúr a bhí millteanach dúchasach ó thaobh teanga dó agus tábhachtach"* [That in particular was infrastructure that was extremely traditional and important with regards to the language]. Another interviewee made a similar comment, referring to one of these closed hotels in particular, an imposing building which overlooks much of the surrounding community and now lies in a very visible state of dereliction:

> C: *Bhí an óstán sin beo beithíoch ar feadh tamaill agus bhíodh go leor cleamhnais déanta ann, deirtear, agus gur casadh daoine óga ar a chéile agus tá cúpla áit eile mar é ann. Agus castar ar a chéile iad istigh i Leitir Ceanainn [anois] agus b'fhéidir nach gcastar dhá Ghaeilgeoir ar a chéile [. . .] Tá briseadh síos ó thaobh cúrsaí teangeolaíoch ann.*
>
> [C: That hotel was very busy for a while and it's said that lots of matchmaking was done there, and that young people met each other and there's a few other places like it. And [now] they meet each other in Letterkenny and maybe two Irish speakers won't meet [. . .] There's a linguistic breakdown.]

A local parent corroborated this sentiment, noting that such closures have led to his teenage daughter socialising outside the Gaeltacht in a way that had not previously been necessary.

A similar pattern pertains to those who have finished their schooling locally and are now at university, with not only the lack of broadband or summer jobs (see 8.2; 8.5.1), but also the lack of opportunities to socialise reducing their inclination to return home during weekends or holidays. A middle-aged interviewee from Donegal who divides his time between his home community and working in Dublin explained this as follows: *"Ní hamháin gur díbríodh ar shiúil iad, seo daoine óga atá ag obair fosta [. . .] ach ansin a mhalairt – cionn is go bhfuil sé mar sin níl daoine ag iarraidh teacht ar ais [chuig a bpobail dhúchais], daoine óga go háiride. Ní raibh sé riamh mar sin, go dtí ceithre nó cúig bliana [ó shin]"* [Not only were they driven away, this is people who are working too [. . .] but then the opposite – because it's like that people aren't coming back [to their native communities], young people in particular. It never used to be like that, until four or five years [ago]].

While the tendency of rural pub closures to increase instances of social isolation amongst older people has been well documented (Cabras and Mount 2017), it is clear that within the Gaeltacht such closures also have linguistic consequences, particularly for the important young adult demographic amongst which linguistic exogamy can have a significant impact on the language's future. As the developer of the "Index of Isolation" which aims to address "the probability that a Welsh speaker will meet another speaker locally" points out, with regard to intergenerational language transmission "the most important group of two is the two parents forming a family. These are usually comparatively young people. The most important spatial distributions, or networks, in that respect are those of young people" (Jones 2007: 28). The loss of much of the social infrastructure key to maintaining such networks is thus far from conducive to Irish-language maintenance.

8.4 Criticisms of the Foreign Direct Investment model

As Kirby and Murphy explain, the neoliberal character of the Irish "competition state" sees its policies favour the requirements of international capital "over the needs of its own citizens", with the Foreign Direct Investment model on which the Irish economy is based providing a clear example of this trend (2011: 21). While ÚnaG has been relatively successful at attracting enterprise to the Gaeltacht since its establishment (Walsh 2011a: 310), the Foreign Direct Investment approach they use was the subject of sharp criticism amongst many of my interviewees. Criticisms of the type of work made available through such investment and the attitude of client companies to the Gaeltacht were particularly common.

The Republic of Ireland's comparatively low wages have been a key selling point through which the state has marketed the country to international capital for many decades (O'Toole 2010: 16), and high rates of unemployment in the Gaeltacht have typically ensured that a large pool of low-cost labour is available therein. This, in combination with the reduction in union density seen in recent decades (McDonough 2010: 452), means that a key attraction of the Gaeltacht to investors is the submissive nature of its workforce, with workers not only unlikely to be unionised, but also rarely having other employment options available. Indeed, several ÚnaG employees told me that they explicitly promote the Gaeltacht on this basis, *"go bhfuil dílseacht ag an bhfoireann dá bhfostóir"* [that the staff are loyal to their employer].

In light of the impression such a sentiment gives, it is unsurprising that companies tend to make only limited efforts at language promotion, knowing that ÚnaG is unable to be overly assertive in insisting on the use of Irish by client companies. This issue was a common cause of complaint amongst interviewees, who frequently claimed that ÚnaG's emphasis on employment creation did not pay sufficient heed to linguistic concerns, as was the fact that a significant minority of positions in ÚnaG client companies are actually staffed by English speakers who commute into the Gaeltacht.

A woman formerly employed by a multinational corporation in Donegal – which has since relocated to the developing world – told me that her workplace was dominated by English, particularly at management level and in more specialised roles, which were usually not filled by Irish speakers. Furthermore, in the absence of a workplace language policy favouring Irish, even fluent Irish speakers defaulted to English with co-workers not previously known to them, as speakers of minoritised languages typically do when meeting strangers. Another interviewee pointed out that client companies operating through English can establish a pattern of speaking English amongst Irish speakers, particularly couples who first meet in the workplace.

Walsh (2011a: 317–335) similarly observes the resistance of client companies to Irish-language promotion measures, with them seemingly being seen as an impediment to commercial success. Nonetheless, Walsh also details ÚnaG's attempts at adopting a more language-focused policy direction in 2005. On the basis of my interviews, conducted over a decade after this supposed re-orientation, it would appear that the effects of their reformed approach are not apparent to many Gaeltacht residents, however.

One interviewee, a man in his mid-20s from Donegal, was particularly frustrated that ÚnaG, in his estimation, funds businesses which function entirely through English but adopt Irish in a tokenistic manner to qualify for grants:

F: Má úsáideann tú ainm Gaeilge ar do ghnó gheobhann tú deontas [. . .] But níl tú ag déanamh fuck all le focal amháin isteach sa fuckin, I dunno, éiceolaíocht Gaeilge [. . .] Ba chóir daofa airgead Gaeilge a úsáid mar is ceart [. . .] Tá an tÚdarás ag déanamh lear rudaí maith, right, lear rudaí maith. But shílim go bhfuil pollaí ann, y'know, pollaí fuckin bómánta [. . .] Like bhfuil tú ag iarraidh é a úsáid mar fuckin, just é a exploiteáil basically? Fuck off.

[F: If you use a name in Irish for your business you get a grant [. . .] But you're not doing fuck all with one word in the fuckin, I dunno, Irish ecology [. . .] They should use money for Irish properly [. . .] The Údarás is doing lots of good things, right, lots of good things. But I think there are holes, y'know, stupid fuckin holes [. . .] Like do you just want to use it as a fuckin, just exploit it basically? Fuck off.]

Although perhaps overstated in this example, such cynicism towards many ÚnaG developments was certainly a common theme during my fieldwork. Indeed, another interviewee from the same area commented that even the symbolic use of Irish was something adopted by a company she worked for only when they were forced to do so, after complaints were made about them having English-only signage in the heart of the Gaeltacht, in an estate run by ÚnaG.

Shockingly, in 2021 Randox, an international healthcare company known for receiving lucrative contracts for Covid testing in recent years, issued a memo to staff in its plant in the Donegal Gaeltacht which stated that "English must be spoken at all times in the workplace", regardless of the nature of the conversation, that all written communication must also be in English, and that "[f]ailing to do so is not acceptable" (The Times 2021, emphasis in original memo – see Figure 2). Considering enticing Randox to this area was publicised as a major victory for ÚnaG a few years prior, the optics of such a move were extremely negative, although very much in line with what I had heard from many of my interviewees. After much outcry, Randox withdrew the memo, claiming it had been "sent in error".

Despite such challenges, several informants did acknowledge there had been a chronic need for employment in Gaeltacht areas before the Foreign Direct Investment strategy had helped overcome this dearth, and noted that in this regard ÚnaG's efforts were to be welcomed, even though the significant social change this caused also helped weaken the language in some ways.

When asked whether the increased pressures of creating employment post-2008 led them to be more lenient in terms of accepting companies regardless of the linguistic implications, an ÚnaG employee told me that this was not the case: *"Ní dhéanann sé difear ar bith [. . .] Achan chomhlacht a thagann isteach tá coinníollacha ann. Dúirt fear [. . .] 'we're not desperate'. We are but ní dhéanann muid sin. No, ní dheanann sé difear ar bith.* [It doesn't make any difference [. . .] Every company that comes has conditions attached to it. A man said [. . .] 'we're not desperate'. We are but we don't do that. No, it doesn't make any difference]. He went on to defend the agency's job creation strategy by comparing a Gaeltacht area in Donegal that had been industrialised to one that had not, and where the language is now in a much weaker position. While a valid point, and one which challenges Mufwene's contention that "language shift is inversely correlated with socioeconomic integration" (2008: 197), it is nonetheless lamentable that this economic foundation was not developed in tandem with more forceful language policies.

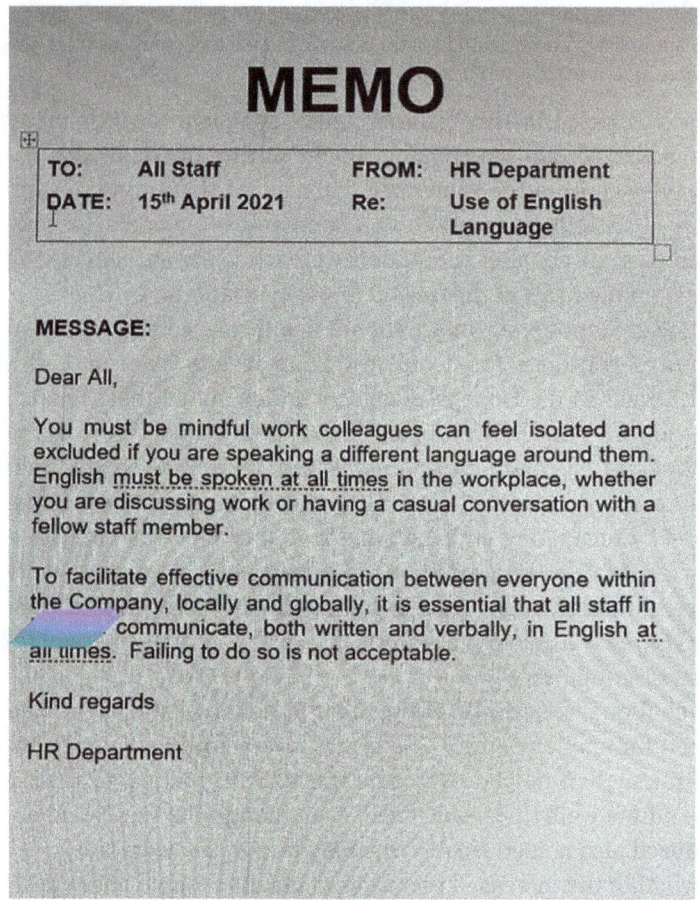

Figure 2: "English must be spoken at all times": memo sent to staff in the Randox plant in the Donegal Gaeltacht. (Source: www.twitter.com/HMFerry/status/1382761686944395266).

Belying the efficaciousness of the conditions mentioned by this executive, in response to a parliamentary question to the minister responsible for the Gaeltacht in 2021 it emerged that ÚnaG do not keep any record of how often these conditions are broken. In explanation for this, the absurd claim was made that this is because they lack the technology to be able to do so. It was also stated that there were not *"mórán cásanna"* [many cases] of them refusing grants on the basis of infractions over the previous decade (Oireachtas Éireann 2021c).

In contrast with the alleged loyalty of the workforce to ÚnaG's client companies which was mentioned above, the fickleness of the companies themselves towards the Gaeltacht was another source of much frustration amongst many of my interviewees, as seen in the following quote from an interviewee in Donegal:

> M: Seo an rud a tharlaíonn – labhrann tú leis an IDA, aimsíonn siad sin comhlacht duit, labhrann tú leis an chomhlacht, tairgíonn tú margadh daofa, glacann siad leis an margadh, tagann siad, imíonn siad, back to square one [. . .] Tá sé ag bualadh seo aríst i gcloigne daoine, más mian leat jab a fháil caithfidh tú Béarla a bheith agat. 'Seo na daoine, tá siad ag déanamh gar mór dhúinn ag teacht [anseo] [. . .] Now ná bígí ag déanamh rudaí amaideacha cosúil le bheith ag iarraidh Gaeilge a labhairt nó goil isteach i gceardchumainn, tá's againn céard a tharlós, imeoidh siad!' But tá's againne céard a tharlós anyway – imeoidh siad!

> [M: This is what happens – you talk to the IDA, they find a company for you, you talk to the company, you make them an offer, they accept the offer, they come, they go, back to square one [. . .] It's hammering home to people again that if you want a job you need English. 'These are the people, they're doing us a big favour coming here [. . .] Now don't do anything stupid like trying to speak Irish or join a trade union, you know what will happen, they'll leave!' But we know what's going to happen anyway – they'll leave!]

When I asked why he felt this model persisted, this interviewee – who was unusually informed politically – went on to explicitly mention neoliberalism, one of very few instances in my corpus of an interviewee doing so: *"Sin an nualiobrálachas. Neoliberalism, déanann sé sin do dhaoine. Má deir tú rud ar bith nach bhfuil ag cloí leis an nualiobrálachas tá tú as do mheabhair [. . .] [Ach] bréag atá ann!"* [That's neoliberalism, it does that to people. If you say anything at all that doesn't adhere to neoliberalism you're out of your mind! [. . .] But it's a lie!]. While not generally so developed, similar frustrations were widespread amongst my interviewees.

Furthermore, the type of industries that the Foreign Direct Investment model most frequently succeeds in attracting often offer relatively poor quality positions, as well as being problematic from a language planning perspective. While there are certainly important exceptions to this trend, the opening of a call centre during my research was illustrative of the type of development which many of my informants found immensely contradictory. In 2016, it was announced that an English telemarketing company was to create 125 jobs in the Donegal industrial estate described above (Údarás na Gaeltachta 2016c). In terms of creating employment in a community which had been hit hard by job losses in previous years, such a development was undoubtedly most welcome. Nonetheless, the work in question presented major challenges in terms of language policy. As has been observed elsewhere, it is difficult to imagine a more inappropriate industry to locate in such a linguistically sensitive area than one that quite literally pays people to speak English all day (Walsh 2011a: 319). Furthermore, adhering to the tendency of such companies to lack any long-term interest in the Gaeltacht, in December 2017 – after just 18 months in operation –

this same call centre announced it was closing immediately, leading to the loss of the 30 jobs it provided (RTÉ 2017), which was itself less than 25% of the total they originally promised to create.

As one interviewee, who had himself worked in another call centre in the same area, quipped: *"níl's agam caidé an focal Gaeilg fá choinne an fhocal 'call centre' ach bheinn níos sásta ag smaoineamh nach raibh focal againn ar an obair sin!"* [I dunno what the Irish word for 'call centre' is but I'd be happier thinking we didn't have a word for that type of work!]. In line with this sentiment, these positions are very often of low prestige, with few parents I talked to wanting their children to take up work in such establishments upon finishing their education. On several occasions I observed that even the most language-conscious of parents have somewhat of a blind spot regarding their own children when it comes to employment and maintaining the population of their communities. One woman, a diligent Irish speaker who I have often heard complain about how few of those activists who are highly committed to the language in urban contexts see fit to relocate to the Gaeltacht, told me during a conversation about her young adult children *"b'fhearr liom muna mbeadh siad fágtha thiar ar an [oileán] sin"* [I'd prefer if they weren't left back on that [island]]. She then stated that they are better off in the cities due to the greater opportunities available there, and was apparently surprised when I brought up the linguistic implications of such migration. Another man, a former member of the Gaeltacht Civil Rights Movement who has been very involved in efforts to promote the vitality of his community, commented that he was happy his own children had moved away to the cities, *"seachas grúpa beag acub a bheith thiar ag caint leob féin. Ag caint leis na faoileáin!"* [instead of a little group of them out west talking to themselves. Talking to the seagulls!].

Such attitudes highlight the depth of the economic challenges faced by the Gaeltacht, with even those parents most committed to the language not wishing to see their children involved in the type of employment that Foreign Direct Investment has been most successful at creating. With the contrast between the "opportunity deprivation" (Haase and Pratschke 2017b: 7) of the Gaeltacht and the aspirations now held by many young people and their parents being so great, the maintenance of vibrant Irish-speaking populations becomes increasingly challenging. This is likely to be especially true with regard to retaining populations which include the ambitious and socially mobile, who, as Holmes notes (2013: 61), are very often the first section of a community to shift to the dominant language as they integrate into the wider economy. Those who pursue higher education – an ever-increasing percentage of school leavers – are even less likely to want to take up precarious, low-paid positions, a fact not lost on parents such as those just quoted. It is worth noting, however, that it may be that the very class background which makes parents such as those quoted above more likely to be interested in language promotion (cf. Wright 1996: 43) also inclines them to have aspirations for their children which necessarily entail them leaving the Gaeltacht. Their opinions may therefore not be wholly representative of the wider Gaeltacht population.

Suggesting intentions of adopting an approach not so dependent on Foreign Direct Investment, in 2014 ÚnaG published a development plan specifically aimed at restoring employment to the Donegal Gaeltacht in which they recognised the need for creating a supportive environment and grant system in which local people would be willing to establish their own businesses (Údarás na Gaeltachta 2014: 18–19). Despite these intentions, several of my interviewees in the area reported that they had received no such support for their proposal to use an ÚnaG-owned building to set up a cultural and linguistic tourism cooperative with the aim of undoing some of the damage done to the area by the closure of five of its six hotels (see 8.3). There was a clear perception amongst several of my interviewees that ÚnaG's strategy of job creation via the attraction of Foreign Direct Investment has led to a bias against such local groups. One interviewee involved in this plan expressed his immense dissatisfaction with ÚnaG's attitude towards their efforts as follows:

> M: Ní bhfuair muid ariamh an mothú tá siad seo linn, tá siad ag tacú linn [. . .] Agus ní hé gur scaifte fuckin lunatics atá ag goil dhó seo [. . .] Tá daoine anseo atá ag obair ar son an phobail agus a dtuigeann go dtig linn fostaíocht a chruthú a bheadh i nGaeilg amháin, a bheadh chun leas an phobail, a bheadh ag cruthú fostaíochta do dhaoine óga agus a bheadh ag dírigh ar riachtanais turasóireachta [. . .] Agus bheadh seo uilig ag tarlú istigh i lár na Gaeltachta [. . .] agus tá siad ag cur achan fuckin bhac os ár gcomhair.

> [M: We never got the feeling that these are on our side, they support us [. . .] And it's not that we're a gang of fuckin lunatics who are involved in this [. . .] There are people here who are working for the community and who understand that we can create employment which would be entirely through Irish, which would be good for the community, which would be creating employment for young people and which would focus on the needs of tourism [. . .] And this would all be happening in the middle of the Gaeltacht [. . .] and they're putting every fuckin obstacle in front of us.]

Although the experience of this group seems to contradict ÚnaG's claims to be supportive of local entrepreneurs, when I asked about the change in the makeup of the local industrial estate, an ÚnaG executive insisted that not only had they always supported smaller-scale indigenous enterprises, but that such companies had become even more important in light of the recent deindustrialisation of the area.

Despite, then, the many criticisms made by my informants and the numerous challenges they face, ÚnaG does attract enterprise and generate employment on both a small and large scale which would not exist in the Gaeltacht without their support. Indeed, the factory owner whom I interviewed was adamant that ÚnaG was responsible for his own business being located in the Gaeltacht: *"Ní bheadh mórán fostaíocht tionscail i ndeisceart Chonamara murach Údarás na Gaeltachta [. . .] Agus déarfainn freisin nach mbeadh [a mhonarcha féin san áit a bhfuil sé] murach Údarás na Gaeltachta. Gan aon dabht"* [There wouldn't be much industrial employment in south Conamara without Údarás na Gaeltachta [. . .] And I'd say as well that [his factory wouldn't be located where it is] without Údarás na Gaeltachta. Without any doubt].

ÚnaG's approach to economic development has thus clearly been successful in creating employment and attracting investment that would otherwise not exist. The industries it attracts, however, often leave the Gaeltacht after a short period, and are generally unsupportive of Irish-language use, if not outright anglicising in their effects. This leads to the common – if contestable – belief amongst my interviewees that ÚnaG offers less support to language vitality than such a specifically Gaeltacht-focused institution should do.

8.5 Further implications of the decline in employment opportunities

8.5.1 Summer work for students

As noted in 8.3, in both Donegal and the more westerly parts of Galway I was told that reduced employment opportunities meant that young adults studying in university no longer had a ready source of summer employment in their home communities, which many interviewees told me was customary before the crash:

> S: *Gabh thuas, cúpla mí obair, agus ansin bhí an t-airgead agam le teacht ar ais go dtí an ollscoil [. . .] Bhí sé iontach tábhachtach. Bhí go leor mic léinn ag obair ann. Agus anois níl sin ann ar char ar bith agus níl's agam caidé an dóigh atá ag tuismitheoirí [. . .] páistí s'acu a chur [chuig an ollscoil].*
>
> [S: Go up, a couple of months work, and then I had the money to come back to university [. . .] It was very important. There were lots of students working there. And now that's not there at all and I don't know how parents will be able to [. . .] send their children [to university].]

Prior to 2008 it was primarily those who had already graduated who were unlikely to return home for work. With such summer employment not being available to students during the recession, however, those who succeeded in getting seasonal jobs where they were studying or elsewhere outside their home communities had their connections to the Gaeltacht weakened even earlier than was previously the case. As with the unappealing social life discussed in 8.3 and the tendency for emigrants to break their link with the language (as discussed in the following chapter), this decline in summer employment thus contributed to the loss of a key demographic in the Gaeltacht.

8.5.2 Community pride

In November 2017 it was reported that of the 516 buildings ÚnaG owns, 106 were empty, with 81 of these having been vacated during the previous decade (Tuairisc.ie, 2017m). 45 such units were in Donegal, where these "white elephants" – as radical architect Brian Anson warned of in his unimplemented Donegal Gaeltacht Development Plan (1982) – stand alongside the abandoned pubs and hotels described above, providing a very visible illustration of the effects of the crisis on the community. As one interviewee stated *"tá an oiread áiteachaí dúnta suas le feiceáil. Níl ann ach áit amháin i ndiaidh áit eile [. . .] Tá sé an-uaigneach [. . .] Ní chuidíonn sé le beocht a chur in áit ar bith"* [you see so many places that are closed up. It's just one place after another [. . .] It looks very forlorn [. . .] It doesn't help to breathe life into any place.]

Similar to the closures discussed in 8.3, this lack of social vitality makes the area less appealing to either live in or visit than it could be. Indeed, interviewees often explicitly told me that such dereliction has had a detrimental impact on community pride, as this quote from a language planner working in Donegal explains:

D: Tá dromchla uafásach ar an mbóthar [. . .] Tá céatadán maith de na foirgnimh dúnta [. . .] Déanann sin dochar do mhuinín an phobail [. . .] Dá mba rud é go raibh mé in ann spreagadh a dhéanamh agus bród na ndaoine a ardú, sin [an] freagra [. . .] Ach arís ní, níl an teanga, níl réiteach na faidhbe [. . .] in a bubble féin ansin [. . .] Fáinne fí atá ann, spreagann sé an seanadhearcadh den Ghaeilge, teanga an bhochtanais [. . .] Níl daoine óga na linne seo tiubh [. . .] Feiceann siad an stuif seo agus déanann siad na nascanna idir fíorscéal an bhaile agus an teanga atá ceaptha le bheith anseo.

[D: There's a terrible surface on the road [. . .] There's a good percentage of the buildings closed [. . .] That damages the community's confidence [. . .] If I could inspire the community and increase their sense of pride, that's the answer [. . .] But again the, the language isn't, the solution to the problem isn't [. . .] in its own bubble [. . .] It's a vicious circle, it encourages the old view of Irish as the language of poverty [. . .] Young people today aren't stupid [. . .] They see this stuff and they make the links between the true story of the town and the language that's meant to be here.]

Dorian has similarly pointed out that community self-confidence is key for "withstand[ing] pressures for ancestral language abandonment". Citing the cases of Wales and Catalonia in evidence, she claims that economic prosperity leads to the development of a middle class with the "social self-confidence to insist on traditional identity and heritage", although also notes that this is precisely the sort of self-confidence which minoritised language communities typically lack (1999: 12–13; see also Walsh 2011a: 111–155). Having been impoverished and marginalised for so many years, such confidence levels were likely quite low in much of the Gaeltacht even pre-2008, with this possibly being one reason why entrepreneurship remained so uncommon in these areas even when the national economy was growing rapidly (Ní Bhrádaigh 2007). In line with the opinions of the interviewee quoted above, however, it would seem probable that the decline in material prosperity experienced post-2008 further damaged the "social self-confidence" of those living in such communities, as well as their loyalty to the language. Section 10.5 offers evidence of this in the linguistic landscape and Chapter 11 elaborates on how the state's suppression of community dissent throughout the crisis has also contributed to this general sense of disempowerment.

8.6 Conclusion

An oft-cited aphorism relating to the maintenance of Gaeltacht communities highlights the primacy of a healthy labour market: "no jobs, no people; no people, no Gaeltacht; no Gaeltacht, no language" (in Dunbar 2016: 466). Employment is clearly very important for the maintenance of the communities I conducted my fieldwork in, and as such much of the attempt to sustain the Gaeltacht has historically focused on economic development, seeing significant success during the Celtic Tiger years, as Chapter 2 described. The post-2008 recessionary period saw much of this work rapidly undone, however, with sectors such as construction, manufacturing and hospitality being hit particularly hard. With a huge increase in unemployment occurring across the country post-2008, peripheral communities such as the Gaeltacht were bound to experience this particularly severely.

While ÚnaG has had some success in countering this trend – and the situation of the Gaeltacht would surely be much worse if not for their efforts – in doing so it has had to contend with a state that has little interest in the development of the periphery and a privatised broadband service which is slow to invest in poor, remote areas, thus making the stimulation of enterprise yet more difficult. Their efforts also see ÚnaG acting against the fundamentally centripetal dynamics of capitalism, which tend towards urbanisation, and having to do so in the face of the huge cuts to their budget and staff numbers that were described in Chapter 3. Furthermore, while certainly welcome in many ways, much of the employment they do create is linguistically problematic and of fairly low quality economically – call centres paying Gaeltacht people to speak English being one striking example.

In addition to unemployment often making it unfeasible for people to continue to live in the Gaeltacht, many of the businesses that closed during the recession contributed to the wider social vibrancy of these communities. The closure of establishments in the hospitality industry (a phenomenon which was particularly pronounced in Donegal) reduced opportunities to socialise in many communities, and likely affected the sort of community pride that authors such as Dorian (1999) have referenced as being crucial for language maintenance. Such closures were also, of course, detrimental for the maintenance of networks of Irish-speakers, who now are much more likely to socialise in English-speaking areas.

In light of the disruptions detailed in this chapter which greatly reduced options to work in or near the Gaeltacht, and in accordance with the "no jobs, no people" adage cited above, emigration rates increased considerably, as the following chapter will describe.

9 Migration

9.1 Introduction

With population mobility being a fundamental trait of globalisation (Appadurai 2005: 3) and economic disruption being known to intensify this mobility, it was almost inevitable that the Republic of Ireland would see extremely high rates of out-migration in the wake of the crash. Examining national patterns post-2008, Glynn and O'Connell state that "[w]hereas 245,900 people left the country in the eight years between 2000 and 2007, nearly 610,000 departed between 2008 and 2015" (2017: 299). As Glynn, Kelly and MacÉinrí (2013: 29–30) have explained, the distribution of emigrants' origins during the recession was heavily skewed towards rural areas such as the Gaeltacht. When one considers that the demographic submersion of minority language speakers as a result of both out- and in-migration is often cited as a major factor contributing to language shift (e.g., Krauss 1992: 6), the potential for this development to negatively impact the vitality of Irish becomes apparent. This chapter will explore how this has been the case in the years since the crash occurred.

9.2 Out-migration

Since the earliest days of the Free State, chronic underdevelopment meant that emigration was a fundamental fact of rural Irish life (Ó Riagáin 1997: 217). This phenomenon was particularly prevalent in the Gaeltacht, its constituent communities being amongst the most peripheral in the country. Indeed, throughout the 1950s and 60s over two thirds of young people in Na Gleannta, an Irish-speaking area in Donegal, had emigrated before they reached their thirties (Glynn, Kelly and MacÉinrí 2013: 7). Many other Gaeltacht areas were similarly depopulated at this time (Ó hÉallaithe 2004: 174).

Faced with such a massive haemorrhage of population, and in accordance with the national move away from the protectionist policies of earlier decades, Gaeltarra Éireann (succeeded by ÚnaG in 1979) set about a programme of "saving the Gaeltacht by industrialisation" (Ó hÉallaithe 2004: 174). As was discussed in the previous chapter, however, despite creating much needed employment, these efforts also impacted negatively on language use in their own way. Further to encouraging both the in-migration and commuting of people from outside the Gaeltacht who were also searching for employment, there was a significant amount of return-migration of people who had left in earlier years and who often brought non-Irish-speaking partners and children with them on their return (see 8.4; also Walsh 2010).

Emigration from the Gaeltacht, then, is long-established, and during the recession this legacy led to the rekindling of chain migration patterns. The chain migration phenomenon has been observed by migration scholars for many years, with it being claimed that "so long as there are people to emigrate the principle cause of emigration is prior emigration" (Peterson, cited in Brody 1974: 7). Being such a central part of life for generations of Gaeltacht people, this pattern means that many (if not most) of those in the Gaeltacht today already have family connections in more economically dynamic areas of the world, thus making moving abroad an appealing option during challenging times. Several of my interviewees commented on this: *"D'imeodh daoine ar imirce an-éasca [. . .] Níl siad ag dul go áit nach bhfuil aithne acub ar éinne, mar a déarfá. Agus de ghnáth má théann siad ann b'fhéidir go bhfuil uncail leob a bheadh in ann post a thabhairt dhóib, nó a bhfuil aithne aige ar dhuine éigeant"* [People would emigrate very easily [. . .] They're not going somewhere where they don't know anyone, y'know. And usually if they go maybe they have an uncle who could give them a job, or who knows someone].

I also repeatedly heard that this phenomenon occurred in an intra- as well as an inter-cohort fashion, whereby an initial emigrant would report back on their improved quality of life, thus inspiring their friends to follow them abroad.

The vast majority of my informants explicitly linked this to the search for employment. While *un*employment was invariably mentioned as driving such departures, other research suggests that emigrants are more likely to be underemployed and/or overqualified for their work at the time of emigration, rather than being unemployed outright (Glynn, Kelly and MacÉinrí 2013: 9). This is likely due to the fact that a significant initial outlay is typically required to emigrate, making it prohibitively costly for poorer sections of society. Trends post-2008 were for people to often go far afield when emigrating, to Australia for instance, making the move particularly expensive – especially when visa requirements necessitate having a considerable bank balance as a minimum requirement for entry. This, I was told, led to a two-stage process of emigration, whereby people first moved to Britain in order to work and save the money to then move further afield, with Britain's proximity and non-requirement of visas for Irish citizens making this initial step much more affordable.

Similar to the observation by Glynn, Kelly and MacÉinrí that recent emigration was more severe in the "most remote areas in Ireland" (2015: 7), and in line with the weak economic status of most peripheral Gaeltacht areas, many of my informants made comments such as the following:

> A: Tá ráta an-ard imirce agus 'sé is faide a théann tú siar 'sé is airde atá an ráta imirce [. . .] Má théann tú siar [go hiarthar na Gaeltachta], tá an áit bánaithe ar fad. Is beag duine óg atá fágtha [. . .] Aon duine singil, óg tá siad bailithe as an áit [. . .] Níl na ceantracha níos giorra go Gaillimh baileach chomh dona, y'know, mar tá roinnt oibre sa gcathair ag daoine. Ach fós féin tá cuid mhaith daoine imithe.

> [A: There's a very high rate of emigration and the further west you go the higher it gets [. . .] If you go back [to the west of the Gaeltacht] the place is totally abandoned. There are hardly any young people left [. . .] Anyone single, young, they've left the place [. . .] The areas nearer to Galway aren't quite as bad, y'know, as there's still some work in the city for people. But still there's a lot of people gone.]

It is, of course, well documented that these areas furthest west are almost always the most strongly Irish-speaking communities (Ó Giollagáin and Charlton 2015a). As another interviewee stated: *"Fós is fíor na háiteacha is mó Gaeilge, 'siad na háiteacha is lú rachmais"* [Still it's the case that the strongest Irish-speaking places are the poorest] (see also 7.2.3).

Those I spoke to frequently lamented such high rates of emigration as being extremely detrimental to the vibrancy of their communities, as the following quote – typical of many others – explains:

> L: Tá tú ag sú nó ag tarraingt anam amach as pobal [. . .] Pobal a raibh creidim láidir in am [. . .] nuair a bhí obair agus fostaíocht agus achan rud ag dul ar aghaidh [. . .] Achan duine a imíonn bheireann siad píosa den phobal leotha [. . .] Nuair a fheiceann tú go díreach na háiteacha atá druidte [. . .] an méid tithe, chan amháin tithe ach áiteacha a raibh fostaíocht iontu san am a chuaigh thart. Má tá tú ag tomaint thart agus má fheiceann tú na háiteacha atá fágtha fuar, fann, folamh a raibh beocht agus solas agus b'fhéidir toit ann am amháin, déarfá leat féin nach mór an trua [. . .] ach mór an náire é fosta.

> [L: You're sucking the soul out of the community [. . .] A community that was once strong [. . .] when the work and employment and everything was going well [. . .] Everyone who leaves takes a part of the community with them [. . .] When you just see the places closed [. . .] the number of houses, not just houses but places where there was employment in the past. If you drive around and see the places left cold, idle, abandoned – places that once had life and light and smoke, you say to yourself isn't it an awful pity, but an awful disgrace too.]

Figure 3 shows a very graphic illustration of the degree to which emigration weighs heavy on one community in Donegal. Titled *Ár nEisimircigh Ionúin* [Our Beloved Emigrants], this display in a Gaeltacht pub shows photos of locals who have moved abroad, and features advertisements for various companies which now employ them – construction firms in Australia or England, for instance. There were more photos on this wall than I could fit in the photo frame.

Figure 3: *"Ár nEisimircigh Ionúin"* – the emigrants' corner in a Donegal pub.

Beyond the search for employment, a further important factor contributing to emigration is the changing of aspirations that accompanies globalised modernity. As noted by Deprez (2000: 464), television – and the internet, one must now add – bombards people in peripheral locations with (often exaggerated) images of all that they are missing out on in urban life, thereby luring them away from their home communities (see also 13.3.1). As Brody explained, these increased aspirations can have very detrimental consequences for rural communities, ultimately meaning that "life in Inishkillane can no longer provide what the Inishkillane people want" (1974: 15). Emigration, then, becomes the natural choice for individuals living in communities which they have "lost faith in", to use Brody's terminology (1974: 16). The increased information flows which are responsible for such expanded conceptions of success are, of course, themselves a fundamental characteristic of globalisation (Castells 2000; Giddens 2002), as too is the trend towards urbanisation which is depopulating rural areas worldwide (section 8.2; OECD 2015).

Relatedly, on several occasions during my fieldwork I noted the social conservatism prevalent in some rural communities and how it contrasts with many of the more progressive images presented to young people in the media. On an island in Donegal I was struck by the large piece of graffiti in the main village reading "[name of island] SAY NO", a reference – in English – to the referendum on permitting same sex marriages which had recently been passed by overwhelming majority, although this island voted strongly against it. In the wake of such a historic vote on a national scale, such attitudes seemed all the more outdated, a fact which, I suspect, would not be lost on younger islanders, a number of whom were preparing to go to university in the autumn.

Several informants commented on the tendency for personal aspiration to prompt people to emigrate, saying that the recession was not the sole reason for emigration: *"Sin sórt caoga faoin gcéad economic. Tá daoine ag iarraidh bogadh thart anyway"* [It's about 50% economic. People want to move around anyway]. While "the lure of modernity in urban centres" (Mufwene 2016: 134) is certainly an important factor in driving the depopulation of minority language community heartlands, the overwhelming majority of my informants nonetheless felt the recession had greatly accelerated this pattern, a contention which other research confirms (Glynn, Kelly and MacÉinrí 2013: 38; Glynn and O'Connell 2017).

Despite high rates of emigration, many young people who I interviewed had positive attitudes about their communities, with one young woman proffering the following praise for her area: *"Tá mise ag ceapadh go bhfuil saol maith anseo. Tá chuile rud atá uainn a'ainn anseo [. . .] Tá na seirbhísí a'ainn, tá an siopa a'ainn, tá an dochtúir a'ainn, tá na scoileannaí a'ainn, tá an páirc peile a'ainn [. . .] Níl mé in ann cuimriú ar rud ar bith atá ag teastáil uainn"* [I think life is good there. We have everything we want [. . .] We have services, there's a shop, we have a doctor, we have schools, we have the football pitch [. . .] I can't think of anything else we'd want].

It is telling, however, that in spite of this recommendation, both she and her two siblings, also young adults, have all "voted with their feet" and moved to cities. It is therefore difficult not to read such a comment more as an example of the parochial pride typical of the west of Ireland and of the nostalgic gaze of someone who now spends most of her time in the city, rather than as a serious personal commitment to life in a rural community.

Although the nostalgia of departed emigrants can in some cases provoke a newfound affection for Irish among those who emigrate, as Harbert points out (2011: 409), such a positive effect is unlikely to outweigh the damage done through the reduction in the social density of speakers in the language's core communities. With those aged 20–34 having comprised 70% of emigrants during the recession (Glynn, Kelly and MacÉinrí 2013: 34), the loss of the cohort which is most likely to form families and so bring up the next generation of Irish speakers can only be seen as most detrimental for the long-term future of Irish in the Gaeltacht (see also 8.3). As one interviewee bluntly observed: *"Mairfidh sé sin an teanga, muna bhfuil daoine óga, cainteoirí dúchais, ag fanacht sa bhaile, sin deireadh"* [That'll kill the language, if young people, native speakers, aren't staying at home, that's the end].

I also was told on many occasions of the tendency for the primary breadwinner in a family to migrate (either in a conventional sense or as "commuter migrants" who spend extended periods working in cities – Glynn, Kelly and MacÉinrí 2013: 31), with partners often being left at home to raise their children alone:

> A: *Baintrí déine go bhféadfaí a rá leob. Mná atá fanta anseo agus a gcuid gasúr, agus na fir imithe ag obair in áiteachaí eile. Bhí col ceathrar liom féin ar an mbunú sin [. . .] D'imigh a fear go New Zealand ar feadh bliana [. . .] agus bhí sé féin ag cur an t-airgead abhaile [. . .] Tá go leor dhó sin ag tarlú. Tá roinnt daoine atá ag commuteáil, atá ag dul anonn is anall go Sasana, agus go dtí an Eoraip fiú, agus beidheadar ag fanacht cúpla seachtain thall agus ag teacht ar ais ansin.*
>
> [A: Austerity widows you could call them. Women that are left here with their children while the men are gone away to work in other places. I had a cousin like that [. . .] Her husband went to New Zealand for a year [. . .] and he was sending the money home [. . .] There's lots of that happening. There are some people commuting, going back and forth to England and to Europe even, and they'll stay a couple of weeks over there and then come back.]

An informant in Donegal commented on this phenomenon in a very impassioned manner, being visibly moved while discussing it: *"chan dóigh ar bith é sin ag teaghlach ar bith a bheith [. . .] Cuireann sé corraigh ort ar dhóigh, ach briseann sé do chroí fosta ar dhóigh eile"* [that's no way for any family to be [. . .] It makes you angry in a way, but it breaks your heart too].

As well as the obvious reduction in language input resulting from one parent emigrating seasonally or commuting long distances – with long-distance commuting having greatly increased since 2008 (Western Development Commission 2018) – parents who remain at home are likely to have less time to spend with their children as they attend to daily chores on their own. Unlike in previous generations when relatives more often helped with child rearing (thereby ensuring Irish-language input was maintained), modern technologies are nowadays likely to become surrogate child minders for parents who have to work overtime and/or without holidays in order to compensate for a loss in their organisation's budget (see 12.1) or to be able to pay bills, as many of my informants were. This tendency has often been reported in sociological research (see 13.3.1) and is, of course, an understandable response to the pressures of daily life. Notably, however, as I discuss in Chapter 13, these very technologies were often cited by interviewees as being key to causing young children to shift to speaking English. Furthermore, those who emigrate or even commute long distances are most likely to be drivers of language shift on returning to their home communities (Tabouret-Keller 1972; Kulick 1992: 4; section 9.3).

While academic literature on emigration post-2008 invariably mentions employment as having been a key factor in prompting an individual to migrate (e.g., Glynn and O'Connell 2017), the issue of debt peonage has very rarely been addressed. On many occasions I was told of people having to emigrate to ensure they could service debts, as the following quote describes:

> A: *An méid tithe a bhí dúnta, dochreidte [. . .] D'fheicfeá teach a bhí nú as a bpíosa agus dúnta agus geata glasáilte agus nuair a chuirfeá ceist cé a bhí anseo is dream óg a thóg an teach b'fhéidir agus a bhfuil riaráistí morgáiste orthu nó a thuig gurb é an t-aon bhealach a bhí acub le morgáiste a íoc ná imeacht agus goil ag obair in áit eicínt agus tá siad ag íoc as teach atá folamh.*
>
> [A: The number of houses closed up, unbelievable [. . .] You'd see a house that was brand new and closed and the gate locked and when you'd ask who was there, it was young people who built the house maybe and had mortgage repayments to make and who knew that the only way they had to pay the mortgage was by going and working somewhere and paying for a house that is empty.]

This high percentage of empty houses was something I also noticed myself on many occasions throughout different parts of the Gaeltacht.

As noted in 8.1, property bubbles are a fundamental feature of neoliberal economics, as are ever-increasing levels of indebtedness, with debt being used to compensate for the low or stagnant wages that neoliberalism offers the majority of the population (Graeber 2014: 361–393). The enormous mortgages which prompted such emigration are therefore themselves intimately connected to the macro-economic forces that brought about the 2008 crash, forces which ultimately left people with no choice but to emigrate in order to keep their homes from being repossessed by recently bailed-out banks.

The immense social cost of mass emigration, and the damage caused to linguistic vitality by such a disruption, is, then, intrinsically linked to neoliberalism in multiple intersectional ways. Several interviewees also linked out-migration to educational achievement, as the following section describes.

9.2.1 Education and out-migration

While typical narratives about emigration focus on the search for work, out-migration of young people from the Gaeltacht in the 21st century is also, I was told, very likely to be initially brought about by the requirements of gaining a third-level education. As with many developed nations, higher-level education is increasingly seen as a basic requirement for most employment in the country's "knowledge economy" (OLRS 2014), a further factor forcing young people to leave their communities once they have finished school.

This trend of education leading people away from their home communities is one that Hindley observed in his 1990 work, although at that time it was primarily islanders pursuing secondary schooling on the nearby mainland that were forced to leave home for such reasons (1990: 69). Secondary level education is now available on all the Gaeltacht islands on which I conducted fieldwork, which is a source of great satisfaction amongst older islanders who remember having to leave at a very young age for boarding schools on the mainland.

The increase in numbers studying at third-level during the recession (Department of Education and Skills 2015) meant, however, that greater numbers of school leavers than ever were likely to leave their home communities in order to obtain an education.

As was true when Hindley was writing, Gaeltacht natives who go on to get a higher level of education are unlikely to find satisfactory employment in their home communities. As an 18-year-old from Galway who had recently finished school and was considering going to university at the time of our interview commented: *"níl tú goil cúrsa a dhéanamh, níl tú goil fáil le bheith i do chócaire agus teacht amach anseo agus goil ag cócaireacht agus pá uafásach"* [you're not going to do a course, to learn how to be a chef and come out here to go cooking for terrible pay].

The tendency for large numbers of young people to pursue higher education – which predates but was intensified by the post-2008 downturn – means that it is most likely to be those who do not have such educational achievements who are left in the remote rural communities that comprise most of the category A Gaeltacht (CEDRA 2014: 30). As pointed out to me by a well-informed interviewee in Galway, this less-educated group were significantly more likely to be employed in those sectors most severely hit by the recession. Many worked either in construction (which all but ceased during the recession), in small businesses (a high percentage of which closed down, particularly in rural areas), or in manufacturing plants (a great many of which moved overseas), as discussed in Chapter 8. As a result of such closures, much of the younger population of the Gaeltacht who had not already left their communities to gain higher education were forced to leave to find work elsewhere in the wake of the crash – meaning that both those with and without higher level qualifications left these areas in recent years.

Historically, the self-confidence and assertiveness gained through higher-level education by native Irish speakers has had an important role in driving revitalisation efforts. Such developments are, however, dependent on there being suitable employment to entice these individuals back to Gaeltacht communities, something which is not currently the case in the majority of the areas where my fieldwork took place, with long established patterns of "brain drain" therefore likely to continue for the foreseeable future.

9.3 In-migration

As noted above, increased population mobility is a fundamental characteristic of globalisation. Consequently, the converse of the huge out-migration seen after 2008 is a simultaneous in-migration, predominantly of people coming from significantly more deprived countries (Healy 2015). While the number of immigrants from such areas that settle in the Gaeltacht is extremely low, it is not unusual for people to migrate from the Galltacht to the Gaeltacht, and the issue of in-migration as a counterpoint to wide-scale emigration is therefore one that must be addressed.

On several occasions in both Donegal and Galway I was told of business owners in strongly Irish-speaking communities employing eastern European immigrants due to the fact that they were vulnerable enough to be willing to work for low pay and under bad conditions:

G:	*Sin an cineál duine a thiocfas amach anseo [tá siad ag iarraidh] ciúnas, introversion sórt, nó Lithuanians le goil ag obair sa hotel.*
Údar:	*An bhfuil mórán Lithuanians san óstán?*
G:	*Chuile bhliain tiocann daoine nú amach.*
Údar:	*Muise, agus cén fáth nach bhfaigheann siad muintir an oileáin?*
G:	*Mar tá siad in ann iad a íoc go dona agus tá siad in ann goil ag béiceacht orthu.*
[G:	That's the kind of person who comes out here [they want] quiet, introversion, sort of, or Lithuanians to go working in the hotel.
Author:	Are there many Lithuanians in the hotel?
G:	Every year more people come out.
Author:	Really, and why don't they get islanders?
G:	Because they can pay them badly and shout at them.]

While such economic immigrants are few in number, in many Gaeltacht communities there is a relatively large cohort of people who have relocated there as a lifestyle choice, as mentioned in the above extract (see also Smith-Christmas 2014). This trend is often a by-product of the tourism sector, with immigrants of this type very frequently having initially visited these communities as tourists (Chapter 10; see also Phillips and Thomas 2001: 75–76).

As explained in 7.2.3, unemployment rates in much of the Gaeltacht are significantly higher than the national average. This fact, when combined with both the low incomes of many of those who are employed and the overinflated price of housing throughout Ireland (itself typical of neoliberal economies – see 8.1), means that locals are often effectively priced out of the property market, leaving existing houses to be bought by people from outside the community. The following extract from an interview with a businessman in Galway explains this phenomenon:

> B: *Tá teach ansin thiar [. . .] [Cheap] an auctioneer go bhfaigheadh sé 145,000-150,000 [. . .] Díoladh é ar 270,000. Agus daoine áitiúla ní raibh an t-airgead acub lena cheannacht. 'Sé a cheannaigh é ná beirt as Gaillimh, [. . .] Daoine áitiúla, go leor acub atá as obair cheana féin [. . .] níl aon rogha acub. Níl siad ag iarraidh fágáil. Tá mise breá compordach le daoine atá ag iarraidh imeacht ar feadh roinnt blianta [. . .] Ach má tá siad ag iarraidh teacht ar ais go mbeadh deis acub sin a dhéanamh. Agus má tá siad ag iarraidh fanacht sa gcéad áit gan imeacht thar sáile go mbeadh sin acub chomh maith.*
>
> [B: There's a house back there [. . .] The auctioneer [thought] it'd get 145,000-150,000 [. . .] It was sold for 270,000. And local people didn't have the money to buy it. It was two people from Galway [city] who bought it [. . .] Local people, many of whom are out of work already [. . .] they have no choice. They don't want to leave. I'm very comfortable with people who want to leave for a few years [. . .] But if they want to come back [they should] have that chance too. And if they want to stay in the first place and not go abroad, they should equally be able to do that.]

Through this process the structural issues that militate against the creation of well-paid employment in the Gaeltacht mean that what available housing there is often comes to be owned by well-off urbanites who are statistically unlikely to speak Irish (Fóram Chois Fharraige um Pleanáil Teanga 2016: 7). A similar phenomenon is well attested in Welsh-speaking areas and on the west coast of Scotland too (see 14.3; Williams 2014: 244).

Another cause for someone to move to the Gaeltacht is exogamy, itself very often a consequence of economic restructuring (Euromosaic 1996: 6). This was frequently noted by informants as a factor contributing to the decline of Irish in recent years, echoing Holmes' observation that "[m]arriage to a majority group member is the quickest way of ensuring shift to the majority group language for the children" (2013: 65). So too was the presence of non-Irish-speaking children whose families had moved to the area seen as one of the reasons that language shift amongst Gaeltacht children was happening so rapidly. Every day while walking past the playground on an island in Donegal I would hear only English, something which the local co-operative manager verified as being the normal state of affairs and linked to the presence of in-migrants in the community:

> M: Labhrann siad [Gaeilge] ar an scoil. But bím ag éisteacht leofa amuigh san ionad súgradh agus ó! [. . .] Nuair a bhogann teaghlach istigh agus Béarla acu, aistríonn na páistí uilig achan áit go Béarla [. . .] Agus tá an scoil iontach maith, Gaeilg go hiomlán a bhíonn ann [. . .] Ach just chíonn muid iad ag teacht amach geata na scoile agus bíonn siad ag caint i mBéarla!
>
> M: They speak [Irish] in school. But I listen to them out in the playground and oh! [. . .] When an English-speaking family moves in, all the children everywhere change to English [. . .] And the school is very good, it's all in Irish [. . .] But we just see them coming out the school gate talking English!]

In a community in Galway that is popular with tourists I was also told that English speakers who moved into the area and have not learned Irish, even after many years, make up a relatively significant portion of the community. As in Donegal, these are often people who have married someone from the area and who allegedly intended to learn Irish, but as time passed and the community became accustomed to interacting with them in English their dedication started to wane. One woman described this challenging situation to me as follows:

> E: Ar dtús cheapfadar go bhfuileadar an-dáiríre faoi agus breathnaíonn sé go mbíonn agus beidheadar ag goil chuig ranganna. Ach taobh istigh de dó nó trí de bhlianta, fiú ann dhá bhliain, beidh sé sin caite san aer – 'tá muid istigh anois agus tá muid glactha leis agus is cuma'. Agus ní bhíonn a fhios a'd an é muid féin is ciontach leis, go ndeireann muid 'á sure tá sibh alright'. Sórt ar dtús beidh tú ag rá 'bhfuil tú ag foghlaim Gaeilge?' agus ansin tar éis scaithimh déanann tú dearmad, is beag nach bhfuil an oiread sin cleachtadh a'd ag labhairt Béarla leob nach gcuimhneoidh tú air.
>
> [E: At first you'd think that they are very serious about it and it looks like they are and they'll be going to classes. But within two or three years, even two years, that'll be abandoned – 'we're in now and they've accepted us and it doesn't matter'. And you don't know is it ourselves that are at fault, that we say 'ah sure you're alright'. At first you'll be saying 'are you learning Irish?' and then after a while you forget, it's as if you're so used to speaking English to them that you don't think of it.]

Despite there being some provision of Irish classes for such incomers in many areas in the form of the *Ionad Seirbhísí Teanga* [Language Service Centres], which are funded by ÚnaG, in accordance with other recent research I was often told that very few of those who moved to the Gaeltacht ever attain fluency in Irish – in Cois Fharraige the figure is just 20% (Fóram Chois Fharraige um

Pleanáil Teanga 2016: 6, 27). In this way, in-migration creates a steadily increasing pool of non-Irish speakers in even the strongest remaining Gaeltacht areas. As discussed in the conclusion of this chapter, in addition to regulating the housing market, provision for teaching Irish to incomers needs to be significantly improved if this issue is to be addressed.

The high levels of emigration seen after 2008 also have the potential for greatly exacerbating this problem in coming years. As mentioned in 8.4 and 9.1, emigrants who returned during previous periods of prosperity and brought English-speaking families often contributed to the anglicisation of the Gaeltacht. Nonetheless, many of the children of migrants who returned in previous decades and who found themselves living in an Irish-dominant community ultimately became Irish speakers themselves. Were a similar phenomenon to occur again in coming years, however, it is unlikely that there is any community where Irish is strong enough to be able to assimilate incomers in this fashion. As one of my interviewees observed: *"Má imíonn siad tamallt fada agus má phósann siad daoine ansin má bhíonn siad thart anseo níl an t-infreastruchtúr ann le cuidiú leo ó thaobh na teanga [. . .] Tá sé cosúil leis an seanrud [. . .] who's immersing whom?"* [If they go for a long time and if they marry someone and they are back around here there isn't the infrastructure to help them with regards to the language [. . .] It's like the old thing [. . .] who's immersing whom?]

Rather than being able to linguistically integrate the families of returned immigrants, it would seem likely that without significant provision to address this issue, such an influx will spur local children to speak English even more than they already do (see Chapter 13). Despite the upturn in the economy post-2016 (at least until the Covid pandemic), thus far there has been no public discourse about this issue, or attempts to plan for the eventuality of large numbers of emigrants possibly returning home in coming years. Although a significant risk, none of those language plans which have thus far been completed in accordance with the *Gaeltacht Act 2012* (see 3.4) make any provisions for dealing with such a possibility – by recommending, for instance, a school integration model similar to that in use in Wales (Ní Thuairisg 2012).

9.4 Conclusion

Emigration from the Gaeltacht was one of the clearest ways in which the effects of the economic crash could be seen in the communities I spent time in, with interviewees often speaking in a very impassioned manner about the damage it had done to their areas. The absence of young adults in particular from community events I attended was very clear, something which was also evident in the census data discussed in 7.2.1. This is an issue of particular concern considering that it is this cohort who would otherwise be most likely to bring up the next generation of Irish speakers in the Gaeltacht. Of course, as with many of the phenomena discussed in this work, the economic crisis served primarily to significantly intensify already existent patterns of rural depopulation, something which has long since been noted as a fundamental trait of both late modernity and the way capitalism's urbanising tendencies operate (see 8.2).

A counterpoint to the mass emigration seen post-2008, however, is the tendency of much of the housing stock in rural areas to come to be owned by well-off retirees who move into the Gaeltacht, and in doing so often outprice locals likely to be employed in the sort of low wage jobs discussed in the previous chapter. As is the case in Wales and Scotland, holiday homes also contribute to this problem enormously. It must be emphasised, however, that arguing against class-based demographic displacement is not to adopt an anti-immigrant position in the way some right-wing commentators are wont to do, but rather to argue for a better distribution of resources to marginal communities which would ensure those who grow up there are not forced to leave against their will. While ultimately the issues which prevent Gaeltacht locals from being able to afford to live in their areas need to be addressed, so long as there continues to be people moving to the Gaeltacht (be they families of returning emigrants or retirees or others moving for lifestyle reasons), a greater effort needs to be made with regards to teaching such incomers Irish. In addition to the insights of research on new speakers (e.g., O'Rourke and Walsh 2020), lessons from Wales are valuable here, with the aforementioned linguistic integration units for the children of immigrants being a particularly good example (Ní Thuairisg 2012). So too could Ireland learn much from the Welsh government-funded *Dysgu Cymraeg/Learn Welsh* body, which provides classes to fit all schedules for adult learners of all levels for relatively nominal costs, and sometimes for free.

Although not something that many of my interviewees addressed, most likely as other economic issues were more pressing at the time of my fieldwork, difficulties with obtaining planning permission for building houses in the Gaeltacht exacerbate the housing crisis therein, and further contribute to people being forced to leave. Much of this is a product of the protected environmental status of a large part of the Gaeltacht. Under EU legislation, the Irish government is required to assign protected status to a certain amount of its territory, and much of the Gaeltacht has been so designated. One of the few interviewees who mentioned this issue, a young man in Donegal, claimed that under current provisions *"Tá níos mó meas ar ainmhithe agus ar éanlaithe an aeir ná atá ar dhaoine an talaimh. So sin ábhar mór frustrachais do phobal ar bith"* [There is more respect for animals and the birds of the sky than for the people of the land. So that's a great source of frustration for any community]. While later acknowledging the importance of environmental protection, he nonetheless felt that the depopulation of his area is not receiving the attention it warrants. This frustration provides a further example of the pattern discussed in 6.4, whereby materialist concerns typically trump the post-materialist (which the environment continues to be for many, although ecological collapse is likely to soon change this – see 14.6). Similar to many of the topics discussed in this work, the housing issue is one that could be greatly alleviated under an economic paradigm other than that of neoliberalism, if more forceful procedures were put in place regarding market regulation and the provision of affordable housing for all.

As mentioned above, a large number of those who move to the Gaeltacht were initially attracted to do so by their experience of it as tourists. Relatedly, and in addition to those which are purchased as private holiday homes, many Gaeltacht properties which had previously been available for long-term lease have recently become Airbnbs, further aggravating the housing situation. Despite tourism creating much needed employment, these issues highlight one aspect of the tension between tourism and community and language maintenance, a tension which I explore in the following chapter.

10 Tourism and the Gaeltacht post-2008: Uneasy bedfellows

10.1 Introduction

Much of the contemporary LPP literature on tourism discusses how minoritised languages can be commodified in the neoliberal economy, particularly through their symbolic use to index "authenticity" (e.g., Pietikäinen 2013; Jaffe and Oliva 2013; Heller, Pujolar and Duchêne 2014). As will be seen in this chapter, however, in the wake of the 2008 crash, the trend in the Gaeltacht, if anything, was to move *away* from the use of Irish as a way of enticing tourists, particularly in the emblematic ways discussed in 10.5. While certainly an important economic sphere, tourism is clearly also linguistically disruptive, as will be seen. I thus present a counterpoint to Moriarty's (2015: 99–115) analysis of the benefits of tourism for the Gaeltacht, which was based primarily on her reading the website for an Irish-language school in Donegal.

Common to many of the peripheral areas across Europe which are home to minoritised language communities is the tendency to be heavily dependent on tourism (Euromosaic 1996: 8), and the Gaeltacht very much follows this trend. This is part of a wider pattern which has seen tourism developed as a key industry throughout Ireland, with it being described as "the single most important industry in the west of Ireland" in academic literature (Anderson, Bakir and Wickens 2015: 78).

Although tourist numbers fell significantly post-2008 – by 18% in 2010 alone (Callaghan and Tol 2013: 106) – by 2015 the sector was growing again, with total revenue from tourism for the year amounting to €7.7 billion. The Central Statistics Office stated that 139,000 people – 7.1% of the national workforce – were employed directly in "accommodation and food service activities", although this percentage is much higher in some areas, particularly in Dublin. Fáilte Ireland, the national tourist board, claimed that in total 220,000 were employed in tourism in 2015 (Fáilte Ireland 2016a). Hoping to expand on this market, one of the five pillars of the government's *Action Plan for Rural Development* is "maximising rural tourism" (Government of Ireland 2017b: 39). A "key deliverable" of this plan was "to develop a Tourism Investment and Development Strategy for the Gaeltacht" during quarter one of 2017 (Government of Ireland 2017b: 42), although as of the time of writing no such strategy had been forthcoming.

Despite being an important industry in the Gaeltacht, as Harbert points out, the experience of the Celtic languages in general with tourism has historically been a rather unhappy one (2011: 419). Although typically only seasonal, large influxes of tourists inevitably alter the linguistic balance of minoritised languages' heartland communities, increasing dominant language use significantly. As discussed in the previous chapter, a key way in which lesser used languages are minoritised is through in-migration, and it is tourism which initially attracts the majority of immigrants to areas where minoritised languages are spoken (Phillips and Thomas 2001: 75–76; see also Euromosaic 1996: 38).

It is unsurprising, then, that concerns regarding tourism's cultural impact have long existed in the Gaeltacht. Well-known author Máirtín Ó Cadhain wrote in 1964 that Dún Chaoin in Kerry was at risk of becoming a tourist park rather than a community (Ó Cadhain 1964) and later proclaimed, with typical rhetorical flair, that "[w]ith regard to tourism in the Gaeltacht, I would hang the first Bord Fáilte [tourist board] official that ventured west of Knocknacarragh from the nearest tree, or from the nearest *sceach* [bush] if a tree was not available" (in Ó Gadhra 2000: 267).

While not so combative in tone, much academic literature on tourism expresses similar reservations about its implications for indigenous cultures. Denvir, for instance, himself a long-time resident in the Galway Gaeltacht, contends that "[t]ourism, by definition, is an invasive activity" which disrupts community life during the tourist season, when "[t]hose in the tourist sector and in related businesses work long hours, there are far greater numbers of people in the area and, while there is a hive of activity around, people in general are so busy that they do not socialize in the same way as during the rest of the year" (Denvir 2002: 39).

Although the expansion of the tourism sector was promoted as a way to overcome the effects of the recession – especially in areas which lost employment in construction or manufacturing – several of my interviewees also raised concerns about the potentially negative implications this could have for Gaeltacht culture. One interviewee in Galway, for instance, was worried that an increase in tourist numbers would see his community become steadily more like a neighbouring island which receives much greater numbers of tourists, and is consequently anglicised to a far greater degree:

> *R: Feicim [an t-oileán béal dorais] agus cuireann sé isteach orm go mór, bhfuil's a'd. Tá fógraí móra Béarla chuile áit – 'bike hire', 'hotel', 'guided tours' [. . .] Agus turasóirí ag siúl thart, cineál, díomách [. . .] ag súil [. . .] leis an rud a chonaiceadar sa bhfógraíocht. Agus b'fhéidir go bhfuil sé sin le feiceáil ach caithfidh tú íoc isteach lena fheiceáil.*
>
> [R: I see [the neighbouring island] and it annoys me a lot, y'know. There are big English signs everywhere – 'bike hire', 'hotel', 'guided tours' [. . .] And tourists walking around, kind of, disappointed [. . .] expecting [. . .] what they saw in the ads. And maybe you can see that, but you have to pay to do so.]

A Donegal islander I talked to worried about a similar issue, saying *"'sé an dearcadh atá agam ó shin go bhfuil an t-oileán seo ag éirí cosúil le áit fá choinne cuairteoirí"* [it seems to me that this island is becoming like a place for tourists]. Important as tourism may be in economic terms, as an informant from the nearby mainland community stated bluntly: *"ní shábhálfaidh turasóirí an teanga, tá siadsan ag fágáil!"* [tourists won't save the language, they're leaving!].

Further to promoting the use of English in commercial sectors, tourism can also significantly affect language practices amongst local children. Indeed, on one memorable occasion I greeted a group of children in Irish while walking past them, only to have one of them (whose family, I subsequently found out, were holidaying there) scream "don't speak that to me!" in response. With this being unlikely to be the only time this visitor expressed such sentiments, the linguistic consequences of spreading such extremely negative language attitudes amongst the area's youngest Irish speakers are clear.

Nonetheless, in the absence of other viable options, tourism has grown to provide the Gaeltacht with a key source of employment. Accordingly, many of those I spoke to felt that the Wild Atlantic Way, a marketing campaign launched in 2014 by Fáilte Ireland to attract visitors to the west coast, was a very positive development which was of much economic benefit to the Gaeltacht.

Beyond the obvious financial benefits, tourism can also be of psychological support to peripheral communities. As Brody explains, tourists can help validate rural ways of life for the locals themselves, offering "reassurance and approval" to populations that may otherwise feel disadvantaged and inferior compared to residents of the developed urban core (1974: 40).

Such is the dependency on tourism in several of the areas in which I conducted my fieldwork, however, that numerous informants commented on the risk created by this lack of economic diversity. One woman in Galway explained the constitution of the local economy as follows:

E: Is turasóireacht uilig cheapfainn a bhun agus a bharr anois [. . .] Scrios an tAontas Eorpach [. . .] an t-iascach. Agus i ndáiríre chuirfeadh sé faitíos ort dá ngabhfadh rud amháin mícheart ó thaobh na turasóireachta dhe...

Údar: Bheadh sibh caillte?

E: Go dona.

[E: It's all tourism now from start to finish [. . .] The European Union destroyed [. . .] the fishing. And really, it'd scare you that if anything went wrong with the tourism...

Author: You'd be sunk?

E: Badly.]

In addition to areas with such a low level of economic diversity being at risk from even extended periods of bad weather or political disruptions like Brexit, this comment takes on a greatly increased salience in light of the Covid pandemic (see section 14.5). Indeed, an article in the Irish Times in January 2021 discussing how the pandemic had affected the Oileáin Árann quoted one islander as saying bluntly "[w]e are down to the last penny" (Irish Times 2021a).

Despite the often excessive level of dependence on this sector, tourism is extremely important to both the Galway and Donegal Gaeltacht areas, as explained in the following sections. As will be seen, however, there are significant contrasts between the two counties, with this distinction being largely the product of geographical centrality/peripherality.

10.2 Tourism in Galway

With Galway city being heavily integrated into the national tourist trail, it receives a very large number of visitors, particularly during the summer. While this generates considerable knock-on benefit to some of the areas west of the city, much of the Gaeltacht, particularly more remote areas, sees relatively few tourists. As an interviewee from one of the strongest Irish-speaking areas on the west coast told me: *"Tá go leor den turasóireacht i dtuaisceart Chonamara, sa gceantar Béarla [. . .] An turasóireacht atá againne níl sé mór ach tá sé roinnte níos fearr, agus sin na coláistí Gaeilge"* [There's lots of tourism in north Conamara, in the English-speaking area [. . .] The tourism we have isn't big but it's shared better, that's the Irish summer colleges]. The summer Irish colleges referred to by this informant are discussed in 10.4.1 below.

One of the stronger Irish-speaking areas which reaps much benefit from tourism, however, are the Oileáin Árann, which receive huge numbers of visitors each year. These islands have a much higher profile in the national consciousness than any of the islands in Donegal – largely due to their proximity to other major tourist attractions, but also the literary heritage associated with the area. Such is the strength of the Oileáin Árann's tourist industry that it left them better off than much of the mainland Gaeltacht during the recession, despite them being more difficult to reach. As observed in the *Galway County Council Gaeltacht Local Area Plan 2008–2018*, "the general decline in population has not been as dramatic [on the islands] as some western districts of the Conamara Gaeltacht and the improved transport services of the ferry companies and [the air service have made possible] access to mainland facilities, including national and international travel routes" (Galway County Council 2008, revised 2013: 48). These transport links, however, were themselves the subject of much dispute during my fieldwork, as section 11.4 recounts.

Despite a certain number of tourists visiting throughout the year, during winter and autumn these are almost all day trippers, with most accommodation being closed at this time. The tourist season on these islands, I was often told, begins in March and continues until late September. Although numbers tend to be low in the early part of the season, during a visit to one of these islands in April I observed a definite increase in the number of tourists arriving compared to my previous visit in December. By mid-summer numbers swell enormously. While I was staying on one of these islands in July 2016 there were up to 2,000 people visiting daily. Despite the fact that many were visiting just for the day, this is nonetheless a huge influx for an island with a population of well under 300. Indeed, there was discussion on RnaG during my stay about there possibly being "too many" tourists visiting the island, with local infrastructure at risk of being overwhelmed.

As described by a woman who runs a small tourist-focused business on the island I stayed on, the surge in tourism during the summer sustains the island financially for the rest of the year, when very few visit the area, something which meant that the effects of the recession were not felt too severely there: *"Ar an gcarraig, tá sé sin coinní' sách réasúnta. Tá sórt forbairt inmharthana ansin ar bhealach mar gheall ar an séasúr turasóireachta agus cuidíonn an turasóireacht go mór leis an áit a choinneáil mar atá sé"* [On the rock [i.e., island] things are half decent. There's a kind of sustainable development there in a way because of the tourist season and the tourism helps a lot in keeping the place as it is].

Indeed, such is the amount of work available during the summer that migrant workers come to the island. While these are often from other parts of Ireland (friends or relatives of the business owners), eastern European workers have also availed of these opportunities, with many of the islands' businesses functioning through English in order to accommodate non-local workers (see also 9.3).

While on this same island in Galway over successive summers I also witnessed young adults who were home from university for the summer being asked to work multiple jobs simultaneously, with several finishing a day's work in one establishment before going straight to work in another. This was a striking counterpoint to national youth employment trends, which showed the unemployment rate amongst young adults to be double the national average at the time of my fieldwork.

Although tourism provides vital opportunities for the local population, this seasonal engagement, when combined with the social welfare payments collected during the off-season, provides an adequate income and means people are often reluctant to work in other sectors of the economy. One informant told me that the islanders liked to "hibernate" in the winter, and said it was therefore difficult to fill fulltime, year-round positions with the local development co-operative, such as the one that was being advertised at the time of our interview.

While I heard that the recession did lead to a decline in tourists coming from abroad, it saw an increase in tourists visiting from within Ireland, as financial constraints meant that Irish people, having grown accustomed to holidaying abroad during the Celtic Tiger, began to holiday at home more. A woman who works in a craft shop explained this "staycationing" phenomenon:

> E: Ní dhéarfainnse go bhfuil an oiread sin Meiriceánaigh ag teacht le cúpla bliain [. . .] An bhliain a raibh siad ag rá linn go raibh an tír an-dona b'shin é ceann de na blianta is fearr a bhí againn [. . .] Agus ó shin tá sé ag feabhsú, ach roimhe sin bhí muid ag díol fíorbheagán. Bhí sé ar nós go raibh Éireannaigh ag rá siod í an tír s'a'ainn féin agus tá muid le goil ar thuras in Éirinn.
>
> [E: I wouldn't say that there are as many Americans coming in the last few years [. . .] The year they were saying that the country was very badly off was the best year we had [. . .] And since then it's improving but before then we were selling very little. It was like Irish people were saying this is our own country and we're going to go on holiday in Ireland.]

A similar phenomenon may have occurred as a result of the Covid pandemic, at least after the most extreme lockdown restrictions were relaxed, although specific research into this matter has yet to be done.

In spite of dependence on tourism leaving local economies at the mercy of external shocks that could lead to a decline in visitor numbers, the prosperity brought to those areas which receive large numbers of visitors is clearly most important. Furthermore, although often linguistically problematic for the reasons discussed above, tourism in Galway has stimulated investment in infrastructure that has not happened in Donegal, particularly on those islands I visited. A small fleet of relatively large and modern boats owned by two different companies service the Oileáin Árann with as many as eight trips a day from two different mainland locations during the summer. While one of these companies is in receipt of state subsidy, the other is run as a private enterprise capitalising on the large number of tourists travelling to the area each year. As the following section describes, such provision is in stark contrast to the service available to the Donegal island where I conducted some of my fieldwork.

Significantly, despite the largest of the Oileáin Árann receiving some 100,000 visitors per year (Galway County Council 2013: 8), it experienced a 9.8% population loss between 2011–2016. While certainly better than it not existing at all, the tourism sector is typically characterised by poor quality and low-paid employment

(Eurostat 2015), with such a decline highlighting the importance of creating attractive jobs which adhere to the conceptions of success that many people nowadays hold (see 8.4 and 9.1).

10.3 Tourism in Donegal

Although seaside towns such as Bundoran in the south of Donegal are well-known as popular tourist destinations, the county in general, particularly the Gaeltacht in the north, is further removed from typical tourist routes than any part of Galway. In 2015 some 289,000 overseas tourists went to Donegal, far less than the 1,354,000 who visited Galway (Fáilte Ireland 2016b: 2). One of my interviewees from Donegal commented on tourism as follows, giving a concise overview of the industry in the area: *"tá sé ann ach níl sé róláidir ag an am céanna. Ní bheadh sé láidir go leor le daoine a choinneáil in san áit. Tá cúpla mí obair sa samhradh, sin an méid"* [it does exist but it's not too strong at the same time. It wouldn't be strong enough to keep people in the area. There's a few months' work in the summer, that's it].

When I asked another interviewee why he felt his area gets so many fewer tourists than the Galway Gaeltacht, I was told that its underdeveloped infrastructure makes it much more difficult to attract tourists:

> L: *Caithfidh an infreastruchtúr a bheith ann [. . .] Ach aríst tagann sé ar ais ag easpa airgid. Tá iarratas ag dul isteach chuig Roinn na Gaeltachta agus níl an roinn ag ceadú airgid ná cibé rud é. So tá sé náireach nuair a smaointíonn tú air [. . .] Tá dream anseo go háitiúil agus tá fochoiste turasóireachta acu, tá mé féin ar an fhochoiste sin [. . .] Ach in amanna bheadh sé chomh maith agat caint leis an bhalla ansin. Nuair a théann tú go dtí na húdaráisí sin agus deir siad yeah tá sin fís ghalánta agus achan rud ar pháipéar but easpa creidim airgead nó easpa cibé rud atá ann.*

> [L: The infrastructure needs to exist [. . .] But again, it comes back to a lack of money. There's an application going in to the Department of the Gaeltacht and the department isn't granting the money or whatever. So it's shameful when you think of it [. . .] There's a group here locally and they have a tourism subcommittee, I'm on that subcommittee [. . .] But sometimes you'd be as well off talking to that wall there. When you go to the authorities and they say yeah that's a lovely vision and everything on paper but a lack of money I think or a lack of whatever it is.]

Several other interviewees in the area echoed this sentiment and noted the chicken-and-egg nature of the problem, whereby tourists are not only attracted to areas with adequate infrastructural provision, but also help ensure its development.

As with my fieldwork in Galway, while in Donegal I had the opportunity to spend time on a strongly Irish-speaking island. Unlike the Galway island which I visited at various times of the year, my time on the Donegal island was all during the middle of the tourist season. As in Galway, tourism provides a key source of income to the islanders. The difference with my experience in Galway was quite dramatic, however. Unlike the crowds that can be seen on the island pier in Galway on a good day in the summer, there was typically only a handful of tourists arriving on the Donegal island daily – an amount very similar, in fact, to that which I witnessed visiting the Galway island during the off season. Indeed, in 2017 visitors to the island numbered just 8,688, according to a report which unfortunately cannot be directly referenced due to issues of anonymity. In the same year the similarly-sized Galway island received an equal amount every few days during the summer.

Unlike in Galway, none of my interviewees in this area observed an increased number of Irish tourists during the recession. Indeed, an owner of tourist accommodation told me that increased unemployment on the nearby mainland meant people were less likely to visit for the weekend as had been the case before the crash, something other interviewees confirmed: "crowds used to come here for weekends who'd be working in places locally. And that seems to have diminished considerably [. . .] They would all have to go away then, maybe to England, Scotland [. . .] Canada or Australia, which has happened".

The decline in tourists visiting the mainland Gaeltacht in Donegal was also severe. As 8.3 described, five out of six hotels in one community closed between 2010–2015, with detrimental consequences for both the social and linguistic vitality of the area. *"Fáinne fí atá ann, cionn is go raibh rudaí go holc dhruid na hóstáin síos, agus níl an saol sóisialta go maith [. . .] Níl ach teach ósta amháin ann. So dá mbeadh dream mór ann ní fhéadfadh muid iad a choinneáilt"* [It's a vicious circle, because things were bad the hotels closed and the social life isn't good [. . .] There's only one pub. So if a large group did come, we'd have nowhere for them to stay], as another interviewee put it.

Similarly, the hotel on the island I visited closed in 2010. It was immediately put on the market but remained unsold for three years. Seeing one of the island's most prominent buildings left boarded up while awaiting a sale had a significant impact on community pride. *"Bhí sé fiánta don oileán [. . .] Nuair a dhruideann rudaí síos cuireann sé cuma olc ar áit"* [It was awful for the island [. . .] When things close it makes the place look bad], a local recounted. Section 8.5.2 discusses the consequences of such closures and the attendant reduction in community pride for linguistic reproduction.

Although the mainland hotels remain closed, the island hotel was eventually bought in 2013 by a well-off retired couple who now open it for three months during the summer. While not locals or Irish speakers themselves, they have an affinity for the area and run the hotel in an attempt "to improve life on the island", as one of them told me. Despite employing approximately ten people – mostly islanders but also some family members – the business does not have a sufficient turnover for them to pay themselves for their work there, with them keeping the hotel open "as a service to the island" rather than for financial gain.

In contrast to Galway's Oileáin Árann, the Donegal island does not have an aeroplane service, despite being further away from the mainland. The one boat that serves the island (which is smaller and older than any boat serving the Galway islands) is often cancelled due to bad weather, even in the summer, with islanders occasionally having to call the coastguard to bring them necessities by helicopter after they have been cut off for several weeks.

This underdeveloped infrastructure is a source of considerable frustration to many of the islanders. As with inhabitants of the nearby mainland, they often told me that this is the main reason tourism has not flourished as it has in Galway: *"Muna fhaigheann muid an bád [nua], ní bheidh sé, ní bheidh an forbairt ceart ar fáil, ní bheidh an líon turasóirí ag teacht [. . .] Tá muid ag iarraidh an sórt céanna bád farantóireachta atá ag freastal ar [Oileáin Árann]. Níos faide, níos compordaí"* [If we don't get a [new] boat, it won't, we won't have proper development, tourists won't come [. . .] We want the same type of ferry that goes to [the Oileáin Árann in Galway]. Longer, more comfortable]. Despite such sentiments being common among islanders in Donegal, as section 11.4.2 describes, 2018 saw a different company granted the tender to service one of the main Irish-speaking islands. Far from improving the service the way the islanders had been demanding, this change saw a decline in its suitability, with a ferry which was widely decried as being even less appropriate than its predecessor taking over the route.

While the low numbers of visitors going to Donegal is likely one of the area's biggest draws for a certain minority of visitors, its peripherality means it is difficult to envision the relative prosperity seen in parts of Galway emerging in such a remote location in the near future. As discussed in the next section, however, the promotion of linguistic tourism may offer the stronger Irish-speaking areas of Donegal an option for expanding their tourism sector in coming years.

10.4 Linguistic tourism

As Ó Laoire explains, state efforts to promote linguistic tourism to the Gaeltacht have existed for many years (2008: 210). The 2017 *Action Plan for Rural Development* includes amongst its Irish-language-related aims "[c]ontinue to develop Irish language based tourism in the Gaeltacht", and the section titled *Promoting the Irish language as a key resource* commits to "[c]ontinu[ing] to support the development of cultural tourism in the Gaeltacht by administering the Irish Language Learners [sic] scheme" (Government of Ireland 2017b: 42, 52).

Despite these laudable goals, with the significant exception of the *coláistí samhraidh* focusing on teenagers (discussed in the following section), linguistic tourism currently makes up only a very small proportion of tourism overall. While now dated, an unpublished study commissioned by ÚnaG in 1999 stated that linguistic tourism to Conamara comprises only 3% of total annual visits (in Denvir 2002: 34). This very much accords with my own observations – I was repeatedly told in both Galway and Donegal that adult linguistic tourists are not at all common. One interviewee in Donegal said the following to me regarding the use of Irish with tourists: *"Thiocfadh leat 'conas atá tú?' [mar a bheadh ag daoine le Gaeilge na scoile] a rá le 300 duine ag teacht isteach ón mbád sin agus is ar éigean go dtuigfeadh cúigear thú, níos lú arís má tá tú ag ráit 'caidé mar atá tú?' [an leagan atá sa gcanúint áitiúil]"* [You could say 'conas atá tú?' [the form of 'how are you' most often taught in Irish schools] to 300 people coming in off that boat and barely five would understand you, less again if you are saying 'caidé mar atá tú?' [the local dialect form]].

He went on to state that *"mothaíonn tú mar amadán má labhrann tú Gaeilg agus muna dtuigeann daoine thú"* [you feel like an idiot if you speak Irish and people don't understand you]. As well as illustrating attitudes towards Irish amongst tourists that visit the island commonly referred to as the strongest Irish-speaking community in Donegal, this rather downhearted sentiment is also very indicative of the language's standing vis-à-vis English, the lingua franca of tourism and, therefore, economic prosperity.

10.4.1 Summer language schools

Although few adults visit the Gaeltacht for linguistic purposes, one area in which linguistic tourism does indeed flourish in much of the Gaeltacht is in the provision of summer courses for teenagers. For over one hundred years *coláistí samhraidh* [summer colleges] have brought large numbers of secondary school students to Gaeltacht communities and provided a significant source of income thereto, particularly to women, who are otherwise marginalised by the traditional economic structure of rural Ireland (Denvir 2002: 48).

Those who attend such courses, which are far from inexpensive, are likely to have parents or guardians with above-average incomes and as a result they constitute a valuable target market for Gaeltacht communities to capitalise on. Fees for a three-week long course including accommodation with a local family generally cost in the region of €1,000. As well as these fees and the money students spend in local businesses during their stay, it is commonplace for parents to come and visit at weekends, often staying overnight in local accommodation, thereby contributing further to what is typically an otherwise depressed local economy.

Many of my interviewees commented on the importance of these courses to their areas, particularly in Galway. The following quote is representative of many others: "*Murach na Gaeilgeoirí [.i. lucht freastail na gcoláistí] ní bheadh tada [sa gceantar] [. . .] Thiocfadh corrthurasóir ach níl an turasóireacht mór*" [Without the Irish learners [i.e., attendees at the summer colleges] there'd be nothing [in the area] [. . .] The odd tourist would come but tourism isn't big].

A language planner I interviewed in Galway claimed the industry is worth some €20 million to the Gaeltacht per annum, a figure also given by Conradh na Gaeilge (2017: 6–7). Indeed, one woman felt that this income is so significant that it means there is little incentive to develop other aspects of the tourist industry in the way that has happened in nearby English-speaking areas. "*Sure cén fáth a ndéanfadh siad é sin nuair atá siad in ann 20 nó 30,000 a dhéanamh leis na Gaeilgeoirí sa samhradh?*" [sure why would they do that when they can make 20 or 30,000 in the summer with the Irish learners?], she commented, offering an insight into a unique form of the so-called "Dutch disease" which, typically, explains how the benefits of a sector like tourism harm other aspects of an area's economy.

While the economic benefit of such colleges is clearly most significant, their linguistic consequences are also of immense importance, with the importance of maintaining the use of Irish in the community being very apparent to those involved in this industry.

The recession led to a significant decline in attendance at these colleges, however. I had the opportunity to interview an employee of the organisation which oversees the industry and ask him about this:

> P: *Feictear dom go raibh titim thubaisteach, dáiríre. Agus ar bhealach go raibh an earnáil seo i mbaol in áiteachaí éagsúla. Is minic a bhímse ag caint le lucht coláistí eile agus feicim go mbíonn na fadhbanna céanna le sonrú ag chuile dhuine. Nuair a iarann tú is dóigh idir 800 agus €1,000 ar dhuine le freastal ar chúrsaí trí seachtainí, nuair a thit an tóin as an tír b'shin é an chéad rud a thit as pócaí na ndaoine [. . .] Bhí muid buailte go tubaisteach.*

[P: I saw a catastrophic decline, really. And in a way that the sector was at risk in different areas. I often talk to people in other colleges and I see that everyone has the same problems. When you charge I suppose between 800 and €1,000 for a three-week course, when the country collapsed that was the first thing people stopped paying for [. . .] We were hit catastrophically.]

This decrease created significant difficulty for communities that had grown largely dependent on this income. The overall reduction of 25% in attendance nationally between 2008–2014 masks an even greater rate of decline in certain areas – with the drop of 37% in Donegal, for instance, being significantly higher, possibly due to the county's peripherality making it costlier to travel to (Tuairisc.ie 2014b). After such a dramatic fall during the worst years of the recession, attendance figures for 2016, while improving on those of recent years, were still, on average, 7% below 2008 levels (Tuairisc.ie 2017n). As discussed in 14.5, the effects of the Covid pandemic were once again severe for this sector.

Despite these courses being the most successful language-based industry in the Gaeltacht, they are still heavily dependent on state support. The *mná tí* [housekeepers] who host students receive a subvention from the department responsible for the Gaeltacht. This allowance, *Scéim na bhFoghlaimeoirí Gaeilge* [the Irish-learners' scheme], is paid per pupil per night and increased in accordance with inflation from 1997–2007, at which point it remained stable at €10.50 per student per night until 2010. It was cut to €10.00 in 2010 and then to €9.50 in 2011, the rate recommended by An Bord Snip Nua (see 3.2). It was frozen at €9.50 for six years, but was increased for the first time in a decade to €10.00 in April 2017, although a return to pre-recession levels was ruled out in 2018 (Tuairisc.ie 2017n, 2018g). These reductions, coupled with the substantial drop in student attendance at the colleges, saved the state over €2 million per annum, but were reported to have cost the Gaeltacht in the region of €10 million when the loss of the multiplier effect associated with spending by students and parents was included (Tuairisc.ie 2014b). While further cuts to the sector were recommended by An Bord Snip Nua, *Guth na Gaeltachta* (see 11.2) was largely successful in resisting these proposals.

Although providing one of the only significant sources of tourism in many Gaeltacht communities, on the Galway island I visited, which receives huge numbers of visitors regardless, the island's one summer college for teenagers has a less visible – although still not negligible – impact. On the Donegal island no such college exists, a fact that frustrates local business owners, who feel a valuable market is not being capitalised on.

Such frustrations notwithstanding, no steps have been taken to establish such a college on the island – which is somewhat surprising considering the nearby mainland has colleges that are over a century old. A narrative I regularly heard regarding summer colleges in various parts of the Gaeltacht, however, was that they were not originally founded by locals, but rather by university lecturers, teachers or Irish-language groups from elsewhere in the country. As noted by Deprez, writing about a Gaeltacht island in Donegal, "the initiative [there] comes from the outside" (2000: 470). Furthermore, the teachers in these colleges are rarely locals, although it is still not clear why revitalisation advocates ignored this island and not other areas nearby. While this is quite probably a sector that could be developed on the island, it would take someone with a strong entrepreneurial drive, something that has historically been slow to emerge in the Gaeltacht (Ní Bhrádaigh and Murray 2006). Such an individual would also have to be very confident in their level of Irish, particularly its written form – which not many Gaeltacht residents are, according to all accounts I have heard. Low rates of literacy in Irish amongst Gaeltacht residents have long been noted as a challenge to revitalisation efforts (Ní Mhianáin 2003).

As such, it seems unlikely that an enterprise of this sort will be developed on a significant scale on this particular island. Nonetheless, in 2015 and 2016 the local co-operative did indeed provide the impetus for a week-long course directed at fluent adult speakers in which I took part, and which continued to occur in subsequent years, except during the Covid lockdowns of 2020 and 2021. Notably, however, the course is organised by a language school based elsewhere in Donegal, which was invited to run the course at the request of the co-operative in order to bring visitors to the island. While this presumably means that much of the profit from the course itself left the island, when I attended it was nonetheless successful in attracting more than 20 diligent Irish speakers who contributed to the local economy over a week when visitor numbers to the island would otherwise most likely have been almost negligible. Although islanders led several afternoon activities, none of the teachers were from the island.

On the much busier Galway island the impact of the courses for adult learners that I taught for many years while researching this book was far less visible. As with the teenagers attending similar courses, those adults visiting the island for explicitly linguistic purposes get submerged in the greater throng of non-linguistic tourists. Here too almost all of those involved in teaching were not islanders. While having 30 Irish learners spending a week on an island with a small population is not insignificant, this number becomes much less striking when there are some 2,000 visitors arriving daily. With such a large majority of tourists seemingly having little interest in Irish, it is unsurprising that the dynamics of local, tourist-dependent economies would quickly become associated with the use of English.

10.5 The linguistic landscape – shifting terrain

One area in which the linguistic consequences of both tourism and, it would seem, the Great Recession, were particularly clear is the "linguistic landscape" (Gorter 2006) of some of the communities in which I conducted my fieldwork, with notable changes having occurred therein in recent years. Despite the relative strength of Irish in these communities, and despite legal stipulations requiring many official signs to be monolingually Irish in the Gaeltacht (Government of Ireland 2003), the linguistic landscape of most of these areas is dominated by English. This in itself is not overly unexpected, with minoritised languages – even in their "heartlands" – often being excluded from those symbolic spaces associated with higher and commercial registers. Of particular interest in the context of this study, however, are the clear moves towards the bottom-up anglicisation of this domain which were visible throughout the duration of my fieldwork, and which were reported by several informants to have accelerated as a direct result of the recession.

Figure 4: A hotel in Galway, photographed first in 2015 and then again in 2016.

The example in Figure 4 of a hotel photographed in Galway in 2015 and again in 2016 provides a particularly clear example of this process. As can be seen, this establishment, which is one of the main sources of accommodation for visitors in the area, went from displaying a sign which was primarily in Irish during the first year of my fieldwork, to a monolingual English one by the time I returned to the island the following year. Even the owner's name, obscured in these images, was translated to English in the new sign. While I have often heard committed native Irish speakers using both the English and Irish versions of their names, the depth of such a symbolic move is nonetheless quite striking.

Figure 5 displays a restaurant, also in Galway. The owners, a couple, one of whom married into the community many years ago and has not learned Irish, are heavily involved in community development initiatives. Despite the Irish-speaking partner being familiar with the *Gaeltacht Act 2012* and criticising it heavily in casual conversation with me, they rebranded their formerly bilingual restaurant name in English only in recent years – something I was told about by a friend of mine from the area.

Figure 5: A restaurant in Galway, bilingual in 2012 but English only in 2014.

One of my interviewees claimed that this development was something which began during the recession and was linked to tourism:

> R: *Tá sé tosaithe anseo anois fiú sna daoine atá ag iarraidh Gaeilge a choinneáil. Feicim iad ag cur suas anois – thosaigh sé ag tarlú le cúig bliana anois go díreach – ag cur suas fógraí i mBéarla amháin agus go bhfuil sé níos éifeachtaí, gur Béarla atá ag cuid is mó de na cuairteoirí nó go bhfuil sé níos fusa. Tá siad ag ceapadh nach bhfuil sé ag déanamh aon dochar agus [. . .] nach bhfuil an teanga i mbaol dáiríre [. . .] agus cén dochar agus, is dóigh. Ach goileann sé orm.*

> [R: It's started here even with the people who want to keep Irish. I see them putting up – it started within just the last five years – putting up signs that are only in English and that it's more effective, that it's mostly English that the tourists speak, or that it's easier. They think it's not doing any damage and [. . .] that the language isn't really in danger [. . .] and what harm, I suppose. But it upsets me.]

10.5 The linguistic landscape – shifting terrain

As noted in section 10.1, the link between tourism and English is particularly evident on one of the other islands in Galway that sees an enormous flow of tourists. The main village there, probably the most developed settlement of any Gaeltacht island, contains many large and seemingly prosperous businesses, although Irish is hardly more visible there than it would be in any small town elsewhere in Ireland.

With tourism being so central to the economy of many Gaeltacht communities, it is understandable that locals would feel the need to facilitate visitors in whatever way possible in light of the tumultuous economic situation they faced, as an employee of a state-funded language promotion body suggested:

> C: Tá sé brónach [. . .] gur tharla sé de léim [. . .] taobh istigh de deich mbliana [. . .] B'fhéidir go bhfuil easpa misnigh nó mórtais nó muinín atá ann agus go gceapann siad go gcaithfidh siad cineál iad féin a dhíol trí Bhéarla. See nuair a thit an tóin ar bhealach as na Gaeilgeoirí a bheith ag goil [go dtí na coláistí samhraidh] [. . .] bhí an cineál t-athrú seo ag teacht isteach i gcloigeann na ndaoine [. . .] níl lucht Gaeilge ag teacht chugainn níos mó, níl na postanna. Agus y'know is rud cineál teibí é ach [. . .] téann sé i bhfeidhm ar dhaoine, cinnte téann sé i bhfeidhm ar dhaoine [. . .] Tá mé ag ceapadh go bhfuil sé psych-, sa psyche is dóigh ar bhealach.

> [C: It's sad [. . .] that it happened suddenly [. . .] within ten years [. . .] Maybe there's a lack of courage or confidence or pride and that they think they have to sell themselves through English. See when the Irish-learners stopped going [to the summer colleges] [. . .] there was this kind of change to people's attitudes [. . .] the Irish-speakers aren't coming anymore, there aren't the jobs. And y'know it's kind of abstract but [. . .] it affects people, it definitely affects them [. . .] I think it's psych-, it's in the psyche in a way.]

As this interviewee notes, the combination of the dramatic decrease in income from the summer colleges and the decline of the ÚnaG-supported industrial sector (see 8.2) saw the economic basis of many Gaeltacht communities removed. This disruption, it seems, contributed to a sense of Irish not having a significant impact on local economic welfare and therefore prompted, at least in part, this turn away from the promotion of the language in such clearly visible ways.

Relatedly, the website of a company in the Kerry Gaeltacht in the south of Ireland which was analysed by Kelly-Holmes (2013) due to its multilingual layout and references to the importance of Irish and the Gaeltacht has also since been redesigned as monolingually English. The only Irish now visible on the site is in the form of three brief taglines which are embedded in images and presented in much smaller text below the dominant English – see www.louismulcahy.com. The Irish-language version of the website, still under construction at the time of the 2013 research, has been entirely removed, with management clearly not agreeing with Kelly-Holmes' assessment that "[n]ot to have an Irish language version, in the context of having linked the business so strongly to its locality, would be a marketing blunder" (2013: 125).

Figure 6: An official sign modified to include English.

While language activism in the Gaeltacht over the last fifty years has often included painting over English-language signs (TG4 2004), Figure 6, showing a sign on a Donegal island, provides an example of English being added unofficially to the linguistic landscape.

Significantly, the handwriting in which this DIY-anglicisation is done is unmistakably that of the elected local community representative on this island. This same individual is extremely pro-Irish in his rhetoric, regularly being heard in the Irish-language media and attending events related to the language. As well as being a vocal proponent of Irish, he is also very forceful in his views regarding island development, feeling that the area has been neglected by the authorities. He frequently discusses the need for improved infrastructure and comments on the lack of employment as an issue of major concern. As a result of these beliefs, it is perhaps to be expected that he would attempt to facilitate tourists as much as possible through making such a sign intelligible to non-Irish speakers, even though the lighthouse mentioned is clearly visible from almost everywhere on the island.

It is quite possible that this marginalisation of Irish in the linguistic landscape does not actually concur with the desires of tourists, at least some of whom are surely attracted to these areas due to their perceived cultural "otherness" and indigeneity, of which the language is a key component. Such changes, however, reflect the long-established link between commerce and English. This oft-referenced association has been a key factor in driving language shift over several centuries: "[t]he conviction that Irish was a badge of backwardness and poverty, or, at least, that English had certain economic advantages over it, which seized a great part of Gaelic-speaking Ireland in the 19th century has never been completely eradicated and remains to some extent in the Gaeltacht today" (Ó Huallacháin 1991: 124).

Although the impact of symbolic actions such as these on community language use is a matter for debate, they provide a vivid example of the ongoing minoritisation of Irish in even its strongest communities. As Gorter points out "the visibility or non-visibility of a language in public is a message in and of itself" (in Sallabank 2011: 503). Conversely, however, all too often "bilingual road-signs and some schooling [. . .] are seen as substitutes for parental or other early-childhood language learning" (Gunther 1989: 64). Nonetheless, the trend described here affords us an insight into a belief which clearly has a certain currency in the Gaeltacht and sees Irish and commercial enterprise as being contraindicated. This opinion was apparently strengthened due to the economic crisis – a finding which starkly contrasts with Brennan and Costa's (2016) discussion of the use of Irish as part of a strategy of "de-homogenisation" elsewhere in the country during the recession.

10.6 Conclusion

Duchêne and Heller (2012) are well known for their commentary on minoritised languages under neoliberalism coming to be understood as a potential source of profit in sectors such as tourism, rather than connected to traditional discourses of nationalist pride. Before 2008 Heller even claimed that "linguistic minorities are suddenly fashionable icons of the new hybridity" (2006: 14). As has been seen, however, at least in the communities where I did my fieldwork, the reality in recent years has been decidedly more sober.

Indeed, tourism in many ways exemplifies the Catch-22 contradiction that defines the minority language condition. While the employment it creates is often very important for stimulating some level of economic activity, the linguistic disruption that it almost invariably entails itself contributes to language shift.

While visitor numbers fell as a consequence of the economic crisis, tourism remained one of the few industries that offered some chance of creating employment in communities hit by the collapse of the construction and industrial sectors which were discussed in Chapter 8, and as such it was promoted by both state and local community efforts. The tendency towards increased staycationing that the crisis prompted was of benefit to areas in Galway in particular, while the more peripheral communities of Donegal saw little such improvement. Even in the most remote areas of Galway tourist numbers remained higher throughout the period under discussion than in Donegal, something which has ensured the maintenance of much better infrastructure in Galway than in the Gaeltacht areas of the north-west of the country.

The tension between tourism and language maintenance was starkly illustrated by the anglicisation of the linguistic landscape documented above, apparently undertaken in an attempt to facilitate tourists, who are rarely attracted to the Gaeltacht primarily for linguistic reasons. While the link between the visibility of Irish in the written landscape of the Gaeltacht and community language use is an under-researched topic, these developments are nonetheless indicative of the problems faced by language advocates when trying to promote tourism as a solution to the Gaeltacht's economic challenges.

The summer schools for teenagers which have been so important both for the creation of new speakers of Irish and for the economic vitality of the Gaeltacht for over a century also suffered a dramatic decline in attendance, with parents understandably reluctant to pay for expensive 3-week long courses during a period of such uncertainty. I return to this issue in 14.5 regarding the Covid pandemic. The development of a similar week-long course for adults on the island I visited in Donegal was a positive development however, and highlights one of the ways in which one community exercised their agency during a trying time, a subject which I explore further in the following chapter.

11 Community responses to austerity

11.1 Introduction: Organised opposition to state policies

Shortly after the first austerity budgets were implemented, many in the Irish media began to comment on the lack of organised resistance to these measures. In the years immediately following the crash this apparent passivity led to the emergence of an oft-repeated assertion that "the Irish don't protest" (Magill 2013; Thejournal.ie 2013b). Despite the lack of more militant actions of the type seen elsewhere in the EU at the time, by 2009 there had nonetheless been several significant mobilizations opposing the cuts, including marches of more than 100,000 people and a one-day strike of over 250,000 public servants. Various sectors of civil society mobilised in defence of their interests during this period, including pensioners, students and the parents and staff of DEIS schools for the disadvantaged. Building on an earlier failed boycott of the household tax that took place between 2011–2013, during the research of this study a mass civil disobedience campaign defeated the imposition of water charges, which were widely understood as stealth taxes designed to facilitate later privatisation of the water infrastructure.

Despite this, resistance to state policies was undeniably more muted in Ireland than elsewhere in Europe during this period, not escalating to the point of large-scale riots or property destruction. Conservative commentators attributed popular impassiveness to the widespread acceptance of the need for fiscal restraint, combined with the legacy of Catholic deference (Irish Independent 2012).

As Grasso and Giugni explain, however, "neoliberal contexts tend to be characterised by more individualised understandings of poverty, thus depressing protest action" (2016: 667). Furthermore, as Allen and Boyle note, "political responses to an economic crisis are shaped by the manner in which the mass of people entered it – their experience of prior struggles and the existence or non-existence of substantial left minorities" (2013: 128). The conditions in which the Irish working class entered the crisis, however, did not in any way prepare them for the challenges of combating austerity. The social partnership model of industrial relations that came to prominence throughout the Celtic Tiger saw a decline in large-scale industrial action, as disputes were dealt with by a professional managerial class employed by the trade unions. Concomitant to the adoption of this conservative, clientelist model of negotiation by the union leadership, union density more than halved between 1980 and 2007 (McDonough 2010: 452). Combined, these developments resulted in the annual average of work days lost per 1,000 salaried employees falling enormously from 501 in 1985 to just 2 in 2011 (OECD 2017: 1). Consequently, by 2008 the vast majority of the Irish working class had little experience of collective action or mobilisations in defence of common causes (Allen and Boyle 2013: 134–143), meaning the only way to create effective resistance "was to start from the ground up" (Bisset 2015: 178), a time-consuming process, albeit one which eventually culminated in the successful water charges campaign.

Although they never had a place at the social partnership negotiating table (unlike other organisations in the voluntary and community development sectors – see Ó Murchú 2003), Irish-language organisations nonetheless adopted a managerial lobbying strategy throughout the 1990s. They were thus arguably in an even weaker position than other sectors to defend their interests when faced with the drastic cuts described in Chapter 4. While the post-2008 period did see some important mobilisations of the Irish-speaking community, these, as will be seen, made no attempt at connecting their sectional struggles with the wider anti-austerity movements that emerged during this time.

In spite of various academic commentators calling for Irish-language activists to link their efforts with those of other social justice and environmental movements both pre- and post-2008 (e.g., McCloskey 2001; Ó Croidheáin 2006; Mac Síomóin 2006; Cronin 2011), such an approach remained very much a minority position throughout this time, as it did before the crash. One organisation that attempted to resist the sectionalism of mainstream language groups was *Misneach*, of which I am an active member. Due, however, to my personal involvement in this group, space constraints, and Misneach being a relatively small group, this organisation will not be discussed in further detail.

While language issues remained relatively marginal, many of the national campaigns against austerity had a notable presence in Gaeltacht areas, including the anti-water charges campaign, which began in the Donegal Gaeltacht, as locals often proudly told me. There was also important localised resistance during the early years of the crisis (against the closure of post offices and health service cuts in Donegal, for instance), although the majority of these single-issue campaigns occurred before I began my research and I have only limited second-hand knowledge of them. As this study is premised on the interconnectedness of language vitality and wider socioeconomic issues, I am reluctant to present an overly linguacentric view of resistance to austerity in the Gaeltacht. Due to space constraints, however, the following sections will focus largely on those campaigns that specifically aimed at maintaining language-focused supports, namely *Guth na Gaeltachta* and *Dearg le Fearg*. I also discuss campaigns regarding transport links for the Árann and Toraigh islands in which I was a participant-observer. While not explicitly linked to recession-induced austerity, such developments are intimately connected to the public procurement regulations of the EU, which, as Kunzlik (2013) demonstrates, are themselves deeply neoliberal, and as such are worthy of attention.

11.2 Guth na Gaeltachta

The *Guth na Gaeltachta* [Voice of the Gaeltacht] group, active 2009–2013, was founded in Donegal in response to the recommendations of An Bord Snip Nua, which proposed extremely severe cuts to Gaeltacht funding (see 3.2). Guth na Gaeltachta explicitly aimed to resist these recommendations, although it also campaigned on the position of the language in the education system and other language-related issues.

The group drew attention to the severity of An Bord Snip Nua's recommendations regarding the Gaeltacht, regularly appearing in the Irish-language media and organising information stalls and meetings in Donegal, Galway and Dublin (although not, to my knowledge, anywhere in Munster). In co-operation with Conradh na Gaeilge, they organised a series of lobbying days which were attended by several dozen politicians and explained the implications of the proposals to abolish ÚnaG, the department responsible for the Gaeltacht and related measures discussed in Chapter 3.

Several of my interviewees spoke of Guth na Gaeltachta with great enthusiasm, as seen in the following extract:

> L: *Bhí tábhacht millteanach ag baint leo [. . .] Ba feachtas ar dóigh a bhí ann, feachtas trasphobail, tras-pháirtí, ní raibh baint ar bith ag páirtithe polaitíochta ann. Ón bhun aníos a tháinig sé [. . .] Fiú cuid de na cruinnithe a raibh mé aige [. . .] bhí scaifte istigh agus bhí fiú atmaisféar, bhí sé go maith don spiorad, don t-anam, don duine féin a bheith i do shuí istigh in seomra. Agus in amantaí bhí díospóireacht te teasaí ag dul ar aghaidh agus bhí daoine ag tabhairt amach, ach é sin ar leataobh bhí sé go maith díreach go raibh comhluadar ann agus daoine ann agus an fhís chomónta seo acu. Agus bhí daoine ag ráit, bhuel, tá muid anseo le chéile, y'know ar scáth a chéile a mhaireann na daoine.*
>
> [L: They were extremely important [. . .] It was a great campaign, a cross-community, cross-party campaign, it had nothing to do with political parties. It came from the grassroots [. . .] Even the meetings I attended [. . .] there was a big crowd and even an atmosphere, it was good for the spirit, for the soul, for the person themselves to be sat in the room. And sometimes there was a heated, tense debate taking place and people were arguing, but that aside it was good just that there was community and people with this common vision. And people were saying, well, here we are together, y'know, united we stand.]

The group was thus clearly a valuable development for the Gaeltacht during a very difficult time. As with the *Dearg le Fearg* movement discussed in the following section and the state-funded language organisations, in their anxiousness to declare themselves a "non-political campaign" to avoid the influence of party politics, Guth na Gaeltachta eschewed links with comparable grassroots organisations which could have aided in building a broad-based campaign of resistance to austerity in general. This sectionalism is typical of other areas of civil society in Ireland, with there being few instances of groups that attempted to draw links between the multitude of single-issue campaigns each expressing their individual grievances (Allen and O'Boyle 2013: 128). One former participant explained his frustration with this position as follows:

> M: Chreid mé go mór i nGuth na Gaeltachta [. . .] Ach [. . .] thóg mise an rud gur chóir do Ghuth na Gaeltachta [. . .] a bheith páirteach sa rud níos leithne in éadan cúrsaí déine [. . .] Bhí mórshiúl mór i Sligeach [. . .] Agus ag an chruinniú dúirt mé gur chóir go mbeadh ionadaí ó Ghuth na Gaeltachta i láthair ag an mhórshiúil. Agus dúirt siad 'ó no, no, níl baint aige sin leis an Ghaeltacht, níl baint aige sin leis an Ghaeilg'. Agus dúirt mé no but tá baint aige le...Y'know tá lucht na Gaeilge iontach maith ag rá caithfidh daoine seasamh linn, agus aontaím leo, ba chóir go seasfadh daoine leis an teanga, ach nuair nach bhfuil lucht na teangan sásta seasamh le daoine eile, then tuigim do na daoine eile fosta: 'caidé a rinn lucht na Gaeilg dúinn?'

> [M: I really believed in Guth na Gaeltachta [. . .] But [. . .] I raised the point that Guth na Gaeltachta should [. . .] be part of the wider thing against austerity [. . .] There was a big march in Sligo [. . .] And at a meeting I said that there should be a representative from Guth na Gaeltachta at the march. And they said 'oh no, no, that isn't to do with the Gaeltacht, it's not to do with Irish'. And I said no but it has to do with...Y'know Irish speakers are very good saying people have to stand with us, and I agree with them, people should stand with the language, but when the Irish-language community isn't willing to stand with other people, then I can understand them too: 'what did the Irish speakers ever do for us?']

As well as reflecting the general tendency towards the sectionalisation of social movements in Ireland, this reluctance to be seen as overtly political may result from the belief occasionally expressed by commentators that the politicisation of Irish (particularly in the North of Ireland) has been to its detriment. The fact that Guth na Gaeltachta began in Ulster, and in an area frequented by republicans seeking respite during the war ("the Troubles"), may have resulted in a heightened sensitivity to such beliefs.

Despite their sectional approach and very moderate tactics, Guth na Gaeltachta was nonetheless clearly seen as a threat by the state. Their first spokesperson, who was employed as a gardener in a national park which is under the management of a state body, received a letter from the department responsible for the Gaeltacht threatening him with dismissal from his job if he did not refrain from publicly criticising state policy. This threat proved effective, leading him to resign his role with the organisation. His successor too was similarly threatened into silence. As a well-informed interviewee in Galway who has long since been involved in Gaeltacht activism told me *"tá an chuma air gurb éard a tharla ná mar gheall go raibh an cheannasaíocht ag obair le Acadamh na hOllscolaíochta Gaeltachta more or less gur dúradh leob bígí ciúin, tá muid ag brath ar Roinn na Gaeltachta agus ar Údarás na Gaeltachta ar airgead so tá bhur bpostanna i mbaol"* [it seems that what happened is that because the leadership were working for Acadamh na hOllscolaíochta Gaeltachta they were more or less told to be quiet, that they were depending on the Department for the Gaeltacht and on Údarás na Gaeltachta for money so your jobs are at risk].

Although these threats were reported in both English- and Irish-language national media (Gaelport.com 2012; Gaelscéal 2013: 2), they provoked no opposition from either the wider Irish-language or trade union movements. While perhaps somewhat hyperbolic in his sentiments, one of my interviewees observed that the small amount of attention this case received was not proportionate to its significance:

> M: *Léirigh sé sin cé chomh imeallach is atá an Ghaeilg agus ceist na Gaeltachta in saol polaitiúil na tíre [. . .] Dá dtarlódh sé sin in áit ar bith eile sa tír, bheadh na ceardchumainn, bheadh an eite chlé, bheadh na páipéirí lán le altannaí [. . .]* But tharla sé! D'éirigh sé as! *Agus an té a ceapadh mar urlabhraí ina dhiaidh, cé go ndearna sé é gan ainm, bagraíodh eisean a bhriseadh as a phost [. . .] Agus cuireadh deireadh le Guth na Gaeltachta.*
>
> [M: That showed how marginal Irish and the Gaeltacht are in the political life of the country. [. . .] If that happened elsewhere in the country, the trade unions, the left, the newspapers would be full of articles [. . .] But it happened! He resigned! And the person who was appointed as a successor after that, even though he did it anonymously, he was threatened with being fired [. . .] And an end was put to Guth na Gaeltachta.]

This lack of solidarity from the wider Irish-language movement highlights the apprehensiveness of the state-funded language organisations to take a confrontational position at a time when they too were facing extreme rationalisation measures (see 4.4), and ensured the state was easily able to control a key opposition movement in the Gaeltacht during the recession.

Such fearfulness of those with careers and incomes at risk is, of course, far from unique to the Irish-language sector. The precarious nature of the employment market and the "atypical" labour conditions that exist under neoliberalism (see 3.4), coupled with a social safety net which has been greatly reduced in recent years, make it much less likely that people will risk their livelihoods by challenging state policies (Grasso and Giugni 2016). Further to being fundamental to the emergence of nation-states and capitalism more generally (Thompson 1991), the suppression of dissent has been a central requirement of neoliberalism since its inception as a political project (Klein 2007), and was notably intensified post-2008 (Bruff 2016), including in the Gaeltacht and elsewhere in the Irish state.

The fact that many of those involved in Irish-language campaigning are employed by state-funded institutions made it particularly straightforward to limit Guth na Gaeltachta's efforts. While it is from the ranks of the middle classes often employed in the public sector that the impetus for language revitalisation has typically come (Wright 1996: 43), such individuals – teachers, for instance – are also easily silenced when their demands come into conflict with state policies. The fact that the implementation of neoliberal measures requires the suppression of dissent therefore sees it inflict a double blow on areas such as the Gaeltacht: it both weakens the supports on which peripheral communities so often depend and simultaneously punishes attempts to resist this attrition.

Containing as it did many individuals committed to the maintenance of the Gaeltacht as a distinct linguistic community, Guth na Gaeltachta may seem to fit the standard description of a post-materialist "new social movement" (Touraine 1981). Due to the state's economic support for the Gaeltacht, however, the group also included many participants who are materially dependent on the vitality of Irish in the Gaeltacht, including those who host attendees at Irish-language summer colleges or who teach Irish in third-level institutions. As such, Guth na Gaeltachta could perhaps more accurately be defined as a materialist, "survival" cause rather than one of "self-expression", to use Inglehart's well-known typology (1997).

As well as seeing issues that communities felt worth raising at the political level totally ignored, such a response from the state destroys the sort of community initiative and self-confidence that is essential for language revitalisation. This was evident in the opinions of several of my interviewees, who noted the general sense of disempowerment pervading their communities. Similarly, in 2018 a RnaG presenter prompted much discussion in the Irish-language media by claiming that the people of the Gaeltacht were utterly *"cloíte"* [defeated], accepting of every insult and disregard from the state (Tuairisc.ie 2018h). Although historical experiences of underdevelopment meant that Gaeltacht communities were probably already somewhat disempowered before the crash, as Cheshire and Lawrence (2005) and Harris (2014) have shown, neoliberalism, and the effects of recent austerity measures, have further disenfranchised groups that were historically marginalised. As with many issues described in this ethnography, disempowerment of Gaeltacht communities has multiple causes, with the recession having exacerbated previously existing tendencies. Such disempowerment, however, clearly links to the decline in community pride described in 8.5.2 and the wider trend towards social atomisation that has become so profound in recent years, a phenomenon itself due in no small part to austerity and the inequality that is a fundamental trait of neoliberalism (Lancee and Werfhorst 2012; Scharf 2015).

It is ironic that at the same time as the state was threatening members of Guth na Gaeltachta, an autonomous initiative to maintain Gaeltacht communities, the *Gaeltacht Act 2012*, which is predicated on voluntary community activism, was being enacted. As a former member of Guth na Gaeltachta told me:

> A: *An teachtaireacht atá muid ag fáil ná déanaigí na rudaí seo [leis an bpleanáil teanga] ach ná bígí ag súil le aon cheannasaíocht nó aon rud uainne. In fact, b'fhéidir gur bagairt a bhfaighfeá. Sin teachtaireacht iontach láidir mar léiríonn sé do dhaoine níl an stát dul a sheasamh leat. Tá sé deacair go leor bheith mar cheannasaí [. . .] teanga [. . .] 'Cause fiú sa Ghaeltacht ní hí an Ghaeilge an chloch is mó ar an phaidrín againn. So na daoine atá ag breathnú amach ar son na teanga [. . .] breathnaíonn daoine orainn mar cranks! [. . .] Cén incentive atá ann do ghrúpaí pobail, nó do dhaoine aonara seasamh suas don teanga?*
>
> [A: The message we're getting is do this stuff [with language planning] but don't expect any leadership or anything from us. In fact, maybe you'll get threatened. That's a very strong message as it shows people that the state isn't going to stand with you. It's hard enough to be a leader with regard to language [. . .] 'Cause even in the Gaeltacht Irish isn't our main concern. So people who are looking out for the language [. . .] people look at us as cranks! [. . .] What incentive are you giving to community groups, or to individuals to stand up for the language?]

The bitterness engendered by the suppression of Guth na Gaeltachta was clearly far from conducive to promoting the voluntarism the state claims to want, and which is necessary for language revitalisation, and is perhaps one further reason why an ÚnaG executive told me that recruiting volunteers has been one of the most challenging aspects of the language planning process described in section 3.4 above.

11.3 Dearg le Fearg

An important development in early 2014 was the emergence of the *Dearg le Fearg* [Red with Anger] movement. Organised primarily by the state-funded lobby group Conradh na Gaeilge, Dearg le Fearg began in response to the unexpected resignation of the Coimisinéir Teanga in protest at the state's inadequate implementation of the *Official Languages Act 2003* and the *20-Year Strategy for the Irish Language* (see Chapter 3 and section 6.2). After a series of large organisational meetings, the first of several marches, titled *Lá Mór na Gaeilge* [The big day of Irish], took place in Dublin in February 2014. With some 6,000 attendees, this was the first language-related march on this scale in almost a decade.

Being largely a product of the language movement outside the Gaeltacht, Dearg le Fearg at times struggled to ensure the participation of Gaeltacht residents, as described below. Nonetheless, a subsequent march which took place in the Galway Gaeltacht was the largest protest in any Gaeltacht area in many years, having some 1,000 attendees (Galway Advertiser 2014).

The Dublin march officially aimed to oppose the merger of the office of the Coimisinéir Teanga with that of the Ombudsman, but also served as an opportunity for those long since dissatisfied with state language policy to voice their frustration. The merger of these two offices, first proposed in 2011 as part of wider public service rationalisation measures (Department of Public Expenditure and Reform 2011 Appendix 2: 7; see also 6.2), ultimately did not take place, with a Seanad [senate] debate on the matter noting that it would not reduce expenditure, instead being likely to increase costs to the state (Seanad Éireann 2011: 8). In addition to the follow-up march in Galway, in the months following the Dublin protest a similar demonstration took place in Belfast, where the focus was on the demand for a language act for the North of Ireland.

Despite the obvious connection between this proposed merger and the public service reform that took place in response to the recession, it is notable that the Dearg le Fearg campaign did not link its demands to the wider economic context being experienced by the country at the time. In early 2014, while still an MA student, I attended the large day-long meeting organised by Conradh na Gaeilge at which the Dearg le Fearg march was first proposed. None of the invited speakers, nor any of the dozens of questions and comments from the floor made any connection between the recession or austerity, then still severe, and the plight of the language. Instead, as with the attitudes towards the use of Irish in the civil service discussed in 6.2, language policy reforms were framed as attacks on *Irish-qua-Irish*, the result of those in power allegedly being personally ill-disposed to the language. The Coimisinéir himself, however, did note during his resignation speech that his office was severely under-resourced and under-staffed, their budget having been cut by 45% since 2008 (Oireachtas Éireann 2013b).

One of my interviewees described the disconnect between the demands of the Irish-language movement and the issues facing Irish society more generally as follows: *"Na heagraíochtaí a roghnaíonn muid le hamharc i ndiaidh na Gaeltachta, is cuma leotha faoin chuid eile den tír. Agus is cuma leis an chuid eile den tír fán Ghaeltacht. Tá cineál symbiotic relationship ansin, tá siad ag déanamh neamhaird ar a chéile!"* [The organisations we choose to look after the Gaeltacht don't care about the rest of the country. And the rest of the country doesn't care about the Gaeltacht. There's a kind of symbiotic relationship there, they ignore each other!].

As with the case of Guth na Gaeltachta described above, the sectional, depoliticised analysis of the language movement highlights the degree to which Irish is understood as an individual, sectoral pursuit, not something to be fought for as part of a broader struggle to resist the individualisation of public goods. This apolitical approach is likely also connected to Conradh na Gaeilge's dependence on state funding, which ensures it will never be particularly confrontational, for fear of meeting a fate similar to that of groups like Pléaráca (see section 12.2).

Reminiscent of the lack of participation in the language planning process (see 3.4; 11.2), an employee of Conradh na Gaeilge from the Gaeltacht discussed at length with me the difficulties faced in mobilising people to attend the Dearg le Fearg marches. This difficulty was, she said, particularly pronounced in her home community in west Galway, with many seeing little need to protest for language rights:

Ú: *Mother of God, I think go raibh daoine ag iarraidh orainn goil thart, iad a thóigeáil ón leaba, an bricfeasta a réiteach dhótha, agus iad a chrochadh ar do dhroim ar feadh an mórshiúil. 'Cause bhí muid ag cur busanna saor in aisce ar fáil. Ba chuma linne cé mhéad busanna a bhí ann [. . .] Chuirfeadh muid imeachtaí ar siúil [le hairgead a bhailiú], but just faigh na daoine.*

[Ú: Mother of God, I think people wanted us to go around, take them out of bed, prepare breakfast for them, and carry them on your back for the whole march. 'Cause we were organising free buses. We didn't care how many buses were necessary [. . .] we'd organise fundraisers, but just get the people.]

The failure of the language movement to impress upon people the severity of the cuts, the extent of the language shift currently taking place or to promote the potential of language planning interventions to benefit Gaeltacht communities as *communities*, regardless of the language issue, was also obvious in her sentiments, which very much accord with my own experiences at the time:

Ú: *Níor thuig siad go raibh baint ar bith acu lena saol féin. Mar gheall bhí siad ag rá 'cén sórt cearta daonna? Tá muid ag labhairt na Gaeilge! Níl siad ag baint uainn an teanga' [. . .] [Ní ba dhéanaí sa mbliain] bhí duine de na mná tí ag tabhairt amach yeah faoin gcaoi nach bhfuil airgead dhá chaitheamh sna Gaeltachtaí [. . .] Agus like mar a deir [a máthair] 'bhuel nuair a bhí agai' a bheith ag an mórshiúil níor sheas sib". Agus 'sé an freagra ceart. Ach an freagra a thug sí ar ais ná 'sure níor thuig mé cén fáth a raibh sib' dhá dhéanamh'.*

[Ú: They didn't think it had anything to do with their own lives. Because they were saying 'what sort of human rights? We're speaking Irish! They're not taking the language from us!' [. . .] [Later that year] one of the women who hosts learners at summer colleges was complaining about money not being spent on the Gaeltacht [. . .] And like as [the interviewee's mother] said, 'well you didn't come on the march when you should have'. And it's the right answer. But the answer she gave back was 'sure I didn't know why ye were doing it'.]

This disjoint between the minority involved in language activism and the wider community of Irish speakers in the Gaeltacht is a fundamental challenge facing revitalisation efforts. As Fennell (1981a) argued, so long as the majority of the population of the Gaeltacht lacks a strong commitment to revitalisation, the best efforts of (often urbanite) language activists are likely to have little impact on the fate of the Gaeltacht. With Irish no longer being the unmarked vernacular of the vast majority of Gaeltacht communities (Ó Giollagáin and Charlton 2015a), there is certainly merit to this sentiment. While originally referring to the situation of the Gaeltacht in the 1970s, when applied in the present day Fennell's argument raises the greater question of what is preventing the development of such a commitment. As discussed in 3.4 and 6.4, the tendency of economic crises to shift people's concern from post-materialist issues such as language to the realm of material survival is well established in the sociological literature on both civic engagement and attitude formation (Putnam 2000: 189–203; Voicu Mochmann and Dülmer: 2016). Furthermore, as seen above, the tendency for crises in neoliberal states to often discourage participation in protest movements rather than radicalise populations into action is also well documented (Grasso and Giugni 2016).

Although the momentum behind Dearg le Fearg eventually petered out over the course of 2014, *An Dream Dearg,* the hugely vibrant campaign group which emerged in 2016 with the goal of securing a language act for the North of Ireland, has, nevertheless, taken some of its cues (at least in terms of branding) from the Dearg le Fearg campaign.

Assessing their impact retrospectively, many of my interviewees who attended the 2014 marches had rather lukewarm evaluations of their success: *"Níl's agam cé mhéad bus a bhí le goil go Bleá Cliath, agus go Béal Feirste tamallt ina dhiaidh. Caidé a tharla? Fuck all"* [I dunno how many buses went to Dublin, and to Belfast a while afterwards. What happened? Fuck all].

While not quite as negative, a Conradh na Gaeilge organiser also expressed mixed feelings regarding the marches:

> B: *Tá sé deacair a rá, I mean nuair a fheiceann tú an rud atá ag tarlú le Aer Árann [féach an chéad rannóg eile], caithfear ceist a chur. Cheapfainn go raibh éisteacht áiride ann [. . .] Fiú ó thaobh cheapachán an choimisinéara nua [. . .] d'fhéadfadh siad duine i bhfad níos laige a cheapadh, bhí ionadh orm go raibh ceapachán mar sin ann. So like, tá sé deacair a rá cén éisteacht a bhí ann.*

> [B: It's hard to say, I mean when you see what's happening with Aer Árann [see the following section], you have to wonder. I think there was some heed paid to us [. . .] Even with regards to the appointment of the new commissioner [. . .] they could have appointed someone much weaker; I was surprised that there was such an appointment. So it's hard to say how much they listened.]

A senior employee in the office of the Coimisinéir Teanga told me himself that Dearg le Fearg was an important development, which, while perhaps not making specific gains, at least helped raise the profile of their office and show the state the support they have from the Irish-speaking community:

> A: Chuidigh sé go mór le láidreacht na hoifige seo, go bhfuil tuiscint ann go bhfuil glór ag an oifig seo, go bhfuil lucht labhairt na Gaeilge ag éisteacht leis an méid atá an oifig seo ag rá, agus go bhfuil tuiscint ag an oifig seo ar céard atá ag teastáil [. . .] Sílim go bhfuil tuiscint in áiteachaí eile air sin anois.

> [A: It helped a lot with the strength of this office, there's an understanding that this office has a voice, that Irish speakers are listening to what this office says, and that this office understands what is necessary [. . .] I think there is an understanding of that in certain places now.]

Despite this, since his appointment a great many of the second Coimisinéir's statements have echoed those of his predecessor, with him frequently claiming that his office is being systematically disregarded and undermined (see 6.2).

While its results were far from decisive, then, and although such small marches in isolation are easily ignored by the state, Dearg le Fearg was still a high point for the language movement during the period discussed in this study. Indeed, the intervening years have seen calls by activists for such protests to be repeated (Tuairisc.ie 2018i), something which has yet to occur.

11.4 Reform of island transport links

Due to the historical progression of English from core to periphery, those islands with Gaeltacht status are generally amongst the strongest remaining Irish-speaking communities. The disruptions to life on several such islands caused by reforms proposed in recent years were therefore most unwelcome developments which were unconducive to the maintenance of these core Gaeltacht communities.

11.4.1 The Oileáin Árann air service

Amongst these proposals was the suggested discontinuation of the aeroplane service which flies several times daily from Conamara to each of the three Oileáin Árann. Unsurprisingly, this proposal was opposed by a sustained community campaign when it was first made public in summer 2015. Despite this service being in place since 1970, the outcome of the department responsible for the Gaeltacht's call for tender in 2015 sought to change this long-established arrangement. The department intended to replace the aeroplane service from Conamara with a helicopter route that would depart from the other side of Galway city, thereby making it very difficult – if not impossible – for people to get the boat in the event of inclement weather preventing flying, as happens on occasion.

Protesting this decision, a large public meeting with several hundred attendees took place in September 2015 in Conamara, followed by a march to the nearby Department of Arts, Heritage, Regional, Rural and Gaeltacht Affairs' office. This action was followed in the following weeks and months by various pickets, lobbying trips to Dublin, etc. Receiving support from all local opposition politicians, the campaign has to date been successful in maintaining the existing air service, although, similar to the issues discussed in 4.4 and 12.1, resisting such proposals detracts significantly from the work that community development groups are meant to be engaged in.

Publicly, the Department's decision to not renew the contract of the airline that has been serving the islands for many years was stated to be the outcome of fair competition in the call for tender (Department of Arts, Heritage and the Gaeltacht 2015). Several of my informants, however, claimed that the proposed helicopter provision was simply a step towards cutting all air provision for the islands by stealth. A number of interviewees contended that by offering such an unsuitable and undesired helicopter service, which was likely to be a commercial failure, it would ultimately be easier in coming years for the state to discontinue all air provision for these islands, which are exceptional amongst Irish islands in having a regular air service. One employee of the Irish-language sector who was involved in the community's protests explained this logic to me as follows:

> B: Sin é mo thuairimse hréis a bheith ag caint le lucht an oileáin inné, le roinnt insiders, le Ó Cuív [iarAire Gaeltachta] agus na polaiteoirí ar fad [. . .] Tuigeann siadsan [. . .] gur sábhailt airgid é. 'Cause is cuimhin liom [. . .] ag plé le Michael Ring [Aire Spóirt agus Turasóireachta na linne] agus bhí seisean ag rá go macánta liom 'I said to Dinny [McGinley, iarAire Gaeltachta eile] just do it, take one big hit and that's it, it'll be forgotten about then'. So sin an t-aon feckin dearcadh atá acu, one big hit, it'll be off your plate. Ba chuma faoin fuckin dochar a bhí á dhéanamh, ba chuma faoi na hoileáin. Just breathnaigh: that'll save you money.

> [B: That's my opinion after talking to the islanders yesterday, to some insiders, to Ó Cuív [former minister for the Gaeltacht] and all the politicians [. . .] They understand [. . .] that it's about saving money. 'Cause I remember [. . .] talking to Michael Ring [then Sport and Tourism minister] and he was saying honestly to me 'I said to Dinny [McGinley, then minister for the Gaeltacht] just do it, take one big hit and that's it, it'll be forgotten about then'. So that's their only concern – one big hit, it'll be off your plate. It didn't matter about the fuckin damage that was being done, it didn't matter about the islands. Just look: that'll save you money.]

In an interview with an employee of the company which provides the current air service, he talked at length about the difficulties of working with civil servants who were, by his account, simply not interested in finding a solution to this controversy: *"Tá siad ag ceapadh gur cur amú airgid é. Muintir Árann, tá an iomarca faighte acub cheana agus bíonn siad ag gearán i gcónaí and to hell with them and that's it"* [They think it's a waste of money. The people of Árann, they've gotten too much already, they're always complaining and to hell with them and that's it].

This is one of very few examples in my data where several interviewees explicitly claimed that there was a covert policy agenda which was linked to budgetary constrictions. When compared to the Toraigh case discussed in the following section, it is very possible that if not for the huge amount of tourism to these islands, which gives their populations a certain amount of sway at the political level, that the service would already have been removed.

The 2015 protests were ultimately successful in getting the government to abandon the proposed helicopter service. Although local opposition was clearly important, it must also be noted that during the public commotion over the new helicopter route, department officials responsible for the decision became aware that Galway County Council intended to close the airport from which the helicopter was to run just six months after the service began. This fact was not, apparently, factored into the original decision to grant the tender to the company proposing to run its service therefrom (Irish Times 2015a).

While these protests were an important success story for community mobilisation against state policy, resistance to the restructuring of the air service in Galway remained a highly localised issue. Similar to the Dearg le Fearg movement described above, at no point that I am aware of in any of the public discourse on the issue – either at public meetings, rallies, or in the media – was the matter explicitly linked to wider issues surrounding reduced state support for the Gaeltacht.

Although aeroplane services continued throughout 2016–2017, in mid-2018 Aer Árann, the company running the service, announced it was intending to surrender its contract and discontinue services at the end of the year. They claimed this was due to their dissatisfaction with the excessive fees which are being imposed on them by the department responsible for the Gaeltacht (RTÉ 2018c). Although a last-minute compromise was eventually reached which saw services continue (Tuairisc.ie, 2018j), in 2019 the minister responsible for the Gaeltacht announced that the state was still considering replacing the aeroplane service with a helicopter one (Dáil Éireann 2019), although this had not been further pursued by the time of writing.

The potential loss of the aeroplane service takes on even greater significance when one considers that in early December 2016 the ferry service to one of these islands was almost discontinued until March, due to the County Council having demanded a significant increase in the fee they charged the ferry company to land on the island (Tuairisc.ie 2016j). While the County Council was adamant that the fee previously being charged was too low, it is easy to see this proposed change as an attempt by the Council to increase their own revenue in the face of the severe cutbacks they too faced (see 6.2). As a community co-operative manager said to me when talking about the Council: *"Jesus, bheifeá ag tarraingt amach do ghruaig ag plé leotha sin! 'Níl muid ábalta seo a dhéanamh, níl airgead ar bith againn, níl airgead ar bith againn, níl airgead ar bith againn'* [Jesus, you'd be pulling out your hair dealing with them! 'We can't do this, we have no money, we have no money, we have no money'].

While it is hard to imagine that it could come to pass that islanders would ever be left stranded for even a short time for want of either sea or air services, such events nonetheless illustrate some of the difficulties faced by island communities in recent years.

11.4.2 The Toraigh ferry service

The reform of the ferry service to Oileán Thoraí in Donegal in 2018 provides another striking example of community wishes being ignored, and the damage caused when this happens. Despite the islanders frequently complaining before 2018 that their ferry was too old and unfit for purpose, tender for this service was granted to a company proposing to use an even older and less suitable boat, with the authorities apparently feeling that it was more important to demonstrate a commitment to free market competition processes than to ensure the maintenance of island communities.

In response to this, a well-supported protest in Dublin was organised, as were two smaller ones in Galway (one in the city and one in Conamara where an office of the department responsible for the Gaeltacht is located). Several families also stated publicly that the imposition of this unsuitable service would prompt them to leave the island. Nonetheless, despite very few being happy about the proposal, a significant portion of the island felt that their best option was to accept the service being offered, likely for want of any better alternative. This led to a deep split in the community and much animosity. Indeed, an outside mediator was eventually brought in to help alleviate tensions, although the degree to which this was successful is far from clear. While a community vote ultimately chose to accept the service being offered, the result of

112 votes in favour versus 102 in opposition illustrates the degree to which the population was divided (Tuairisc.ie 2018k). All this amounts, of course, to a severe blow for an island which has the highest rate of Irish speaking of any Language Planning Area in Donegal, albeit a community that had seen a 17.4% decline in its population between 2011–2016 (see 7.2.1).

Freedom of Information requests by news site Tuairisc.ie showed that although the *National Development Plan*, which was launched at the time of this controversy, included a commitment to build a new ferry for the island sometime before 2027 (Government of Ireland 2018b: 51), this was added just days before the plan's publication, seemingly in response to protests which were ongoing at the time. Furthermore, the Department of Public Expenditure agreed to the inclusion of this point "on the strict understanding that the costs are met from within your Department's stated allocation", with no additional funding to be made available for the building of such a vessel (Tuairisc.ie 2018l). In light of the greatly reduced budget the department responsible for the Gaeltacht has, as was discussed in Chapter 4, it seems unlikely that they will be able to meet the required costs during the lifetime of this plan.

As with the funding for language plans being taken from the budget that had funded the maintenance of Gaeltacht roads (see 3.4), this case thus offers yet another illustration of the cynical attitude state institutions hold towards the provision of fundamental community infrastructure in the Gaeltacht. It also highlights the immense damage done to communities which bear the brunt of a neoliberal logic enforced on them by a state deeply reluctant to offer adequate support to such marginalised, deprived parts of the periphery.

11.5 "Corporate Social Responsibility" and the Gaeltacht – fighting neoliberalism with neoliberalism?

In addition to the oppositional movements detailed above, during my fieldwork I noted several instances of communities attempting to overcome the difficulties caused by decreased state subventions via recourse to unorthodox means, including turning to non-state actors and corporate sources of funding in order to finance important local infrastructure.

While staying in a Donegal community during my fieldwork I was enthusiastically told by several locals that a new pre-school was to be opened in a few months. Shortly after I left the area, an online crowdfunding campaign was started by the community co-operative to fund this initiative. Being in some ways a 21st century variation of the long-established tradition of getting financial and material aid from those who have emigrated, this effort could be seen as having significant cultural precedent. Traditionally, clothing packages were sent home by departed relatives, as were so-called "American letters" – which often included money to pay the emigration passage of younger relatives (Brody 1974: 84).

As opposed to aiding immediate family members, however, this crowdfunding campaign was attempting to finance important infrastructure for the whole community, a service which one would expect to have been eligible for state funding. Nonetheless, this approach clearly indicates that those who started the campaign have an awareness that it is, to a degree, up to themselves to seek out unconventional funding methods in order to finance such initiatives as a result of the greatly reduced budget for the Gaeltacht. It is also, I believe, indicative of the extent to which the neoliberal understanding of state functions has been internalised by these populations. Despite initially garnering attention on both social and traditional media, over six months after the campaign was launched only a little over a sixth of the target had been reached, €645 of a €3,000 goal.

Similarly, several schools have had to resort to asking parents to pay for the recruitment of an additional teacher to ensure that a new Gaeltacht education policy launched in 2016 can be effectively implemented, a process which has been made particularly challenging due to the cuts to staff numbers in small rural schools since 2008 (Tuairisc.ie 2017o).

An even more striking example of the neoliberalisation of the financing of public infrastructure occurred in summer 2015 in Inis Meáin in Co. Galway. A change in the Department of Education's policy regarding student-staff ratios – itself allowing for expenditure on rural schools to be cut (Irish Times 2011b) – left Inis Meáin's school, with under twenty pupils, no longer eligible for a second teacher. This decision led to a community campaign to have this second teacher re-instated, involving public meetings and lobbying efforts in Dublin (Irish Times 2015b). The issue was ultimately resolved when Zurich Insurance Group, which as of 2017 was the 127th largest company in the world (Forbes 2017), committed to funding the second teacher's position for two years. As part of their "investing in communities" programme, Zurich claimed they were anxious to fund the school due to the fact that "Inis Meáin is a stronghold of the Irish language. The language, and the very sustainability of the island, is under threat if families there cannot avail of a good level of education for their children" (Irish Times 2015b). In light of their involvement in the hedge fund scandals (Reuters 2007) that ultimately helped precipitate the global crash which led the Irish state to cut funding for small rural schools, it is not without irony that Zurich have seized on the Inis Meáin case as a way to bolster their image. Indeed, one newspaper at the time described them as a "white knight" riding in to save the Gaeltacht (Connacht Tribune 2015). Fortunately, however, an increase in pupil numbers after this two-year period of funding was concluded saw the Department of Education concede to funding the second teacher's position once more.

Similarly, in a language school in Galway I heard conversations in which management discussed applying for grants from corporations such as Google under their corporate social responsibility schemes. While there was also discussion of applying for support from ÚnaG, it was observed that the cuts meant they had very little left to give to small businesses.

The fact that corporate and other unorthodox funding was being discussed so widely illustrates not only the extent of the cutbacks but also the success with which neoliberalism has framed the concerns of such peripheral communities as an issue for charitable schemes by corporations seeking good publicity, rather than the responsibility of the state which governs these areas. While there is undoubtedly potential for short-term gain for Gaeltacht communities by adopting such strategies, as Watson has observed, it is the policy legacy of the earlier protectionist and liberal eras (c. 1922–1985) that continues to support Irish. The neoliberal era that has emerged since the late 1980s, on the other hand, has seen this support steadily dismantled (Watson 2016: 71). As such, by engaging with the neoliberal project on its own terms and conceding, perhaps, that it is not necessarily the responsibility of the state to provide important community infrastructure, minority language communities potentially sow the seeds of their own destruction. Through such actions, the neoliberal vision of society gradually becomes normalised on a micro-level, with states largely absolved of their previously existing responsibilities to the periphery.

11.6 Conclusion

Austerity negatively affected Irish society to an enormous degree, and as such significant popular resistance was almost inevitable in response. While this was not as militant as elsewhere in the world, as has been seen, common narratives popular in the media during the worst years of austerity about Irish people's supposedly innate aversion to protest are simplistic and misleading. Despite the individualism that is so central to neoliberalism creating a popular understanding of poverty and other hardships that centres personal rather than structural forces, even this can be challenged when movements have the time and space to develop, as groups like Guth na Gaeltachta and Dearg le Fearg evidence in Irish-speaking Ireland.

Nonetheless, movements connected to Irish and the Gaeltacht remained sectional and avoided making links with comparable groups from anglophone Irish society, which likely limited their efficacy, as well as the ability of the broader anti-austerity movement to challenge the ideological rationale for the cuts. As well as echoing the "divided and conquered" nature of the official language groups discussed in 4.4, this sectionalism further highlights the degree to which Irish has been depoliticised, seen as unconnected to other issues of social justice or inequality.

Of course, a central duty of the state is ensuring that resistance movements do not threaten the status quo – something which is all the more pressing in a time of crisis – and the most significant of the movements relevant to this work, Guth na Gaeltachta, was therefore repressed. In addition to neoliberalism creating precarious employment conditions which are often inconducive to people getting involved in opposition movements (see 6.4), those who have some level of material security are often employed in the public sector, and they are therefore relatively easy to threaten into inaction should they challenge the state, as the Guth na Gaeltachta case highlights.

The disruptions faced by various island communities in both Galway and Donegal regarding the degradation of transport links further highlights the disregard the Irish competition state has for the development of community infrastructure in the periphery. These developments were likely part of the reason – in addition to all that has been discussed previously – for the various instances I saw of communities attempting to secure alternate forms of funding to finance infrastructure, including "Corporate Social Responsibility" grants and crowdfunding campaigns – a striking illustration of the internalising of neoliberal approaches to rural development.

The two case studies presented in the following chapter continue the discussion begun above, examining in detail how austerity affected community co-operatives and the *Pléaráca* group, which was also, seemingly, targeted for cuts due to it challenging state policy and dominant narratives at a time when the state was intent on forcing through deeply unpopular policies.

12 Cuts to other community projects

Further to those already discussed, many other Gaeltacht support structures were also heavily rationalised in the wake of the 2008 crash. While the full extent of state withdrawal of such provisions is too great to cover systematically in a work of this length, two detailed case studies that are worthy of attention and illustrative of wider patterns are discussed in this chapter – those of community development co-operatives and the arts and culture group *Pléaráca*. As will be seen, the reduction in official support for each of these has damaged the social vitality of the communities they serve and also weakened the strength of Irish in the Gaeltacht in very direct ways.

12.1 Community co-operatives

Having first emerged in the 1960s and 70s as a grassroots reaction to the failure of state-sponsored efforts at Gaeltacht development (Breathnach 1986: 80), community co-operatives (hereafter "co-ops") have since become central to the socioeconomic life of many Gaeltacht communities. Serving primarily as local development agencies, co-ops typically oversee services such as waste collection, day care centres for the elderly, pre-school groups, employment schemes, etc. In most cases it is to the local co-op that responsibility for the language planning process required by the *Gaeltacht Act 2012* has been delegated, with them overseeing the voluntary committees described in 3.4. While initially financed by subscriptions from local households, the co-ops are now funded by the state through ÚnaG. Co-ops are widely understood to be very important for life in the Gaeltacht, with one informant stating simply that *"tá siad uafásach, uafásach lárnach i bhforbairt pobail agus forbairt eacnamaíochta"* [they are extremely, extremely central to community and economic development].

Referring to the problematic nature of employment based on Foreign Direct Investment, which typically leaves the Gaeltacht once an end comes to ÚnaG-supplied grants (see 8.4), another interviewee commented on the value for money co-ops present to the state, with them being certain not to re-locate overseas in search of cheaper labour: *"Dá n-éireodh le trian de na comharchumainn, gheobhadh siad luach a gcaiteachais"* [If a third of co-ops succeeded, they'd get value for their money].

Although ostensibly based on local democratic empowerment, I repeatedly heard that only a small number of people play an active role in these co-ops:

> R: Má théann tú ag an gcruinniú cinn bhliana ní bheidh ann ach b'fhéidir deichniúr, cúig-, cúig dhuine dhéag, mar sin níl sé [. . .] mar ba mhaith leat é a bheith [. . .] D'fhéadfá a rá gur eagraíocht de chuid an státa atá ann agus atá coinnithe ag imeacht ag airgead an státa agus, agus gur ó, gurb shin é an dearcadh atá ag daoine.
>
> [R: When you go to the AGM there'll only be ten or fifteen people, so it's not [. . .] like you would want it to be [. . .] You could say it's a state organisation and it's financed by state money and, and that's the attitude people have.]

As well as echoing common discourses around the problematic nature of the professionalization of what were previously voluntary sectors, this lack of significant community co-operation with so many co-ops is reflective of the wider breakdown of civic engagement in post-industrial western societies over recent decades (see 3.4; Chapter 11). Similar to language planning committees, it appears that this tendency has also affected Gaeltacht co-ops. With the state now funding full-time employees, other community members seemingly feel they no longer have a personal duty towards these institutions, and that all related work should be done by those supposedly paid to do it – a particularly problematic situation in light of the cutbacks to staff funding described below.

In interviews with the managers of co-ops in Galway and Donegal, they commented at length about the severity of the cutbacks to their budgets. These budgets are provided by ÚnaG, which passed the major cuts it received on to the co-ops in the form of a 40% cut to their funding.

Despite facing such significant cuts, in both Galway and Donegal I was told that rather than discontinuing essential services, this reduction in funding was absorbed on a personal basis by staff members – foregoing holidays, working an unpaid day every week, etc.:

> C: Chuir sé an-bhrú orm féin, like I mean ní bhínn ag tógáil saoire nó tada, níor thóg mé saoire le blianta [. . .] An duine a thiocfas i mo dhiaidh ní bheidheadar ag iarraidh an saol sin agus beidh an ceart acu [. . .] Fiú ann bliain amháin [. . .] bhí mé sásta pá le ceithre lá agus ansin lá saor a dhéanamh don chomharchumann [. . .] mar tá an comharchumann fiorthábhachtach don [phobal].
>
> [C: It really put a lot of pressure on me, like I mean I didn't used to take holidays or anything, I haven't taken a holiday in years [. . .] The person who comes after me won't want that life and they'll be right [. . .] Even one year [. . .] I was willing to [receive] four days' pay and then do a free day for the co-op [. . .] because the co-op is vital for the community.]

The manager in Donegal told me of a similar experience, having taken significant cuts to her own salary in order to save money for other key services. While certainly a very altruistic responses to the crisis, this personal absorption of the cutbacks is perhaps partly a pragmatic response to life in small communities.

Rather than turning the community against them due to the collapse of vital services that are under their direction, these managers may have simply found it easier to accept such personal tribulations as the price of satisfying their communities.

Beyond the negative effects for local socioeconomic development, cuts to staffing in co-ops very directly weaken the standing of Irish in these communities. Unlike the majority of state-supported employment in the Gaeltacht (see 8.4), co-ops in stronger Gaeltacht areas provide a professional environment in which Irish is the default language, and as such they play a very important role in ensuring the dominance of the language in domains beyond the home and educational contexts.

The worsening of conditions in the sector makes what was traditionally one of the better paid and more stable jobs in many Gaeltacht communities much less appealing to those who might otherwise be interested in working in this area. Somewhat unsurprisingly, shortly after our interview, the co-op manager who I interviewed on an island in Donegal resigned to take up work unrelated to the Gaeltacht. Although a replacement has now been found, this process took some time and there was less interest in the position than might once have been expected. Indeed, despite unemployment being the main issue raised by locals when asked about the challenges of island life, when the manager's position was eventually filled it was by someone from the mainland.

As well as the financial difficulties of continuing to fund important services on a day-to-day basis despite budget cuts, I was also told that these austerity measures have impinged on the time that co-ops have to focus on local development. While quite possibly only ever announced as part of a project of political "kite-flying" to make the cuts that were implemented seem more reasonable, the proposed discontinuation of many other services in these communities has meant that a great deal of staff time was spent trying to resist even more severe cuts (see also 4.4):

> C: Bhí mé ar nós fear tine [. . .] Chuile chruinniú a bhí mé ag goil bhí mé ag iarraidh an tine seo a mhúchadh seachas ag déanamh forbairt pobail [. . .] Bhí go leor den bhliain seo caite ag goil ag cruinneachaí, troid, troid, troid, mar a bhíonn tú, ag rá le daoine, 'y'know, tá sé goil an-dochar a dhéanamh don [phobal] má leanann sibh ar aghaidh leis seo' [. . .] Dá gcuirfeadh sé aon rud i gcoinne dream óg a bheith ag maireachtáil [anseo]...

> [C: I was like a firefighter [. . .] Every meeting I was going to I was trying to put out this fire instead of doing community development [. . .] A lot of last year was spent going to meetings, fighting, fighting, fighting, as you do, saying to people, 'y'know, this is going to do awful damage to [the community] if you continue with this' [. . .] If it did anything to stop young people being able to stay [here]...]

Further to the co-ops' role in providing critical local infrastructure, the delegation of much of the language planning duties in the *Gaeltacht Act 2012* to such groups has seen them receive a very significant extra duty. As with the other institutions charged with implementing this Act (see 3.4), in apparent indifference to the already overworked and under-resourced nature of the co-ops, this duty has been imposed on them at the same time as their budgets were substantially reduced.

By 2016, the average budget a Gaeltacht co-op received was €54,000, significantly lower than the €85,000 average received by comparable Community Development Programmes outside the Gaeltacht. An umbrella group representing the co-ops consequently demanded total funding be increased by €600,000 in the 2018 budget (CCCP 2017). Despite the department responsible for the Gaeltacht also requesting significantly increased funding for the co-ops (Tuairisc.ie 2018c), in 2018 the minister responsible for Gaeltacht policy confirmed during Dáil questions that the funding increase for 2018 was just €100,000. When divided amongst all 32 Gaeltacht co-ops, the average budget increase was therefore just €3,125 – a meagre amount compared to the extent of the cuts received since the recession began (Dáil Éireann 2018b).

12.2 Pléaráca

Conamara-based Pléaráca began as a voluntary initiative in the early 1990s, receiving state funding in 1996 which allowed for the employment of two full-time staff. While primarily an arts and culture group, Pléaráca also explicitly aimed to combat social exclusion and the above-average levels of deprivation prevalent in much of the Conamara Gaeltacht (see 7.2.3). As well as providing opportunities for adults likely to be socioeconomically disadvantaged, Pléaráca conducted a wide range of youth outreach work, including summer camps, book festivals, drama and writing workshops, and generally played an important part in the social life of the Galway Gaeltacht (Tuairisc.ie 2015b). For many years the group organised a festival of "sean nós singing, dancing, poetry readings, plays, community art, and sporting and children's activities" which was held in September "when all the tourists are gone . . . [as] a celebration of selfhood, of personal and community identity, and not [as] a contrived pseudo-cultural show put on to satisfy the tourist gaze" (Denvir 2002: 40). Furthermore, "[a] festival such as Pléaráca illustrates that the Gaeltacht has not (or not yet, at least) gone the moribund touristic route of the staged folkloric or pseudo-traditional event" (Denvir 2002: 40). While primarily based in Conamara, Pléaráca regularly toured many of their events to other Gaeltacht areas, and indeed, to Wales and the *Gàidhealtachd* islands of Scotland as well.

Many of my informants in Galway spoke very fondly of Pléaráca, often commenting on its importance to the community as a whole. The following quote from a woman in her early thirties is typical of such accounts:

> G: Bhíodh an Pléaráca ag tíocht ag an scoil, bhíodh muid ag déanamh comórtais ealaíona, comórtais filíochta [. . .] Bhí an oiread deiseannaí a'ainn [. . .] Agus an rud a thaitnigh liomsa faoi sin, Pléaráca, mar shampla, bhí idir shean agus óg páirteach ann [. . .] Is cuimhneach liom go raibh ceolchoirm acub ar an gCeathrú Rua. Bhí mise óg go maith, rud ollmhór. Tháinig daoine as chuile áit [. . .] Thóg sé an pobal uilig le chéile [. . .] Cineál Glastonbury na Gaeltachta!

> [G: Pléaráca used to come to the school, we used to have art competitions, poetry competitions [. . .] We had so many opportunities [. . .] And the thing I liked about that, Pléaráca, for example, both young and old were involved [. . .] I remember they had a concert in An Cheathrú Rua. I was pretty young, a huge thing. People came from everywhere [. . .] It brought the whole community together [. . .] Like the Gaeltacht Glastonbury!]

The organisation, then, was clearly of great importance to the vitality of the Gaeltacht in Galway, with there being obvious positive linguistic implications to bringing the generations together, as described by this interviewee, as well as great social value in their work reaching out to the most underprivileged members of the community. Like a great number of the "community sector" groups involved in fighting social exclusion (Bisset 2015), however, Pléaráca had its funding drastically reduced post-2008.

Amongst the recommendations of An Bord Snip Nua was the proposal to save €44 million by cutting both the *Local Development Social Inclusion Programme* and the *Community Development Programme*, the schemes which funded groups such as Pléaráca. Noting that "these programmes aim to counter disadvantage [with] projects funded includ[ing] adult education courses, support for local enterprise initiatives and information provision for target groups", An Bord Snip Nua claimed that "[t]here is little evidence of positive outcomes for these initiatives" and as such they could be cut with minimal adverse effect (McCarthy et al. 2009b: 38; see also section 3.2).

With their funding severely reduced, Pléaráca's directors took the decision in April 2015 to disband the organisation rather than continue in a substandard fashion, stating that their decreased budget meant that the organisation's continued existence was no longer tenable (RnaG 2015).

As with the discontinuation of other community development projects throughout the country (Bisset 2015), the liquidation of Pléaráca has had a detrimental effect on the community, as a parent of two young adults brought up during the organisation's heyday described: *"Tá bearna an-mhór fágtha, tá. An bearna is measa ar fad atá fágtha [. . .] ná sna scoileanna [. . .] Bhíodar ag déanamh an-obair ar fad agus tá sé sin ar fad imithe. Tá an fhéile imithe, tá rudaí eile imithe freisin"* [There's a huge gap left, there is. The worst gap is [. . .] in the schools [. . .] They used to do great work altogether and it's all gone. The festival is gone, other things are gone too].

Further to being engaged in such important development of young people's linguistic repertoires, the multiplier effect of groups such as Pléaráca for local businesses was noted by another Conamara resident:

> A: Tá an infreastruchtúr pobal bainte óna chéile [. . .] Cuid mhaith den infreastruchtúr sin bhí rudaí eile crochta air. So abair na heagraíochtaí cosúil le MFG [Meitheal Forbartha na Gaeltachta], Cumas, Pléaráca – ní hamháin go raibh siad ag comhlíonadh na ndualgais a bhain leis an scéim áirithe a bhí siad ag fáil maoiniú uaidh, ach bhíodar ag cur isteach ar scéimeanna eile agus ag déanamh [. . .] tograí a bhí ag fostú daoine eile agus bhí airgead ag goil thart sa bpobal. Bhí sé ag coinneáil siopaí oscailte.

> [A: The community infrastructure has been dismantled [. . .] Other things were dependent on a lot of that infrastructure. So, say the organisations like MFG [Meitheal Forbartha na Gaeltachta, the Gaeltacht development working group], Cumas, Pléaráca – not only were they fulfilling the duties of the specific scheme they were being funded by, but they were applying for other schemes and doing other [. . .] projects that were employing people and money was going around in the community. It was keeping shops open.]

One of my other informants, who himself was involved in founding Pléaráca, contended that the creation of an unfavourable environment for such groups was a result of the then government being anti-community empowerment, rather than being connected to budgetary restrictions:

> S: Rinne an rialtas sin scrios ar an earnáil dheonach [. . .] Ní bhaineann sé le airgead. Baineann sé le idé-eolaíocht mar bhí na dreamannaí seo róchriticiúil faoi pholasaí poiblí maidir le cúrsaí bochtanais i ndáiríre. Níor thaithnigh sé sin leis an rialtas [. . .] Agus rinne siad scrios i ndáiríre ar an earnáil [. . .] Ba chuid den brief a bhí [ag Pléaráca] ná déileáil le cúrsaí bochtanais agus social exclusion [. . .] Agus sa deireadh ní raibh siad sásta airgeadú a dhéanamh ar an rud [. . .] agus thit an rud as a chéile. Agus bhí sé sin ag déanamh go leor maitheas ó thaobh na Gaeilge [. . .] Ní dóigh liom gur thit sé sin as a chéile mar gheall ar chúrsaí airgeadais.

> [S: That government destroyed the voluntary sector [. . .] It's not to do with money. It's to do with ideology as really these groups were too critical of public policy with regards to poverty. The government didn't like that [. . .] And they destroyed that sector really [. . .] Part of [Pléaráca's] brief was to deal with poverty and social exclusion [. . .] And in the end they weren't willing to fund it [. . .] and it fell apart. And it was doing a lot of good for Irish [. . .] I don't think it fell apart because of money.]

This distinction between ideology and economics is overly simplistic, however: further to ignoring the significant financial savings resulting from cutting such programmes, this argument overlooks the fact that an allegiance to neoliberal economics and efforts to quash dissent and grassroots community empowerment are ultimately two sides of the same coin, as discussed in Chapter 11. A 2014 report on "government funding and social justice advocacy" (also referred to in 4.5 and 6.3) does, nonetheless, confirm the belief that the suppression of subversive voices was indeed a key factor in the cutting of funding for groups such as Pléaráca:

> there was a compelling body of evidence of the manner in which the state had suppressed or actively prohibited advocacy, crossing the border from inhibition to an element of deliberation. The prime example was the Community Development Programme [which funded Pléaráca], where detailed documentation and case studies pointed to dissent as the most convincing explanation for its closure [. . .] It was evident that some issues were especially sensitive, such as development, education, women, childcare and corruption, with examples of organizations that had spoken out of turn having to repay grants.
>
> (Harvey 2014: 4)

While ultimately tracing the origins of this approach to before the onset of the crisis, the report goes on to detail a great number of strategies that were adopted by the state post-2008 to silence oppositional groups, similar to the examples in the previous chapter. As discussed above, in times of crisis the suppression of organised dissent is particularly crucial to the maintenance of the status quo, and the dramatic restructuring of the community sector is just one more example of the way in which the state used the 2008 crash as an opportunity to remake Irish society by strengthening the hold of neoliberalism thereon. In doing so it has, as Bisset argues, "maintain[ed] the power and privilege of some while extending and deepening the suffering of others" (2015: 175; see also Mercille and Murphy 2015).

The informant who noted the link between Pléaráca's social justice work and its defunding went on to explain that such restructuring has led to a reduction of community ownership of other groups similar to Pléaráca:

> S: Le cuid mhaith de na heagraíochtaí seo tá siad bainte ar ais ón bpobal. Bhíodh siad [. . .] i bhfad níos pobalbhunaithe ná atá anois. Tá siad curtha faoin gComhairle Contae, agus tá córas coistí ag an gComhairle Contae atá ag breathnú daonlathach ach tá rud chomh bloody casta, fiú ann mise, abair, agus tá spéiseanna agamsa sna rudaí sin, ní thuigim fós cén chaoi a n-oibríonn sé! [. . .] Tá an oiread coistí anois éagsúil ag an gComhairle Contae agus tá na coistí sin mar buffer zone idir an Chomhairle Contae agus an pobal.

> [S: With a lot of these organisations they've been taken back from the community. They used to be [. . .] much more community-based than they are now. They're put under the charge of the County Council, and the County Council has a system of committees that looks democratic but is so bloody complicated, even me, say, and I'm interested in these things, I still don't understand how it works! [. . .] The council has so many different committees now and those committees are like a buffer zone between the County Council and the community.]

As described in 4.2 regarding the abolition of the ÚnaG election, this increasing of the democratic deficit and centralisation of power was a key method used by the state to manage the implementation of austerity. The removal of local level democratic accountability and the abolition of groups such as Pléaráca is thus readily interpreted as yet another example of the broader trend of neoliberalisation described throughout this work.

Fishman's sceptical attitude towards cultural festivals in which participants have such a good time that they forget afterwards that nothing much has changed in terms of the language's wider prospects is well known (1991: 91, 110, 398). As Fettes has explained, however, while surely insufficient in themselves, groups like Pléaráca and the events they organise are a key part of language revitalisation efforts, ensuring that the language is no longer "heard only at funerals" (1997: 315). By operating primarily in Conamara, Pléaráca also contributed significantly to the area's socioeconomic vitality, itself key to language maintenance. The group's dissolution, however, surely marked a low point for community vitality, and many of my informants hoped that a similar group will emerge in coming years. Like the case of the inner city Community Development Programmes described by Bisset, "in a community where educational equality is extreme, the removal of such infrastructure has significant consequences" for all age groups (2015: 177). Groups like Pléaráca, as the Irish Congress of Trade Unions' report on the rationalisation of the community sector described, "[b]uild social capital, active citizenship and participation in a democratic society" (B. Harvey 2012: 9) and as such their suppression provides yet another example of the detrimental consequences of austerity not just for the Gaeltacht, but for Irish society as a whole.

12.3 Conclusion

Striking as they at times appear, the issues described in this and previous chapters are only a microcosm of the enormous suffering caused by austerity since 2008. Although much of the literature on neoliberalism conceptualises it as the hollowing out of the state (cf. Weller, Bavis and Rhodes 1997), as has been seen, in reality its effects often amount to the hollowing out of society, with a great many of the social structures key to the vibrancy of Gaeltacht (and other) communities having been eroded considerably in recent years.

In *Reversing Language Shift* Fishman stated that "[f]ostering small-scale community life is difficult but crucial for RLS" (1991: 6). Many other well-known authors in the field have made similar statements, including Romaine's observation that "arguments in favor of doing something to reverse language death are ultimately about preserving and sustaining viable communities" (2006: 456; see also Crystal 2000: 154; Spolsky 2004: 8; Williams 2014: 243; etc.). As has been demonstrated, however, the Great Recession and the intensification of neoliberal policies that accompanied it had the exact opposite effect on the Gaeltacht, negatively impacting the "home-family-neighbourhood-community" nexus (Fishman 1991: 95) so key to language maintenance in a huge variety of ways, some of the most notable of which have been discussed in this and the preceding chapters. While explicitly language-focused revitalisation programmes were adversely affected since 2008, so too were many of the supports for the wider community vitality called for by Fishman, Romaine, et al., thereby presenting enormous challenges for sustaining Irish-speaking communities in the coming years.

Commenting on the difficulties of creating environments suitable for the maintenance of threatened languages such as Irish, Mufwene has observed that

> Linguists and language teachers have no control over the conditions that sustain a language, despite their expertise. That is, revitalization efforts should also address the nonlinguistic factors that produced the socioeconomic ecologies that are disadvantageous to the relevant languages. Just think how unproductive it would be if environmentalists only provided food to an endangered species while keeping it in the same deleterious ecosystem. (Mufwene 2017: e308)

Although greatly improved by being informed by the expertise of linguists of various types, as has been shown, language revitalisation policies (like so much of public policy) are ultimately subservient to the requirements of international capital. Part 3 of this work has so far explored how the tension between these interests and minoritised language promotion has recently played out in the Republic of Ireland, a country which is supposedly committed to revitalising its "first national language", but which has readily adapted itself to become a prototypical "competition state" which serves the needs of capital above those of its inhabitants (Kirby and Murphy 2011). It is hoped that by drawing attention to the mutually constitutive nature of the local and global factors affecting language vitality, I have helped provide evidence for the position expressed by Mufwene and others, and illustrated some of the causal mechanisms through which the neoliberal hegemony that is enacted by competition states impacts threatened language communities like the Gaeltacht.

The final chapter of this section offers some additional comments on language use, including ways in which language shift was visible during my fieldwork and some explanations for this which have not yet been discussed in detail.

13 Further observations on language use

13.1 Introduction

In addition to the material discussed thus far, during my fieldwork various other issues regarding language use arose that are also worthy of mention. As described in 1.3.3, detailed quantitative work published in recent years identifies the strongest remaining Irish-speaking areas where over 67% of the population speak Irish daily outside of the education system, and it was in such "category A" communities that this research was conducted (Ó Giollagáin et al. 2007a; Ó Giollagáin and Charlton 2015a). While previous quantitative studies offer important insights into language practices in the Gaeltacht, ethnographic research adds a further degree of granularity to our understanding, complementing statistical work with an additional level of epistemological "thickness".

The quantitative data (which cannot be directly referenced here due to ethical constraints requiring anonymity) show that in almost all the areas I studied over 50% of those aged 3–18 speak Irish daily outside the education system, which, from my own observations, does not seem implausible. Based on all my experiences, however, it is beyond doubt that it is overwhelmingly to their elders that children and teenagers speak Irish. Amongst themselves, English is clearly the socially dominant language (see also Ó Giollagáin et al. 2007a: 321–338). While several informants told me that at least some members of this age cohort speak Irish together in the absence of older people, throughout the entire duration of my fieldwork I did not see a single peer-to-peer interaction in Irish amongst the under-18 age group when they were not in the company of an older person. Coughlan's ethnographic work on Irish-medium education in the Gaeltacht does, however, document youth interactions through Irish in the absence of authority figures, although reports these to be the exception rather than the norm (Coughlan 2021).

In this chapter I present some additional data regarding language use, shift, and how this was perceived during my fieldwork by both those I interviewed and by myself. In doing so I hope to extend the discussion of how a macro-level change such as the economic disruption that followed 2008 acts as an *ultimate* cause which triggers or intensifies various additional *proximate* causes of language shift (cf. Gal 1979: 3; Kulick 1992: 8–9).

13.2 Language practices of young people: A family vignette

While Ó Giollagáin et al. described the dominance of English amongst young people in many category A areas in 2007, the data presented in this section would suggest that language shift has taken place very rapidly in the intervening years. In Galway I was fortunate enough to be able to interview three siblings in one family, all young adults, in whose home I was staying and whose comments on language use I quote throughout this section. While this data is clearly very limited and not automatically generalisable to wider contexts, it is nonetheless informative, especially considering, as noted below, the degree to which it aligns with other observations made during my fieldwork.

This first extract is from an interview with the oldest sibling, a 25-year-old woman who lives and works in a city away from the Gaeltacht, but returns periodically:

Údar: Céard faoin dream a bhí ar scoil leatsa, an labhrann sibh Gaeilge lena chéile nó an mbeadh níos mó Béarla ann?

S: Ó Gaeilge i gcónaí, yeah Gaeilge i gcónaí [. . .] Tá sé an-nádúrtha againn Gaeilge a labhairt lena chéile mar sin an chaoi a d'fhás muid suas.

[Author: What about those who were at school with you, do ye speak Irish to each other or would it be more English?

S: Oh, always Irish, yeah always Irish [. . .] It's very natural for us to speak Irish as that's the way we grew up.]

This response indeed reflects both what I witnessed of informal social interactions in the area and what others reported to be the case, with it not being unusual to see those in their mid-to-late twenties speak Irish to each other, as well as to other age groups.

The middle sibling, a woman aged 20 who also spends most of the year working in an urban environment, answered a similar question as follows:

Údar: Agus céard faoin dream ar tháinig tú aníos leofa, an labhrann tú Gaeilge leofa sin?

M: Labhraim Gaeilge leis na leaids.

[Author: What about those who you grew up with, do you speak Irish to them?

M: I speak Irish to the lads.]

Although the term "lads" is often used in Ireland to refer to mixed-gender groups, the interviewee confirmed that she did indeed mean that Irish was more common amongst the males in her peer group. In the relatively small age gap between this woman and her older sister, it would thus appear that at least some of the females in this community have shifted away from Irish – a point on which this interviewee later elaborated. When discussing one of her female peers who is particularly reluctant to speak Irish she said:

> M: Nuair atá an cailín seo ann ní labhrann muid Gaeilge mar ní labhróidh sí linn é. Agus tá sé chomh aisteach mar tá an Ghaeilge aici. Bheadh cúpla lá labhródh muid cúpla focal Gaeilge léi [. . .] ach ní labhródh sí linne é unless go gcuirfeadh muid brú uirthi [. . .] Níor thaitin sé léi riamh, 'níl mé ag iarraidh é a fhoghlaim, tá mé ag iarraidh Béarla a labhairt, níl sé goil tada a dhéanamh dhom, labhrann chuile dhuine Béarla, ní labhrann mórán daoine Gaeilge', an sórt sin rud.

> [M: When this girl is around we don't speak Irish because she wouldn't speak it to us. And it's so strange because she can speak Irish. The odd day we'd speak a few words of Irish to her [. . .] but she wouldn't speak it to us unless we pressured her [. . .] She never liked it, 'I don't want to learn it, I want to speak English, it's not gonna do anything for me, everyone speaks English, not many people speak Irish', that kind of thing.]

Such an instrumental view of languages is, of course, far from uncommon and is something Rojo (2020) has claimed to be itself connected to neoliberal subjectivity and self-management (a topic which I discuss further in the following section). The propagation of such sentiments amongst younger speakers in a minoritised language community is, however, likely a sign that intergenerational transmission is beginning to break down.

The gendered dynamic reported by this informant is also notable. While, again, this is just one example from one small community (albeit one of the strongest Gaeltacht areas in Galway), it recalls Ó Curnáin's observation about the *"claonadh mór"* [strong tendency] amongst young females in the contemporary Gaeltacht to shift to English (Ó Curnáin 2012b: 107). This is at least partly due to the nature of the local labour market, which sees males more likely to work in industries where Irish in maintained (farming or fishing, for instance) and therefore slower to shift to the dominant language (see also Gal 1979: 167; Labov 2001: 292; section 8.2 above). As Edwards (2009: 134–135) observes, shifting to the dominant language can also be a logical response to the greater levels of social precarity that women tend to experience. This particular gendered dynamic with regards to language shift and maintenance, is, of course, far from a universal principle, but contingent on both individual disposition and the way in which gender interacts with other factors in a given context. Kulick (1992: 7, 20), for instance, notes that due to emigration and commuting patterns, males were faster to switch to the dominant language in the community he researched in Papua New Guinea. Clyne (2003: 34, 36), on the other hand, reports instances of both male- and female-led shift in various immigrant communities in Australia, with language use patterns again tracking other factors such as exogamy. Holmes (2013: 61) also discusses how gendered employment patterns determine the degree of language shift.

The third and youngest sibling who I interviewed, a man aged 18, told me that his peer group in the area was entirely English-speaking during in-group interactions:

> Údar: Nuair atá tú ag caitheamh ama le do chuid cairde thíos ag imirt pool san óstán, an labhrann sibh Gaeilge?
>
> G: Á Béarla i gcónaí.
>
> [Author: When you're spending time with your friends playing pool down in the hotel, do ye speak Irish?
>
> G: Ah always English.]

As above, this response tallies with all my own observations – including talking to others of the same age, asking their parents, etc. I also often saw his peer group socialise in both single and mixed gender groups, with language patterns not notably different in either case. We can thus see a dramatic shift in both reported and observed language use within a very short time frame, an observation which accords with other statistical evidence for ongoing language shift in the Gaeltacht (e.g., Ó Giollagáin and Charlton 2015a). While a family vignette such as that given here cannot, of course, be immediately extrapolated to wider Gaeltacht society, the above extracts largely accord with the language use patterns I observed throughout my fieldwork in various category A Gaeltacht communities. Within a space of seven years, to judge from the age gap between these informants, Irish appears to have gone from being the unmarked language spoken by even the youngest adults, to no longer being used in typical peer-to-peer interactions. Of course, this data must still be approached cautiously – further research on this topic with a larger sample size and wider geographical spread would be essential before definitive conclusions about the breadth and pace of language shift in recent years were drawn.

The same young man quoted above elaborated on the language dynamics of the local pub where he socialises regularly:

> G: Labhródh na seandaoine Gaeilge amongst themselves agus dá mbeadh's acu gur muide atá ann agus tá's acu go bhfuil Gaeilge againn, ansin caithfidh tú b'fhéidir dhá nóiméad ag caint Gaeilge leo agus cúpla soicind small talk agus imíonn tú, sin é, sin an t-aon Ghaeilge a labhrós tú agus ar ais ar an mBéarla.

[G: The older people would speak Irish amongst themselves and if they knew it was us and that we know Irish, then you'll spend maybe two minutes speaking Irish to them and a few seconds of small talk and you leave, that's it, that's the only Irish you'll speak and then back to English.]

Again, this is something I observed myself quite regularly in this pub. Outside of the tourist season when it was only locals present the age-graded patterns of Irish-language use were stark: older people would only speak Irish together, while the youngest present (in their late teens and early 20s) spoke no more Irish when interacting with each other than might be seen anywhere else in Ireland – next to none. Of course, the interactional nature of language socialisation has long since been noted (e.g., Ochs 1986: 2; Kulick 1992: 13), and intragenerational communication is a key form of reinforcement for minoritised languages, particularly among adolescents and children (McLeod 2022: 360). While it is possible that some of these teenagers may develop an interest in Irish in later life and begin to use the language more often, this will most likely be, at best, a minority of them. The language use patterns amongst younger speakers that are currently present therefore hardly bode well for the long-term prospects for Irish-language maintenance in the area where these three siblings live.

13.3 Additional explanations of language shift

Further to the multitude of social disruptions discussed throughout this work, including the cutting of a huge range of schemes focused directly or indirectly on the maintenance of Irish, several other distinct but mutually reinforcing explanations were offered by my informants for why language shift was occurring in the Gaeltacht, as discussed in the following sections.

13.3.1 Information and communications technology

Several of my interviewees mentioned information and communications technology as being a cause for language shift in their families and communities, a factor which has frequently been referenced in literature in this field (e.g., Crystal 2000: 78; Fishman 2001: 473). Notably, though, research on language loss, revival and technological change rarely gives much consideration to the wider forces which are responsible for increasing dependence on technology – nor, it must be admitted, was this something any of my informants discussed. As will be seen, however, here too can the effects of economic change and neoliberalisation be seen to play a role in a number of important ways.

The youngest of the three siblings I interviewed described the anglicising influence of digital media and technology on his own linguistic trajectory:

> G: Tá teilifís i mBéarla, tá idirlíon i mBéarla, má tá tú ag iarraidh goil ar Facebook, tá na posts ar fad i mBéarla [. . .] Bhí mé ar an X-bosca agus ag labhairt i mBéarla le chuile dhuine air sin. So bhí, chaill mise an Ghaeilge níos luaithe ná [a dheirfiúracha]. Chaill mise é nuair a bhí mé timpeall 13 – stop mise á labhairt den chuid is mó. Tháinig an teicneolaíocht isteach i mo shaol.
>
> [G: Television is in English, the internet is in English, if you go on Facebook all the posts are in English [. . .] I was on the X-box and speaking English with everyone on that. So I lost Irish sooner than [his sisters]. I lost it when I was about 13 – I mostly stopped speaking it. Technology came into my life.]

This narrative accords with Cunliffe's description of younger speakers of minoritised languages, who are more likely than older speakers to be early adopters of information and communications technology, seeing the relevance of the minoritised language to their lives undermined as a result of heavy engagement with these platforms (2021: 75; see also Eisenlohr 2004).

Significantly, the two older siblings who I interviewed, who each told me they use Irish with at least some of their peers, both conceded that they only used English when on social media. Quantitative survey data collected in a Gaeltacht community in County Cork echoes this finding, showing that social media are overwhelmingly used through the medium of English by young people in that area too (Ó hIfearnáin 2022: 128). The pervasive lack of confidence amongst native Irish speakers regarding the written version of the language which was noted in section 10.4.1 may be partly responsible for this trend, although this would, of course, only apply to social media that are primarily text based.

Another possible explanation for Irish speakers defaulting to English on social media is what has been termed "context collapse", whereby different domain networks merge online to create a composite network which can only be addressed as one audience. With this in mind, if we consider the tendency for speakers to switch to the majority language when in the company of people who do not know the minoritised language (Thomas and Roberts 2010: 105), the likelihood of interactions on social media taking place in English becomes apparent. However, as Cunliffe's valuable discussion of this topic has described, context collapse can be avoided through compartmentalising personal networks by platform, with speakers using different forms of social media to address specific groups, or by consciously using the minority language to connect with only certain contacts within their audience (2021: 79; see also Szabla and Blommaert 2018 on "addressee selection").

Of course, the most popular forms of social media are all owned by largely unregulated private companies who engineer their platforms to maximise the time people spend engaging with them, to the point of intentionally cultivating user addiction (Berthon, Pitt and Campbell 2019; Zuboff 2019: 449–451; Seymour 2020). The fact that this process leads to speakers of minoritised languages engaging with ever more majority language material is an additional negative effect of this process which, while unintended, is significant. So too is the fact that social media have been extensively analysed as important factors in the creation of the neoliberal subject (Gershon 2011, 2016; Roberts 2014: 93–112; Marwick 2015), with users conditioned to apply the logic of neoliberalism to even their most intimate sense of personal identity.

In light of the data presented in section 7.2.3 regarding economic precarity in the Gaeltacht, it is also worth noting that research in Britain has shown that those on the lower end of the class spectrum make proportionately greater use of social media, despite often using the internet less overall (Yates, Kirby and Lockley 2015; Simeon and Lockley 2018). To my knowledge no such research has been done in the Gaeltacht, or in Ireland more generally, although a similar trend is quite likely to exist.

While the use of technology was sure to have increased regardless of the 2008 economic crash, it must be remembered that, as many studies have shown (e.g., Warren 2005; Piotrowski et al. 2015: 169; Domoff et al. 2017: 279), overworked parents and those in lower income households are much more likely to have no choice but to use television and computers as surrogate child minders. In doing so, they expose their children to more of the very technologies which are so often charged with being key drivers of language shift. As discussed in 9.2, information and communication technologies are also a source of the rising expectations which can prompt emigration from rural areas like the Gaeltacht.

Although research on the effects of the Covid lockdowns on the Gaeltacht has yet to be done, the immense increase in online social interaction brought about by the pandemic likely exacerbated these tendencies. A countervailing force may also have operated here, however, with furloughed parents and children who were being home-schooled due to lockdown perhaps having *increased* time to interact with each other through Irish – a topic surely ripe for further exploration (see also section 14.5).

Many interviewees also saw broadcast media as another instance of information and communications technology weakening the use of Irish in their families. Memorably, a father I interviewed in Donegal recounted the shocked conversation he had with his five-year-old upon hearing her advanced level of English for the first time during a family holiday in England: "'Cá háit a d'fhoghlaim tú do chuid Béarla? Ní raibh's agamsa go bhfuil Béarla mar sin agat!' 'Á a dheaide, tá *scoil bheag Béarla agamsa mé féin thíos i mo sheomra leapan ag coimhead Netflix'".* ['Where did you learn English? I didn't know you could speak English like that!' 'Ah daddy, I have my own little English school down in my bedroom watching Netflix'].

Similarly, a grandfather to young children in west Galway told me with patent dismay that *"Feicim na gasúir atá ag [a iníon], Béarla acub ó bhí siad dhá bhliain d'aois. Agus gur Gaeilge uilig a labhrann sí leob sa mbaile agus an t-athair freisin. Agus ina dhiaidh sin tá...Mar chuile nóiméad a fhaigheann siad deis tá siad ag breathnú ar video eicínt nó tá siad ar an ríomhaire"* [I see [the informant's grandchildren], they know English from when they're two years old. Even though [their mother] only speaks Irish to them at home, and their father as well. And still...Because every minute they get they're looking at some video or they're on the computer].

Despite sometimes being dismissed as merely a product of the oppositional nature of teenage identity in Irish society, the pattern of English dominance is clearly, then, also evident amongst much younger children, and was something I often witnessed myself. During my stay on an island in Donegal I would get a lift every day from the local minibus driver, who would usually have his two-year-old son with him. Despite living on the far side of a remote island with a majority Irish-speaking population and having two local parents who speak Irish to each other and their child, this young boy would invariably respond to his father's Irish – and to mine – in English. His father seemed unconcerned by this, stating nonchalantly that his son will learn Irish at school, and that it was from television he learned English, because, as the father claimed, *"níl teilifís ar bith i nGaeilg"* [there's no television in Irish]. While there is, as Chapter 5 discussed, a predominantly Irish-language television station, to this informant at least, this was irrelevant in comparison with the enormous volume of English-language material. Regardless, the striking linguistic behaviour of his son brought to mind Harrison's description of the youngest speakers in a minoritised language community acting as "tiny social barometers" which gauge the value of the languages they hear around them and tailor their linguistic behaviour accordingly (2007: 8). This and the other sentiments quoted above also recall Krauss' oft-cited line about one of the main causes driving the mass loss of linguistic diversity being "electronic media bombardment, especially television, an incalculably lethal new weapon (which I have called 'cultural nerve gas')" (1992: 6).

As with the discussion of competence in the following section, and in accordance with Ó Curnáin's (2012a, 2015) assessment of those born post-1960 as being speakers of "post-traditional" Irish, this same bus driver, who was in his 30s, told me that his parents' generation had a much wider vocabulary and used far less English while speaking Irish. Similar opinions were expressed by others in his peer group in different settings. Again according with Ó Curnáin's assessment, we could expect to see the children of such post-traditional speakers having a significantly reduced competency in Irish themselves, or shifting outright to English, as the bus driver's young son appears to have done.

While avoidance is all but impossible for even the most dedicated of minority language activists, broadcast media are increasingly responsible for bringing hegemonic languages into the home domain, which had traditionally been seen as the last sanctuary for a minoritised language (Grenoble 2011: 35). As Ó Riagáin (1997: 107) has pointed out, though, the home, contrary to typical understandings in the field, can in fact be the first domain lost in the process of language shift, rather than the last – with exogamy often having been the main cause of this change in the past. Technological omnipresence has since greatly exacerbated this possibility, reducing the importance of the parental role in language input and ultimately leading to greater use of the dominant language in most cases (McLeod 2022: 362). This arguably makes domains such as the school, which can be engineered so as to reduce input in English, all the more important in revitalisation contexts.

It is, of course, often easier for informants to see the effects of technology in anglicising their family language practices than to comment in detail on the way in which fiscal policy and associated disruptions impact the vitality of Irish in their communities. As such it is perhaps not overly surprising that technology was often cited when I asked about why language shift was occurring in the Gaeltacht. That is not, however, to deride its relevance, which is clearly significant. Indeed, as Hicks et al. (2018: 1) state, without substantive policies to protect "digital language diversity", speakers of minoritised languages "are facing a digital time-bomb", which on current trajectories of digital development will leave them "excluded from using their own language in an increasingly digitized society", a prospect which has been termed "digital language death" by Kornai (2013).

For all the challenges presented to language revitalisation efforts by traditional and social media, it must be remembered that, as discussed in Chapter 5, broadcast and online print media can play an important role in language promotion. Furthermore, as King and Wang describe (2021: 125, 127), although often increasing access to enticing majority language content, social media can also help overcome the linguistic isolation of individuals or families which may be brought about as a result of emigration. Cunliffe (2021) has also demonstrated the potential of social media to offer useful "breathing spaces" in language revitalisation contexts. As has been seen, however, while naturalised to a huge degree, we must also remember that information and communications technologies and their proliferation are not neutral forces, but are themselves connected to the wider trends that have been discussed throughout this work. Nonetheless, with these technologies now such an enormous part of so many of our lives, future research on the use of minoritised languages will find it "increasingly necessary to consider online and offline social networks" (Cunliffe 2021: 91; see also King and Wang 2021: 127).

13.3.2 Irish-language competence of young people

Another issue proposed by several informants as a discrete factor driving language shift was the limited Irish-language competence of many young Gaeltacht people. The youngest of the three siblings that I interviewed in Galway commented on this as follows:

> G: Tá Gaeilge sórt briste ag go leor acu, go leor acub.
>
> Údar: Muise? D'aoisghrúpa?
>
> G: Yeah, I mean breathnaigh ar mo chaighdeán [. . .] Níl mé in ann sentence a chuir le chéile gan focal Béarla ann [gáire].
>
> Údar: Agus an mbeifeá ar chomhchaighdeán leis an dream eile?
>
> G: Ó bheadh caighdeán níos measa ag go leor acub! [. . .] Yeah, i bhfad níos measa.
>
> [G: A lot of them speak sort of broken Irish.
>
> Author: Really? Your age group?
>
> G: Yeah, I mean look at my standard [. . .] I can't put a sentence together without it having an English word in it [informant laughed – probably as he said the word for "sentence" in English].
>
> Author: Would you be at the same level as the rest of the group?
>
> G: Oh, lots of them would be much worse! [. . .] Yeah, much worse.]

This interviewee's standard of Irish is indeed lower than his older sisters, with a much greater use of functional codeswitching and unconventional grammatical forms not used by his siblings, a code reminiscent of the "reduced Irish" described by Ó Curnáin (2012a; see also Lenoach 2012; Ó Giollagáin et al. 2007a: 300–320). While it is not uncommon for the youngest sibling in a bilingual context in which language shift is taking place to acquire a lower competence in the minoritised language than their older siblings (Dorian 1981: 107), the interviewee was clear that others in his peer group (and presumably they are not all the youngest members of their respective families) have limited expressive capacity in Irish. Having informally interacted with many of these peers during my fieldwork, hearing the informant make this point was not a surprise.

This reduced acquisition is, of course, itself connected to the dominance of information and communication technology which was discussed in the previous section, as well as various issues explored above, such as cuts for language enrichment projects, population mobility, etc.

Ensuring sufficient input in a minoritised language is surely one of the fundamental challenges connected to its maintenance. This challenge has been explored by Montrul (2008), who explains how native speakers of a minoritised language can ultimately develop greater competence in the majority language, despite acquiring it later, as a result of the greater amount of input they receive therein:

> Children exposed to family bilingualism [only], or who are members of an ethno-linguistic minority culture, do not usually get the full benefits of substantial linguistic exposure and use of the two languages. Typically, the less frequently used language lags behind in development and becomes functionally, psycholinguistically, and structurally weaker.
>
> (Montrul 2008: 107)

With adults, as Montrul explains, a weaker level of ability in their native language can be a result not just of such incomplete acquisition, but also attrition brought about through lack of use (2008: 108). Relatedly, Dressler (1996: 206) has made the important point that this lesser degree of expressive capacity in the minoritised language ultimately prompts speakers to shift towards the dominant language, something which is exacerbated by the lack of intragroup peer reinforcement of the language amongst young people which was discussed in 13.2. Similar findings regarding acquisition and usage have been reported in Gathercole and Thomas (2009), Péterváry et al. (2014), O'Toole and Hickey (2017) and Ó Giollagáin et al. (2020).

The middle of the three siblings who I interviewed also described her use of English as being a product of her greater fluency therein. While discussing the tendency of many of her peers to predominantly speak English she commented as follows, clearly stating that her own use of English was not due to any attitudinal disposition against the language:

> M: Déanaim féin é amantaí [. . .] Ach is maith liom an Ghaeilge [. . .] Nuair a bheas páistí a'm, táim ag iarraidh iad a thógáil le Gaeilge. Ach braithim orm féin go n-athraím ar an mBéarla cuid den am. Fiú ann ag caint cuid den am bím ag caitheamh isteach focla Béarla

ar nós nach n-úsáidim mo chloigeann ag soláthar an focal Gaeilge mar tá sé a'm i mBéarla. Tá sé aisteach.

[M: I do it sometimes myself [. . .] But I like Irish [. . .] When I have children, I want to raise them with Irish. But I feel that sometimes I switch to English. Even sometimes I throw in English words like I don't use my brain to find the word in Irish as I have it in English. It's strange.]

Indeed, later on in our interview this informant told me that she was making a concerted effort to minimise codeswitching while talking to me (itself an interesting illustration of the way at least some informants interact with researchers), and that doing so was difficult for her, but that she was happy to do so as she knew I have a professional interest in the language.

While, as Olsen-Reeder observed in a recent discussion of language revitalisation in Aotearoa New Zealand, high proficiency does not automatically guarantee frequent use of a minoritised language, speakers tend to "choose English when they feel their own proficiency is not high enough to sustain conversation in Māori" (2022: 175). This dynamic would appear to be equally relevant to many young people in today's Gaeltacht. Olsen-Reeder also makes the important point, however, that "[l]ower proficiency speakers [including learners] can contribute much to language revitalisation if they are using what they know, as much as they can, as soon as they possibly can" (2022: 176), something which bears frequent repeating in all communities attempting to revitalise a language.

13.3.3 Reconstruction of youth identities

A language's indexical function as a salient identity marker has often been seen as key to ensuring its maintenance (e.g., Kulick 1992: 2; Edwards 2009: 247). Serving to correct some of the positions seen in earlier sociolinguistic literature, authors such as Ochs (1993), Jaffe (2007), Dorian (2010: 89) and Dunmore (2019: 17–23), however, have noted that the relationship between language and identity is not as simple as was often traditionally assumed. Nonetheless, García (2012: 88) claims that a strong link between ethnic identity and language is "a necessary pre-requisite for language policies" aiming to promote the use of an endangered language. In the Gaeltacht communities where I conducted my fieldwork, however, this important link would seem to be breaking down – something several of my informants commented on – with local identity being renegotiated under the influence of the various other forces discussed throughout this text.

The youngest of the three siblings I talked to explained in considerable detail that when he was younger there was a group of young adults in his area who aspired to seem older than they were, as young adults are wont to do. He told me that they demonstrated this by being diligently Irish-speaking, as the use of Irish was seen as characteristic of older community members:

> G: Ní gheobhadh tú [é] ach ó na daoine a bhí idir, idir 18-24 agus a bhí ag iarraidh a bheith ag breathnú sórt, a bhí ag iarraidh a bheith níos mó ar nós [daoine níos sine]. So bhíodar i gcónaí ag cur béim ar an nGaeilge mar bheadh Gaeilge i gcónaí á labhairt ag [daoine níos sine] le chéile, agus bhíodar ag iarraidh go mbeadh chuile dhuine sórt níos cosúil leo.

> [G: You'd only get it from people who were between 18-24 and wanted to look, who wanted to be more like [older people]. So they were always emphasising Irish because [older people] would always speak Irish together, and they wanted to be more like them.]

I asked others in the area about this phenomenon and they corroborated it – indeed, I was told they even had a nickname for such individuals, *na seanleaids óga:* "the young old lads". When pressed as to whether any of his peer group had such a mindset the young interviewee replied as follows:

> G: No, níl níos mó [. . .] Is mise an generation anois atá 18, níl muide mar sin ar chor ar bith.
>
> Údar: Éinne?
>
> G: Nah, not duine.
>
> [G: No, not anymore [. . .] I'm the generation who's now 18, we're not like that at all.
>
> Author: Anyone?
>
> G: Nah, no one.]

The implications of such a reconstruction of local identity for the maintenance of Irish in the area are clear. This data echoes recent research in Scotland, where Ó Giollagáin et al. (2020) show that in the few remaining island communities where Scottish Gaelic is spoken by a considerable percentage of the population, young people are far less likely to either speak Scottish Gaelic or identify strongly with the ethnolinguistic category of "Gael" (see also Dunmore 2019: 123–126).

Writing about the Gaeltacht, Lenoach (2012: 23) convincingly argues that such a breakdown in seeing Irish as a strong marker of identity is itself inherently linked to the lack of communicative ability such individuals have in the language, which was discussed above. This renegotiation of youth identities in recent years is also reminiscent of Giddens' work on reflexive identity construction as a trait of globalised modernity, with increased information flows and the destabilisation of traditional social roles seeing people express their identities in new ways, particularly via consumerism (Giddens 1991). More optimistically, however, O'Rourke and Walsh (2020) discuss ways in which new speakers can be attracted to Irish as part of such a project of identity construction.

Of course, as mentioned in 13.3.1, neoliberalism itself is often claimed to impact people on the most intimate level of identity construction, acting to shape our very sense of who we are as individuals. This "entrepreneur of the self" concept is addressed in some of the recent LPP literature that discusses neoliberalism. Rojo, for instance, has explored "the dynamics that turn market-governing processes into modes of social organisation and of self-constitution" (2020: 179), leading the third-level students in Madrid who were surveyed in her research to construct their identity, in part at least, as what they perceived to be the model language learner, and, therefore, employee. They also, as stated in 13.2, come to view languages largely for their instrumental value in the marketplace, something which some of Rojo's informants connected to the economic crisis which recently caused such disruption for the local labour force (2020: 171). Gao and Park (2015) have addressed neoliberal political economy and language learning in a similar fashion.

While a fuller discussion of youth identities, language and the Gaeltacht is, unfortunately, beyond the scope of this work, the following observation by Pavlenko and Blackledge is of clear relevance to this topic:

> language choice and attitudes are inseparable from political arrangements, relations of power, language ideologies, and interlocutors' views of their own and others' identities. Ongoing social, economic, and political changes affect these constellations, modifying identity options offered to individuals at a given moment in history and ideologies that legitimize and value particular identities more than others.
>
> (Pavlenko and Blackledge 2004: 1–2)

Again, while further research on this topic would be welcomed, with such enormous disruptions having occurred on a global scale since 2008, and Irish no longer being a central identity marker for many young people in the Gaeltacht, further language shift in these heartland communities would seem likely.

13.4 Conclusion

Much of the information presented in this chapter is, certainly, indicative of longer-term trends regarding technological proliferation and established patterns of language shift, and as such it is quite likely that the data would not be vastly different if not for the 2008 crash. As stated in Chapter 1, however, counterfactuals are all but impossible in the social sciences, leaving us with only the ethnographic insights that can be inferred from the data we do have access to. This data, as this and previous chapters have shown, demonstrates that the Great Recession and associated disruption clearly exacerbated what was an already difficult situation regarding the maintenance of Irish in the Gaeltacht.

Although largely based on the reported behaviour of only one family and my observations of the community they live in, it is of significance that the picture presented above would seem to suggest that language shift has taken place very rapidly in recent years. Indeed, most of my youngest informants' formative teenage years coincided directly with the recession. While this time frame should not, perhaps, be afforded undue salience, it is nonetheless an interesting point, considering the well-attested tendency for macro-level economic changes to impact people's ideologies, even on an unconscious level (Malmendier and Nagel 2011; Inglehart 2018: 173–199; Giuliano and Spilimbergo 2014 for discussion of psychology's "impressionable years hypothesis" and recessionary periods). Echoing my commentary in section 6.4 regarding the tendency for precarity to push people away from pluralist values of tolerance and support for redistributive causes like language revitalisation, in a discussion of economic change and the revitalisation of Manx, Wilson explains that one of the principles behind the concept of post-materialism is the "socialisation hypothesis". "This", he states, "contends that people's values and attitudes develop during their formative years and remain with them throughout their life. Furthermore, these values and attitudes are profoundly influenced by a person's economic circumstances during that formative period" (2011: 61). In light of such an understanding of ideological formation, it would seem probable the economic developments of recent years have contributed to language shift amongst young people in the Gaeltacht by strengthening the instrumentalist view of language discussed above.

Relatedly, King and Wang (2021: 128–130) have pointed out that the high levels of economic inequality which neoliberalism engenders can affect the ideological dispositions of not just those going through their formative developmental years, but parents too. Authoritarian, "pushier" parenting styles which place a great deal of focus on academic achievement are more prevalent in unequal societies. This, as King and Wang note, may well have detrimental implications for the valuing of minoritised languages as, even when supported by the education system, they are typically understood by parents to be of less importance than other school subjects.

Much of the discussion here clearly remains conjectural, of course, for want of further research on the specific matter of economic instability and language attitudes in the Irish case. Economic disruption bringing about a change in ideologies relating to language and identity is, however, something which is documented in other literature on language shift (e.g., Mufwene 2008: 245–250).

Further to the cuts and social disruption described above, an awareness amongst young people in the Gaeltacht of the recession and its implications for marginal communities may well help explain Ó Giollagáin and Charlton's finding in their 2015 update to the 2007 *Comprehensive Linguistic Study* that language shift had occurred at an even more rapid rate than the 2007 research predicted (2015a: 2). Of course, as discussed in the final chapter, I do not mean to imply that economic disruption is the sole factor behind the complex issue of language shift, which is almost always overdetermined, but rather that such economic forces play a key role, as detailed throughout this text.

Through weakening the social fabric in which Irish survives, the 2008 crash clearly contributed to the decline of the language. The 2016 census results illustrated this starkly, with the 11.2% decrease in the number of daily speakers outside the education system in the Gaeltacht being in dramatic contrast with the modest growth seen for the same category during the Celtic Tiger (see 7.2.2). While significant reductions in coming years were predicted by the *Comprehensive Linguistic Study* in 2007 (Ó Giollagáin et al. 2007a), the economic crisis that began the following year exacerbated these trends by removing or diminishing much of the support infrastructure on which the Gaeltacht had come to depend. In light of all that has been described in Parts 2 and 3 of this book, it can hardly be a surprise that the standing of Irish in the Gaeltacht therefore went from bad in 2008, to even worse in the years that have followed the crash.

Part 4: **Conclusion**

14 Summary and conclusion

14.1 Introduction

This book has sought to address a significant deficit in LPP research to date – our limited understanding of how exactly economic forces drive language loss, a phenomenon often alluded to in the literature, but rarely explained in detail. Examining the relationship between neoliberalism and the vitality of Irish, I have investigated how economic developments since 2008 have affected Irish-speaking communities and Irish-language policy in the Republic of Ireland. Through doing so, it has become apparent that even in a state which is ostensibly committed to language revitalisation, dominant economic orthodoxies play a key role in shaping language policies, a point seldom discussed by LPP scholars.

This conclusion will offer an overview of the key findings that emerged from this research and examine some international parallels. I will reflect on the implications of these findings for language revitalisation in Ireland, explore how the Covid pandemic may alter or exacerbate the picture presented above, and offer some general thoughts on the intersection of language loss and economic forces in a time of immense social, political and economic upheaval.

14.2 Summary of findings

Writing five years after the 2008 crash, Williams stated that

> the question to be asked is whether or not such minority language groups are experiencing disproportionally more cutbacks and more than their due share of pain at the expense of collective gain. That is, is there anything particular about the nature of language policies and programmes that make them particularly vulnerable to the fiscal demands of austerity and budget reduction. (Williams 2013: 10)

This book has taken up Williams' challenge and endeavoured to answer this question by examining the ways in which the Great Recession and its consequences resulted in significant reforms of both overt and covert Irish-language policy, and how the socioeconomic disruptions of this period affected Irish-speaking communities in Galway and Donegal. It has explained that the neoliberal hegemony which has dominated global economic development for decades rejects many of the principles on which language revitalisation has traditionally been premised, and it is this that leaves such efforts so vulnerable to disproportionate suffering in an era of capitalist retrenchment.

Adopting an expansive conception of ethnographic methodology, my fieldwork and interviews for this study were buttressed by policy analysis and use of extant quantitative data. This was described in Part 1, where I also presented an overview of Irish-English language shift and revitalisation efforts pre-2008 and discussed the nature of neoliberalism as an economic hegemony opposed to both social planning and redistributive economic policies – key components of almost all language revitalisation efforts. As was explained, the crisis of neoliberalism which began in 2008 was the second most severe in the history of industrial capitalism and was particularly bad in the Republic of Ireland, where all manner of public policy was rationalised as a result.

In Part 2 I detailed the intense process of neoliberalisation that language revitalisation policies in the Republic underwent as a result of this crisis. Although having initially proposed many of the key reforms that were ultimately implemented in Irish-language policy since 2008, the report of An Bord Snip Nua – the main roadmap for the state's austerity policies – has previously received very little attention in discussions of Irish LPP. As discussed in Chapter 3, this report and the *Memorandum of Understanding* agreed with the IMF, the European Central Bank and the European Commission "Troika" which supervised the running of the Irish economy between 2010–2013 fundamentally informed subsequent LPP developments. Indeed, two of the most significant reforms of overt Irish-language policy in the last several decades – the *20-Year Strategy for the Irish Language 2010–2030* and the *Gaeltacht Act 2012* – were both introduced while the economy was under the direction of the Troika, a fact which even literature most critical of these policies fails to address.

These trying economic circumstances clearly affected both the content and implementation of these and other policies – with the *20-Year Strategy* being largely unimplemented since its introduction and the *Gaeltacht Act* being voted through the Dáil by the governing coalition despite significant disapproval from language groups and opposition parties. Although over 150 amendments were proposed to the bill that became the *Gaeltacht Act*, all of these were rejected by the government. Given that this legislation constituted an official response to the well-documented sociolinguistic crisis facing the Gaeltacht, the lack of engagement with such proposals does not bode well for the long-term viability of the language in its heartland communities, particularly when combined with the fraught nature of the Act's implementation, an account of which was offered in 3.4.

As Chapters 4 and 5 detailed, such challenges regarding "overt" language policy have been exacerbated by developments in "covert" policy (Shohamy 2006), not least the severe, disproportionate budgetary cutbacks that many Gaeltacht institutions received, including the Gaeltacht development authority

ÚnaG, which lost 73.7% of its budget between 2008–2015. Tellingly, comparable non-Gaeltacht institutions such as Enterprise Ireland and the IDA were not targeted in anything like the same manner during this time. Austerity also left its mark on numerous other language support structures, seeing the closure of 13 of 19 language promotion groups and very damaging cuts to Irish-language media funding. Raidió na Gaeltachta and TG4 each saw audience numbers decline, seemingly related to budgetary contraction, which prompted numerous scheduling issues. The majority of print media in Irish became defunct after 2008, and the remaining publications are continuing to have their funding cut as of the time of writing.

Overall, by 2017 capital expenditure on the Gaeltacht and islands was €10.9 million, having fallen from €75.7 million in 2008. This was the case despite total public expenditure reaching 90% of its 2008 level by 2018. Furthermore, proposed expenditure in this area for 2018–2027 is only slightly more than *half* the 2006–2016 spend, the severe post-2008 cuts that occurred during this time notwithstanding. Irish, however, continues to be taught as a compulsory subject in schools throughout the state and it must be noted that this aspect of language revitalisation policy did not receive significant cutbacks, as education budgets, while reduced, were not cut as severely as other sectors. Regardless, figures regarding Gaeltacht-specific expenditure clearly highlight the extent of state "rollback" in the field of language policy in the Republic of Ireland, a development eminently characteristic of neoliberal policy regimes (Peck and Tickell 2002).

Another area in which austerity had indirect, but very significant implications for top-down language policies was in public service reform, as described in Chapter 6. In recent years an oft-repeated discourse amongst Irish speakers is that significant numbers of public servants are "opposed" to Irish and thus work to render top-down language policies ineffective. Such opinions are expressed in both popular and academic commentary. Challenging this belief as being overly simplistic, I offered a detailed study of the neoliberal "New Public Management" rationalisation measures implemented in the public sector since 2008. In contrast to common individualist accounts, this "unprecedented change for the Irish public service" (MacCarthaigh 2017: 161) was proposed as being a much more plausible, structural explanation for the failure of policies such as the *Official Languages Act*. The non-implementation of the Act has increased significantly since 2008 (Coimisinéir Teanga 2017b), seemingly due to increased workloads and reduced resources meaning public servants simply have more pressing concerns than implementing Irish-language schemes.

As neoliberalism is a hegemonic ideological force which conditions behaviour at both the individual and state level, various other ways in which this ideology conflicts with key requirements of language revitalisation were also discussed in Chapter 6. Not only is neoliberalism fundamentally opposed to social planning (cf. Hayek 2006 [1944]), of which language planning is, of course, a form, but it also actively dismantles the sort of redistributive economic policies that are so often necessary to sustain linguistic minorities. Furthermore, the precarious living conditions neoliberalism generates for so much of the world's population tend to turn people away from the pluralist values that are fundamental to arguments in favour of defending cultural diversity, a point well documented in sociological and political science literature on attitude formation (e.g., Inglehart 2018: 173–199).

Building on the policy analysis presented in Part 2, the results of extensive ethnographic fieldwork, including 52 interviews, conducted in some of the strongest remaining "category A" Gaeltacht areas in Galway and Donegal were detailed in Part 3. In addition to examining the micro-level consequences of many of the macro-level policy reforms documented in the preceding chapters, discussion also focused on various socioeconomic consequences of the crisis not related to language policy per se, but with distinct implications for language vitality. Chief amongst these, perhaps, were transformations in the labour market, particularly the collapse of the construction sector, deindustrialisation and the closure of businesses in the hospitality industry, as examined in Chapter 8. In addition to the rise in unemployment caused by such developments, the closure of pubs and hotels has led to an increase in young people socialising outside the Gaeltacht, a trend obviously detrimental for language reproduction.

With emigration having increased enormously throughout Ireland as a result of the recession, particularly in rural areas, peripheral communities such as the Gaeltacht areas of Galway and Donegal inevitably experienced significant population loss post-2008, as was seen in Chapter 9. The disproportionate emigration of the young adult cohort which is most likely to form families (making them crucial for the continued intergenerational transmission of Irish) was one particularly negative consequence of the recession in terms of community and linguistic vitality which I discussed.

The tourist industry was also hit hard by the recession, with attendance at summer language colleges in particular falling sharply as disposable incomes declined – a troubling development considering that such colleges are one of the few segments of the Gaeltacht economy that is explicitly language-based. Tensions between tourism and language promotion could be seen elsewhere, too: evidence was presented which suggests that the recent increase in the use of English in the "linguistic landscape" of various Gaeltacht communities occurred as part of an attempt to attract tourists in light of reduced employment opportunities and supports for other sectors. This, of course, belies much of the contemporary LPP literature on minoritised languages being used in the tourism sector as a source of profit due to their indexing of "authenticity".

While drastic, the reduction of funding for the Gaeltacht did not go unchallenged. As seen in Chapter 11, many communities attempted to resist state policies through the anti-austerity campaigns of groups such as Guth na Gaeltachta. Although met with some success, the state was quick to clamp down on these efforts and the organisation was thus relatively short-lived. Furthermore, Guth na Gaeltachta received little solidarity from official Irish-language promotion groups who, in a classic example of divide and rule tactics, were preoccupied with (and seemingly fearful of being abolished under) the process of rationalisation they were undergoing at the same time (see 4.4). The disbanding of the Pléaráca arts and social outreach group (discussed in 12.2) was a further example of both the effects of the cutbacks and how dissent against official policy measures is treated in the Gaeltacht – a phenomenon echoed throughout many other areas of Irish society during the era of cutbacks (Harvey 2014).

With state support for the Gaeltacht having fallen so severely post-2008, many communities and groups I witnessed attempted to overcome the difficulties this caused via recourse to unorthodox measures such as "Corporate Social Responsibility" grants and crowdfunding campaigns. Despite being another way in which community agency was exercised positively in the face of the cuts, by conceding almost entirely to neoliberal notions of the role of the state and seeing the maintenance of rural communities as a matter for corporate charity, not concerted policy, this tendency potentially sees communities sow the seeds of their own destruction.

According with the widespread disruption detailed in this study, the 2016 census reported an 11.2% decrease in daily speakers of Irish in the Gaeltacht outside the education system since 2011, a drop which dramatically contrasts with the modest growth in the same category shown in the previous census. While this decline in the vitality of Irish is to a large degree the continuation of centuries of marginalisation, the immense social turmoil caused by the recession in a short time frame clearly exacerbated this trend, with the 2016 figures providing quantitative demonstration of this fact. Chapter 13 discussed some of the additional ways in which language shift was visible during my fieldwork, as well as some further factors exacerbating it, including increased use of information and communication technology, the reduced Irish-language competence of many young Gaeltacht people, and the weakening of Irish as a key identity marker – phenomena discussed discretely for the sake of clarity, but which are clearly intimately connected.

The vast majority of Irish society, of course, suffered under austerity. So extensive were the cuts to Gaeltacht support schemes, however, that Machiavelli's infamous advice that "injuries should be done all together" is brought to mind (2003: 38). Referring to work by Klein (2007), Mirowski (2013) and Krugman (2015), it was argued that the Great Recession presented an instance of "punctuated equilibrium" whereby the state had the opportunity to radically intensify an incrementalist process of withdrawal from the sphere of language revitalisation which had been taking place over the preceding decades. While the reduction in support for the Gaeltacht was both severe and rapid, rather than demonstrating a particularly anti-Irish sentiment on behalf of the political class, I have argued that these cuts reflect the extent of neoliberal hegemony. In order to maintain economic growth, the "competition states" (Kirby and Murphy 2011) neoliberalism produces are constantly forced to vie with each other to demonstrate their suitability for capitalist investment (Block 2020 [1977]), and therefore generally have little interest in such "culturalist" spheres as language revitalisation, which, at best, are of limited interest to major investors. The fact that much of the Gaeltacht population, particularly in stronger Irish-speaking areas, is on the lower end of the class scale made them all the more likely to be affected disproportionately by the cuts, with research both in Ireland and internationally showing austerity hits more vulnerable sections of society hardest (Bisset 2015: 175–177; Varoufakis 2016). This class bias is, of course, itself another aspect of the internal logic of neoliberalism described in 2.6, whereby facilitating the increased opulence of those in the upper sections of the economic strata is seen as the most efficient way of enhancing the conditions of the worse off, who, it is assumed, will reap the benefits of trickle-down economics in their turn. In reminding us of these dynamics which are so key to the way neoliberal states work, the Irish case thus clearly illustrates the precarious position that minoritised languages that are dependent on state support can find themselves in during times of financial crisis.

Despite the communities I conducted my fieldwork in having had high concentrations of relative deprivation before 2008 (see 7.2.3), "[r]elative poverty", as Harbert et al. note, "does not in itself lead to language death unless a disruptive factor comes into play" (2009: 11). The Great Recession, of course, offers an example *par excellence* of a disruptive factor, and one which exacerbated previous socioeconomic marginalisation, acting as an ultimate cause for many of the proximate causes of recent language shift discussed throughout this book.

While much literature on Irish-language revitalisation since 2008 has focused on linguistic issues (e.g., Lenoach, Ó Giollagáin and Ó Curnáin 2012; Ó hIfearnáin and Walsh 2018), as Edwards has stated "failure to fully come to grips with external facts, pressures and attitudes is tantamount to treating language in isolation – the cardinal sin committed in so many treatments [of LPP]" (2007: 116). With the greatest economic crisis in the history of the state occurring in the years after 2008, I have attempted to move away from the tendency to look at Irish-language policy "in isolation" and examine the wider structural issues that are of crucial importance to the success of almost all efforts to reverse language shift. In doing so, I have sought to avoid what Beck, Bonss and Lau (2003: 23) have termed "methodological nationalism", defined as an "insistence on interpreting every social phenomenon within . . . the frame of reference of the nation-state". In examining the various links between macroeconomic disruption and micro-level social change, it has become clear that such is the totalising nature of capitalism in the 21st century that the actions of a relatively small number of individuals in the boardrooms of various banking conglomerates and the offices of Wall Street can have profound consequences for language vitality in remote communities thousands of miles away.

Although attention has been drawn to the role of transnational economic forces in determining the success or failure of language revitalisation efforts, this is not to imply a totally deterministic reading of the sociology of language. As is well-documented, the success of language revitalisation efforts invariably depends on a multitude of elements (Fettes 1997). This work does, however, add empirical weight to the great many allusions in LPP literature to the centrality of economic forces in driving language loss and endangerment, some of which were referenced in section 1.1. In doing so, it has echoed Engels' contention that

> it is not, as people try here and there conveniently to imagine, that the economic position produces an automatic effect. Men make their history themselves, only in given surroundings which condition it and on the basis of actual relations already existing, among which the economic relations, however much they may be influenced by the other political and ideological ones, are still ultimately the decisive ones. (Engels 1894)

While the success of Irish-language policy is most undeniably dependent on a host of various factors, in light of the findings demonstrated in this work, Engels' position would appear to be of distinct relevance to the field of Irish LPP.

14.3 International comparisons: Scottish Gaelic and Welsh

Detailed comparison with international examples has, regrettably, not been possible in a work of this length. Nonetheless, the data presented here certainly have parallels in other contexts. Considering the international nature of the crisis which began in 2008 and the near-universal adoption of austerity measures as a response, many other linguistic minorities inevitably experienced at least some of the same challenges as Irish speakers did. While there is very little detailed research about other cases, some nearby examples – Scottish Gaelic and

Welsh, both members of the same Celtic language family as Irish – are nonetheless worthy of mention. As a speaker of each of these languages, and having lived and worked in both Scotland and Wales during the research of this book, I have some knowledge of their situations. Although the cuts for Irish-language expenditure have been more severe than in these or any of the other examples I have heard of, this can readily be explained as resulting from the vigour with which the Republic of Ireland adopted neoliberal policies since the early 1990s and the severity of the austerity that this produced.

Scottish Gaelic makes for an easy comparison with Irish due to the close linguistic relationship of the languages, their geographic proximity and the fact that Gaelic too has a small speaker base (some 57,375 speakers – 1.1% of the Scottish population according to the 2011 census). Also similar to the Irish case is the fact that the remaining Gaelic-speaking communities are remote, rural areas on the west coast, particularly in the Western Isles, although even there the language is in an extremely precarious situation. Echoing many of the developments discussed in Part 2 of this work, between 2010–2017 the budget for Comhairle nan Eilean Siar, the Western Isles council, was cut more severely than any other local authority in Scotland, when its funding was reduced by 29% in real terms. It was consequently classed as one of the most deprived councils in Scotland in a government report (Comhairle nan Eilean Siar n.d.: 1; Gannon et al. 2016: 51), which is particularly concerning in light of the very weak nature of all local government in Scotland (Bort, McAlpine and Morgan 2012; Wightman 2014; Rae, Hamilton and Faulds 2019). 16% of council staff were laid off between 2011–2018, a blow which was very damaging for an area where public sector employment is of great importance (Press and Journal 2018). Furthermore, those who are employed in the Western Isles receive some of the lowest rates of remuneration in Scotland, with wages dropping there and in just one other local authority area between 2009–2016 (Skills Development Scotland 2017: 60–61). The area also has "by far the lowest level of permanent employment of all 32 local authorities" (National Health Service n.d.: 25). Despite expenditure on the Gaelic television station comprising the largest section of the Gaelic budget, the channel's 2020/21 annual report noted it faces a "severe funding challenge" (MG Alba 2021: 8; Scottish Government 2022). The £12.8 million it receives from the devolved Scottish Government comprises the totality of its budget since the Westminster government cut 100% of its £1 million contribution in 2015. While ostensibly ringfenced for protection from funding cuts, when inflation is accounted for, the budget of national Gaelic promotion body *Bòrd na Gàidhlig* decreased by 30% between 2008–2019 (Misneachd 2021). Accordingly, the Bòrd stated in its 2018–2023 corporate plan that financial pressures "continue to be a major test of our resilience" (Bòrd na

Gàidhlig 2018: 12), an issue further exacerbating what was already a very challenging situation for the Gaelic-speaking community.

While Welsh has a significantly larger community of speakers than either Irish or Scottish Gaelic (562,000 speakers in Wales as of 2011 – 19% of the population), and consequently a much greater deal of official protection, austerity measures have affected the language's heartland communities in similar ways to those discussed above, with many crucial local services being cut (Tomos 2021). Funding for language-specific supports was also reduced during the period discussed in this work. The *Welsh for Adults* programme, for instance, was forced to cut €700,000 in the space of just four weeks in 2014 (Cymdeithas yr Iaith Gymraeg 2014), and the Welsh-medium television channel, S4C, also experienced cuts of "at least 36%", which were seen as "severe and disproportionate" by the parliamentary committee which oversees the station (Culture, Welsh Language and Communications Committee 2017: 10). In a statement from the station in 2014 it was noted that they had already lost 25% of their staff as a result of these reductions (S4C 2014: 2). Although a much larger body than its Irish equivalent, the Welsh Language Commissioner's office experienced cuts similar to those faced by the office of the Coimisinéir Teanga (see 6.2; 11.3), receiving a cut of 23% between 2014–2020. This meant that by 2019 "budget and resources were the highest risk to the organisation", with vacant positions being left unfilled due to budgetary pressures, thereby increasing workloads for the remaining staff (Welsh Language Commissioner 2020: 46; Culture, Welsh Language and Communications Committee 2020). Reminiscent of the issues discussed in section 9.4, the structural inequities in the housing market which are so characteristic of neoliberalism are the source of much contention in Welsh-speaking communities, as they are in Scotland as well (Anwyl 2021; The Guardian 2022; Mac a' Bhàillidh 2022).

Despite there likely being many parallels with other languages further afield and outside the Celtic language family, the lack of research done on this topic means it is unfortunately impossible to make any further comparative comments (although, as noted in 5.3, one of the very few academic articles addressing austerity and minoritised languages explains that Basque and Catalan broadcasting also received significant cuts). With many language revitalisation programmes dependent on some form of state support, a deeper understanding of how major economic fluctuations, including those caused by Covid (see 14.5), affect this provision in contexts outside Ireland would surely give us a better appreciation of the challenges that linguistic minorities are likely to face in the near future. It is, of course, only by first understanding the nature of these challenges that we can have any hope of overcoming them.

14.4 The loss of the Gaeltacht and the threat of further recessions

Irish, as Fishman noted (1991: 122), is in many ways exceptional for a language of its size, having an institutional support network that few other minoritised languages can hope for. The years since 2008 have seen an immense weakening of these supports, however, as the state in the Republic moved ever closer to the laissez-faire disinterest which characterises so many states' attitudes to the fate of linguistic minorities within their territories. Nonetheless, despite the extensiveness of recent reforms, Irish still has an array of supports that leave it in a stronger position than many other languages with similarly sized speaker populations. If the neoliberalisation of Irish-language policy which was explored in this work continues, however, Irish may be an exceptional case no longer, becoming instead yet another example of the inability of most nation-states to adequately support endangered language communities (cf. Fishman 1991: 3).

While the economy in the Republic of Ireland had returned to rapid growth by 2016, the structural challenges which caused such disruption for Irish-language revitalisation continue to loom large over this field. Indeed, the continuation of the trend towards state rollback from supporting revitalisation measures is likely to be the case. Further to planned expenditure on the Gaeltacht for 2018–2027 being much lower than the amount spent between 2006–2016, further periods of economic turmoil will quite probably see further cuts to state expenditure on social policy. As the following section discusses, although the long-term economic outcomes of the Covid crisis remain to be seen at the time of writing, it may well be the case that the costs associated with the pandemic result in further austerity. Even if that is avoided, though, whenever the next economic downturn occurs – and it is well-established in economics that another major crash will undoubtedly occur in due course – further cuts to institutions such as ÚnaG or the department responsible for the Gaeltacht could well leave them essentially defunct, being that they are now so much weaker than they were in 2007. Indicating the troubles that may lie ahead, as early as 2018 the IMF was issuing warnings about the state of the global economy, as protectionist trade policies began to take effect globally and the increase in consumer debt that helped overcome the Great Recession approached unsustainable levels (IMF 2018; see also IMF 2022). Furthermore, with language shift continuing apace, were another economic crisis to befall the state, cuts to Gaeltacht expenditure will be all the easier to justify as we approach a "post-Gaeltacht" era in which such communities are not significantly distinct linguistically from the rest of Ireland. Such a development is unlikely to be met with increased state support for language revitalisation elsewhere in the country.

Nonetheless, despite the extent of the forces which minoritised the language historically and the magnitude of the threats currently stacked against it, Irish continues to be transmitted within its heartland communities, albeit tenuously. Many Gaeltacht activists continue to do extremely valuable work to support the language and its speakers. Moreover, there are still tens of thousands of "new speakers" of the language throughout the rest of Ireland, although the challenges of the Gaeltacht have distinct repercussions for these as well. While recent research on new speakers shows that the Gaeltacht is not universally seen as essential, as Hindley has noted, "much of the romantic appeal for learning Irish will die with the Gaeltacht" (1990: 253; see also O'Rourke and Walsh 2020: 176). Further to the end of this "romantic appeal", the loss of these distinct linguistic communities – surely a tragedy for all who care about the language, regardless of whether their view "challenges the Fishmanian paradigm" (Ó hIfearnáin 2018: 163) – will see a key opportunity to learn the language outside of a classroom setting disappear. Such extra-curricular experience in Irish-speaking communities has been vital to the creation of many tens of thousands of new speakers of Irish over the last century, this author included. Even the more positive developments regarding overt Irish LPP which occurred towards the end of the writing of this book, such as the EU adopting Irish as a full working language and the strengthening of the *Official Languages Act,* are unlikely to have any great impact on the intergenerational transmission of Irish (cf. Dunbar 2011: 63). Indeed, they amount to exactly the sort of "higher order props" that have been for so long favoured in Ireland and elsewhere (Fishman 1991: 143, 380). With there being few examples internationally of languages that continue to be transmitted on a substantial scale once they are no longer spoken as a vernacular in any bounded territorial community (see, however, Hornsby and McLeod 2022), the long-term prospects for the survival of Irish therefore remain far from certain.

14.5 The Covid pandemic

The global pandemic caused by the Covid-19 virus is ongoing at the time of writing. While the long-term consequences of this are as yet unknown and further detailed research is required to fully understand how the pandemic affected the vitality of Irish, some points are worthy of mention. Coming on the tail of over a decade of austerity, these unprecedented events saw states rush to *restrict* economic activity, rather than revive it as was the case in previous crises. Shockingly, the immediate effects of the resulting economic disruption were even greater than after 2008, as "global output declined about three times as much as during the global financial crisis in half the time", although the preservation of a certain degree of financial stability has meant that the long-term "scarring" of this is expected to be less than during the Great Recession (IMF 2021: 43). Unlike the austerity measures so prominent previously, this crisis necessitated an enormous increase in state support policies in a very short period, with some commentators therefore believing that this moment may mark the emergence of a new phase in capitalism (Blakeley 2020). It must be remembered, though, that neoliberalism has always been committed to a strongly interventionist state, albeit one that operates to maintain capitalist social relations, and so these emergency intercessions are not necessarily the divergence that some have assumed (Šumonja 2021).

As Covid restrictions began to relax in July 2021, the Irish government published its *Economic Recovery Plan 2021*, which politicians were anxious to announce as being the "opposite of austerity" (Irish Times 2021b). While this plan extended Pandemic Unemployment Payments for an additional six months, by the time they wind down the Central Bank estimated that some 100,000 people will have lost their jobs due to Covid (cf. 300,000 between 2008–2012). Although many of these were jobs likely to be lost over the coming years due to automation, the pandemic accelerated this trend greatly.

Notable in the context of this study, the *Economic Recovery Plan's* €3.5 billion stimulus includes an allocation of €0.2 billion "to address the significant impacts of the COVID-19 pandemic on the tourism, cultural, sport, Gaeltacht and media sectors" (Government of Ireland 2021: 59), although how this will be allocated is unclear. Of course, as with the rest of the world, the Gaeltacht has suffered a great deal as a result of this crisis, and while additional investment is undoubtedly to be welcomed, it is almost certain that the funding it will receive under the *Economic Recovery Plan 2021* will be insufficient to compensate for previous cuts.

It is significant, however, that interest in Irish seemingly increased during lockdown (Conradh na Gaeilge 2021: 14), with many people suddenly having free time and a certain level of income support which allowed them to pursue post-material interests. A similar pattern was also visible in Wales, where numbers registered for taster courses run by the government-funded body *Dysgu Cymraeg/Learn Welsh* in 2020 were greater than the three previous years combined (Culture, Welsh Language and Communications Committee 2020: 16). Such developments offer a glimpse of one of the ways in which policies such as Universal Basic Income and Universal Basic Services could support minoritised languages enormously, and offer a stark contrast to the effects of precarity discussed in sections 3.4 and 6.4.

In terms of the Gaeltacht economy, however, many of the challenges discussed throughout this work were exacerbated by the Covid crash. Not least amongst these were the issues faced by the tourism sector, which totally shut down for most of 2020 and 2021. Courses run by the summer colleges which saw such a decline in attendance during the Great Recession were cancelled both years, and supports offered by the state for those in the industry were widely derided as being inadequate. While the newly-granted permission to work remotely meant some Gaeltacht people could avoid the long commutes or emigration discussed above, this also increased demand for housing from non-Irish speakers relocating to rural areas, exacerbating the housing crisis which is a source of such concern in so many communities (RTÉ 2021). The accelerated move towards online communication that emerged during lockdown may also impact the use of Irish as a vernacular language negatively, based on the precedents described in section 13.3.1. While many learners and language enthusiasts surely enjoyed the increased availability of Irish-language events online, the majority of Irish speakers in the Gaeltacht are very unlikely to have sought out events purely due to them being in Irish, and as such will likely have defaulted to engaging with the vastly greater quantity of English-language content online. Although no link was made with the pandemic during discussion of the matter in Irish-language media, or in the reports of the Coimisinéir Teanga, an additional consequence of Covid-induced financial pressures for language policy would seem to be that the reduced revenue for county councils contributed to their neglect of Irish-language provision, as discussed in 6.2.

Another sad fact of a virus more dangerous to the elderly is that it has, of course, been more lethal to Irish speakers in the Gaeltacht, considering the age-graded patterns of language use detailed in Chapter 13, a fact which is surely equally true for a huge number of the world's minoritised languages. Needless to say, the overall lethality of the virus was itself amplified by the cuts to healthcare budgets that had been implemented in so many countries before the pandemic began.

Notably, despite their new found "opposite of austerity" rhetoric, the government in the Republic was deeply reluctant to commit to an increase in the corporate tax rate from 12.5% to 15%, the international minimum which was proposed by the G7 and OECD at the same time as the *Economic Recovery Plan 2021* was launched (Irish Times 2021c). Nonetheless, under much international and popular pressure in light of the Pandora Papers' leak (which exposed again the enormous, systemic scale of tax avoidance by transnational corporations and high wealth individuals), they were later forced to concede to this 15% figure for companies that make over €750 million a year – itself a very low rate in comparison with pre-neoliberal trends (Irish Times 2021d). Despite this small positive step, however, the overall trend towards maintaining pre-Covid economic arrangements on a global scale is apparent in research done by Oxfam, which notes that "84% of the IMF's COVID-19 loans were encouraging, and in some cases requiring, countries to adopt austerity measures in the aftermath of the health crisis" (Oxfam 2021: 26). It would seem that reports of neoliberalism's death from coronavirus have so far, then, been exaggerated.

Considering the trajectory of global economic development before the pandemic, none of this is overly surprising, despite much vaunted claims about "building back better" and opinion polls showing majorities in many parts of the world not wanting to return to the pre-Covid status quo. Unless there is a significant escalation of working-class organisation and militancy in coming years, it would seem likely that any discussion of a move away from neoliberalism's "essence" as a "utopia of endless exploitation" (Bourdieu 1998) is sure to remain in the realm of fantasy, with attendant social and sociolinguistic consequences worldwide.

Nonetheless, despite having increased the fortunes of the richest enormously, the fact that the pandemic saw the implementation of so many measures which seemed to contradict the economic logic of the previous decade may have opened the door to increased expectations with regard to health care, eviction moratoriums, minimum income guarantees and so on. Such expectations may yet prompt the sort of movement building that is so urgently needed. When combined with the other catastrophes which are threatening communities all over the world, the pandemic and the measures needed to curb its spread may yet be one factor leading to a resurgence of grassroots organising which resists neoliberal dictates (Ó Ceallaigh 2022: 41–43).

14.6 Conclusion: Language revitalisation in a time of crises

The vast extent of language loss occurring throughout the 21st century which was discussed in 1.1 is, of course, far from the only drastic challenge facing humanity at this juncture. Indeed, we currently face enormous, existential threats to the very future of our species – with runaway climate change, loss of biodiversity, soil erosion and the risk of nuclear armageddon ranking high amongst these in the estimation of many analysts and international bodies.

While the triumphalist ascendency of neoliberal capitalism was seriously challenged by the 2008 crash, and although policy makers have had to adopt some unprecedented measures in response to the Covid pandemic, neoliberalism remains dominant, albeit in an increasingly "zombified" form (Green and Lavery 2017: 79). International political developments since 2016, including Brexit and the resurgence of various nativist and fascist movements across the planet, have led commentators such as Blyth and Matthijs (2017: 218–219) to interpret the political crisis currently befalling neoliberalism as the lagged response to the economic crisis of 2008. Indeed, the resultant tension between the economic compulsion of capitalism to globalise (cf. Friedman's "golden straitjacket" [2000: 101–111]) and the political drive towards "neo-nationalism" which is currently present in many states (Blyth and Matthijs 2017: 222) is emerging as a fundamental conflict of our age. As many authors have described, the political turmoil resulting from this conflict is inherently linked not just to the Great Recession, but to the wider emergence of neoliberalism as a global hegemony over the last four decades (Blyth 2016; Inglehart 2018: 173–199).

In the face of challenges of such immense proportions, the most powerful argument for being involved in language revitalisation is now surely that it requires us to challenge the "runaway civilization" (Fettes 1997; see also Giddens 2002) that is responsible for so many of the difficulties humanity currently faces. Without developing large-scale systemic solutions to our current crises as a matter of urgency, we face not just the continued loss of linguistic and ecological diversity on an extraordinary scale, but potentially the collapse of our very civilization.

Unfortunately, a discussion of the sort of alternative political and economic models that may help overcome these major, totalising catastrophes as well as the challenges faced by speakers of minoritised languages has been beyond the scope of this work. Examples such as the "democratic confederalism" of the Autonomous Administration of North and East Syria offer a glimpse, however, of what a society based on direct democracy, environmentalism, feminism and explicit protection for linguistic minorities may look like (Jones 2018). In light of the findings of this study, it is clear that this topic is ripe for future research.

Although language revitalisation is certainly a worthy cause in and of itself, as Audre Lorde reminds us "[t]here is no such thing as a single-issue struggle because we do not live single-issue lives" (2007 [1982]: 138), and so attempts to secure justice and recognition in the field of LPP will necessarily intersect with other areas of progressive social struggle. Indeed, without engaging with such wider struggles, as this work has attempted to show, the best efforts of language revitalisation advocates can have little hope of being effective long-term. Language revitalisation is therefore best understood as a "good problem" (Fishman 1991: 6), one whose resolution can contribute to solving the many other challenges we face. Without recognising this fact and acting accordingly, activist efforts at reversing language shift can only be destined to remain a hopelessly peripheral endeavour in an age of such enormous, intersectional crises, meaning that the mass extinction of linguistic diversity may thus come to be seen as just one more of the many melancholic characteristics that have so far defined the 21st century.

Bibliography

Activism.com. 2012. *Don't Destroy the Irish language Voluntary Sector.* https://web.archive.org/web/20130517084212/http://www.activism.com/en_IE/petition/don-t-destroy-the-irish-language-voluntary-sector/16962 (Accessed 16 September 2021)

Allen, Kieran & Brian O'Boyle. 2013. *Austerity Ireland: The Failure of Irish Capitalism.* London: Pluto Press.

Allen, Kieran. 2012. The model pupil who faked the test: Social policy in the Irish crisis. *Critical Social Policy* 32(3). 422–439.

An Coimisiún um Athbheochan na Gaeilge. 1963. *An Tuarascáil Dheiridh* [The final report]. Dublin: Stationery Office.

Anderson, Benedict. 1991 [1983]. *Imagined communities: Reflections on the origin and spread of nationalism*, revised edn. London: Verso.

Anderson, Elizabeth, Ali Bakir & Eugenia Wickens. 2015. Rural Tourism Development in Connemara, Ireland. *Tourism Planning and Development* 12(1). 73–86.

Anson, Brian. 1982. *North West Donegal Gaeltacht: A Social and Environmental Study.* Unpublished report for Údarás na Gaeltachta. Summary available online at http://www.craiceailte.com/imleacan2/ansonbearla.htm (Accessed 16 September 2021)

Anwyl, Llinos. 2021. Priced out Via Pinterest – Cottagecore and the Second Homes Crisis. *Planet: The Welsh Internationalist* 242. https://planetmagazine.org.uk/planet-online/242/llinos-anwyl (Accessed 30 April 2022)

Appadurai, Arjun. 2005. *Modernity at large: Cultural Dimensions of Globalization.* Minneapolis: University of Minnesota Press.

Bachrach, Peter & Morton S. Baratz. 1963. Decisions and Nondecisions: An Analytical Framework. *The American Political Science Review* 57(3). 632–642.

Bachrach, Peter & Morton S. Baratz. 1970. *Power and Poverty.* Oxford: Oxford University Press.

Bacon, Peter & Associates. 2009. *Over-Capacity in the Irish Hotel Industry and Required Elements of a Recovery Programme.* https://www.ihf.ie/documents/HotelStudyFinalReport101109.pdf (Accessed 16 September 2021)

Bakan, Joel. 2005 [2004]. *The Corporation: The Pathological Pursuit of Profit and Power*, revised edn. London: Constable.

Baker, Colin. 2011 [1993]. *Foundations of Bilingual Education and Bilingualism*, 5th edn. Clevedon: Multilingual Matters.

Bank of Ireland. 2007. *The Wealth of the Nation: Updated for 2007.* http://www.finfacts.ie/biz10/WealthNationReportJuly07.pdf (Accessed 16 September 2021)

Barry, Frank & Adele Bergin. 2017. Business. In William K. Roche, Philip J. O'Connell & Andrea Prothero (eds.), *Austerity and Recovery in Ireland: Europe's Poster Child and the Great Recession*, 62–84. Oxford: Oxford University Press.

BBC. 2010. *Irish unveil tough four-year austerity plan.* http://www.bbc.co.uk/news/business-11829811 (Accessed 16 September 2021)

Beck, Ulrich, Wolfgang Bonss & Christoph Lau. 2003. The Theory of Reflexive Modernization: Problematic, Hypotheses and Research Programme. *Theory, Culture & Society* 20(2). 1–33.

Bergin, Osborn. 1911. *Irish spelling: A Lecture.* Dublin: Browne and Nolan Ltd.

Berthon, Pierre, Leyland Pitt & Colin Campbell. 2019. Addictive De-Vices: A Public Policy Analysis of Sources and Solutions to Digital Addiction. *Journal of Public Policy & Marketing* 38(4). 451–468.

Bew, Paul & Henry Patterson. 1982. *Seán Lemass and the making of modern Ireland, 1945–66*. Dublin: Gill & Macmillan.

Bisset, John. 2015. Defiance and Hope: austerity and the community sector in the Republic of Ireland. In Colin Coulter & Angela Nagle (eds.), *Ireland Under Austerity: Neoliberal Crisis, Neoliberal Solutions*, 171–191. Manchester: Manchester University Press.

Blakeley, Grace. 2020. *The Corona crash: How the pandemic will change capitalism*. London: Verso.

Block, David, John Gray & Marnie Holborow. 2012. *Neoliberalism and Applied linguistics*. New York: Routledge.

Block, David. 2018a. *Political Economy and Sociolinguistics: Neoliberalism, Inequality and Social Class*. London: Bloomsbury.

Block, David. 2018b. Inequality and Class in Language Policy and Planning. In James W. Tollefson & Miguel Pérez-Milans (eds.), *The Oxford Handbook of Language Policy and Planning*, 568–588. Oxford: Oxford University Press.

Block, Fred. 2020 [1977]. *The Ruling Class Does Not Rule*. https://jacobinmag.com/2020/04/ruling-class-capitalist-state-reform-theory (Accessed 5 March 2022).

Blyth, Mark & Matthias Matthijs. 2017. Black Swans, Lame Ducks, and the mystery of IPE's missing macroeconomy. *Review of International Political Economy* 24(2). 203–231.

Blyth, Mark. 2013. *Austerity: The History of a Dangerous Idea*. Oxford: Oxford University Press.

Blyth, Mark. 2016. Policies to overcome stagnation: the crisis, and the possible futures, of all things euro. *European Journal of Economics and Economic Policies: Intervention* 13(2). 215–228.

Bohane, Caren. 2005. The Official Languages Act 2003. *Cork Online Law Review 4*. https://docs.wixstatic.com/ugd/724adb_e8baf22f74ea4986be7414ece74af88e.pdf (Accessed 16 September 2021)

Bòrd na Gàidhlig. 2018. *Bòrd na Gàidhlig Corporate Plan 2018–23*. https://www.gaidhlig.scot/en/our-work/corporate/corporate-information/ (Accessed 16 September 2021)

Bort, Eberhard, Robin McAlpine & Gordon Morgan. 2012. *The Silent Crisis: Failure and Revival in Local Democracy in Scotland*. https://www.bl.uk/britishlibrary/~/media/bl/global/social-welfare/pdfs/non-secure/s/i/l/silent-crisis-failure-and-revival-in-local-democracy-in-scotland-summary-report.pdf (Accessed 9 May 2022)

Bourdieu, Pierre. 1998. 8 December. Utopia of endless exploitation: The essence of neoliberalism. *Le Monde diplomatique*. https://mondediplo.com/1998/12/08bourdieu (Accessed 14 May 2022)

Boyle, Richard. 2015. *Public sector trends 2015 [State of the public service series, research paper no. 17]*. Dublin: Institute of Public Administration.

Boyle, Richard. 2017. Public Sector Reform. In William K. Roche, Philip J. O'Connell & Andrea Prothero (eds.), *Austerity and Recovery in Ireland: Europe's Poster Child and the Great Recession*, 214–231. Oxford: Oxford University Press.

Breathnach, Proinnsias. 1986. Structural and functional problems of community development cooperatives in the Irish Gaeltacht. In Diarmuid Cearbhaill (ed.), *The organisation and development of local initiative*, 78–108. Galway: The International Society for the Study of Marginal Regions.

Brennan, Sarah C. & James Wilson Costa. 2016. The Indexical Reordering of Language in Times of Crisis: Nation, Region, and the Rebranding of Place in Shetland and Western Ireland. *Signs and Society* 4(1). 106–137.

Bresser-Pereira, Luiz Carlos. 2010. The Global Financial Crisis, Neoclassical Economics, and the Neoliberal Years of Capitalism. *Revue de la Régulation* (7). https://journals.openedition.org/regulation/7729 (Accessed 16 September 2021)
Brody, Hugh. 1974. *Inishkillane: Change and decline in the west of Ireland*. Harmondsworth: Penguin.
Bruff, Ian. 2016. Neoliberalism and Authoritarianism. In Simon Springer, Kean Birch & Julie MacLeavy (eds.), *The Handbook of Neoliberalism*, 107–117. New York: Routledge.
Bryman, Alan. 2008. *Social Research Methods*. Oxford: Oxford University Press.
Buckley, Helen & Caroline O'Nolan. 2013. *An examination of recommendations from inquiries into events in families and their interactions with State services, and their impact on policy and practice*. Dublin: Department of Children and Youth Affairs.
Byrne, Seán. 2018. *An Plean Forbartha Náisiúnta agus an Ghaeltacht 2018–2027* [The National Development Plan and the Gaeltacht 2018–2027]. https://teachtaniar.eu/proxy/pdf/anaili-s-ar-chaiteachas-an-rialtais-ar-an-ngaeltacht-agus-an-ghaeilge-leagan-deif-22052018-g/ (Accessed 16 September 2021)
Cabras, Ignazio & Matthew Mount. 2015. Economic Development, Entrepreneurial Embeddedness and Resilience: The Case of Pubs in Rural Ireland. *European Planning Studies* 24(2). 254–276.
Cabras, Ignazio & Matthew Mount. 2017. How third places foster and shape community cohesion, economic development and social capital: The Case of Pubs in Rural Ireland. *Journal of Rural Studies* 55(5). 71–82.
Cairney, Paul. 2012. *Understanding Public Policy*. Basingstoke: Palgrave Macmillan.
Callaghan, Niamh & Richard S. J. Tol. 2013. UK Tourists, the Great Recession and Irish Tourism Policy. *Economic and Social Review* 44(1). 103–116.
Canagarajah, Sureash & Phiona Stanley. 2015. Ethical Considerations in Language Policy Research. In Francis Hult & David Cassels Johnson (eds.), *Research Methods in Language Policy and Planning: A Practical Guide*, 33–44. London: Wiley.
Casado Del Río, Miguel Ángel, Josep Ángel Guimerà i Orts & Juan Carlos Miguel De Bustos. 2016. The impact of the cuts to regional public service broadcasters on the audiovisual industry: The Basque Country and Catalonia (2007–2014). *Communication & Society* 29(4). 9–27.
Castells, Manuel. 2000. Information technology and global capitalism. In Anthony Giddens & Will Hutton (eds.), *Global Capitalism*, 52–74. New York: The New Press.
CCCP. 2017. *Request: What is required to save Gaeltacht Co-op's [sic] and Community Development Companies*. http://www.ccpb.ie/%C3%A9%C3%ADleamh (Accessed 12 September 2021)
CEDRA. 2014. *Energising Ireland's rural economy: Report of the commission for the economic development of rural areas*. https://www.teagasc.ie/media/website/rural-economy/CEDRA_Report.pdf (Accessed 16 September 2021)
Central Statistics Office. 2007a. *Gaeltacht – Galway*. http://census.cso.ie/sapmap2006results/Results2.aspx?Geog_Type=Gael&Geog_Code=26/27%20Galway (Accessed 16 September 2021)
Central Statistics Office. 2007b. *Gaeltacht – Donegal*. http://census.cso.ie/sapmap2006results/Results2.aspx?Geog_Type=Gael&Geog_Code=33%20Donegal (Accessed 16 September 2021)

Central Statistics Office. 2007c. *Census 2006 Volume 9: Irish language.* http://www.cso.ie/en/media/csoie/census/census2006results/volume9/volume_9_irish_language_entire_volume.pdf (Accessed 16 September 2021)

Central Statistics Office. 2012a. *Daonáireamh na hÉireann 2011: Cainteoirí Gaeilge* [Irish census 2011: Irish speakers]. http://www.cso.ie/en/media/csoie/census/documents/census2011profile9/Profile_9_Irish_speakers_-_Combined_document.pdf (Accessed 16 September 2021)

Central Statistics Office. 2012b. *Gaeltacht Area Galway.* http://census.cso.ie/sapmap2011/Results.aspx?Geog_Type=GA&Geog_Code=03 (Accessed 16 September 2021)

Central Statistics Office. 2012c. *Gaeltacht Area Donegal.* http://census.cso.ie/sapmap2011/Results.aspx?Geog_Type=GA&Geog_Code=02 (Accessed 16 September 2021)

Central Statistics Office. 2012d. *Statistical Product - Profile 9 What we Know - A study of Education and Skills in Ireland: Tables CD964, CD965, CD959 & CD960.* https://web.archive.org/web/20171025073536/http://www.cso.ie/px/pxeirestat/Database/eirestat/Profile%209%20What%20we%20Know%20-%20A%20study%20of%20Education%20and%20Skills%20in%20Ireland/Profile%209%20What%20we%20Know%20-%20A%20study%20of%20Education%20and%20Skills%20in%20Ireland_statbank.asp?SP=Profile%209%20What%20we%20Know%20-%20A%20study%20of%20Education%20and%20Skills%20in%20Ireland&Planguage=0 (Accessed 16 September 2021)

Central Statistics Office. 2017a. *Census 2016 Summary Results – Part 1.* http://www.cso.ie/en/media/csoie/newsevents/documents/census2016summaryresultspart1/Census2016SummaryPart1.pdf (Accessed 16 September 2021)

Central Statistics Office. 2017b. *Census 2016 Sapmap Area: Gaeltacht Ghaeltacht Na Gaillimhe* [sic] [Galway Gaeltacht]. http://census.cso.ie/sapmap2016/Results.aspx?Geog_Type=GAEL&Geog_Code=372FEC7C-DB30-4853-B7D4-BA6C2DCAF0F2 (Accessed 17 September 2021)

Central Statistics Office. 2017c. *Census 2016 Sapmap Area: Gaeltacht Ghaeltacht Dhún Na Ngall* [sic] [Donegal Gaeltacht] http://census.cso.ie/sapmap2016/Results.aspx?Geog_Type=GAEL&Geog_Code=865CD4F3-B2D8-4405-841E-0AB4CEA25B7B (Accessed 17 September 2021)

Central Statistics Office. 2017d. *Census of Population 2016, E2021: Population of Islands off the Coast 2011 to 2016 by Islands, Census Year and Sex.* https://web.archive.org/web/20190418044735/http://www.cso.ie/px/pxeirestat/Statire/SelectVarVal/Define.asp?maintable=E2021&PLanguage=0 (Accessed 16 September 2021)

Central Statistics Office. 2017e. *EA055: Irish Speakers Aged 3 Years and Over 2011 to 2016 by Sex, Frequency of Speaking Irish, Gaeltacht Areas, Age Group and Census Year.* https://data.cso.ie/table/EA055 (Accessed 16 September 2021)

Central Statistics Office. 2017f. *Census 2016 Summary Results – Part 2.* http://www.cso.ie/en/media/csoie/newsevents/documents/census2016summaryresultspart2/Census_2016_Summary_Results_%E2%80%93_Part_2.pdf (Accessed 16 September 2021)

Central Statistics Office. 2018a. *Seasonally Adjusted Monthly Unemployment Rates.* https://web.archive.org/web/20191114061450/https://statbank.cso.ie/multiquicktables/quickTables.aspx?id=mum01 (Accessed 16 September 2021)

Central Statistics Office. 2018b. *Monthly Unemployment: April 2018.* https://www.cso.ie/en/releasesandpublications/er/mue/monthlyunemploymentapril2018/ (Accessed 16 September 2021)

Chaeyoon, Lim & James Laurence. 2015. Doing good when times are bad: Volunteering behaviour in economic hard times. *British Journal of Sociology* 66. 319–344.
Chang, Ha-Joon. 2007. *Bad Samaritans: The Guilty Secrets of Rich Nations & the Threat to National Prosperity*. London: Random House.
Chang, Ha-Joon. 2016. *Owen Jones meets Ha-Joon Chang | The economic argument against neoliberalism*. https://www.youtube.com/watch?v=ti3rjogF_VU (Accessed 16 September 2021)
Cheshire, Lynda & Geoffrey Lawrence. 2005. Neoliberalism, Individualisation and Community: Regional Restructuring in Australia. *Social Identities* 11(5). 435–445.
Chomsky, Noam. 2012. *How the World Works*. London: Hamish Hamilton.
CILAR. 1975. *Report: Committee on Irish language Attitudes Research*. Dublin: Stationery Office.
Clarke, Tom & Anthony Heath. 2014. *Hard times: The divisive toll of the economic slump*. New Haven: Yale University Press.
Clyne, Michael G. 2003. *Dynamics of Language Contact: English and Immigrant Languages*. Cambridge: Cambridge University Press.
Coakley, Maurice. 2012. *Ireland in the World Order: A History of Uneven Development*. London: Pluto Press.
Coimisinéir Teanga. 2013. *Tuarascáil Bhliantúil/Annual Report 2012*. http://coimisineir.ie/user files/files/Tuarascail_Bhliantuil_2012.pdf (Accessed 13 September 2021)
Coimisinéir Teanga. 2014. *Tuarascáil Bhliantúil/Annual Report 2013*. http://coimisineir.ie/user files/files/Tuarascail_Bhliantuil_2013.pdf (Accessed 13 September 2021)
Coimisinéir Teanga. 2015. *Tuarascáil Bhliantúil/Annual Report 2014*. http://coimisineir.ie/user files/files/Tuarascail_Bhliantuil_Iomlan_2014.pdf (Accessed 13 September 2021)
Coimisinéir Teanga. 2017a. *Tuarascáil Bhliantúil/Annual Report 2016*. http://coimisineir.ie/ userfiles/files/24_05_17_Oifig_an_Choimisinear_Teanga_Tuarascail_Bhliantuil_Annual_ Report_2016.pdf?lang=GA (Accessed 13 September 2021)
Coimisinéir Teanga. 2017b. *Tráchtaireacht ar Chóras na Scéimeanna Teanga* [Commentary on the system of language schemes]. https://www.coimisineir.ie/userfiles/files/Trachtair eacht-Leagan-Gaeilge.pdf (Accessed 13 September 2021)
Coimisinéir Teanga. 2018. *Ráiteas ón gCoimisinéir Teanga ar fhoilsiú: Tuarascáil Chomhchoiste na Gaeilge, na Gaeltachta agus na nOileán ar Scéim Ghinearálta Bhille na dTeangacha Oifigiúla (Leasú), 2017* [Statement from the Language Commissioner on the publication of the report on the General Scheme of the Official Languages Bill (Amendment), 2017 by the Committee on the Irish language, the Gaeltacht and the Islands]. https://www.coimisineir.ie/userfiles/files/Raiteas_on_gCoimisineir_Teanga.pdf (Accessed 13 September 2021)
Coimisinéir Teanga. 2019a. *Tuarascáil Bhliantúil/Annual Report 2019*. https://www.coimisi neir.ie/userfiles/files/CT_TuarascailBhliantuil2019.pdf (Accessed 13 September 2021)
Coimisinéir Teanga. 2019b. *Tuarascáil Faireacháin/Monitoring Report 2018*. https://www.coi misineir.ie/userfiles/files/Tuarascail_Faireachain_2018.pdf (Accessed 13 September 2021)
Coimisinéir Teanga. 2021. *Tuarascáil Faireacháin/Monitoring Report 2020/21*. https://www.coi misineir.ie/userfiles/files/Tuarascail_Faireachain_2020-2021.pdf (Accessed 13 September 2021)

Coimisiún na Gaeltachta. 1926. *Report of Coimisiún na Gaeltachta*. https://aran.library.nuigal way.ie/bitstream/handle/10379/2586/CnaGReport.pdf?sequence=1 (Accessed 16 September 2021)

Coimisiún na Gaeltachta. 2002. *Tuarascáil/Report*. Dublin: Department of Arts, Heritage, Gaeltacht and Islands.

Cois Life. 2018. *Ráiteas ó Cois Life* [Statement from Cois Life]. https://web.archive.org/web/ 20210423083711/https://www.coislife.ie/raiteas-o-cois-life/ (Accessed 16 September 2021)

Comhairle nan Eilean Siar. n.d. *Local Government and Communities Committee Draft Budget 2018-19 Submission from Comhairle nan Eilean Siar*. https://archive2021.parliament. scot/parliamentarybusiness/currentcommittees/106441.aspx (Accessed 16 September 2021)

Connacht Tribune. 2015. 27 August. *White knight rides in to save Galway island school*. https://connachttribune.ie/white-knight-rides-in-to-save-galway-island-school-098/ (Accessed 16 September 2021)

Connacht Tribune. 2017. 27 May. *Grants will help Gaeltacht firms assess impact of Brexit*. https://connachttribune.ie/grants-will-help-gaeltacht-firms-assess-impact-of-brexit-434/ (Accessed 16 September 2021)

Connolly, James. 1898. *The Language Movement*. https://www.marxists.org/archive/con nolly/1898/10/language.htm (Accessed 22 June 2022)

Conradh na Gaeilge. 2013. *Cén Fáth Go bhfoghlaimeodh aon státseirbhíseach an Ghaeilge a thuilleadh?* [Why would any civil servant learn Irish anymore?] https://cnag.ie/ga/ nuacht/508-c%C3%A9n-f%C3%A1th-go-bhfoghlaimeodh-aon-st%C3%A1t-seirbh%C3%ADseach-an-ghaeilge-a-thuilleadh.html (Accessed 16 September 2021)

Conradh na Gaeilge. 2015. *Céard é an scéal? Dearcthaí an Phobail i leith na Gaeilge* [What's the story? Public opinions on the Irish language]. Dublin: Conradh na Gaeilge.

Conradh na Gaeilge. 2017. *Investment in the Irish language and in the Gaeltacht from 2018 onwards – The case for additional funding. Version 5.0*. https://cnag.ie/images/GaelV% C3%B3ta/24SA2017_Plean_MaoiniuBreise.pdf (Accessed 16 September 2021)

Conradh na Gaeilge. 2021. *Céard é an scéal?* [What's the story?]: *Public Opinions on the Irish Language. Annual Analysis 7*. https://peig.ie/wp-content/uploads/2022/03/06NO2021_ Ce%CC%81ard-e%CC%81-an-Sce%CC%81al_RP-2.pdf (Accessed 14 April 2021)

Cooper, Robert L. 1989. *Language Planning and Social Change*. Cambridge: Cambridge University Press.

Cooper, Vickie & David Whyte. 2017. *The Violence of Austerity*. London: Pluto Press.

Cormack, Mike 2007. The Media and Language Maintenance. In Mike Cormack & Niamh Hourigan (eds.), *Minority Language Media: Concepts, Critiques and Case Studies*, 52–68. Clevedon: Multilingual Matters.

Costigan, Bosco & Seán Ó Curraoin. 1987. *De Ghlaschloich an Oileáin: Beatha agus Saothair Mháirtín Uí Chadhain* [Of the greenstone of the island: the life and works of Máirtín Ó Cadhain]. Indreabhán: Cló Iar-Chonnacht.

Coughlan, Eileen. 2021. *Identity, place and legitimate language: a comparative study of language attitudes among teenagers in two Irish-medium schools*. Oxford: Unpublished PhD in the Department of Linguistics, University of Oxford.

Coulter, Colin & Angela Nagle. 2015. *Ireland under Austerity: Neoliberal Crisis, Neoliberal Solutions*. Manchester: Manchester University Press.

Crang, Mike & Ian Cook. 2007. *Doing Ethnographies*. Norwich: Geobooks.

Crenson, Matthew A. 1971. *The Un-politics of Air Pollution: A Study of Non-decision making in the Cities*. London: Johns Hopkins Press.
Creswell, John W. 2013 [2009]. *Research design: Qualitative, Quantitative, and Mixed Methods Approaches*, 4th edn. London: SAGE.
Cronin, Michael. 2011. An Ghaeilge agus cultúr na hInbhuanaitheachta [Irish and a culture of sustainability] in Breandán Mac Cormaic (ed.), *Féiniúlacht, Cultúr agus Teanga i Ré an Domhandaithe* [Identity, culture and language in an era of globalisation], 228–235. Dublin: Coiscéim.
Crowe Horwath. 2013. *Review of Funding for Public Service Broadcasters 23rd May 2013*. https://web.archive.org/web/20200603143001/https://dccae.gov.ie/en-ie/communications/publications/Documents/71/Five%20Year%20Review%20of%20Funding%20of%20Public%20Service%20Broadcasting.pdf (Accessed 16 September 2021)
Crowley, Frank. 2018. *Why Project Ireland 2040 is doomed to fail*. https://www.rte.ie/brainstorm/2017/1206/925347-irelands-national-development-plan-is-doomed-for-failure/ (Accessed 9 May 2022)
Crystal, David. 2000. *Language Death*. Cambridge: Cambridge University Press.
Culture, Welsh Language and Communications Committee. 2017. *Outside the Box: The Future of S4C*. https://senedd.wales/laid%20documents/cr-ld11157/cr-ld11157-e.pdf (Accessed 14 July 2021)
Culture, Welsh Language and Communications Committee. 2019. *Supporting and Promoting the Welsh Language*. https://senedd.wales/media/hpbpjiga/cr-ld12636-e.pdf (Accessed 14 July 2021)
Culture, Welsh Language and Communications Committee. 2020. *Annual scrutiny of the Welsh Language Commissioner*. https://record.assembly.wales/Committee/5706#C220662 (Accessed 14 July 2021)
Culture, Welsh Language and Communications Committee. 2021. *The impact of the COVID-19 outbreak on the Welsh language*. https://senedd.wales/media/e1jpzqa3/cr-ld13874-e.pdf (Accessed 17 August 2021)
Cunliffe, Daniel. 2021. Minority Languages in the Age of Networked Individualism: From Social Networks to Digital Breathing Spaces. In Huw Lewis & Wilson McLeod (eds.), *Language Revitalisation and Social Transformation*, 67–97. Cham: Palgrave Macmillan. https://doi.org/10.1007/978-3-030-80189-2_3
Curtis, Liz. 1993 [1985]. *Nothing but the same old story: The roots of anti-Irish racism*, 3rd edn. London: Information on Ireland.
Cymdeithas yr Iaith Gymraeg. 2014. *Lack of investment in the Welsh language: Welsh Government draft budget proposals for 2015-16. Response from Cymdeithas yr Iaith Gymraeg (The Welsh Language Society)*. https://business.senedd.wales/documents/s30197/FIN4%20-%202015-16WGDB17%20The%20Welsh%20Language%20Society.pdf (Accessed 9 September 2021)
Dáil Éireann. 2010. *Dáil Éireann debate – Wednesday, 7 Jul 2010. Question 110. Departmental Reports*. https://www.oireachtas.ie/en/debates/debate/dail/2010-07-07/59/?highlight%5B0%5D=42&highlight%5B1%5D=full&highlight%5B2%5D=103&highlight%5B3%5D=part#s110 (Accessed 16 September 2021)
Dáil Éireann. 2017. *Dáil Éireann Debate, Tuesday – 11 April 2017. Question 470. Scéim na mBóithre Pobail* [Community roads scheme]. https://www.oireachtas.ie/en/debates/question/2017-04-11/470/?highlight%5B0%5D=na (Accessed 16 September 2021)

Dáil Éireann. 2018a. *Straitéis 20 Bliain don Ghaeilge* [The 20-Year strategy for the Irish Language]: *Dáil Éireann Debate, Tuesday – 23 January 2018*. https://www.oireachtas.ie/ga/debates/question/2018-01-23/67/?highlight%5B0%5D=plean&highlight%5B1%5D=gn%C3%83%C2%ADmh&highlight%5B2%5D=c%C3%83%C2%BAig&highlight%5B3%5D=bliana&highlight%5B4%5D=na (Accessed 16 September 2021)

Dáil Éireann. 2018b. *Dáil Éireann debate – Wednesday, 28 Feb 2018 Vol. 966 No. 2 Other Questions: Maoiniú Údarás na Gaeltachta* [Údarás na Gaeltachta funding]. https://www.oireachtas.ie/en/debates/debate/dail/2018-02-28/9/ (Accessed 16 September 2021)

Dáil Éireann. 2019. *Aerfoirt Réigiúnacha* [Regional airports]. *Dáil Éireann Debate, Thursday – 21 February 2019*. https://www.oireachtas.ie/ga/debates/question/2019-02-21/10/?highlight%5B0%5D=ceist&highlight%5B1%5D=ann&highlight%5B2%5D=f%C3%83%C2%B3s&highlight%5B3%5D=f%C3%83%C2%B3s&highlight%5B4%5D=ceist&highlight%5B5%5D=ann&highlight%5B6%5D=ann (Accessed 16 September 2021)

Daltún, Séamus. 2018. *Tuairisc ar an anailís ar na meáin Ghaeilge atá maoinithe ag Foras na Gaeilge* [Report on the analysis of the Irish-language media that are funded by Foras na Gaeilge]. https://www.forasnagaeilge.ie/wp-content/uploads/2019/06/6fa367509ddbfc41f29f514b21205cef.pdf (Accessed 26 July 2021)

Del Percio, Alfonso, Mi-cha Flubacher & Alexandre Duchêne. 2017. Language and Political Economy. In Ofelia García, Nelson Flores & Massimiliano Spotti (eds.), *The Oxford Handbook of Language and Society*, 55–75. Oxford: Oxford University Press.

Delap, Breandán. 2008. Irish and the media. In Caoilfhionn Nic Pháidín & Seán Ó Cearnaigh (eds.), *A New View of the Irish Language*, 152–163. Dublin: Cois Life.

Delap, Breandán. 2015. *Buille fill ar an teanga* [A treacherous blow for the language]. https://www.irishtimes.com/culture/treibh/buille-fill-ar-an-teanga-1.2479493 Accessed (Accessed 16 September 2021)

Denvir, Gearóid. 2002. The Linguistic Implications of Mass Tourism in Gaeltacht Areas. *New Hibernia Review/Iris Éireannach Nua: A Quarterly Record of Irish Studies* 6(3). 23–43.

Department of Arts, Heritage and the Gaeltacht. 2015. *Aran Islands Air Service*. https://web.archive.org/web/20201012223844/https://www.chg.gov.ie/aran-islands-air-service/ (Accessed 16 September 2021)

Department of Culture, Heritage and the Gaeltacht. 2017. *Amharcóir Pleanála Teanga* [Language planning viewer]. https://dahg.maps.arcgis.com/apps/webappviewer/index.html?id=7090794ee2ca4b53bb785b84c2bd9ad80 (Accessed 16 September 2021)

Department of Culture, Heritage and the Gaeltacht. 2019. *Treoirlínte Pleanála Teanga* [Language planning guidelines]. https://assets.gov.ie/86337/c907b60a-5a0d-4374-83d9-aad86260c5bd.pdf (Accessed 11 April 2022)

Department of Education and Skills. 2015. *Projection of demand for full-time Third-level Education, 2015-2029*. https://assets.gov.ie/26633/acbcc00c33334d7181acf417963ab26e.pdf (Accessed 12 September 2021)

Department of Finance. 2010. *Infrastructure Investment Priorities 2010-2016: A Financial Framework*. http://edepositireland.ie/bitstream/handle/2262/79898/infrastructure%20investment%20priorites%202010-2016.pdf?sequence=1&isAllowed=y (Accessed 12 September 2021)

Department of Public Expenditure and Reform. 2011. *Public service reform, 17th November 2011*. https://assets.gov.ie/35067/7f1d75ab9ccf47ab9ed13ae80e73b502.pdf (Accessed 16 September 2021)

Department of the Taoiseach. 2015. *20-Year Strategy for the Irish Language 2010-2030 Progress Report: 2010-2015 Department of the Taoiseach*. https://web.archive.org/web/20171024012519/https://www.taoiseach.gov.ie/eng/Irish_Language_Policy/20-Year_Strategy_for_the_Irish_Language_2010_2030_Progress_Report_2010_2015_Department_of_the_Taoiseach.pdf (Accessed 13 September 2021)

Deprez, Kas. 2000. Who wants to Save Oileán Thoraigh [sic]. In Peter Wynn Thomas & Jayne Mathias (eds.), *Developing Minority Languages: The Proceedings of the Fifth International Conference on Minority Languages* (ICML), 464–475. Cardiff: Department of Welsh, Cardiff University.

DIGI. 2014. *DIGI Opening Statement to the Joint Committee on Transport and Communications 17th December 2014*. https://wayback.archive-it.org/10702/20180504185644/https://www.oireachtas.ie/parliament/media/committees/transport/archivesept2016-transportandcommunications/Presentation-from-DIGI-to-JOC.docx (Accessed 17 September 2021)

Domoff, Sarah E., Alison L. Miller, Neeaz Khalatbari, Megan H. Pesch, Kristen Harrison, Katherine Rosenblum & Julie C. Lumeng. 2017. Maternal beliefs about television and parental mediation in a low-income United States sample. *Journal of Children and Media* 11(3). 278–294.

Dorian, Nancy C. 1977. The Problem of the Semi-Speaker in Language Death. *Linguistics* 15 (191). 23–32.

Dorian, Nancy C. 1981. *Language Death: The Life Cycle of a Scottish Gaelic Dialect*. Philadelphia: University of Pennsylvania Press.

Dorian, Nancy C. 1999. Western Language Ideologies & Small Language Prospects. In Lenore A. Grenoble & Lindsay J. Whaley (eds.), *Endangered languages: language loss and community response*, 3–21. Cambridge: Cambridge University Press.

Dorian, Nancy C. 2010 [1999]. Linguistic and ethnographic fieldwork. In Joshua A. Fishman & Ofelia García (eds.), *Handbook of Language and Ethnic Identity: Disciplinary and Regional Perspectives (Vol. I)*, 2nd edn., 89–106. Oxford: Oxford University Press.

Doyle, Aidan. 2015. *A History of the Irish Language: From the Norman Invasion to Independence*. Oxford: Oxford University Press.

Dressler, Wolfgang U. 1996. Language death. In Rajendra Singh (ed.), *Towards a Critical Sociolinguistics*, 195–210. Amsterdam: John Benjamins.

Duchêne, Alexandre & Monica Heller. 2007. *Discourses of Endangerment: Ideology and Interest in the Defence of Languages*. New York: Continuum.

Duchêne, Alexandre & Monica Heller. 2012. *Language in late capitalism: Pride and profit*. New York: Routledge.

Dukelow, Fiona. 2015. 'Pushing against an open door': Reinforcing the neo-liberal policy paradigm in Ireland and the impact of EU intrusion. *Comparative European Politics* 13(1). 93–111.

Dunbar, Robert. 2003. Gaelic medium broadcasting, reflection on the legal framework from a sociolinguistic perspective. In John M. Kirk & Dónall P. Ó Baoill (eds.), *Towards our goals in broadcasting, the press, the performing arts and the economy: minority languages in Northern Ireland, the Republic of Ireland, and Scotland*, 73–82. Belfast: Cló Ollscoil na Banríona.

Dunbar, Robert. 2011. An tèid aig an lagh cleachdadh mion-chànain a bhrosnachadh? Achd na Gàidhlig agus achdan chànan eile fon phrosbaig [Can the law be used to promote minority language use? The Gaelic act and other language acts under examination]. In

Richard A. V. Cox & Timothy Currie Armstrong (eds.), *A' Cleachdadh na Gàidhlig: Slatan-tomhais ann an dìon cànain sa choimhearsnachd* [Using Gaelic: Criteria for language protection in the community], 51–72. Ostaig: Clò Ostaig.

Dunbar, Robert. 2016. Language Legislation and Policy in the UK and Ireland: Different Aspects of Territoriality in a 'Celtic' Context. *International Journal on Minority and Group Rights* (23). 454–484.

Dunmore, Stuart. 2019. *Language Revitalisation in Gaelic Scotland: Linguistic Practice and Ideology*. Edinburgh: Edinburgh University Press.

Dye, Thomas R. 1972. *Understanding Public Policy*. Englewood Cliffs, N.J.: Prentice Hall.

Eckert, Penelope & Sally McConnell-Ginet. 2003. *Language and Gender*. Cambridge: Cambridge University Press.

Edwards, John. 1984. Language diversity and identity. In Edwards, John (ed.), *Linguistic Minorities, Policies and Pluralism*, 277–310. London: Academic Press.

Edwards, John. 2007. Language Revitalization and its Discontents: An essay and review of *Saving languages: An introduction to language revitalization. Canadian Journal of Applied Linguistics* 10(1). 101–120.

Edwards, John. 2009. *Language and Identity: An Introduction*. Cambridge: Cambridge University Press.

Eisenlohr, Patrick. 2004. Language Revitalization and New Technologies: Cultures of Electronic Mediation and the Refiguring of Communities. *Annual Review of Anthropology* 33. 21–45

Engels, Friedrich. 1894. *Marx-Engels Correspondence 1894: Engels to Borgius*. https://www.marxists.org/archive/marx/works/1894/letters/94_01_25.htm (Accessed 16 September 2021)

Enterprise Ireland. 2009. *Annual Report & Accounts 2008*. https://www.enterprise-ireland.com/en/Publications/Reports-Published-Strategies/Annual-Reports/2008-Annual-report-eng.pdf (Accessed 16 September 2021)

Enterprise Ireland. 2016. *Annual Report & Accounts 2015*. https://www.enterprise-ireland.com/en/Publications/Reports-Published-Strategies/Annual-Reports/2015-Annual-Report-and-Accounts-English.pdf (Accessed 16 September 2021)

Euromosaic. 1996. *The Production and Reproduction of the Minority Language Groups in the European Union*. Luxembourg: Euromosaic Office for Official Publications of the European Communities.

Eurostat. 2015. *Tourism industries – employment*. http://ec.europa.eu/eurostat/statistics-explained/index.php/Tourism_industries_-_employment#Jobs_are_less_stable_in_tourism_than_in_the_rest_of_the_economy (Accessed 16 September 2021)

Fáilte Ireland. 2016a. *Tourism facts 2015*. http://www.failteireland.ie/FailteIreland/media/WebsiteStructure/Documents/3_Research_Insights/3_General_SurveysReports/Failte-Ireland-s-tourism-facts-2015.pdf?ext=.pdf (Accessed 16 September 2021)

Fáilte Ireland. 2016b. *Regional tourism performance in 2015*. http://www.failteireland.ie/FailteIreland/files/c4/c42b5249-242d-4860-b3b5-8720df101d4c.pdf (Accessed 16 September 2021)

Fennell, Deasún. 1981a. Can a shrinking linguistic minority be saved? Lessons from the Irish experience. In Einar Haugen, Derrick J. McClure & Derick Thomson (eds.), *Minority Languages Today*, 32–39. Edinburgh: Edinburgh University Press.

Fennell, Deasún. 1981b. The Last Years of the Gaeltacht. *The Crane Bag: Irish Language and Culture – an t-eagrán Gaelach* [the Gaelic edition] 5(2). 8–11.

Fetterman, David M. 1989. *Ethnography Step by Step*. London: SAGE.
Fettes, Mark. 1997. Stabilizing what? An ecological Approach to Language Renewal. In Reyhner, Jon (ed.), *Teaching Indigenous Languages*, 301–318. Flagstaff: Northern Arizona University.
Financial Times. 2013. *One Irish person emigrates every six minutes*. https://www.ft.com/content/d27e950a-10bf-11e3-b291-00144feabdc0 (Accessed 17 September 2021)
Fishman, Joshua A. 1991. *Reversing Language Shift*. Clevedon: Multilingual Matters.
Fishman, Joshua A. 2001. *Can Threatened Languages be Saved?* Clevedon: Multilingual Matters.
Fitzgerald, Garret. 1984. Estimates for Baronies of Minimum Level of Irish-Speaking Amongst Successive Decennial Cohorts: 1771-1781 to 1861–1871. *Proceedings of the Royal Irish Academy. Section C: Archaeology, Celtic Studies, History, Linguistics, Literature* 84C. 117–155.
Fóram Chois Fharraige um Pleanáil Teanga. 2016. *Achoimre agus Moltaí Plean Teanga 2017–2023* [Summary and recommendations language plan 2017–2023]. https://www.coisfharraige.ie/cumann-forbartha/wp-content/uploads/2014/07/PleanTeangaCF2016.pdf (Accessed 13 September 2021)
Foras na Gaeilge. 2013. *Réamhrá ar thuarascáil ar thórthaí an phróisis chomhairliúcháin maidir le seirbhís nuachta Gaeilge* [Introduction to the report on the findings of the consultation process regarding an Irish-language news service]. http://www.forasnagaeilge.ie/wp-content/uploads/2016/06/Anail%C3%ADs-agus-molta%C3%AD-faoi-sheirbh%C3%ADs-nuachta.pdf (Accessed 16 September 2021)
Foras na Gaeilge. 2019. *Tuairisc ar Chomhairliúchán Poiblí Fhoras na Gaeilge ar athbhreithniú ar earnáil na meán Gaeilge Clóite agus ar líne Meitheamh – Lúnasa 2019* [Report on Foras na Gaeilge's public consultation on the review of the Irish-language print and online media sector June – August 2021]. https://www.forasnagaeilge.ie/comhairliuchan-ar-earnail-na-mean-tuarascail/ (Accessed 7 July 2021)
Foras Teanga. 2009. *The North/South Language Body Annual Report and Accounts for the year ended 31 December 2008*. https://web.archive.org/web/20171031041223/https://www.forasnagaeilge.ie/wp-content/uploads/2016/02/Tuarasc%C3%A1il-Bhliant%C3%BAil-%E2%80%93-An-Foras-Teanga-2008.pdf (Accessed 16 September 2021)
Foras Teanga. 2017. *The North/South Language Body Annual Report and Accounts For the year ended 31 December 2016*. http://www.forasnagaeilge.ie/wp-content/uploads/2016/02/06d5a821e60cc329c5325959075b08d3.pdf (Accessed 16 September 2021)
Forbes. 2017. *The World's Biggest Public Companies*. https://www.forbes.com/companies/zurich-insurance-group/ (Accessed 16 September 2021)
Foucault, Michel. 2008. *The Birth of Biopolitics: Lectures at the College de France, 1978–79*. Basingstoke: Palgrave Macmillan.
Friedman, Milton. 2002 [1962]. *Capitalism and Freedom*. Chicago: Chicago University Press.
Friedman, Milton. 2007 [1970]. The Social Responsibility of Business is to increase its profits. In Walther C. Zimmerli, Marcus Holzinger & Klaus Richter (eds.), *Corporate Ethics and Corporate Governance*, 173–178. Berlin: Springer.
Friedman, Thomas. 2000. *The Lexus and the Olive Tree*. London: HarperCollins.
Future of Media Commission. 2021a. *Aighneacht don Choimisún [sic] Um Thodhchaí na Meán ó Cheardchumann na nIriseóirí RTE Raidió na Gaeltachta* [Submission to the Future of Media Commission from the RTÉ Raidió na Gaeltachta Journalists' Union].

https://futureofmediacommission.ie/wp-content/uploads/341.-Raidio-na-Gaeltachta-Union-of-Journalists.pdf (Accessed 24 July 2021)

Future of Media Commission. 2021b. *Comhar: Aighneacht don Choimisiún um Thodhchaí na Meán in Éirinn* [Comhar: submission to the Future of Media in Ireland Commission]. https://futureofmediacommission.ie/wp-content/uploads/812.-Comhar.pdf (Accessed 24 July 2021)

Gaelport.com. 2012. Gardener gagged by the state. *Irish Daily Mail* 17 July 2012. https://web.archive.org/web/20171224091854/http://www.gaelport.com/nuacht/Gardener-gagged-by-the-State/ (Accessed 24 July 2021)

Gaelscéal. 2013. 20 February. Aighneas san Acadamh [Argument in the Acadamh]. https://cs.slu.edu/~scannell/gaelsceal/2013-02-20.pdf (Accessed 16 September 2021)

Gal, Susan. 1979. *Language Shift: Social Determinants of linguistic change in Bilingual Austria*. New York: Academic Press.

Galway Advertiser. 2014. *One thousand take part in Spiddal 'Slán le Séan'* [sic] *Irish language rights march*. https://www.advertiser.ie/galway/article/67348/one-thousand-take-part-in-spiddal-sl%C3%a1n-le-s%C3%a9an-irish-language-rights-march (Accessed 24 July 2021)

Galway County Council. 2013 [2008]. *Gaeltacht Local Area Plan 2008-2018 Adopted 25th February 2008, Amendment and Extension Adopted 25th March 2013*. http://www.galway.ie/en/media/Gaeltacht%20LAP%202008%20-2018%20(Amended%2025%20March%202013).pdf (Accessed 12 September 2021)

Gamble, Andrew. 1994 [1988]. *The Free Economy and the Strong State: The Politics of Thatcherism*, 2nd edn. Basingstoke: Palgrave Macmillan.

Gamble, Andrew. 2009. *The Spectre at the Feast: Capitalist Crisis and the Politics of Recession*. Basingstoke: Palgrave Macmillan.

Gannon, Maria, Ailsa Burn-Murdoch, Andrew Aiton, Nick Bailey, Glen Bramley, Allan Campbell, Kayleigh Finnigan, Laura Gilman, Annette Hastings. 2017. *The social impact of the 2017–18 local government budget*. https://digitalpublications.parliament.scot/ResearchBriefings/Report/2017/12/5/The-social-impact-of-the-2017-18-local-government-budget (Accessed 10 August 2021)

Gao, Shaugh & Joseph Sung-Yul Park. 2015. Space and language learning under the neoliberal economy. *L2 Journal* 7(3). 78–96.

García, Ofelia. 2012. Ethnic identity and language policy. In Bernard Spolsky (ed.), *The Cambridge Handbook of Language Policy*, 79–99. Cambridge: Cambridge University Press.

Garvin, Tom. 1987. *Nationalist Revolutionaries of Ireland 1858–1928*. Oxford: Oxford University Press.

Gathercole, Virginia C. Mueller & Enlli Môn Thomas. 2009. Bilingual First-Language Development: Dominant Language Takeover, Threatened Minority Language Take-Up. *Bilingualism* 12(2). 213–237.

Geertz, Clifford. 1973. *The Interpretation of Cultures: Selected Essays*. London: Fontana Press.

Geertz, Clifford. 1988. *Works and Lives: The Anthropologist as Author*. Stanford: Stanford University Press.

Gershon, Ilana. 2011. Un-Friend My Heart: Facebook, Promiscuity, and Heartbreak in a Neoliberal Age. *Anthropological Quarterly* 84(4). 865–894.

Gershon, Ilana. 2016. "I'm not a businessman, I'm a business, man": Typing the neoliberal self into a branded existence. *Hau: Journal of Ethnographic Theory* 6(3). 223–246.

Giddens, Anthony. 1991. *Modernity and self-identity: Self and society in the late-modern age.* Cambridge: Polity Press.
Giddens, Anthony. 2002 [1999]. *Runaway World: How Globalisation is Reshaping Our Lives*, revised edn. London: Profile.
Gille, Zsuzsa & Seán Ó Riain. 2002. Global Ethnography. *Annual Review of Sociology.* 281(1). 271–295.
Giuliano, Paola & Antonio Spilimbergo. 2014. Growing up in a Recession. *Review of Economic Studies* 81(2). 787–817.
Glynn, Irial & Philip J. O'Connell. 2017. Migration. In William K. Roche, Philip J. O'Connell & Andrea Prothero (eds.), *Austerity and Recovery in Ireland: Europe's Poster Child and the Great Recession*, 290–310. Oxford: Oxford University Press.
Glynn, Irial, Thomas Kelly & Piaras MacÉinrí. 2013. *Irish Emigration in an Age of Austerity.* https://www.ucc.ie/en/media/research/emigre/Emigration_in_an_Age_of_Austerity_Final.pdf (Accessed 16 September 2021)
Gorter, Durk. 2006. *Linguistic Landscape: A New Approach to Multilingualism.* Clevedon: Multilingual Matters.
Government of Ireland. 1965. *White paper on the Restoration of the Irish language.* Dublin: Stationery Office.
Government of Ireland. 2003. *Official Languages Act 2003.* http://www.irishstatutebook.ie/eli/2003/act/32/enacted/en/pdf (Accessed 16 September 2021)
Government of Ireland. 2006. *Statement on the Irish Language 2006.* Dublin: Stationery Office.
Government of Ireland. 2009. *Broadcasting Act 2009.* http://www.irishstatutebook.ie/eli/2009/act/18/enacted/en/pdf (Accessed 16 September 2021)
Government of Ireland. 2010. *20-Year Strategy for the Irish Language 2010–2030.* Dublin: Stationery Office.
Government of Ireland. 2011. *Programme for Government 2011–2016.* https://web.archive.org/web/20190128115619/https://www.taoiseach.gov.ie/eng/Work_Of_The_Department/Programme_for_Government/Programme_for_Government_2011-2016.pdf (Accessed 16 September 2021)
Government of Ireland. 2012. *Gaeltacht Act 2012 and Explanatory and Financial Memorandum.* https://www.oireachtas.ie/documents/bills28/bills/2012/5312/b5312s.pdf (Accessed 16 September 2021)
Government of Ireland. 2017a. *Official Languages (Amendment) Bill 2017 General Scheme and Draft Heads of Bill.* https://web.archive.org/web/20201010165343/https://www.chg.gov.ie/app/uploads/2015/07/official-language-amendment-bill-2017-general-scheme-and-draft-heads-of-bill.pdf (Accessed 16 September 2021)
Government of Ireland. 2017b. *Realising our Rural Potential: Action Plan for Rural Development.* https://web.archive.org/web/20201012041659/https://www.chg.gov.ie/app/uploads/2017/01/162404-rural-ireland-action-plan-web-2-1.pdf (Accessed 16 September 2021)
Government of Ireland. 2018a. *Plean Gníomhaíochta 2018–2022* [Action plan 2018–2022]. https://web.archive.org/web/20201010151026/https://www.chg.gov.ie/app/uploads/2018/06/ghaeltacht_report_screen.pdf (Accessed 16 September 2021)
Government of Ireland. 2018b. *Project Ireland 2040: National Development Plan 2018–2027.* http://www.per.gov.ie/wp-content/uploads/NDP-strategy-2018-2027_WEB.pdf (Accessed 16 September 2021)

Government of Ireland. 2021. *Economic Recovery Plan 2021*. https://assets.gov.ie/136523/03f31f12-10eb-4912-86b2-5b9af6aed667.pdf (Accessed 17 August 2021)

Graeber, David. 2004. *Fragments of an Anarchist Anthropology*. Chicago: Prickly Paradigm Press.

Graeber, David. 2014 [2011]. *Debt: The First 5,000 Years*, revised edn. New York: Melvin House.

Graeber, David. 2018. *Bullshit Jobs: A Theory*. London: Allen Lane.

Gramsci, Antonio. 1992. *Prison Notebooks*. New York: Columbia University Press.

Grasso, Maria T. & Marco Giugni. 2016. Protest participation and economic crisis: The conditioning role of political opportunities. *European Journal of Political Research* 55. 663–680.

Green, Jeremy & Scott Lavery. 2017. After neoliberalisation? Monetary indiscipline, crisis and the state. *Transactions of the Institute of British Geographers* 43(1). 79–94.

Greider, William. 1981. The Education of David Stockman. *The Atlantic* December 1981. https://www.theatlantic.com/magazine/archive/1981/12/the-education-of-david-stockman/305760/?single_page=true (Accessed 16 September 2021)

Grenoble, Lenore A. & Lindsay J. Whaley. 1998. Toward a typology of language endangerment. In Lenore A. Grenoble & Lindsay J. Whaley (eds.), *Endangered languages: language loss and community response*, 22–54. Cambridge: Cambridge University Press.

Grenoble, Lenore A. 2011. Language ecology and endangerment. In Peter Austin & Julia Sallabank (eds.), *The Cambridge Handbook of Endangered Languages*, 27–44. Cambridge: Cambridge University Press.

Grin, Francois. 1999. Market Forces, Language Spread and Linguistic Diversity. In Miklos Kontra, Robert Phillipson, Tove Skutnabb-Kangas & Tibor Varády (eds.) *Language: A right and a resource: Approaching linguistic human rights*, 169–186. Budapest: Central European University Press.

Grin, Francois. 2006. Economic Considerations in Language Policy. In Thomas Ricento (ed.), *An Introduction to Language Policy*: Theory and Method, 77–94. Oxford: Blackwell.

Gunther, Wilf. 1989. Language conservancy or: Can the anciently established British minority languages survive? In Durk Gorter, Jarich F. Hoekstra, Lammert G. Jansma & Jehannes Ytsma (eds.), *Fourth International Conference on Minority Languages. Volume II: Western and Eastern European Papers*, 53–68. Clevedon: Multilingual Matters.

Guth na Gaeltachta. 2010. *Open letter to An Taoiseach and An Tánaiste about the future of the Gaeltacht*. https://web.archive.org/web/20130709031701/http://guthnag.com/summary.html (Accessed 16 September 2021)

Haase, Trutz & Jonathan Pratschke. 2017a. *The 2016 Pobal HP Deprivation Index for Small Areas (SA): Introduction and Reference Tables*. https://www.pobal.ie/Publications/Documents/The%202016%20Pobal%20HP%20Deprivation%20Index%20-%20Introduction%202007.pdf (Accessed 16 September 2021)

Haase, Trutz & Jonathan Pratschke. 2017b. *The 2016 Pobal HP Deprivation Index for Small Areas (SA): Introduction and Key Findings*. http://trutzhaase.eu/wp/wp-content/uploads/1The-2016-SA-Pobal-HP-Deprivation-Index-Introduction-and-Key-Findings-26.ppt (Accessed 16 September 2021)

Hall, Peter A. 1993. Policy Paradigms, Social Learning, and the State: The Case of Economic Policymaking in Britain. *Comparative Politics* 25(3). 275–296.

Harbert, Wayne, Sally McConnell-Ginet, Amanda Miller & John Whitman. 2009. *Language and Poverty*. Bristol: Multilingual Matters.

Harbert, Wayne. 2011. Endangered languages and economic development. In Peter K. Austin & Julia Sallabank (eds.), *The Cambridge Handbook of Endangered Languages*, 403–422. Cambridge: Cambridge University Press.

Hardiman, Niamh & Aidan Regan. 2012. The politics of austerity in Ireland. *Intereconomics* 48 (1). 9–13.

Harris, Carl. 2014. The impact of austerity on a British council estate. *Psychologist* 27(4). 250–253.

Harrison, K. David. 2007. *When Languages Die: The Extinction of the World's Languages and the Erosion of Human Knowledge*. Oxford: Oxford University Press.

Harvey, Brian. 2012. *Downsizing the Community Sector: Changes in employment and services in the voluntary and community sector in Ireland, 2008-2012*. https://www.ictu.ie/download/pdf/downsizingcommunitysector.pdf (Accessed 16 September 2021)

Harvey, Brian. 2014. *Are we paying for that?* Dublin: The Advocacy Initiative.

Harvey, David. 2005. *A Brief History of Neoliberalism*. Oxford: Oxford University Press.

Harvey, David. 2007. Neoliberalism as Creative Destruction. *Annals of the American Academy of Political and Social Science* 610. 22–44.

Harvey, David. 2008. The Right to the City. *New Left Review* 53. 23–40.

Harvey, David. 2012a. *The urban roots of financial crises: reclaiming the city for anti-capitalist struggle*. Socialist Register 48. https://socialistregister.com/index.php/srv/article/view/15644/12768 (Accessed 8 October 2021)

Harvey, David. 2012b. *Rebel Cities: From the Right to the City to the Urban Revolution*. London: Verso.

Hay, Colin. 2002. *Political Analysis: A Critical Introduction*. Basingstoke: Palgrave Macmillan.

Hayek, Friedrich. 1988. *The Fatal Conceit: The Errors of Socialism*. New York: Routledge.

Hayek, Friedrich. 2006 [1944]. *The Road to Serfdom*. New York: Routledge.

Hayek, Friedrich. 2011 [1960]. *The Constitution of Liberty: The definitive edition*. Chicago: University of Chicago Press.

Healy, Tom. 2015. *Emigration has taken its toll*. https://web.archive.org/web/20191009214751/http://www.nerinstitute.net/blog/2015/07/03/emigration-has-taken-its-toll/ (Accessed 17 September 2021)

Heller, Monica & Bonnie S. McElhinny. 2017. *Language, Capitalism, Colonialism: Toward a Critical History*. Toronto: University of Toronto Press.

Heller, Monica, Joan Pujolar & Alexandre Duchêne. 2014. Linguistic Commodification in Tourism. Journal of sociolinguistics 18 (4). 539–566.

Heller, Monica. 2006. *Linguistic minorities and modernity: A sociolinguistic ethnography*. New York: Continuum.

Hicks, Davyth, Paola Baroni, Klara Ceberio Berger, Antton Gurrutxaga Hernaiz, Eleonore Kruse, Valeria Quochi, Irene Russo, Tuomo Salonen, Anneli Sarhimaa, Claudia Soria. 2018. *Roadmap to Digital Language Diversity*. http://www.dldp.eu/sites/default/files/documents/DLDP_Roadmap.pdf (Accessed 23 April 2022)

Hill, Jane H. 1987. Women's speech in modern Mexicano. In Susan U. Phillips, Susan Steele & Christine Tanz (eds.), *Language, gender and sex in comparative perspective*, 121–160. Cambridge: Cambridge University Press.

Hindley, Reg. 1990. *The Death of the Irish Language: A Qualified Obituary*. New York: Routledge.

Holmes, Janet. 2013 [1992]. *An Introduction to Sociolinguistics*, 4th edn. New York: Routledge.

Homburg, Vincent, Christopher Pollitt & Sandra van Thiel. 2007. Introduction. In Christopher Pollitt, Sandra van Thiel & Vincent Homburg (eds.), *New Public Management in Europe: Adaptation and Alternatives*, 1–9. Basingstoke: Palgrave Macmillan.

Hornberger, Nancy H. & David Cassels Johnson. 2011. The Ethnography of Language Policy. In Teresa L. McCarty (ed.), *Ethnography and Language Policy*, 273–289. New York: Routledge.

Hornberger, Nancy H. 2006. Frameworks and Models in Language Policy and Planning. In Thomas Ricento (ed.), *An Introduction to Language Policy: Theory and Method*, 24–41. Oxford: Blackwell.

Hornsby, Michael & Wilson McLeod. 2022. *Transmitting Minority Languages: Complementary Reversing Language Shift Strategies*. Basingstoke: Palgrave Macmillan.

Hult, Francis M. & David Cassels Johnson. 2015. *Research Methods in Language Policy and Planning: A Practical Guide*. London: Wiley.

Hult, Francis M. 2010. Analysis of Language Policy Discourses Across the Scales of Space and Time. *International journal of the sociology of language*. 202. 7–24.

Hyndman, Noel & Irvine Lapsley. 2016. New Public Management: The Story Continues. *Financial Accountability & Management* 32(4). 385–408.

ICTU. 2011. *Privatisation: Learning from the Eircom debacle*. https://www.ictu.ie/download/pdf/learning_from_the_eircom_debacle.pdf (Accessed 17 September 2021)

IDA. 2010. *Annual Report & Accounts 2009*. https://www.idaireland.com/IDAIreland/media/docs/About-IDA/IDA-AR09-24-June(lr).pdf (Accessed 17 September 2021)

IDA. 2016. *Annual Report & Accounts 2015*. https://www.idaireland.com/IDAIreland/media/docs/About-IDA/annual_report_2015.pdf (Accessed 17 September 2021)

IMF. 2010. *Ireland: Letter of Intent, Memorandum of Economic and Financial Policies, and Technical Memorandum of Understanding*. https://www.imf.org/external/np/loi/2010/irl/120310.pdf (Accessed 17 September 2021)

IMF. 2012. *Systemic banking crises database: An update*. https://www.imf.org/external/pubs/ft/wp/2012/wp12163.pdf (Accessed 17 September 2021)

IMF. 2013. *Ireland: Ninth Review under the Extended Arrangement, IMF Country Report No. 13/93*. https://www.imf.org/external/pubs/ft/scr/2013/cr1393.pdf (Accessed 17 September 2021)

IMF. 2016. *The IMF's Role in Ireland: Background Paper for the Independent Evaluation Office of the International Monetary Fund*. https://ieo.imf.org/~/media/IEO/Files/evaluations/completed/07-28-2016-the-imf-and-the-crises-in-greece-ireland-and-portugal/eac-bp-16-02-04-the-imf-s-role-in-ireland-v5.ashx (Accessed 17 September 2021)

IMF. 2018. *A Decade after the Global Financial Crisis: Are We Safer? Global Financial Stability Report World Economic and Financial Surveys October 2018*. https://www.imf.org/en/Publications/GFSR/Issues/2018/09/25/Global-Financial-Stability-Report-October-2018 (Accessed 17 September 2021)

IMF. 2019. *The Rise of Phantom Investments*. https://www.imf.org/external/pubs/ft/fandd/2019/09/the-rise-of-phantom-FDI-in-tax-havens-damgaard.htm (Accessed 8 August 2021)

IMF. 2021. *After-effects of the Covid-19 pandemic: Prospects for medium-term economic damage*. https://www.elibrary.imf.org/view/books/081/29821-9781513575025-en/ch02.xml (Accessed 8 August 2021)

IMF. 2022. *World Economic Outlook April 2022: War Sets Back the Global Recovery*. https://www.imf.org/en/Publications/WEO/Issues/2022/04/19/world-economic-outlook-april-2022 (Accessed 25 April 2022)

Indecon. 2016. *Public Funding Review of Public Service Broadcasters.* https://web.archive.
    org/web/20200603170132/https://www.dccae.gov.ie/en-ie/communications/publica
    tions/Documents/67/Annual%20Review%20of%20Public%20Funding%202015.PDF
    (Accessed 17 September 2021)
Indecon. 2017. *Public Funding Review of Public Service Broadcasters.* http://opac.oireachtas.
    ie/AWData/Library3/CCAEdoclaid160518B_115854.pdf (Accessed 17 September 2021)
Indymedia.ie. 2009. *The Phoenix on Colm McCarthy of An Bord Snip.* http://www.indymedia.
    ie/article/93211 (Accessed 17 September 2021)
Inglehart, Ronald. 1997. *Modernization and Postmodernization: Cultural, Economic, and
    Political Change in 43 Societies.* Princeton: Princeton University Press.
Inglehart, Ronald. 2018. *Cultural Evolution: People's Motivations are Changing, and
    Reshaping the World.* Cambridge: Cambridge University Press.
Irish Examiner. 2012. 20 July. *Opposition TDs stage walkout... over Gaeltacht.* http://www.iri
    shexaminer.com/ireland/politics/opposition-tds-stage-walkout-over-gaeltacht-201372.
    html (Accessed 17 September 2021)
Irish Examiner. 2013. 24 September. *20% have less than €150 a month after bills.* http://www.
    irishexaminer.com/ireland/20-have-less-than-150-a-month-after-bills-244077.html
    (Accessed 17 September 2021)
Irish Independent. 2010. 22 December. *Vow to triple our Irish speakers Government unveils its
    20-year strategy.* http://www.independent.ie/irish-news/vow-to-triple-our-irish-speakers-
    26608582.html (Accessed 17 September 2021)
Irish Independent. 2012. 17 November. *The burning question: Why don't we protest?*
    https://www.independent.ie/lifestyle/the-burning-question-why-dont-we-protest-
    28902901.html (Accessed 17 September 2021)
Irish Independent. 2014. 12 September. *Pubs in crisis as over 2,000 locals call last orders.*
    https://www.independent.ie/regionals/herald/news/pubs-in-crisis-as-over-2000-locals-
    call-last-orders-30583527.html (Accessed 17 September 2021)
Irish Independent. 2017. April. *Rich List 2017.* http://www.independent.ie/business/irish/rich-
    list-2017/ (Accessed 17 September 2021)
Irish Independent. 2018. 15 March. *'Lost decade' is over as number in work looks to hit new
    high.* https://www.independent.ie/business/irish/lost-decade-is-over-as-number-in-
    work-looks-to-hit-new-high-36706902.html (Accessed 16 September 2021)
Irish Times. 2010. 18 November. *TG4 paused for thought as it awaits post-budget fate.*
    https://www.irishtimes.com/business/media-and-marketing/tg4-paused-for-thought-as-
    it-awaits-post-budget-fate-1.678319 (Accessed 16 September 2021)
Irish Times. 2011a. 25 November. *McGinley says €500,000 could be saved with no Údarás
    elections.* https://www.irishtimes.com/news/politics/oireachtas/mcginley-says-500-000-
    could-be-saved-with-no-%C3%BAdar%C3%A1s-elections-1.16019 (Accessed
    16 September 2021)
Irish Times. 2011b. 16 April. *The smallest schools in Ireland.* http://www.irishtimes.com/
    news/the-smallest-schools-in-ireland-1.574073 (Accessed 16 September 2021)
Irish Times. 2015a. 25 September. *Tender procedure for Aran Island air service cancelled.*
    https://www.irishtimes.com/business/transport-and-tourism/tender-procedure-for-aran-
    island-air-service-cancelled-1.2367197 (Accessed 16 September 2021)
Irish Times. 2015b. 16 July. *Community in crisis: Extra teacher 'vital' to Inis Meáin.* http://www.
    irishtimes.com/news/education/community-in-crisis-extra-teacher-vital-to-inis-
    me%C3%A1in-1.2286218 (Accessed 16 September 2021)

Irish Times. 2016a. 23 June. *Arts now a 'Frankenstein department'*, says Sinn Féin. https://www.irishtimes.com/news/politics/oireachtas/arts-now-a-frankenstein-department-says-sinn-f%C3%A9in-1.2695535 (Accessed 16 September 2021)

Irish Times. 2016b. 3 August. *State to buy almost 2,000 hectares in Dublin Mountains.* https://www.irishtimes.com/news/environment/state-to-buy-almost-2-000-hectares-in-dublin-mountains-1.2743804 (Accessed 16 September 2021)

Irish Times. 2017. 28 September. *More Irish people still emigrating than moving back.* https://www.irishtimes.com/life-and-style/abroad/more-irish-people-still-emigrating-than-moving-back-1.3236979 (Accessed 16 September 2021)

Irish Times. 2018a. 17 March. *Give me a crash course in ... Irish economic growth.* https://www.irishtimes.com/business/economy/give-me-a-crash-course-in-irish-economic-growth-1.3429505 (Accessed 16 September 2021)

Irish Times. 2018b. 25 February. *An Post takes 11,693 to court over nonpayment of TV licence in 2017.* https://www.irishtimes.com/news/crime-and-law/an-post-takes-11-693-to-court-over-nonpayment-of-tv-licence-in-2017-1.3405139 (Accessed 16 September 2021)

Irish Times. 2018c. 10 April. *Government to invest €178m in Gaeltacht and Irish language.* https://www.irishtimes.com/news/ireland/irish-news/government-to-invest-178m-in-gaeltacht-and-irish-language-1.3457467 (Accessed 16 September 2021)

Irish Times. 2018d. 19 January. *Western community highlights loss of GAA players in bid to revitalise area.* https://www.irishtimes.com/news/social-affairs/western-community-highlights-loss-of-gaa-players-in-bid-to-revitalise-area-1.3361825 (Accessed 16 September 2021)

Irish Times. 2018e. 29 January. *Údarás supported employment in Gaeltacht regions returns to Celtic Tiger highs.* https://www.irishtimes.com/business/economy/%C3%BAdar%C3%A1s-supported-employment-in-gaeltacht-regions-returns-to-celtic-tiger-highs-1.3372129?mode=amp (Accessed 16 September 2021)

Irish Times. 2020a. 17 October. *Women 'far from achieving gender equality', says Citizens' Assembly.* https://www.irishtimes.com/news/ireland/irish-news/women-far-from-achieving-gender-equality-says-citizens-assembly-1.4383153 (Accessed 14 April 2021)

Irish Times. 2020b. 12 October. *Local authorities say they will have to cut services over collapse in revenues.* https://www.irishtimes.com/news/politics/local-authorities-say-they-will-have-to-cut-services-over-collapse-in-revenues-1.4378106 (Accessed 26 July 2021)

Irish Times. 2021a. 4 January. *'We are down to the last penny': Aran islanders on their pandemic year.* https://www.irishtimes.com/news/ireland/irish-news/we-are-down-to-the-last-penny-aran-islanders-on-their-pandemic-year-1.4449232 (Accessed 26 July 2021)

Irish Times. 2021b. 1 June. *Economic recovery plan 'the opposite of austerity', says Taoiseach.* https://www.irishtimes.com/news/ireland/irish-news/economic-recovery-plan-the-opposite-of-austerity-says-taoiseach-1.4580899 (Accessed 17 August 2021)

Irish Times. 2021c. 15 July. *Ireland cannot be part of current global tax reform proposals, Donohoe says.* https://www.irishtimes.com/business/economy/ireland-cannot-be-part-of-current-global-tax-reform-proposals-donohoe-1.4621213 (Accessed 17 August 2021)

Irish Times. 2021d. 7 October. *Ireland's corporate tax rate set to rise to 15%, as part of global deal.* https://www.irishtimes.com/news/politics/ireland-s-corporate-tax-rate-set-to-rise-to-15-as-part-of-global-deal-1.4693782 (Accessed 16 August 2021)

Jackson, Alvin. 2010 [1999]. *Ireland 1798-1998: War, Peace and Beyond*, 2nd edn. Chichester: Wiley-Blackwell.

Jaffe, Alexandra & Cedric Oliva. 2013. Linguistic Creativity in Corsican Tourist Context. In Sari Pietikäinen & Helen Kelly-Holmes (eds.), *Multilingualism and the Periphery*, 95–117. Oxford: Oxford University Press.
Jaffe, Alexandra. 2007. Discourses of endangerment: Contexts and consequences of essentializing discourses. In Alexandre Duchêne & Monica Heller (eds.), *Discourses of Endangerment: Ideology and Interest in the Defence of Languages*, 57–75. New York: Continuum.
Johnson, David Cassels. 2010. Implementational and ideological spaces in bilingual education language policy. *International Journal of Bilingual Education and Bilingualism* 13(1). 61–79.
Johnson, David Cassels. 2013. *Language Policy*. Basingstoke: Palgrave Macmillan.
Jones, Hywel. 2007. The implications of changes in the ages of Welsh speakers and their spatial distribution: translation from Welsh of paper in *Gwerddon*, 1(2).
Jones, Owen. 2018. *Kurdish Afrin is democratic and LGBT-friendly. Turkey is crushing it with Britain's help*. https://www.theguardian.com/commentisfree/2018/mar/16/turkey-democracy-kurdish-afrin-britain-syria-arming (Accessed 17 September 2021)
Jordan, A. Grant & Jeremy John Richardson. 1987. *British Politics and the Policy Process: An arena approach*. London: Allen & Unwin.
Judt, Tony. 2010. *Ill fares the Land: A Treatise on Our Present Discontents*. London: Penguin.
Kalecki, Michał. 1943. Political aspects of full employment. *The Political Quarterly* 14(4). 322–330.
Kaplan, Robert B. & Richard B. Baldauf Jr. 1997. *Language Planning: From Practice to Theory*. Clevedon: Multilingual Matters.
Kay, Adrian. 2005. A Critique of the use of Path Dependency in Policy Studies. *Public Administration* 83(3). 553–571.
Kelly, Adrian. 2002. *Compulsory Irish: Language and Education in Ireland 1870s-1970s*. Dublin: Irish Academic Press.
Kelly, Liz, Sheila Burton & Linda Regan. 1994. 'Researching Women's Lives or Studying Women's Oppression? Reflections on what Constitutes Feminist Research'. In Mary Maynard & June Purvis (eds.), *Researching Women's Lives From A Feminist Perspective*, 27–48. London: Taylor & Francis.
Kelly-Holmes, Helen. 2013. 'Translation in Progress': Centralizing and Peripheralizing Tensions in the Practices of Commercial Actors in Minority Language Sites. In Sari Pietikäinen & Helen Kelly-Holmes (eds.), *Multilingualism and the Periphery*, 118–132. Oxford: Oxford University Press.
Khoo, Su-ming. 2006. Development education, citizenship and civic engagement at third level and beyond: Capacity building for development education in third level education. *Policy and Practice: A Development Education Review – Special Issue on Citizenship* 3. 26–39.
King, Kendall A. & Adam C. Rambow. 2012. Transnationalism, migration and language education policy. In Bernard Spolsky (ed.), *The Cambridge Handbook of Language Policy*, 399–416. Cambridge: Cambridge University Press.
King, Kendall A. & Ling Wang. 2021. Family Language Policy and Language Transmission in Times of Change. In Huw Lewis & Wilson McLeod (eds.), *Language Revitalisation and Social Transformation*, 119–140. Cham: Palgrave Macmillan.
Kirby, Peadar & Mary Murphy. 2011. Globalisation and Models of State: Debates and Evidence from Ireland. *New Political Economy* 16(1). 19–39.

Kirby, Peadar, Luke Gibbons & Michael Cronin. 2002. Introduction: The Reinvention of Ireland: A Critical Perspective. In Peadar Kirby, Luke Gibbons & Michael Cronin (eds.), *Reinventing Ireland: Culture, Society, and the Global Economy*, 1–18. London: Pluto Press.

Kirby, Peadar. 2010 [2002]. *Celtic Tiger in Collapse: Explaining the Weaknesses of the Irish Model*, 2nd edn. Basingstoke: Palgrave MacMillan.

Klein, Naomi. 2007. *The Shock Doctrine: The Rise of Disaster Capitalism*. London: Allen Lane.

KOF. 2017. *Index of Globalization*. https://www.ethz.ch/content/dam/ethz/special-interest/dual/kof-dam/documents/Globalization/rankings_2017.pdf (Accessed 17 September 2021)

Kornai, A. 2013. Digital language death. *PLoS ONE* 8(10). e77056–e77056. https://doi.org/10.1371/journal.pone.0077056.

Krauss, Michael. 1992. The World's Languages in Crisis. *Language* 68(1). 4–10.

Krugman, Paul. 2015. *The Austerity Delusion*. http://www.theguardian.com/business/ng-interactive/2015/apr/29/the-austerity-delusion (Accessed 17 September 2021)

Kulick, Don. 1992. *Language Shift and Cultural Reproduction: Socialization, Self, and Syncretism in a Papua New Guinean Village*. Cambridge: Cambridge University Press.

Kunzlik, Peter. 2013. Neoliberalism and the European Public Procurement Regime. *Cambridge Yearbook of European Legal Studies* 15. 283–356.

Labov, William. 2001. *Principles of Linguistic Change, Volume 2: Social Factors*. Oxford: Blackwell.

Lancee, Bram & Herman G. Van de Werfhorst. 2012. Income inequality and participation: A comparison of 24 European countries. *Social science research* 41(5). 1166–1178.

Lee, J. J. 1989. *Ireland 1912-1985: Politics and Society*. Cambridge: Cambridge University Press.

Lenoach, Ciarán, Conchúr Ó Giollagáin & Brian Ó Curnáin. 2012. *An Chonair Chaoch: An Mionteangachas sa Dátheangachas* [The blind alley: the minority language condition in bilingualism]. Indreabhán: Leabhar Breac.

Lenoach, Ciarán. 2012. An Ghaeilge Iarthraidisiúnta agus a Dioscúrsa [Post-traditional Irish and its discourse]. In Ciarán Lenoach, Conchúr Ó Giollagáin & Brian Ó Curnáin (eds.), *An Chonair Chaoch: An Mionteangachas sa Dátheangachas* [The blind alley: the minority language condition in bilingualism], 19-109. Indreabhán: Leabhar Breac.

Lin, Angel M. Y. 2015. Researcher Positionality. In Francis Hult & David Cassels Johnson (eds.), *Research Methods in Language Policy and Planning: A Practical Guide*, 21–32. London: Wiley.

Lorde, Audre. 2007. *Sister Outsider: Essays & Speeches by Audre Lorde*. Berkeley: Crossing Press.

Lowi, Theodore J. 1964. An American Business, Public Policy, Case-Studies, and Political Theory. *World Politics* 16(4). 677–715.

Lukes, Steven. 1974. *Power: A Radical View*. London: Macmillan.

Lumsden, Karen. 2009. 'Don't Ask a Woman to Do Another Woman's Job': Gendered Interactions and the Emotional Ethnographer. *Sociology* 43(3). 497–513. https://doi.org/10.1177/0038038509103205.

Lynch, Kathleen. 2012. On the Market: Neoliberalism and New Managerialism in Irish Education. *Social Justice Series* 12(5). 88–102.

Mac a' Bhàillidh, Màrtainn. 2022. *The Highland Clearances, 2022*. https://bellacaledonia.org.uk/2022/06/02/the-highland-clearances-2022/ (Accessed 10 June 2022)

Mac Cóil, Liam. 2021. An Fhírinne Neamhráite [The unstated truth]. *Comhar* (January) 81 (1). https://comhar.ie/iris/81/1/an-fhirinne-neamhraite/ (Accessed 25 July 2021)

Mac Cormaic, Breandán. 2011. *Étrange défaite*, nó an Chíor Tuathail Éireannach agus an Ghaeilge [*Étrange défaite:* the cultural context of the Irish economic crisis of 2008]. In Breandán Mac Cormaic (ed.), *Leas na Gaeilge, Leas an Stáit* [The good of Irish, the good of the state], 13–31. Dublin: Coiscéim.
Mac Donnacha, Joe. 2014. *The Death of a Language*. http://www.drb.ie/essays/the-death-of-a-language (Accessed 17 September 2021)
Mac Donnacha, Seosamh. 2008. TG4: Seirbhís Chraolacháin nó Seirbhís Phleanála Teanga? [TG4: a broadcasting service or a language planning service?]. In Eithne O'Connell, John Walsh & Gearóid Denvir (eds.), *TG4@10: Deich mbliana de TG4* [TG4@10: ten years of TG4], 103–113. Indreabhán: Cló Iar-Chonnacht.
Mac Giolla Chríost, Diarmait. 2005. *The Irish language in Ireland: From Goídel to Globalisation*. New York: Routledge.
Mac Giolla Chríost, Diarmait. 2008. Micro-level Language Planning in Ireland. In Anthony J. Liddicoat & Richard B. Baldauf Jr. (eds.), *Language Planning and Policy: Language Planning in Local Contexts*, 75–94. Clevedon: Multilingual Matters.
Mac Ionnrachtaigh, Feargal. 2013. *Language, Resistance and Revival: Republican prisoners and the Irish language in the North of Ireland*. London: Pluto Press.
Mac Síomóin, Tomás. 2006. *Ó Mharsa go Magla: Straitéis nua don Ghaeilge* [From antiquarianism to revival: a new strategy for Irish]. Dublin: Coiscéim.
MacCarthaigh, Muiris. 2017. Reforming the Irish public service: A multiple streams perspective. *Administration* 65(2). 145–164.
Machiavelli, Niccolò. 2003. *The Prince and other writings*. New York: Barnes & Noble.
Mackey, William F. 2001. The ecology of language shift. In Alwin Fill & Peter Mühlhäusler (eds.), *The Ecolinguistics Reader*, 67–74. London: Continuum.
MacLeavy, Julie. 2012. The Lore of the Jungle: Neoliberalism and Statecraft in the Global-Local Disorder. *Area* 44. 250–253.
Magill. 2013. *Why don't Irish people protest more?* https://magill.ie/comment/why-dont-irish-people-protest-more (Accessed 17 September 2021)
Malmendier, Ulrike & Stefan Nagel. 2011. Depression Babies: Do Macroeconomic Experiences Affect Risk Taking? *Quarterly Journal of Economics* 126(1). 373–416.
Marcus, George E. 1998. *Ethnography Through Thick and Thin*. Princeton: Princeton University Press.
Marwick, Alice Emily. 2015. *Status Update: Celebrity, Publicity, and Branding in the Social Media Age*. New Haven: Yale University Press.
McCabe, Connor. 2013 [2011]. *Sins of the Father: The Decisions that Shaped the Irish Economy*, 2nd edn. Dublin: The History Press Ireland.
McCarthy, Colm, Donal McNally, Pat McLaughlin, Maurice O'Connell, William Slattery & Mary Walsh. 2009a. *Report of the Special Group on Public Service Numbers and Expenditure Programmes Volume I*. Dublin: Government of Ireland Publications Office.
McCarthy, Colm, Donal McNally, Pat McLaughlin, Maurice O'Connell, William Slattery & Mary Walsh. (2009b). *Report of the Special Group on Public Service Numbers and Expenditure Programmes Volume II: Detailed Papers*. Dublin: Government of Ireland Publications Office.
McCarty, Teresa L. 2011. *Ethnography and Language Policy*. New York: Routledge.
McCarty, Teresa L. 2015. Ethnography in Language Planning and Policy Research. In Francis Hult & David Cassels Johnson (eds.), *Research Methods in Language Policy and Planning: A Practical Guide*, 81–93. London: Wiley.

McCloskey, James. 2001. *Guthanna in Éag: An mairfidh an Ghaeilge beo? / Voices Silenced: Has Irish a Future?* Dublin: Cois Life.
McColl Millar, Robert. 2005. *Language, Nation and Power: An Introduction.* Basingstoke: Palgrave Macmillan.
McDonough, Terence. 2010. The Irish Crash in Global Context. *World Review of Political Economy* 1(3). 442–462.
McLeod, Wilson. 2002. Language Planning as Regional Development? The Growth of the Gaelic Economy. *Scottish Affairs* 38. 51–72.
McLeod, Wilson. 2022. Conclusion. In Michael Hornsby & Wilson McLeod (eds.), *Transmitting Minority Languages: Complementary Reversing Language Shift Strategies*, 357–368. Cham: Palgrave Macmillan. https://doi.org/10.1007/978-3-030-87910-5_14
McMahon, Timothy G. 2008. *Grand Opportunity: The Gaelic Revival and Irish Society, 1893-1910.* New York: Syracuse University Press.
Mediatique. 2020. *Annual Review of Performance and Public Funding of Public Service Broadcasters, 2019: A report for the Broadcasting Authority of Ireland.* https://opac.oireachtas.ie/Data/Library3/Documents%20Laid/2021/pdf/TCAGSMdocslaid030621_030621_152907.pdf (Accessed 17 September 2021)
Mendoza, Kerry-Anne. 2015. *Austerity: The Demolition of the Welfare State and the Rise of the Zombie Economy.* Oxford: New Internationalist Publications.
Mercille, Julien & Enda Murphy. 2015. *Deepening Neoliberalism, Austerity and Crisis: Europe's Treasure Ireland.* Basingstoke: Palgrave Macmillan.
MG Alba. 2021. *Annual report & statement of accounts 20/21.* https://mgalba.com/wp-content/uploads/2021/06/MG-ALBA-Annual-Report-2020-21-2.pdf (Accessed 12 August 2021)
Mills, Charles Wright. 2000 [1956]. *The Power Elite.* Oxford: Oxford University Press.
Mirowski, Phillip & Edward Nik-Khah. 2017. *The Knowledge We Have Lost in Information: The History of Information in Modern Economics.* Oxford: Oxford University Press.
Mirowski, Phillip. 2013. *Never Let a Serious Crisis go to Waste: How Neoliberalism Survived the Financial Meltdown.* London: Verso.
Misneachd. 2021. *Empowering Gaelic Communities: A New Deal for Gaelic Language Community Development: Discussion paper.* https://drive.google.com/file/d/1kWBw6y_OP_dskF9Yebt4dJeY4x-Ut9C5/view (Accessed 10 August 2021)
Monbiot, George. 2016. *How did we get into this mess? Politics, Equality, Nature.* London: Verso.
Montrul, Silvina A. 2008. *Incomplete Acquisition in Bilingualism: Re-examining the Age Factor.* Amsterdam: John Benjamins.
Moriarty, Máiréad. 2015. *Globalizing Language Policy and Planning: An Irish Perspective.* Basingstoke: Palgrave Macmillan.
Mufwene, Salikoko S. 2008. *Language Evolution: Contact, Competition and Change.* New York: Continuum International Publishing Group.
Mufwene, Salikoko S. 2016. A cost-and-benefit approach to language loss. In Martin Pütz & Luna Filipović (eds.), *Endangered Languages and Languages in Danger: Issues of documentation, policy, and language rights*, 115–143. Amsterdam: John Benjamins.
Mufwene, Salikoko S. 2017. It's still worth theorizing on LEL, despite the heterogeneity and complexity of the processes (Response to commentators). *Language*, 93(4). e306-e316.
Muller, Janet. 2010. *Language and Conflict in Northern Ireland and Canada: A Silent War.* Basingstoke: Palgrave Macmillan.

Murphy, Mary P. & Fiona Dukelow. 2016. *The Irish Welfare State in the Twenty-First Century.* Basingstoke: Palgrave MacMillan.
Murphy, Mary P. 2014. Ireland: Celtic Tiger in Austerity – Explaining Irish Path Dependency. *Journal of Contemporary European Studies* 22(2). 132–142.
Murray Charles. 1990. *The Emerging British Underclass. Choice in Welfare Series No. 2.* London: Institute of Economic Affairs.
National Health Service. n.d. *Strategic Health and Social Care Needs Assessment – epidemiological overview and service utilisation review.* https://ijbwesternisles.scot/application/files/3814/9451/7072/E_Item_5C_-_Part_1_of_2_Strategic_Health__Social_Care_Needs_Assessment.pdf (Accessed 9 May 2022)
National Treasury Management Agency. 2014. *Review of RTÉ for the Department of Communications, Energy and Natural Resources.* https://web.archive.org/web/20200624011955/https://www.dccae.gov.ie/en-ie/communications/publications/Documents/71/NewERA%20Review%20of%20RT%C3%89.pdf (Accessed 17 September 2021)
NERI. 2012. *Quarterly Economic Facts.* Dublin: NERI.
Nettle, Daniel & Susan Romaine. 2000. *Vanishing Voices: The Extinction of the World's Languages.* Oxford: Oxford University Press.
Neville, Patricia. 2015. Organised Voluntarism in Ireland. *International Journal of Voluntary and Nonprofit Organizations* 27(2). 724–745.
Ní Bhrádaigh, Emer & John A. Murray. 2006. On the Emergence of Entrepreneurial Activity – a longitudinal regional study 1891-2003. In Andrew Zacharakis (ed.), *Frontiers of Entrepreneurial Research: Proceedings of the Twenty-Sixth Annual Entrepreneurship Conference*, 516–530. Babson College, MA: Arthur M. Blank Center for Entrepreneurship.
Ní Bhrádaigh, Emer. 2007. Gaeltacht Entrepreneurship: An Opportunity for Integrated Development, Yet Peripheral in Many Ways. *Irish Journal of Management* 28(2). 221–226.
Ní Chuaig, Neasa. 2021. Polasaí don oideachas Gaeltachta 2017-2020 sa chóras bunscolaíochta: Deiseanna agus dúshláin [The policy for Gaeltacht education 2017-2020 in the primary school system: Opportunities and challenges]. In T.J. Ó Ceallaigh & Muiris Ó Laoire (eds.), *An Tumoideachas: Deiseanna agus dea-chleachtais* [Immersion education: opportunities and good practices], 316–323. Dublin: An Chomhairle um Oideachas Gaeltachta agus Gaelscolaíochta.
Ní Dhoimhín, Hannah & Dónall P. Ó Baoill. 2016. *Plean Teanga do Limistéar Pleanála Teanga Ghaoth Dobhair, Anagaire, Rann na Feirste agus Loch an Iúir* [Language plan for the Gaoth Dobhair, Anagaire, Rann na Feirste and Loch an Iúir Language Planning Area]. http://mptiarthuaiscirt.ie/wp-content/uploads/2016/12/Plean-Teanga-do-LPT-Ghaoth-Dobhair-Anagaire-Rann-na-Feirste-agus-Loch-an-I%C3%BAir.pdf (Accessed 17 September 2021)
Ní Ghearáin, Helena. 2018. 'Bagairt' na teagmhála teanga: creidimh an phobail i dtaca le meascadh na Gaeilge agus an Bhéarla [The 'threat' of language contact: community beliefs regarding the mixing of Irish and English]. In Tadhg Ó hIfearnáin & John Walsh (eds.), *An Meon Folaithe: Idé-eolaíochtaí agus iompar lucht labhartha na Gaeilge in Éirinn agus in Albain* [The covert attitude: ideologies and language practices of Irish and Scottish Gaelic speakers in Ireland and Scotland], 39–73. Dublin: Cois Life.
Ní Mhianáin, Róisín. 2003. *Idir Lúibíní: Aistí ar an Léitheoireacht agus ar an Litearthacht* [Between brackets: essays on reading and literacy]. Dublin: Cois Life.
Ní Thuairisg, Laoise. 2012. Ionaid Sealbhaithe Teanga na Breataine Bige: Eiseamláir don Ghaeltacht? [Welsh-language acquisition units: examples for the Gaeltacht?]. In Ciarán

Lenoach, Conchúr Ó Giollagáin & Brian Ó Curnáin (eds.), *An Chonair Chaoch: An Mionteangachas sa Dátheangachas* [The blind alley: the minority language condition in bilingualism], 171–192. Indreabhán: Leabhar Breac.
Nic Craith, Máiréad & Hill, Emma. 2015. Relocating the Ethnographic Field: From Being *There* to *Being* There. *Anthropological Journal of European Cultures* 24(1). 42–62.
Niskansen, William A. 1971. *Bureaucracy and Representative Government.* Chicago: Aldine-Atherton.
NUJ. 2017. *NUJ calls for review of pay and contracts at RTÉ.* https://web.archive.org/web/20201029103806/https://www.nuj.org.uk/news/nuj-calls-for-review-of-pay-and-contracts-at-rt/ (Accessed 17 September 2021)
Ó Broithe, Éamonn. 2012. Scéim Labhairt na Gaeilge: Feidhm agus Mífheidhm [The Irish-speaking scheme: use and misuse]. In Ciarán Lenoach, Conchúr Ó Giollagáin & Brian Ó Curnáin (eds.), *An Chonair Chaoch: An Mionteangachas sa Dátheangachas* [The blind alley: the minority language condition in bilingualism], 237–268. Indreabhán: Leabhar Breac.
Ó Buachalla, Séamus. 1994. Structural inequalities and the State's policy on the Irish language in the education system. *Studies in Education* 10(1). 1–6.
Ó Cadhain, Máirtín. 1964. *Mr Hill: Mr. Tara.* Dublin: J.B. Houston.
Ó Catháin, Máirtín. 2018. *Géarchéim Chonamara: Tá lá an phíce imithe agus níl tada curtha ina áit* [Conamara's crisis: the day of the hayfork is gone and nothing is put in its place]. https://tuairisc.ie/gearcheim-chonamara-ta-la-an-phice-imithe-agus-nil-tada-curtha-ina-ait/ (Accessed 17 September 2021)
Ó Ceallaigh, Ben. 2020. *Plean Teanga do Limistéar Pleanála Teanga Oirthear Chathair na Gaillimhe – "An Bruach Thoir"* [Language plan for the east Galway city language planning area – "The East Bank"]. https://udaras.ie/assets/uploads/2019/07/19-Oirthear-Chathair-na-Gaillimhe-Leagan-Laghdaithe.pdf (Accessed 11 April 2022)
Ó Ceallaigh, Ben. 2022. Economic disruption and language shift – some ethnographic data from Ireland after the 2008 crash. *Studia Celtica Posnaniensia* 6(21). 21–49. https://doi.org/10.2478/scp-2021-0002
Ó Clochartaigh, Trevor. 2013. *Budget 2014: FG & Labour follow the cuts to Gaeltacht pioneered by FF – Ó Clochartaigh.* https://web.archive.org/web/20171218042006/http://www.trevoroc.com/nuachtnews/fg-lo-ag-leanint-polasaithe-ciorruithe-don-ghaeltacht-a-thosaigh-fianna-filfg-labour-follow-the-cuts-to-gaeltacht-pioneered-by-ff-clochartaigh (Accessed 17 September 2021)
Ó Conchubhair, Brian. 2009. *Fin de Siècle na Gaeilge: Darwin, an Athbheochan agus Smaointeoireacht na hEorpa* [The fin de siècle of Irish: Darwin, the revival and European thought]. Indreabhán: An Clóchomhar.
Ó Croidheáin, Caoimhghin. 2006. *Language from Below: The Irish language, Ideology and Power in 20th Century Ireland.* Oxford: Peter Lang.
Ó Cuaig, Seosamh. 2018a. *Pobal 'uirbeach' is mó atá sa tír anois? Cleas leis an status quo a chosaint…* [Predominantly urban communities in the country now? A trick to protect the status quo…]. https://tuairisc.ie/pobal-uirbeach-is-mo-ata-sa-tir-anois-cleas-leis-an-status-quo-a-chosaint/ (Accessed 17 September 2021)
Ó Cuaig, Seosamh. 2018b. *'Do chuala scéal do chéas gach ló mé' – feall náisiúnta an leathanbhanda* ['I heard a story that tormented me each day' – the national failure regarding broadband]. https://tuairisc.ie/do-chuala-sceal-do-cheas-gach-lo-me-feall-naisiunta-an-leathanbhanda/ (Accessed 17 September 2021)

Ó Cuív, Brian. 1951. *Irish dialects and Irish-speaking districts: Three lectures*. Dublin: Dublin Institute for Advanced Studies.
Ó Cuív, Brian. 1969. Irish in the modern world. In Brian Ó Cuív (ed.), *A View of the Irish Language*, 122–132. Dublin: Stationery Office.
Ó Curnáin, Brian. 2007. *The Irish of Iorras Aithneach County Galway Volume I*. Dublin: Dublin Institute for Advanced Studies.
Ó Curnáin, Brian. 2009. Mionteangú na Gaeilge [The minoritisation of Irish]. In Brian Ó Catháin (ed.), *Sochtheangeolaíocht na Gaeilge, Léachtaí Cholmcille XXXIX* [The sociolinguistics of Irish, Colmcille lectures XXXIX], 90–153. Maigh Nuad: An Sagart.
Ó Curnáin, Brian. 2012a. An Ghaeilge Iarthraidisiúnta agus an Phragmataic Chódmheasctha Thiar agus Theas [Post-traditional Irish and codemixed pragmatics in the west and south]. In Ciarán Lenoach, Conchúr Ó Giollagáin & Brian Ó Curnáin (eds.), *An Chonair Chaoch: An Mionteangachas sa Dátheangachas* [The blind alley: the minority language condition in bilingualism], 284–364. Indreabhán: Leabhar Breac.
Ó Curnáin, Brian. 2012b. An Chanúineolaíocht [Dialectology]. In Tadhg Ó hIfearnáin & Máire Ní Neachtain (eds.), *An tSochtheangeolaíocht: Feidhm agus Tuairisc* [Sociolinguistics: function and account], 83–109. Dublin: Cois Life.
Ó Curnáin, Brian. 2015. Cróineolaíocht na Gaeilge Iarthraidisiúnta i gConamara, 1950-2004 [The chronology of post-traditional Irish in Conamara, 1950-2004]. *Éigse* 39. 1–43.
Ó Flatharta, Peadar, Siv Sandberg & Colin Williams. 2014. *From Act to Action: Implementing Language Legislation in Finland, Ireland and Wales*. http://doras.dcu.ie/19655/ (Accessed 17 September 2021)
Ó Gadhra, Nollaig. 2000. Bearna agus na Forbacha [Bearna and na Forbacha]. In Gearóid Ó Tuathaigh, Liam Lillis Ó Laoire & Seán Ua Súilleabháin (eds.), *Pobal na Gaeltachta: A Scéal agus a Dhán* [The Gaeltacht community: its story and its fate], 265–288. Indreabhán: Raidió na Gaeltachta with Cló Iar-Chonnacht.
Ó Gairbhí, Seán Tadhg. 2017. *Súil Eile* [Another look]. Dublin: Cois Life.
Ó Giollagáin, Conchúr & Brian Ó Curnáin. 2016. *Beartas Úr na nGael: Dálaí na Gaeilge san Iar-Nua-Aoiseachas* [A new deal for the Gaels: the conditions of Irish in post-modernity]. Indreabhán: Leabhar Breac.
Ó Giollagáin, Conchúr & Martin Charlton. 2015a. *Nuashonrú ar an Staidéar Cuimsitheach Teangeolaíoch ar Úsáid na Gaeilge sa Ghaeltacht* [Update to the Comprehensive Linguistic Study of the use of Irish in the Gaeltacht]. https://www.udaras.ie/assets/uploads/2020/11/002910_Udaras_Nuashonrul%C2%81_FULL_report_A4_FA.pdf (Accessed 17 September 2021)
Ó Giollagáin, Conchúr & Martin Charlton. 2015b. *Nuashonrú ar an Staidéar Cuimsitheach Teangeolaíoch ar Úsáid na Gaeilge sa Ghaeltacht: Moltaí agus Beartais Fhéideartha* [Update to the Comprehensive Linguistic Study of the use of Irish in the Gaeltacht: recommendations and possible policies]. http://www.soillse.ac.uk/wp-content/uploads/4.2-Beartais-Nuashonr2.pdf (Accessed 17 September 2021)
Ó Giollagáin, Conchúr, Gòrdan Camshron, Pàdruig Moireach, Brian Ó Curnáin, Iain Caimbeul, Brian MacDonald & Tamás Péterváry. 2020. *The Gaelic Crisis in the Vernacular Community: A Comprehensive Sociolinguistic Study of Scottish Gaelic*. Aberdeen: Aberdeen University Press.
Ó Giollagáin, Conchúr, Seosamh Mac Donnacha, Fiona Ní Chualáin, Aoife Ní Shéaghdha & Mary O'Brien. 2007a. *Staidéar Cuimsitheach Teangeolaíoch ar Úsáid na Gaeilge sa*

Ghaeltacht [Comprehensive Linguistic Study of the use of Irish in the Gaeltacht]. Dublin: Stationery Office.

Ó Giollagáin, Conchúr, Seosamh Mac Donnacha, Fiona Ní Chualáin, Aoife Ní Shéaghdha & Mary O'Brien. 2007b. *Staidéar Cuimsitheach Teangeolaíoch ar Úsáid na Gaeilge sa Ghaeltacht: Príomhthátal agus Moltaí* [Comprehensive Linguistic Study of the Use of Irish in the Gaeltacht: main conclusion and recommendations]. Dublin: Stationery Office.

Ó Giollagáin, Conchúr. 2014a. From Revivalist to Undertaker: New Developments in Official Policies and Attitudes to Ireland's 'First Language'. *Language Problems & Language Planning* 38(2). 101–127.

Ó Giollagáin, Conchúr. 2014b. Unfirm Ground: A re-assessment of language policy in Ireland since Independence. *Language Problems and Language Planning* 38(1). 19–41.

Ó Giollagáin, Conchúr. 2016. Gnéithe de Stair Theorainn na Gaeltachta: Coimhlint Idir Dhá Riachtanas [Aspects of the history of the Gaeltacht boundaries: a conflict between two necessities]. In Conchúr Ó Giollagáin & Brian Ó Curnáin (eds.), *Beartas Úr na nGael: Dálaí na Gaeilge san Iar-Nua-Aoiseachas* [A new deal for the Gaels: the conditions of Irish in post-modernity], 69–106. Indreabhán: Leabhar Breac.

Ó Giollagáin, Conchúr. 2017. *Ceansú na Gaeltachta i ndul i léig na Gaeilge* [The pacification of the Gaeltacht and the decline of Irish]. https://www.youtube.com/watch?v=pRa-G2u6IFk (Accessed 13 September 2021)

Ó Giollagáin, Conchúr. 2018. *Tús áite d'fhealsúnacht na bhfoghlaimeoirí Gaeilge seachas do riachtanais an phobail Ghaelaigh i bplean nua an Rialtais* [Primacy given to Irish learners instead of the necessities of the Gaelic community in the government's new plan]. https://tuairisc.ie/tus-aite-dfhealsunacht-na-bhfoghlaimeoiri-gaeilge-seachas-do-riachtanais-an-phobail-ghaelaigh-i-bplean-nua-an-rialtais/ (Accessed 17 September 2021)

Ó hAoláin, Pádraig. 2002. Regional Development and the Role of Údarás na Gaeltachta. In John McDonagh (ed.), *Economy, Society and Peripherality: Experiences from the West of Ireland*, 23–36. Dublin: Arlen House.

Ó hÉallaithe, Donncha. 2004. From Language Revival to Language Survival. In Ciarán Mac Murchaidh (ed.), *Who needs Irish? – Reflections on the Importance of the Irish Language Today*, 159–192. Dublin: Veritas.

Ó hÉallaithe, Donncha. 2017a. *Athraímis na teorainneacha, ach 'cultural appropriation' a bheadh i stádas Gaeltachta do leithéid Chluain Dolcáin* [Let's change the boundaries, but it would be 'cultural appropriation' to give Gaeltacht status to the likes of Clondalkin]. http://tuairisc.ie/athraimis-na-teorainneacha-ach-cultural-appropriation-a-bheadh-i-stadas-gaeltachta-do-leitheid-chluain-dolcain/ (Accessed 17 September 2021)

Ó hÉallaithe, Donncha. 2017b. *Daonáireamh 2016: Beidh a ndóthain le déanamh ag lucht pleanála teanga sna croíchathair Ghaeltachta* [Census 2016: language planners will have their work cut out for them in the Gaeltacht heartlands]. http://tuairisc.ie/daonair eamh-2016-beidh-a-ndothain-le-deanamh-ag-lucht-pleanala-teanga-sna-croicheantair-ghaeltachta/ (Accessed 17 September 2021)

Ó hIfearnáin, Tadhg & John Walsh. 2018. *An Meon Folaithe: Idé-eolaíochtaí agus iompar lucht labhartha na Gaeilge in Éirinn agus in Albain* [The covert attitude: ideologies and language practices of Irish and Scottish Gaelic speakers in Ireland and Scotland]. Dublin: Cois Life.

Ó hIfearnáin, Tadhg. 2010. Irish-speaking society and the state. In Martin J. Ball & Nicole Müller (eds.), *The Celtic Languages*, 2nd edn, 539–586. New York: Routledge.

Ó hIfearnáin, Tadhg. 2013. Family language policy, first language Irish speaker attitudes and community-based response to language shift. *Journal of Multilingual and Multicultural Development* 34(4). 348–365.

Ó hIfearnáin, Tadhg. 2018. The Ideological Construction of Boundaries Between Speakers, and Their Varieties. In Cassie Smith-Christmas, Noel P. Ó Murchadha, Michael Hornsby & Máiréad Moriarty (eds.), *New Speakers of Minority Languages Linguistic Ideologies and Practices*, 151–164. Basingstoke: Palgrave Macmillan.

Ó hIfearnáin, Tadhg. 2022. Wider Community Stance and Irish-Speaking Families in the Gaeltacht. In Michael Hornsby & Wilson McLeod (eds.), *Transmitting Minority Languages: Complementary Reversing Language Shift Strategies*, 105–135. Cham: Palgrave Macmillan. https://doi.org/10.1007/978-3-030-87910-5_5

Ó Huallacháin, Colmán. 1991. *The Irish Language in Society*. Coleraine: University of Ulster.

Ó Huallacháin, Colmán. 1994. *The Irish and Irish: A sociolinguistic analysis of the relationship between a people and their language*. Dublin: Irish Franciscan Provincial Office.

Ó Laoire, Lillis. 2002. *Ar Chreag i Lár na Farraige: Amhráin agus Amhránaithe i dToraigh* [On a rock in the middle of the ocean: songs and singers in Toraigh]. Indreabhán: Cló Iar-Chonnacht.

Ó Laoire, Muiris. 2008. The Language Situation in Ireland. In Robert B. Kaplan & Richard B. Baldauf Jr. (eds.), *Language planning and policy in Europe, vol. 3: The Baltic States, Ireland and Italy*, 193–255. Clevedon: Multilingual Matters.

Ó Murchú, Helen. 2003. *Limistéar na Sibhialtachta: Dúshlán agus Treo d'Eagraíochtaí na Gaeilge* [The area of civility: challenge and direction for Irish-language organisations]. Dublin: Coiscéim.

Ó Murchú, Helen. 2008. *More Facts about Irish volume 1* [extended electronic version]. https://web.archive.org/web/20191210122207/http://www.gaelport.com/MFAI2014B (Accessed 17 September 2021)

Ó Murchú, Helen. 2014. *More Facts About Irish, volume 2*. https://web.archive.org/web/20191210122207/http://www.gaelport.com/MFAI2014B (Accessed 17 September 2021)

Ó Murchú, Máirtín. 1970. *Urlabhra agus Pobal/Language and Community*. Dublin: Stationery Office.

Ó Murchú, Máirtín. 2001. *Cumann Buan-Choimeádta na Gaeilge: Tús an Athréimnithe* [The society for the preservation of the Irish language: the beginning of the revival]. Dublin: Cois Life.

Ó Murchú, Máirtín. 2002. *Ag Dul Ó Chion? Cás na Gaeilge 1952-2002* [In decline? The situation of Irish 1952-2002]. Dublin: Coiscéim.

Ó Neachtain, Éamonn. 2014. The Irish Gaeltacht: the limitations of regional development and linguistic autonomy. In Levente Salat, Sergiu Constantin, Alexander Osipov & István Gergő Székely (eds.), *Autonomy Arrangements around the World: A Collection of Well and Lesser Known Cases*, 367–415. Editura Institutului pentru Studierea Problemelor Minorităților Naționale.

Ó Riagáin, Pádraig. 1996. Reviving the Irish language: 1893–1993: The first one hundred years. In Máiréad Nic Craith (ed.), *Watching one's tongue: Issues in Language Planning*, 33–55. Liverpool: Liverpool University Press.

Ó Riagáin, Pádraig. 1997. *Language Policy and Social Reproduction: Ireland 1893–1993*. Oxford: Oxford University Press.

Ó Riagáin, Pádraig. 2008. Irish-language Policy 1922–2007: Balancing Maintenance and Revival. In Caoilfhionn Nic Pháidín & Seán Ó Cearnaigh (eds.), *A New View of the Irish Language*, 55–65. Dublin: Cois Life.

Ó Torna, Caitríona. 2005. *Cruthú na Gaeltachta, 1893-1922: Samhlú agus Buanú Chonstráid na Gaeltachta i rith na hAthbheochana* [Creating the Gaeltacht, 1893–1922: imagining and perpetuating the construct of the Gaeltacht during the revival]. Dublin: Cois Life.

Ó Tuathaigh, Gearóid. 1990. *The Development of the Gaeltacht as a Bilingual Entity*. Occasional Paper No. 8. Dublin: Dublin Institute of Technology.

Ó Tuathaigh, Gearóid. 2008. The State and the Irish Language. In Caoilfhionn Nic Pháidín & Seán Ó Cearnaigh (eds.), *A New View of the Irish Language*, 26–42. Dublin: Cois Life.

Ó Tuathaigh, Gearóid. 2011. An Stát, an Féiniúlacht [sic] Náisiúnta agus an Teanga: Cás na hÉireann [The state, national identity and the language: the case of Ireland]. In Breandán Mac Cormaic (ed.), *Féiniúlacht, Cultúr agus Teanga i Ré an Domhandaithe* [Identity, culture and language in an era of globalisation], 76–112. Dublin: Coiscéim.

O'Connell, Eithne, John Walsh & Gearóid Denvir. 2008. *TG4@10: Deich mbliana de TG4* [TG4@10: ten years of TG4]. Indreabhán: Cló Iar-Chonnacht.

O'Connell, Philip J. 2017. Unemployment and Labour Market Policy. In William K. Roche, Philip J. O'Connell & Andrea Prothero (eds.), *Austerity and Recovery in Ireland: Europe's Poster Child and the Great Recession*, 232–251. Oxford: Oxford University Press.

O'Connor, Pat. 2008. The Irish Patriarchal State: Continuity and Change. In Maura Adshead, Peadar Kirby & Michelle Millar (eds.), *Contesting the State: Lessons from the Irish Case*, 142–164. Manchester: Manchester University Press.

O'Donoghue, Cathal, Paul Kilgarriff & Mary Ryan. 2017. *The Local Impact of the Economic Recovery*. https://www.teagasc.ie/media/website/publications/2017/The-Local-Impact-of-the-Economic-Recovery.pdf (Accessed 5 August 2021)

O'Donoghue, Cathal. 2014. Introduction. In Cathal O'Donoghue, Ricky Conneely, Deirdre Frost, Kevin Heanue, Brian Leonard & David Meredith (eds.), *Rural Economic Development in Ireland*, 18–33. Carlow: Teagasc: The Irish Agriculture and Development Authority.

O'Rourke, Bernadette & Joan Pujolar. 2013. From native speakers to "new speakers" – problematizing nativeness in language revitalization contexts. *Histoire Épistémologie Langage*, 35(2). 47–67.

O'Rourke, Bernadette & John Walsh. 2020. *New Speakers of Irish in the Global Context: New Revival?* New York: Routledge.

O'Toole, Ciara & Tina M. Hickey. 2017. Bilingual language acquisition in a minority context: using the Irish–English Communicative Development Inventory to track acquisition of an endangered language. *International Journal of Bilingual Education and Bilingualism* 20(2). 146–162.

O'Toole, Fintan. 2010. *Ship of Fools: How Stupidity and Corruption Sank the Celtic Tiger*. London: Faber.

O'Toole, Fintan. 2017. The smearing of Maurice McCabe. https://www.irishtimes.com/news/politics/fintan-o-toole-the-smearing-of-maurice-mccabe-1.2971456 (Accessed 17 September 2021)

Ochs, Elinor. 1986. Introduction. In Bambi B. Schieffelin & Elinor Ochs (eds.), *Language Socialization Across Cultures*, 1–14. Cambridge: Cambridge University Press.

Ochs, Elinor. 1993. Constructing social identity: A language socialization perspective. *Research on Language and Social Interaction* 26. 287–306.

OECD. 2008. *Ireland: Towards an Integrated Public Service*. Paris: OECD Publishing.

OECD. 2015. *The Metropolitan Century: Understanding Urbanisation and its Consequences*. Paris: OECD Publishing.
OECD. 2017. *Trends in Industrial Disputes*. http://www.oecd.org/els/emp/Industrial-disputes.pdf (Accessed 1 September 2021)
Oireachtas Éireann. 2013a. *Committee of Public Accounts: Correspondence from Aidan Dunning, General Secretary Department of Communications, Energy and Natural Resources*. https://web.archive.org/web/20180509025911/https://www.oireachtas.ie/parliament/media/committees/pac/correspondence/2013meetings/2013-meeting852305/[PAC-R-937]-Correspondence-3A.1.pdf (Accessed 17 September 2021)
Oireachtas Éireann. 2013b. *Joint Committee on Public Service Oversight and Petitions debate – Wednesday, 4 Dec 2013. Annual Report 2012: Discussion with An Coimisinéir Teanga* [The Language Commissioner]. https://www.oireachtas.ie/en/debates/debate/joint_committee_on_public_service_oversight_and_petitions/2013-12-04/2/ (Accessed 17 September 2021)
Oireachtas Éireann. 2014. *An Fochoiste um an Straitéis 20 Bliain don Ghaeilge 2010–2030 agus Rudaí Gaolmhara, 23 January 2014. Straitéis 20 Bliain don Ghaeilge: An Coimisinéir Teanga* [The subcommittee for the 20-Year Strategy for the Irish Language 2010–2030 and related matters, 23 January 2014, 20-Year Strategy for the Irish Language: the Language Commissioner]. https://www.oireachtas.ie/en/debates/debate/an_fochoiste_um_an_straiteis_20_bliain_don_ghaeilge_2010-2030_agus_rudai_gaolmhara/2014-01-23/2/ (Accessed 17 September 2021)
Oireachtas Éireann. 2016. *Comhchoiste na Gaeilge, na Gaeltachta agus na nOileán debate – Tuesday, 4 Oct 2016. Athbhreithniú ar Acht na dTeangacha Oifigiúla 2003: An Coimisinéir Teanga* [The committee on the Irish language, the Gaeltacht and the islands debate – Tuesday, 4 Oct 2016. Review of the Official Languages Act 2003: The Language Commissioner]. https://www.oireachtas.ie/en/debates/debate/comhchoiste_na_gaeilge_na_gaeltachta_agus_na_noilean/2016-10-04/2/ (Accessed 17 September 2021)
Oireachtas Éireann. 2017a. *Report of the Joint Committee on the Future Funding of Public Service Broadcasting. Laid before both Houses of the Oireachtas 28 November 2017*. https://data.oireachtas.ie/ie/oireachtas/committee/dail/32/joint_committee_on_communications_climate_action_and_environment/reports/2017/2017-11-28_report-on-the-future-funding-of-public-service-broadcasting_en.pdf (Accessed 17 September 2021)
Oireachtas Éireann. 2017b. *Houses of the Oireachtas Joint Committee on Communications, Climate Action and Environment Report of the Joint Committee on the Future Funding of Public Service Broadcasting*. http://opac.oireachtas.ie/AWData/Library3/Future_Funding_of_PSB_REPORT_Laid_13_Dec_2017_104152.pdf (Accessed 17 September 2021)
Oireachtas Éireann. 2017c. *Comhchoiste na Gaeilge, na Gaeltachta agus na nOileán: Ráitis Oscailte, Alan Esslemont, TG4, Cur i láthair. 26th September 2017* [The committee on the Irish language, the Gaeltacht and the islands: Opening Statement, Alan Esslemont, TG4, Presentation. 26th September 2017] https://data.oireachtas.ie/ie/oireachtas/committee/dail/32/comhchoiste_na_gaeilge_na_gaeltachta_agus_na_noilean/submissions/2017/2017-09-26_raitis-oscailte-alan-esslemont-tg4-cur-i-lathair_en.pdf (Accessed 17 September 2021)
Oireachtas Éireann. 2017d. *Comhchoiste na Gaeilge, na Gaeltachta agus na nOileán: Aitheasc maidir leis na hábhair: 'Na dúshláin a bhaineann le craoltóireacht in Éirinn trí mheán na Gaeilge agus na dualgais atá ar TG4 faoin reachtaíocht' agus 'Soláthar fotheidil agus foscríbhinní as Gaeilge agus as Béarla'. 26 Meán Fómhair 2017* [The committee on the

Irish language, the Gaeltacht and the islands: address regarding the matters: 'the challenges of broadcasting through the medium of Irish and TG4's obligations under the legislation' and 'provision of subtitles and captions in Irish and English']. https://web.archive.org/web/20180509052728/https://www.oireachtas.ie/parliament/media/committees/irishlanguage/TG4-Aitheasc.pdf (Accessed 17 September 2021)

Oireachtas Éireann. 2018a. *Joint Committee on Culture, Heritage and the Gaeltacht debate – Wednesday, 9 May 2018.* https://www.oireachtas.ie/ga/debates/debate/joint_committee_on_culture_heritage_and_the_gaeltacht/2018-05-09/3/?highlight%5B0%5D=f%C3%83%C2%ADb%C3%83%C2%ADn&highlight%5B1%5D=f%C3%83%C2%ADb%C3%83%C2%ADn&highlight%5B2%5D=f%C3%83%C2%ADb%C3%83%C2%ADn (Accessed 17 September 2021)

Oireachtas Éireann. 2018b. *Comhchoiste na Gaeilge, na Gaeltachta agus na nOileán díospóireacht – Dé Máirt, 20 Márta 2018* [The committee on the Irish language, the Gaeltacht and the islands debate – Tuesday 20 March 2018]. https://www.oireachtas.ie/ga/debates/debate/comhchoiste_na_gaeilge_na_gaeltachta_agus_na_noilean/2018-03-20/1/ (Accessed 17 September 2021)

Oireachtas Éireann. 2018c. *Comhchoiste na Gaeilge, na Gaeltachta agus na nOileán debate – Tuesday, 17 Apr [sic] 2018* [The committee on the Irish language, the Gaeltacht and the islands debate Tuesday 17 April 2018]. https://www.oireachtas.ie/ga/debates/debate/comhchoiste_na_gaeilge_na_gaeltachta_agus_na_noilean/2018-04-17/3/ (Accessed 17 September 2021)

Oireachtas Éireann. 2018d. *Comhchoiste na Gaeilge, na Gaeltachta agus na nOileán díospóireacht – Tuesday 6 Mar [sic] 2018* [The committee on the Irish language, the Gaeltacht and the islands debate Tuesday 6 March 2018]. https://www.oireachtas.ie/ga/debates/debate/comhchoiste_na_gaeilge_na_gaeltachta_agus_na_noilean/2018-03-06/3/ (Accessed 17 September 2021)

Oireachtas Éireann. 2019. *Comhchoiste na Gaeilge, na Gaeltachta agus na nOileán: Tuarascáil ar na dúshláin a bhaineann le craoltóireacht na Gaeilge* [The committee on the Irish language, the Gaeltacht and the islands: report on the challenges of broadcasting in Irish]. https://data.oireachtas.ie/ie/oireachtas/committee/dail/32/comhchoiste_na_gaeilge_na_gaeltachta_agus_na_noilean/reports/2019/2019-06-11_tuarascail-ar-na-dushlain-a-bhaineann-le-craoltoireacht-na-gaeilge_en.pdf (Accessed 17 September 2021)

Oireachtas Éireann. 2020a. *Ráiteas tosaigh, Liam Mac Cóil, Scríbhneoir* [Beginning statement, Liam Mac Cóil, writer]. https://data.oireachtas.ie/ie/oireachtas/committee/dail/33/comhchoiste_na_gaeilge_na_gaeltachta_agus_phobal_labhartha_na_gaeilge/submissions/2020/2020-12-10_raiteas-tosaigh-liam-mac-coil-scribhneoir_en.pdf (Accessed 25 July 2021)

Oireachtas Éireann. 2021a. *Committee of Public Accounts debate – Tuesday, 25 May 2021.* https://www.oireachtas.ie/en/debates/debate/committee_of_public_accounts/2021-05-25/2/?highlight%5B0%5D=raidi%C3%83%C2%B3&highlight%5B1%5D=na&highlight%5B2%5D=gaeltachta&highlight%5B3%5D=forbes&highlight%5B4%5D=raidi%C3%83%C2%B3&highlight%5B5%5D=na&highlight%5B6%5D=gaeltachta&highlight%5B7%5D=forbes (Accessed 25 July 2021)

Oireachtas Éireann. 2021b. *Comhchoiste na Gaeilge, na Gaeltachta agus Phobal Labhartha na Gaeilge debate – Wednesday, 21 Jul [sic] 2021* [The committee on the Irish language, the Gaeltacht and the islands: debate – Wednesday, 21 July 2021]. https://www.oireachtas.

ie/en/debates/debate/comhchoiste_na_gaeilge_na_gaeltachta_agus_phobal_labhartha_na_gaeilge/2021-07-21/3/ (Accessed 25 July 2021)
Oireachtas Éireann. 2021c. *Údarás na Gaeltachta Dáil Éireann Debate, Thursday – 6 May 2021*. https://www.oireachtas.ie/en/debates/question/2021-05-06/53/ (Accessed 30 August 2021)
OLRS. 2014. *Higher education in Ireland: For Economy and Society?* https://web.archive.org/web/20210423152916/https://webarchive.oireachtas.ie/parliament/media/housesoftheoireachtas/libraryresearch/spotlights/spotlight_higher_education_for_upload_155719.pdf (Accessed 17 September 2021)
OLRS. 2016. *The Irish Language: A Linguistic Crisis?* https://web.archive.org/web/20180504034253/https://data.oireachtas.ie/ie/oireachtas/libraryResearch/2016/2016-11-07_the-irish-language-a-linguistic-crisis_en.pdf (Accessed 17 September 2021)
Olsberg SPI & Nordicity. 2017. *Economic Analysis of the Audiovisual Sector in the Republic of Ireland*. https://web.archive.org/web/20201009162941/https://www.chg.gov.ie/app/uploads/2018/06/economic-analysis-of-the-audiovisual-sector-in-the-republic-of-ireland.pdf (Accessed 17 September 2021)
Olsen-Reeder, Vincent Ieni. 2022. Creating Language Shift: Factors Behind the Language Choices of Māori Speakers. In Michael Hornsby & Wilson McLeod (eds.), *Transmitting Minority Languages: Complementary Reversing Language Shift Strategies*, 165–190. Cham: Palgrave Macmillan. https://doi.org/10.1007/978-3-030-87910-5_7
Ortner, Sherry B. 2010. Access: Reflections on studying up in Hollywood. *Ethnography* 11(2). 211–233.
Oxfam. 2021. *The Inequality Virus*. https://oxfamilibrary.openrepository.com/bitstream/handle/10546/621149/bp-the-inequality-virus-250121-en.pdf (Accessed 17 August 2021)
Parenti, Michael. 2016. *The Face of Imperialism*. New York: Routledge.
Paskov, Marii & Caroline Dewilde. 2012. *Income inequality and solidarity in Europe: Gini discussion paper 33*. http://www.gini-research.org/system/uploads/379/original/DP_33_-_Paskov_Dewilde.pdf?1345621096 (Accessed 17 September 2021)
Pavlenko, Aneta & Adrian Blackledge. 2004. *Negotiation of Identities in Multilingual Contexts*. Clevedon: Multilingual Matters.
Pearse, Padraic [Patrick] H. 1976 [1912]. *The Murder Machine and Other Essays*. Dublin: Mercier Press.
Peck, Jamie & Adam Tickell. 2002. Neoliberalizing Space. *Antipode* 34. 380–404.
Péterváry, Tamás, Brian Ó Curnáin, Conchúr Ó Giollagáin & Jerome Sheahan. 2014. *Iniúchadh ar an gCumas Dátheangach: An sealbhú teanga i measc ghlúin óg na Gaeltachta – Analysis of Bilingual Competence: Language acquisition among young people in the Gaeltacht*. Dublin: An Chomhairle um Oideachas Gaeltachta agus Gaelscolaíochta.
Phillips, Dylan & Catrin Thomas. 2001. *The Effects of Tourism on the Welsh Language in Northwest Wales*. Aberystwyth: University of Wales Centre for Advanced Welsh and Celtic Studies.
Phillips, Graham. 2017. *Fragile areas in the Highlands & Islands*. https://medium.com/@gp_50794/fragile-areas-in-the-highlands-islands-b3668dd87651 (Accessed 17 September 2021)
Phillipson, Robert. 2008. The Linguistic Imperialism of Neoliberal Empire. *Critical Inquiry in Language Studies* 5(1). 1–43.

Pierson, Paul. 2002. Coping with permanent austerity: welfare state restructuring in affluent democracies. *Revue Française de Sociologie: L'Europe Sociale en Perspectives* 43(2). 369–406.

Pietikäinen, Sari. 2013. Heteroglossic Authenticity in Sámi Heritage Tourism. In Sari Pietikäinen & Helen Kelly-Holmes (eds.), *Multilingualism and the Periphery*, 77–94. Oxford: Oxford University Press.

Piketty, Thomas. 2014. *Capital in the Twenty-first Century*. Cambridge, Massachusetts: Harvard University Press.

Piller, Ingrid & Jinhyun Cho. 2013. Neoliberalism as Language Policy. *Language in Society* 42 (1). 23–44.

Piotrowski, Jessica Taylor, Amy B. Jordan, Amy Bleakley & Michael Hennessy. 2015. Identifying Family Television Practices to Reduce Children's Television Time. *Journal of Family Communication* 15(2). 159–174.

Pobal.ie. 2017. *Deprivation Indices*. https://maps.pobal.ie/WebApps/DeprivationIndices/index.html (Accessed 10 September 2021)

Potowski, Kim. 2013. Language Maintenance and Shift. In Robert Bayley, Richard Cameron & Ceil Lucas (eds.), *The Oxford Handbook of Sociolinguistics*, 321–339. Oxford: Oxford University Press.

Powell, Kathy. 2017. Brexit positions: neoliberalism, austerity and immigration – the (im) possibilities of political revolution. *Dialectical Anthropology* 41(3). 225–240.

Press and Journal. 2018. *Revealed: The "staggering" true scale of council job cuts*. https://www.pressandjournal.co.uk/fp/news/aberdeen/1380355/revealed-the-staggering-true-scale-of-council-job-cuts/ (Accessed 10 August 2021)

Putnam, Robert D. & Kristin A. Goss. 2002. Introduction. In Robert D. Putnam (ed.), *Democracies in Flux: The Evolution of Social Capital in Contemporary Society*, 3–20. Oxford: Oxford University Press.

Putnam, Robert D. 2000. *Bowling Alone: The Collapse and Revival of American Community*. New York: Simon & Schuster.

Rae, Alasdair, Ruth Hamilton & Allan Faulds. 2019. *Too big to be local, too small to be strategic? Scotland's Councils and the question of local government boundary reform*. https://pure.strath.ac.uk/ws/portalfiles/portal/87071556/FEC_43_1_2019_RaeAHamiltonRFauldsA.pdf (Accessed 9 May 2022)

Randma-Liiv, Tiina & Walter Kickert. 2017. The Impact of the Fiscal Crisis on Public Administration Reforms: Comparison of 14 European Countries. *Journal of Comparative Policy Analysis: Research and Practice* 19(2). 155–172.

Reuters. 2007. *Zurich Fin'l unit settles U.S. market-timing case*. http://www.reuters.com/article/zurichfinancial-sec-idUSN0735226620070507 (Accessed 17 September 2021)

Ricento, Thomas. 2000. Historical and theoretical perspectives in language policy and planning. *Journal of Sociolinguistics* 4(2). 196–213.

Ricento, Thomas. 2006. *An Introduction to Language Policy: Theory and Method*. Oxford: Blackwell Publishing.

Ricento, Thomas. 2015. *Language Policy and Political Economy: English in a Global Context*. Oxford: Oxford University Press.

RnaG. 2015. *Interview on Raidió na Gaeltachta: Iris Aniar Dé Máirt 7 Aibreán 2015* [Tuesday April 7th 2015]. http://www.rte.ie/rnag/iris-aniar/programmes/2015/0407/692512-iris-aniar-d-mirt-7-aibren-2015/?clipid=1849120 (Accessed 17 September 2021)

Roberts, John Michael. 2014. *New media and public activism: Neoliberalism, the state and radical protest in the public sphere.* Bristol: Policy Press.

Roche, William K., Philip J. O'Connell & Andrea Prothero. 2017. *Austerity and Recovery in Ireland: Europe's Poster Child and the Great Recession.* Oxford: Oxford University Press.

Rojo, Luisa Martín. 2020. The "self-made speaker": The neoliberal governance of speakers. In Luisa Martín Rojo & Alfonso Del Percio (eds.), *Language and Neoliberal Governmentality*, 162–189. New York: Routledge.

Romaine, Susan. 2006. Planning for the survival of linguistic diversity. *Language Policy* 5(4). 443–475.

Romaine, Susan. 2008. Irish in the Global Context. In Caoilfhionn Nic Pháidín & Seán Ó Cearnaigh (eds.), *A New View of the Irish Language*, 11–25. Dublin: Cois Life.

Rouse, Paul & Mark Duncan. 2015. *Should public policy be guided by research? Evidently.* https://www.irishtimes.com/news/education/should-public-policy-be-guided-by-research-evidently-1.2178595 (Accessed 17 September 2021)

Rowland, Hugh. 2016. An choimhlint idé-eolaíochta idir Misneach agus an LFM le linn chomóradh 50 bliain an Éirí Amach [The ideological conflict between Misneach and the LFM during the 50 year commemoration of the rising]. *COMHARTaighde* 2 (1). https://doi.org/10.18669/ct.2016.07 Accessed 17 September 2021)

RTÉ. 2009a. *Press release: RTÉ radio keeps the nation talking!* https://presspack.rte.ie/2006/05/18/press-release-rte-radio-keeps-the-nation-talking/ (Accessed 17 September 2021)

RTÉ. 2009b. *Annual Report & Group Financial Statements 2008.* https://www.rte.ie/documents/about/annual_report_2008_eng.pdf (Accessed 17 September 2021)

RTÉ. 2017. *32 jobs lost in Donegal as SLM Connect closes.* https://www.rte.ie/news/ulster/2017/1221/929099-jobs-losses-donegal/ (Accessed 17 September 2021)

RTÉ. 2018a. *Annual Report & Group Financial Statements 2017.* https://web.archive.org/web/20190526221234/https://www.rte.ie/annualreport/pdfs/RTE_Annual_Report_2017.pdf (Accessed 17 September 2021)

RTÉ. 2018b. *Laghdú 90% ar líon na mac léinn in ionaid Ghaeltachta an Acadaimh* [90% decrease in the number of students in the Acadamh's Gaeltacht centres]. https://www.rte.ie/news/nuacht/2018/0501/959563-laghdu-90-ar-lion-na-mac-leinn-in-ionaid-ghaeltachta-an-acadaimh/ (Accessed 17 September 2021)

RTÉ. 2018c. *More turbulence over Aran Islands air route.* https://www.rte.ie/news/analysis-and-comment/2018/0610/969412-aer-arann/ (Accessed 17 September 2021)

RTÉ. 2021. *Why the housing crisis poses a threat to the Gaeltacht.* https://www.rte.ie/news/primetime/2021/1007/1252390-housing-crisis-gaeltacht/ (Accessed 13 May 2022)

S4C. 2021. *S4C written evidence to the Communities, Equality and Local Government Committee before evidence session 27. 3.2014.* https://business.senedd.wales/documents/s25604/CELG4-10-14%20Paper%201.pdf (Accessed 10 August 2021)

Saad-Filho, Alfredo & Deborah Johnston. 2006. *Neoliberalism: A Critical Reader.* London: Pluto Press.

Saarikivi, Jaane & Heiko F. Marten. 2012. Introduction to the Special Issue: Political and Economic Obstacles of Minority Language Maintenance. *Journal on Ethnopolitics and Minority Issues in Europe* 11(1). 1–16.

Sallabank, Julia. 2011. Language Endangerment. In Ruth Wodak, Barbara Johnstone & Paul Kerswill (eds.), *The SAGE Handbook of Sociolinguistics*, 496–512. London: SAGE.

Savage, Mike. 2015. *Social class in the 21st century.* London: Penguin Books.

Save Our Small Schools. 2012. *About*. https://ruralscoilnet.wordpress.com/ (Accessed 17 September 2021)
Scharf, Thomas. 2015. Between inclusion and exclusion in later life. In Keiran Walsh, Gemma M. Carney & Áine Ní Léime (eds.), *Ageing through Austerity: Critical Perspectives from Ireland*, 113–129. Bristol: Policy Press.
Scott, Allen J. 2007. Capitalism and Urbanization in a New Key? The Cognitive-Cultural Dimension. *Social Forces* 85(4). 1465–1482.
Scottish Government. 2022. *Spending breakdown of Gaelic language projects and initiatives: FOI release*. https://www.gov.scot/publications/foi-202200286004/ (Accessed 29 April 2022)
Seanad Éireann. 2011. *Seanad Éireann debate – Thursday, 24 Nov 2011 Vol. 211 No. 12, Adjournment Matters Oifig an Choimisinéara Teanga* [The office of the Language Commissioner] https://www.oireachtas.ie/en/debates/debate/seanad/2011-11-24/25/#s26 (Accessed 13 September 2021)
Seanad Éireann. 2017. *Seanad Éireann debate - Thursday, 2 Feb 2017 Vol. 249 No. 14 Irish Language: Statements*. https://www.oireachtas.ie/en/debates/debate/seanad/2017-02-02/12?highlight%5B0%5D=irish&highlight%5B1%5D=language&highlight%5B2%5D=statements (Accessed 13 September 2021)
Seymour, Richard. 2020. *The Twittering Machine*. London: Verso.
Shannon, Laura. 2016. *Local and regional bodies in Ireland 2012–2016 [Local government research series, no. 12]*. Dublin: Institute of Public Administration.
Share, Perry, Hilary Tovey & Mary P. Corcoran. 2007. *A Sociology of Ireland*. Dublin: Gill & Macmillan.
Shohamy, Elana. 2006. *Language Policy: Hidden Agendas and New Approaches*. New York: Routledge.
Skills Development Scotland. 2017. *Jobs and Skills in Scotland: The Evidence*. https://www.skillsdevelopmentscotland.co.uk/media/43852/jobs-and-skills-in-scotland-2017-main-report.pdf (Accessed 9 May 2022)
Skutnabb-Kangas, Tove. 2000. *Linguistic Genocide in Education, or Worldwide Diversity and Human Rights?* London: Lawrence Erlbaum Associates.
Smith-Christmas, Cassie. 2014. *Language and Integration: Migration to Gaelic-Speaking Areas in the Twenty-First Century*. http://www.soillse.ac.uk/wp-content/uploads/Language-and-Integration-Migration-to-Gaelic-Speaking-Areas-in-the-Twenty-First-Century.pdf (Accessed 17 September 2021)
Sparke, Matthew. 2016. Health and the embodiment of neoliberalism: pathologies of political economy from climate change to austerity to personal responsibility. In Simon Springer, Kean Birch & Julie MacLeavy (eds.), *The Handbook of Neoliberalism*, 237–251. New York: Routledge.
Spillane, Alison. 2015. The Impact of the crisis on Irish women. In Colin Coulter & Angela Nagle (eds.), *Ireland Under Austerity: Neoliberal Crisis, Neoliberal Solutions*, 151–170. Manchester: Manchester University Press.
Spolsky, Bernard. 2004. *Language Policy*. Cambridge: Cambridge University Press.
Spolsky, Bernard. 2009. *Language Management*. Cambridge: Cambridge University Press.
Springer, Simon, Kean Birch & Julie MacLeavy (2016). *The Handbook of Neoliberalism*. New York: Routledge.
Standing, Guy. 2014. *The Precariat: The New Dangerous Class*. London: Bloomsbury.

Steger, Manfred B. 2002. Robert Putnam, Social Capital and a Suspect called Globalization. In Scott L. McLean, David A. Schultz & Manfred B. Steger (eds.), *Social Capital: Critical Perspectives on Community and "Bowling Alone"*, 260–280. New York: New York University Press.
Strubell, Miquel. 2001. Catalan a decade later. In Joshua A. Fishman (ed.), *Can Threatened Languages Be Saved?*, 260–283. Clevedon: Multilingual Matters.
Šumonja, Miloš. 2021. Neoliberalism is not dead – On political implications of Covid-19. *Capital & Class* 45(2). 215–227.
Sweeney, Paul. 2004. *Selling Out? Privatisation in Ireland*. Dublin: TASC/New Island.
Szabla, Malgorzata & Jan Blommaert. Does context really collapse in social media interaction? *Applied Linguistics Review* 11(2). 251–279. https://doi.org/10.1515/applirev-2017-0119
Tabouret-Keller, Andrée. 1968. Sociological factors of language maintenance and language shift: a methodological approach based on European and African examples. In Joshua A. Fishman, Charles A. Ferguson & Jyotirindra Das Gupata (eds.), *Language Problems of Developing Nations*, 107–127. New York: John Wiley & Sons.
Tabouret-Keller, Andrée. 1972. A contribution to the sociological study of language maintenance and language shift. In Joshua A. Fishman (ed.), *Advances in the sociology of language, Vol. 2: Selected studies and applications*, 365–376. The Hague: Mouton.
Taft, Michael. 2016a. *Rural Stagnation in the Marketplace*. http://notesonthefront.typepad.com/politicaleconomy/2016/06/some-commentators-have-recently-challenged-the-assertion-that-there-is-no-recovery-outside-dublin-dan-obrien-does-up-the.html (Accessed 17 September 2021)
Taft, Michael. 2016b. *The Decade Long Income Recession*. http://notesonthefront.typepad.com/politicaleconomy/2016/06/the-decade-long-income-recession.html (Accessed 17 September 2021)
Taft, Michael. 2018. *Austerity's Hangover*. https://notesonthefront.typepad.com/politicaleconomy/2018/01/austerity-hangover.html (Accessed 17 September 2021)
TG4. 2004. *Splanc Deireadh na Gaeltachta* [Last spark of the Gaeltacht]. https://www.youtube.com/watch?v=SELbYVMpTzo (Accessed 17 September 2021)
TG4. 2009. *Tuarascáil Bhliantúil 2008* [Annual report 2008]. https://d1og0s8nlbd0hm.cloudfront.net/tg4-redesign-2015/wp-content/uploads/2015/07/TB2008-G.pdf (Accessed 17 September 2021)
TG4. 2016a. *Tuarascáil Bhliantúil 2015* [Annual report 2015]. https://d1og0s8nlbd0hm.cloudfront.net/tg4-redesign-2015/wp-content/uploads/2015/08/TG4-Tuarascail-15-G.pdf (Accessed 17 September 2021)
TG4. 2016b. *Joint Committee on Communications, Climate Action and Environment: Public Consultation on Funding of Public Service Broadcasting in Ireland. 22nd November 2016*. https://web.archive.org/web/20180429152034/http://www.oireachtas.ie/parliament/media/committees/communicationsclimatechangenaturalresources/publicservicebroadcasting/opening-statements/TG4-PaipearCulraComhchoisteOireachtais.docx (Accessed 17 September 2021)
TG4. 2017. *Anseo i lár an Ghleanna* [Here in the middle of the glen]. https://web.archive.org/web/20180428025622/http://www.tg4.ie/ga/clair/anseo-i-lar-an-ghleanna/ (Accessed 17 September 2021)
TG4. 2018. *Cáipéis Straitéise TG4* [TG4 strategy document]. https://d1og0s8nlbd0hm.cloudfront.net/tg4-redesign-2015/wp-content/uploads/2018/07/Tuairisc-TG4-2017_B%C3%89ARLA.pdf (Accessed 17 September 2021)

TG4. n.d. *Background*. https://www.tg4.ie/en/corporate/background/ (Accessed 17 September 2021)
The Guardian. 2011. 1 February. *Ireland's 'ghost hotels' to be boarded up*. https://www.theguardian.com/business/ireland-business-blog-with-lisa-ocarroll/2011/feb/01/ireland-ghost-hotels-closure-nama (Accessed 17 September 2021)
The Guardian. 2022. 12 March. *Hello £200k beach huts, goodbye primary school – the Welsh village hollowed out by second homes*. https://www.theguardian.com/uk-news/2022/mar/12/abersoch-second-homes-holiday-wales Accessed 20 April 2022.
The Times. 2021. 17 April. *Don't speak Irish, company that accepts gaeltacht [sic] grant tells staff*. https://www.thetimes.co.uk/article/dont-speak-irish-company-that-accepts-gaeltacht-grant-tells-staff-wmntxsvtr (Accessed 25 April 2022)
Thejournal.ie. 2013a. *What's the future for Irish and do politicians want to preserve it?* http://www.thejournal.ie/readme/irish-language-coimisineir-teanga-sean-o-cuirreain-1215147-Dec2013/ (Accessed 17 September 2021)
Thejournal.ie. 2013b. *Five years older and deeper in debt... So why don't the Irish protest more?* http://www.thejournal.ie/protests-ireland-why-1102930-Sep2013/ (Accessed 17 September 2021)
Thejournal.ie. 2014. *More than 1,000 Irish pubs have had to shut down since 2007*. http://www.thejournal.ie/ireland-pubs-closing-1572963-Jul2014/ (Accessed 17 September 2021)
Thomas, Enlli Môn & Dylan Bryn Roberts. 2011. Exploring bilinguals' social use of language inside and out of the minority language classroom. *Language and Education* 25(2). 89–108.
Thompson, Edward Palmer. 1991. *The Making of the English Working Class*. London: Penguin.
Tollefson, James W. 1991. *Planning Language, Planning Inequality: Language Policy in the Community*. London: Longman.
Tollefson, James W. 2006. Critical theory in language policy. In Thomas Ricento (ed.), *An Introduction to Language Policy: Theory and Method*, 42–59. Oxford: Blackwell Publishing.
Tomos, Angharad. 2021. Everything Must Change: Welsh Language Policy and Activism. In Daniel Evans, Kieron Smith & Huw Williams (eds.), *The Welsh Way: Essays on Neoliberalism and Devolution*, 150–161. Cardigan: Parthian.
Tooze, Adam. 2018. *Crashed: how a decade of financial crises changed the world*. London: Penguin.
Touraine, Alain. 1981. *The Voice and the Eye: An analysis of Social Movements*. Cambridge: Cambridge University Press.
Tuairisc.ie. 2014a. *Cóipeáil, comhtharlú nó comhcheilg?* [Copying, coincidence or conspiracy?]. http://tuairisc.ie/coipeail-comhtharlu-comhcheilg/ (Accessed 17 September 2021)
Tuairisc.ie. 2014b. *Titim mhór ar éileamh ar choláistí samhraidh* [Large fall in demand for summer colleges]. http://tuairisc.ie/titim-thubaisteach-ar-eileamh-ar-cholaisti-samhraidh/ (Accessed 17 September 2021)
Tuairisc.ie. 2015a. *'Mórcheisteanna' ag Roinn na Gaeltachta faoi mholtaí i Staidéar Teanga a choimisiúnaigh ÚnaG* [Department of the Gaeltacht has 'big questions' about recommendations in language study that ÚnaG commissioned]. http://tuairisc.ie/morcheisteanna-ag-roinn-na-gaeltachta-faoi-mholtai-i-staidear-teanga-a-choimisiunaigh-unag/ (Accessed 17 September 2021)

Tuairisc.ie. 2015b. *Pléaráca Teoranta le scor ceal maoinithe* [Pléaráca LTD to close due to lack of funding]. http://tuairisc.ie/plearaca-teoranta-le-scor-ceal-maoinithe/ (Accessed 17 September 2021)

Tuairisc.ie. 2016a. *An caidreamh idir foireann agus bainistíocht an Údaráis 'at an all-time low'* [The relationship between staff and management of Údarás 'at an all-time low']. http://tuairisc.ie/an-caidreamh-idir-foireann-agus-bainistiocht-an-udarais-at-an-all-time-low/ (Accessed 17 September 2021)

Tuairisc.ie. 2016b. *Ardú pá d'fhoireann Údarás na Gaeltachta agus 'comhstádas' bainte amach acu* [Pay rise for Údarás na Gaeltachta staff as they achieve 'equal status']. http://tuairisc.ie/ardu-pa-dfhoireann-udaras-na-gaeltachta-agus-comhstadas-bainte-amach-acu/ (Accessed 17 September 2021)

Tuairisc.ie. 2016c. *Plean do chóras nua chun taighde a dhéanamh faoi lucht éisteachta RTÉ Raidió na Gaeltachta caite i dtraipisí* [Plan for a new system to research RTÉ Raidió na Gaeltacht listenership abandoned]. http://tuairisc.ie/plean-do-choras-nua-chun-taighde-a-dheanamh-faoi-lucht-eisteachta-rte-raidio-na-gaeltachta-caite-i-dtraipisi/ (Accessed 17 September 2021)

Tuairisc.ie. 2016d. *Córas á lorg ag RTÉ chun tabhairt faoi 'easnamh mór' taighde maidir le héisteoirí RnaG* [RTÉ looking for a system to address the 'large deficit' of research regarding RnaG's listenership]. http://tuairisc.ie/coras-a-lorg-ag-rte-chun-tabhairt-faoi-easnamh-mor-taighde-maidir-le-heisteoiri-rnag/ (Accessed 17 September 2021)

Tuairisc.ie. 2016e. *Díomá léirithe faoi ghearradh siar ar ábhar Gaeilge san Irish Times* [Disappointment shown regarding cutbacks to Irish-language material in Irish Times]. https://tuairisc.ie/dioma-leirithe-faoi-ghearradh-siar-ar-abhar-gaeilge-san-irish-times/ (Accessed 17 September 2021)

Tuairisc.ie. 2016f. *Óráid Uachtarán na hÉireann ag Cóisir Gaeilge Áras an Uachtaráin...* [The president's speech from the Áras an Uachtaráin Irish-language party...]. https://tuairisc.ie/oraid-uachtaran-na-heireann-ag-coisir-gaeilge-aras-an-uachtarain/ (Accessed 17 September 2021)

Tuairisc.ie. 2016g. *Amhras ar Uachtarán na hÉireann faoi thiomantas an státchórais don Ghaeilge* [President doubtful about diligence of civil service towards Irish]. http://tuairisc.ie/amhras-ar-uachtaran-na-heireann-faoi-thiomantas-an-statchorais-don-ghaeilge/ (Accessed 17 September 2021)

Tuairisc.ie. 2016h. *Deireadh á chur le riachtanas Gaeilge do phost an Uachtaráin in Ollscoil na hÉireann, Gaillimh* [Irish-language requirement being abolished for job of president in National University of Ireland, Galway]. http://tuairisc.ie/deireadh-a-chur-le-riachtanas-gaeilge-do-phost-an-uachtarain-in-ollscoil-na-heireann-gaillimh/ (Accessed 17 September 2021)

Tuairisc.ie. 2016i. *Indreabhán ar an tríú baile is measa in Éirinn maidir le luas leathanbhanda* [Indreabhán the third worst town in Ireland regarding broadband]. http://tuairisc.ie/indreabhan-ar-an-triu-hait-is-measa-in-eirinn-maidir-le-luas-leathanbhanda/ (Accessed 17 September 2021)

Tuairisc.ie. 2016j. *Cuirfear deireadh leis an tseirbhís farantóireachta go Cill Rónáin ar an 1 Nollaig* [Ferry service to Cill Rónáin will be stopped on December 1st]. http://tuairisc.ie/cuirfear-deireadh-leis-an-tseirbhis-farantoireachta-go-cill-ronain-ar-an-1-nollaig/ (Accessed 17 September 2021)

Tuairisc.ie. 2016k. *'Ní féidir maoiniú a chur ar fáil do bhóithre Gaeltachta agus do phleananna teanga araon'* – Kyne ['Funding cannot be made available for both Gaeltacht roads and language planning' – Kyne]. https://tuairisc.ie/ni-feidir-maoiniu-a-chur-ar-fail-do-bhoithre-gaeltachta-agus-do-phleananna-teanga-araon-kyne/ (Accessed 17 September 2021)

Tuairisc.ie. 2017a. *Imní ar phríomhoidí Gaeltachta faoi easpa múinteoirí do chur i bhfeidhm an pholasaí oideachais Gaeltachta* [Gaeltacht principals worried about lack of staff for implementing Gaeltacht education policy]. https://tuairisc.ie/imni-ar-mhuinteoiri-gaeltachta-faoin-easpa-muinteoiri-ata-a-gcur-ar-fail-do-chur-i-bhfeidhm-an-pholasai-oideachais-gaeltachta/ (Accessed 17 September 2021)

Tuairisc.ie. 2017b. *'Chinn an rialtas neamhaird a thabhairt ar an Stráitéis 20 Bliain agus tá sé in am tosú as an nua' – Ó Cuív* ['The government decided to ignore the 20-Year Strategy and it is time to start anew' – Ó Cuív]. http://tuairisc.ie/fisean-chinn-an-rialtas-neamhaird-a-thabhairt-ar-an-straiteis-20-bliain-agus-ta-se-in-am-tosu-as-an-nua-o-cuiv/ (Accessed 17 September 2021)

Tuairisc.ie. 2017c. *Coiste Gaeilge an Rialtais ag bun an tábla maidir le cruinnithe – figiúirí nua* [Government Irish-language committee at bottom of table regarding meetings – new figures]. http://tuairisc.ie/coiste-gaeilge-an-rialtais-ag-bun-an-tabla-maidir-le-cruinnithe-figiuiri-nua/ (Accessed 17 September 2021)

Tuairisc.ie. 2017d. *Rinne Údarás na Gaeltachta agus Roinn na Gaeltachta 'cinsireacht' ar thuarascáil Ghaeltachta – Ó Giollagáin* [Údarás na Gaeltachta and the Department of the Gaeltacht 'censored' Gaeltacht report – Ó Giollagáin]. http://tuairisc.ie/rinne-udaras-na-gaeltachta-agus-roinn-na-gaeltachta-cinsireacht-ar-thuarascail-ghaeltachta/ (Accessed 17 September 2021)

Tuairisc.ie. 2017e. *Titim 40% ar lucht éisteachta Raidió na Gaeltachta le trí bliana anuas* [Decline of 40% in Raidió na Gaeltachta listeners in the last three years]. http://tuairisc.ie/titim-40-ar-lucht-eisteachta-raidio-na-gaeltachta-le-tri-bliana-anuas/ (Accessed 17 September 2021)

Tuairisc.ie. 2017f. *Suim léirithe ag roinnt mhaith fostaithe in RTÉ RnaG agus Nuacht TG4 éirí as luath* [Interest in early retirement expressed by large number of staff in RTÉ RnaG and TG4 news]. http://tuairisc.ie/suim-leirithe-ag-roinnt-mhaith-fostaithe-in-rte-rnag-agus-nuacht-tg4-eiri-as-luath/ (Accessed 17 September 2021)

Tuairisc.ie. 2017g. *Ba í Gaeltacht na nDéise an t-aon cheantar inar tuairiscíodh fás i líon na gcainteoirí laethúla sa Daonáireamh. Cén fáth?* [The Waterford Gaeltacht was the only area where an increase in daily speakers was registered in the Census. Why?]. https://tuairisc.ie/ba-i-gaeltacht-na-ndeise-an-t-aon-cheantar-inar-tuairisciodh-fas-i-lion-na-gcainteoiri-laethula-sa-daonaireamh-cen-fath/ (Accessed 17 September 2021)

Tuairisc.ie. 2017h. *Cláir chainte TG4 le cur ina dtost. An maith é?* [TG4 chat shows to be cut. Is that good?]. https://tuairisc.ie/clair-chainte-tg4-le-cur-ina-dtost-an-maith-e/ (Accessed 17 September 2021)

Tuairisc.ie. 2017i. *Aire Stáit na Gaeltachta chun aghaidh a thabhairt ar theip chóras earcaíochta Gaeilge an Stáit* [Minister of State for the Gaeltacht to address failure of State's Irish-language recruitment system]. http://tuairisc.ie/aire-stait-na-gaeltachta-chun-aghaidh-a-thabhairt-ar-theip-choras-earcaiochta-gaeilge-an-stait/ (Accessed 17 September 2021)

Tuairisc.ie. 2017j. *Níl Gaeilge líofa ag Ard-Rúnaí nua na Roinne Gaeltachta, ach socrú déanta cheana aici 'chun líofacht a bhaint amach'* [New secretary of Gaeltacht Department cannot speak Irish, but has made decision 'to achieve fluency']. http://tuairisc.ie/nil-gaeilgeliofa-ag-ard-runai-nua-na-roinne-gaeltachta-ach-socru-deanta-cheana-aici-chun-liofacht-a-bhaint-amach/ (Accessed 17 September 2021)

Tuairisc.ie. 2017k. *Físeán: Tá ag 'éirí leis an Straitéis 20 Bliain' a deir Aire Stáit na Gaeltachta, in ainneoin figiúirí daonáirimh* [Video: 'The 20-Year Strategy is succeeding' says Minister of State for the Gaeltacht, despite census figures]. http://tuairisc.ie/fisean-ta-ag-eiri-leis-an-straiteis-20-bliain-a-deir-aire-stait-na-gaeltachta-in-ainneoin-figiuiri-daonairimh/ (Accessed 17 September 2021)

Tuairisc.ie. 2017l. *Na 10 gceantar Gaeltachta is measa as agus na 10 gceantar Gaeltachta is fearr as...* [The 10 worst off and the 10 best off Gaeltacht areas...]. https://tuairisc.ie/na-10-gceantar-gaeltachta-is-measa-as-agus-na-10-gceantar-gaeltachta-is-fearr-as/ (Accessed 17 September 2021)

Tuairisc.ie. 2017m. *Cé mhéad foirgneamh folamh atá ag Údarás na Gaeltachta, cá bhfuil siad agus cén fhad atá siad le ligean?* [How many Údarás na Gaeltachta buildings are empty, where are they and for how long are they to let?]. https://tuairisc.ie/ce-mhead-foirgneamh-folamh-ata-ag-udaras-na-gaeltachta-ca-bhfuil-siad-agus-cen-fhad-ata-siad-le-ligean/ (Accessed 17 September 2021)

Tuairisc.ie. 2017n. *Ardú den chéad uair le 10 mbliana anuas ar dheontas na 'mná tí' fógartha ag Kyne* [Increase for the first time in 10 years for the grants for women who host summer college students announced by Kyne]. http://tuairisc.ie/ardu-den-chead-uair-le-10-mbliana-anuas-ar-dheontas-na-mna-ti-fogartha-ag-kyne/ (Accessed 17 September 2021)

Tuairisc.ie. 2017o. *'Táimid inár n-aonar, ag snámh in aghaidh easa' – tuismitheoirí ag íoc iad féin as an tríú múinteoir do scoil Ghaeltachta* ['We're on our own, swimming against the tide' – parents paying themselves for third teacher in Gaeltacht school]. https://tuairisc.ie/taimid-inar-n-aonar-ag-snamh-in-aghaidh-easa-tuismitheoiri-ag-ioc-iad-fein-as-an-triu-muinteoir-do-scoil-ghaeltachta/ (Accessed 17 September 2021)

Tuairisc.ie. 2017p. *'Teipfidh ar na pleananna teanga cheal maoinithe agus ceannaireachta' – Ollamh* ['Language plans will fail due to lack of funding and leadership' – professor]. https://tuairisc.ie/teipfidh-ar-na-pleananna-teanga-cheal-maoinithe-agus-ceannaireachta-ollamh/ (Accessed 17 September 2021)

Tuairisc.ie. 2017q. *Deimhnithe ag Roinn na Gaeltachta gur €100,00 a bheidh ar fáil do phleananna teanga* [Department of the Gaeltacht confirm that €100,000 will be available for language plans]. https://tuairisc.ie/deimhnithe-ag-roinn-na-gaeltachta-gur-e100000-a-bheidh-ar-fail-do-phleananna-teanga/ (Accessed 17 September 2021)

Tuairisc.ie. 2017r. *Grúpaí pleanála teanga i dtrí cheantar Gaeltachta ag tacú leis an gcur chuige gan glacadh le maoiniú an Údaráis* [Language planning groups in three Gaeltacht areas backing plan to refuse Údarás funding]. https://tuairisc.ie/diultu-no-glacadh-le-maoiniu-do-phlean-teanga-le-ple-i-ngaoth-dobhair-anocht/ (Accessed 17 September 2021)

Tuairisc.ie. 2017s. *Iarracht Roinn na Gaeltachta géarchéim na pleanála teanga a réiteach á meas ag Fóram Chois Fharraige* [Department of Gaeltacht's efforts to resolve language planning crisis being assessed by Cois Fharraige forum]. https://tuairisc.ie/iarracht-roinn-na-gaeltachta-gearcheim-na-pleanala-teanga-a-reiteach-a-meas-ag-foram-chois-fharraige/ (Accessed 17 September 2021)

Tuairisc.ie. 2017t. *Ní chuirfidh an phleanáil teanga mar atá le saolré na Gaeilge sa Ghaeltacht – duine d'údair an Staidéir Theangeolaíoch* [Language planning won't add to lifespan of Irish in the Gaeltacht – one of the Linguistic Study's authors]. https://tuairisc.

ie/molta-ag-misneach-bliain-eiri-amach-na-ngael-a-dheanamh-de-bhliain-na-gaeilge/ (Accessed 17 September 2021)

Tuairisc.ie. 2017u. *Post fógartha ag an Roinn Talmhaíochta i gceartlár na Gaeltachta – 'English essential, Irish desirable'* [Job announced by Department of Agriculture in heart of Gaeltacht – *'English essential, Irish desirable'*]. https://tuairisc.ie/post-fogartha-ag-an-roinn-talmhaiochta-i-gceartlar-na-gaeltachta-english-essential-irish-desirable/ (Accessed 17 September 2021)

Tuairisc.ie. 2018a. *Níl feidhm ar bith le haon chuid den struchtúr a bhí in ainm is an Straitéis 20 Bliain don Ghaeilge a chur i gcrích – taighde nua* [None of the structures that were meant to implement the 20-Year Strategy operational – new research]. https://tuairisc.ie/nil-feidhm-ar-bith-le-haon-chuid-den-struchtur-a-bhi-in-ainm-is-an-straiteis-20-bliain-don-ghaeilge-a-chur-i-gcrich-taighde-nua/ (Accessed 17 September 2021)

Tuairisc.ie. 2018b. *Gan aon chinneadh fós faoi cathain a thabharfar maoiniú breise d'Údarás na Gaeltachta* [No decision yet regarding when extra funding will be given to Údarás na Gaeltachta]. https://tuairisc.ie/gan-aon-chinneadh-fos-faoi-cathain-a-thabharfar-maoiniu-breise-project-ireland-2040-dudaras-na-gaeltachta/ (Accessed 17 September 2021)

Tuairisc.ie. 2018c. *Leath an méid airgid bhreise a mheas siad a bhí ag teastáil don Ghaeilge a fuair Roinn na Gaeltachta do 2018* [Department of the Gaeltacht received half the amount they thought necessary in 2018]. https://tuairisc.ie/leath-an-meid-airgid-breise-a-mheas-siad-a-bhi-ag-teastail-don-ghaeilge-a-fuair-roinn-na-gaeltachta-do-2018/ (Accessed 17 September 2021)

Tuairisc.ie. 2018d. *Deireadh le plé faoi chúrsaí nuachta am lóin ar Raidió na Gaeltachta agus ciorrú le déanamh ar 'Nuacht a hAon'* [End to lunchtime discussion of news on Raidió na Gaeltachta as cuts are made to 'News at One']. https://tuairisc.ie/deireadh-le-ple-faoi-chursai-nuachta-am-loin-ar-raidio-na-gaeltachta-agus-ciorru-le-deanamh-ar-nuacht-a-haon/ (Accessed 17 September 2021)

Tuairisc.ie. 2018e. *'Tá earnáil na foilsitheoireachta Gaeilge an-leochaileach agus tá gá le réimse beart' – Príomhfheidhmeannach Fhoras na Gaeilge* ['Irish-language publishing is very vulnerable and a selection of measures are needed' – Foras na Gaeilge CEO]. https://tuairisc.ie/ta-earnail-na-foilsitheoireachta-gaeilge-an-leochaileach-agus-ta-ga-le-reimse-beart-priomhfheidhmeannach-fhoras-na-gaeilge/ (Accessed 17 September 2021)

Tuairisc.ie. 2018f. *An Coimisinéir Teanga chun éirí as monatóireacht a dhéanamh ar scéimeanna teanga mar gur 'cur amú acmhainní' é* [Language Commissioner to stop monitoring language schemes as it is a 'waste of resources']. https://tuairisc.ie/an-coimisineir-teanga-chun-eiri-as-monatoireacht-a-dheanamh-ar-sceimeanna-teanga-mar-gur-cur-amu-acmhainni-e/ (Accessed 17 September 2021)

Tuairisc.ie. 2018g. *Ardú i liúntas 'mná tí' na Gaeltachta curtha as an áireamh ag McHugh* [Increase in grants for women who host summer college students ruled out by McHugh]. https://tuairisc.ie/ardu-i-liuntas-mna-ti-na-gaeltachta-curtha-as-an-aireamh-ag-mchugh/ (Accessed 17 September 2021)

Tuairisc.ie. 2018h. *'Is léir go bhfuil pobal na Gaeilge cloíte agus iad sásta cur suas le gach sórt masla' – Cormac Ó hEadhra* ['Obvious that Irish speaking community is defeated as they are happy to accept every type of insult' – Cormac Ó hEadhra]. https://tuairisc.ie/is-leir-go-bhfuil-pobal-na-gaeilge-agus-iad-sasta-cur-suas-le-gach-sort-masla-cormac-o-headhra/ (Accessed 17 September 2021)

Tuairisc.ie. 2018i. *Molta ag Misneach 'Bliain Éirí Amach na nGael' a dhéanamh de Bhliain na Gaeilge* [Misneach recommend making 'Year of the Uprising of the Gaels' from the Year of

Irish]. https://tuairisc.ie/molta-ag-misneach-bliain-eiri-amach-na-ngael-a-dheanamh-de-bhliain-na-gaeilge/ (Accessed 17 September 2021)

Tuairisc.ie. 2018j. *Aersheirbhís Árann slán go dtí an fómhar seo chugainn agus conradh nua bronnta ar Aer Arann* [Árann air service safe until next autumn as a Aer Arann receive new contract]. https://tuairisc.ie/aersheirbhis-arann-slan-go-dti-an-fomhar-seo-chugainn-agus-conradh-nua-bronnta-ar-aer-arann/ (Accessed 17 September 2021)

Tuairisc.ie. 2018k. *Scoilt mhór i measc phobal Thoraí faoin vótáil ar son glacadh leis an 'Queen of Aran'* [Big split in Toraigh community over vote to accept 'Queen of Aran']. https://tuairisc.ie/scoilt-mhor-i-measc-phobal-thorai-faoin-votail-ar-son-glacadh-leis-an-queen-of-aran/ (Accessed 17 September 2021)

Tuairisc.ie. 2018l. *Gealltanas faoi bhád nua d'oileán Thoraí curtha sa Phlean Forbartha Náisiúnta ar an tuiscint nach mbeadh aon airgead breise ar fáil dó* [Promise of new boat for Toraigh added to National Development Plan on understanding no extra money would be made available for it]. https://tuairisc.ie/gealltanas-faoi-bhad-nua-doilean-thorai-curtha-sa-phlean-forbartha-naisiunta-ar-an-tuiscint-nach-mbeadh-aon-airgead-breise-ar-fail-do/ (Accessed 17 September 2021)

Tuairisc.ie. 2019a. *'Tubaisteach', 'maslach' 'suarach' agus 'náireach' – buiséad na Gaeilge do 2020* ['Disastrous', 'insulting', 'pitiful' and 'shameful' – the Irish-language budget for 2020]. https://tuairisc.ie/tubaisteach-maslach-suarach-agus-naireach-buisead-na-gaeilge-do-2020/ (Accessed 17 September 2021)

Tuairisc.ie. 2019b. *'Cúngú agus tachtadh seachas fás agus bláthú' – tuairimí faoi phlean Fhoras na Gaeilge do na meáin* ['Contraction and choking instead of growth and flourishing' – opinions about Foras na Gaeilge's plan for the media]. https://tuairisc.ie/cungu-agus-tachtadh-seachas-fas-agus-blathu-tuairimi-faoi-phlean-fhoras-na-gaeilge-do-na-meain-ghaeilge/ (Accessed 17 September 2021)

Tuairisc.ie. 2019c. *Ní 'leithscéal' an Breatimeacht gan reachtaíocht Ghaeilge a bheith foilsithe* [Brexit no 'excuse' for not publishing Irish-language legislation]. https://tuairisc.ie/ni-leithsceal-an-breatimeacht-gan-reachtaiocht-ghaeilge-a-bheith-foilsithe/ (Accessed 17 September 2021)

Tuairisc.ie. 2021a. *Foireann Údarás na Gaeltachta le méadú den chéad uair le breis is deich mbliana* [Údarás na Gaeltacht staff to be increased for first time in more than ten years]. https://tuairisc.ie/foireann-udaras-na-gaeltachta-le-meadu-den-chead-uair-le-breis-is-deich-mbliana/ (Accessed 17 September 2021)

Tuairisc.ie. 2021b. *An Rialtas chun toghchán Údarás na Gaeltachta a thabhairt ar ais* [Government to reintroduce Údarás na Gaeltachta election]. https://tuairisc.ie/an-rialtas-chun-toghchan-udaras-na-gaeltachta-a-thabhairt-ar-ais/ (Accessed 17 September 2021)

Tuairisc.ie. 2021c. *Laghdú eile déanta ar an maoiniú a chuireann RTÉ ar fáil do sheirbhís nuachta TG4* [Another reduction in funding RTÉ provides for TG4 news]. https://tuairisc.ie/laghdu-eile-deanta-ar-an-maoiniu-a-chuireann-rte-ar-fail-do-sheirbhis-nuachta-tg4/ (Accessed 17 September 2021)

Tuairisc.ie. 2021d. *'Níl seirbhís nuachta TG4 ag feidhmiú' – ceannasaí TG4* ['TG4 news service not functional' – head of TG4]. https://tuairisc.ie/nil-seirbhis-nuachta-tg4-ag-feidhmiu-ceannasai-tg4/ (Accessed 17 September 2021)

Tuairisc.ie. 2021e. *Gaeilge riachtanach do phost amháin as gach 500 sa státseirbhís le trí bliana anuas – figiúirí nua* [Irish necessary for one job out of every 500 in civil service in last three years]. https://tuairisc.ie/gaeilge-riachtanach-do-phost-amhain-as-gach-500-sa-statseirbhis-le-tri-bliana-anuas-figiuiri-nua/ (Accessed 17 September 2021)

Tuairisc.ie. 2021f. *Deireadh curtha ag Ollscoil na hÉireann, Gaillimh le riachtanas Gaeilge do phostanna riaracháin* [National University of Ireland, Galway ends Irish requirement for administrative roles]. https://tuairisc.ie/deireadh-curtha-ag-ollscoil-na-heireann-gaillimh-le-riachtanas-gaeilge-do-phostanna-riarachain/ (Accessed 17 September 2021)

Tuairisc.ie. 2021g. *Gan gá le Gaeilge ag Leas-Uachtarán Comhionannais in Ollscoil na hÉireann, Gaillimh* [Vice-president of equality in National University of Ireland, Galway does not need Irish]. https://tuairisc.ie/gan-ga-le-gaeilge-ag-leas-uachtaran-comhionannais-in-ollscoil-na-heireann-gaillimh/ (Accessed 17 September 2021)

Turley, Gerard, Stephen McNena & Geraldine Robbins. 2018. Austerity and Irish Local Government Expenditure since the Great Recession. *Administration* 66(4). 1–24.

Tusting, Karin & Janet Maybin. 2007. Linguistic ethnography and interdisciplinarity: Opening the discussion. *Journal of Sociolinguistics* 11(5). 575–583.

Údarás na Gaeltachta. 2009a. *Tuarascáil Bhliantúil agus Cuntais 2008/Annual Report and Accounts 2008*. https://web.archive.org/web/20171218085514/http://www.udaras.ie/wp-content/uploads/2012/06/2009-Annual-Report-and-Accounts.pdf (Accessed 17 September 2021)

Údarás na Gaeltachta. 2009b. *Táblaí 2008: Aguisín don Tuarascáil Bhliantúil/Tables 2008: Appendix to the Annual Report*. https://web.archive.org/web/20171024064313/http://www.udaras.ie/wp-content/uploads/2012/06/2008-Annual-Report-Tables.pdf (Accessed 17 September 2021)

Údarás na Gaeltachta. 2010. *Tuarascáil Bhliantúil agus Cuntais 2009/Annual Report and Accounts 2009*. https://web.archive.org/web/20171218085514/http://www.udaras.ie/wp-content/uploads/2012/06/2009-Annual-Report-and-Accounts.pdf (Accessed 17 September 2021)

Údarás na Gaeltachta. 2014. *Ag Forbairt na Fiontraíochta ar Pháirc Ghnó Ghaoth Dobhair/Enterprise Development on the Gaoth Dobhair Business Park*. https://web.archive.org/web/20171218091025/http://www.udaras.ie/wp-content/uploads/2015/04/Ag-Forbairt-na-Fiontra%C3%ADochta-ar-Ph%C3%A1irc-Ghn%C3%B3-Ghaoth-Dobhair.pdf (Accessed 13 September 2021)

Údarás na Gaeltachta. 2015. *Údarás na Gaeltachta: 2015 Review*. https://www.udaras.ie/assets/uploads/2021/02/End_of_Year_Review_2015_Raiteas.docx (Accessed 13 September 2021)

Údarás na Gaeltachta. 2016a. *Tuarascáil Bhliantúil agus Cuntais 2015/Annual Report and Accounts 2015*. https://www.udaras.ie/assets/uploads/2021/02/Tuarascail-Bhliantuil-2015-D.pdf (Accessed 13 September 2021)

Údarás na Gaeltachta. 2016b. *Táblaí 2015: Aguisín don Tuarascáil Bhliantúil/Tables 2015: Appendix to the Annual Report*. https://www.udaras.ie/assets/uploads/2021/02/Tuarascail-Bhliantuil-Tablai-2015-D-1.pdf (Accessed 13 September 2021)

Údarás na Gaeltachta. 2016c. *UK Digital Marketing company to create 125 jobs in Gaoth Dobhair, Co. Donegal*. https://udaras.ie/en/news/uk-digital-marketing-company-to-create-125-jobs-in-gaoth-dobhair-co-donegal/ (Accessed 13 September 2021)

Údarás na Gaeltachta. 2017. *Údarás na Gaeltachta: Athbhreithniú 2017* [Údarás na Gaeltachta: 2017 review]. https://www.udaras.ie/assets/uploads/2021/02/Athbhreithniu%C2%81-Deireadh-Bliana-2017-ra%C2%81iteas.pdf (Accessed 13 September 2021)

Uí Chollatáin, Regina, Aoife Uí Fhaoláin & Ruth Lysaght. 2011. *Tuarascáil ar straitéis úr maidir le Foras na Gaeilge i leith earnáil na meán Gaeilge clóite agus ar líne: Athláithriú agus athshealbhú teanga*. https://web.archive.org/web/20201213043149/https://www.foras

nagaeilge.ie/wp-content/uploads/2016/06/Tuarasc%C3%A1il-R.-U%C3%AD-Chollat%C3%A1in-2011.pdf (Accessed 25 July 2021)
Uí Chollatáin, Regina. 2016. Language Shift and Language Revival in Ireland. In Hickey, Raymond (ed.), *Sociolinguistics in Ireland*, 176–197. Basingstoke: Palgrave Macmillan.
UNESCO. 2018. *UNESCO Interactive Atlas of the World's Languages in Danger: Irish*. http://www.unesco.org/languages-atlas/index.php (Accessed 17 September 2021)
UNESCO. n.d. *Frequent Asked Questions on Endangered Languages*. http://www.unesco.org/new/en/culture/themes/endangered-languages/faq-on-endangered-languages/ (Accessed 17 September 2021)
Urla, Jacqueline. 2020. Towards an ethnography of linguistic governmentalities. In Luisa Martín Rojo & Alfonso Del Percio (eds.), *Language and Neoliberal Governmentality*, 211–221. New York: Routledge.
Varoufakis, Yanis. 2016. *And the Weak Suffer What They Must? Europe, Austerity and the Threat to Global Stability*. London: Bodley Head.
Verhaeghe, Paul. 2014. *What about me? The struggle for identity in a market-based society*. Melbourne: Scribe.
Voicu, Malina, Ingvill C. Mochmann & Hermann Dülmer. 2016. *Values, economic crisis and democracy*. New York: Routledge.
Wall, Maureen. 1969. The Decline of the Irish language. In Brian Ó Cuív (ed.), *A View of the Irish Language*, 81–90. Dublin: Stationery Office.
Wallerstein, Immanuel. 2004. *World-systems Analysis: An Introduction*. Durham: Duke University Press.
Walsh, John & Wilson McLeod. 2008. An overcoat wrapped around an invisible man? Language legislation and language revitalisation in Ireland and Scotland. *Language Policy* 7(1). 21–46.
Walsh, John. 2010. From Industrial Development to Language Planning – the Evolution of Údarás na Gaeltachta. In Helen Kelly-Holmes & Gerlinde Mautner (eds.), *Language and the Market*, 123–134. Basingstoke: Palgrave MacMillan.
Walsh, John. 2011a. *Contests and Contexts: The Irish Language and Ireland's socio-economic development*. Oxford: Peter Lang.
Walsh, John. 2011b. An Straitéis 20 Bliain Don Ghaeilge: Ní bheidh deis níos fearr ar fáil [The 20-Year Strategy for Irish: there won't be a better chance available]. *Comhar* (February). 3–6.
Walsh, John. 2011c. Fál ar an nGort tar éis na Foghla? Athneartú na Gaeilge agus Acht na dTeangacha Oifigiúla 2003 [Closing the stable door after the horse has bolted: the revitalisation of Irish and the Official Languages Act 2003]. *Bliainiris* 10. 88–130.
Walsh, John. 2012a. Sainiú na Gaeltachta agus an Rialachas Teanga [Defining the Gaeltacht and language governance]. In Tadhg Ó hIfearnáin & Máire Ní Neachtain (eds.), *An tSochtheangeolaíocht: Feidhm agus Tuairisc* [Sociolinguistics: function and account], 177–194. Dublin: Cois Life.
Walsh, John. 2012b. Language Policy and Language Governance: A Case-Study of Irish Language Legislation. *Language Policy* 11(4). 323–341.
Walsh, John. 2014a. Pushing an open door? Aspects of Language Policy at an Irish University. In Virve-Anneli Vihman & Kristiina Praakli (eds.), *Negotiating Linguistic Identity*, 301–325. Oxford: Peter Lang.
Walsh, John. 2014b. An ceart ag an gCoimisinéir. *Comhar* (January). 10–11.

Walsh, John. 2021. The Governance of Irish in the Neoliberal Age: The Retreat of the State Under the Guise of Partnership. In Huw Lewis & Wilson McLeod (eds.), *Language Revitalisation and Social Transformation*, 311–342. Basingstoke: Palgrave Macmillan.

Ward, Steven C. 2011. The machinations of managerialism: New public management and the diminishing power of professionals. *Journal of Cultural Economy* 4(2). 206–215.

Warren, Carol A. B. & Jennifer Kay Hackney. 2000 [1988]. *Gender Issues in Ethnography*, 2nd edn. London: SAGE.

Warren, Ron. 2005. Parental Mediation of Children's Television Viewing in Low-Income Families. *Journal of Communication* 55(4). 847–863.

Watson, Iarfhlaith. 2003. *Broadcasting in Irish: Minority Language, Radio, Television and Identity*. Dublin: Four Courts.

Watson, Iarfhlaith. 2016. The Irish Language and the Media. In Raymond Hickey (ed.), *Sociolinguistics in Ireland*, 60–80. Basingstoke: Palgrave Macmillan.

Weller, Patrick, Herman Bavis & R. A. W. Rhodes. 1997. *The Hollow Crown: Countervailing Trends in Core Executives*. Basingstoke: Macmillan.

Welsh Language Commissioner. 2020. *Annual Report 2018-19*. https://senedd.wales/laid%20documents/gen-ld12792/gen-ld12792%20-e.pdf (Accessed 10 August 2021)

Western Development Commission. 2018. *Travelling from the Western Region to work in Dublin: How has it changed and why?* https://www.wdc.ie/travelling-from-the-western-region-to-work-in-dublin-how-has-it-changed-and-why/ (Accessed 17 September 2021)

Whelan, Karl. 2013. Ireland's Economic Crisis: The Good, the Bad and the Ugly. *Journal of Macroeconomics* 39(Part B). 424–440.

Wightman, Andy. 2014. *Renewing Local Democracy in Scotland*. http://www.andywightman.com/docs/RenewingLocalDemocracy_final_v2.pdf (Accessed 9 May 2022)

Wilkinson, Richard & Kate Picket. 2010. *The Spirit Level: Why greater equality makes societies stronger*. New York: Bloomsbury Press.

Williams, Colin H. 1991. *Linguistic Minorities, Society and Territory*. Clevedon: Multilingual Matters.

Williams, Colin H. 2013. *Minority Language Promotion, Protection and Regulation: The Mask of Piety*. Basingstoke: Palgrave Macmillan.

Williams, Colin H. 2014. The Lightening Veil: Language Revitalization in Wales. *Review of Research in Education* 38(1). 242–272.

Williams, Glen & Delyth Morris. 2000. *Language Planning and Language Use: Welsh in a Global Age*. Cardiff: University of Wales Press.

Wilson, Gary N. 2011. Social change and language revitalization in the Isle of Man: A post-materialist perspective. *Language Documentation and Description* 9. 58–74.

Wolf, Nicholas M. 2014. *An Irish-speaking Island: State, Religion, Community and the Linguistic Landscape in Ireland, 1770-1870*. Madison: The University of Wisconsin Press.

World Bank. 2009. *Reshaping Economic Geography*. https://documents1.worldbank.org/curated/en/730971468139804495/pdf/437380REVISED01BLIC1097808213760720.pdf (Accessed 9 May 2022)

Wright, Sue. 1996. *Language and the State: Revitalization and Revival in Israel and Eire* [sic]. Clevedon: Multilingual Matters.

Wright, Sue. 2016. Language Choices: Political and Economic Factors in Three European States. In Victor Ginsburg & Shlomo Weber (eds.), *The Palgrave Handbook of Economics and Language*, 447–488. Basingstoke: Palgrave Macmillan.

Yates, Simeon & Eleanor Lockley. 2018. Social Media and Social Class. *American Behavioral Scientist* 62(9). 1291–1316.
Yates, Simeon, John Kirby & Eleanor Lockley. 2015. Digital Media Use: Differences and Inequalities in Relation to Class and Age. *Sociological Research Online* 20(4). 1–21.
Zuboff, Shoshana. 2019. *The Age of Surveillance Capitalism: The Fight for a Human Future at the New Frontier of Power*. London: Profile Books.

Index

20-Year Strategy for the Irish Language 2010–2030 32, 47–50, 72, 78, 91, 96, 183

Acadamh na hOllscolaíochta Gaeilge [division of the National University of Ireland, Galway] 8, 13, 56, 86–87, 181

bail out, of banks 39, 53, 109–110, 150
Basque 88, 231
Brexit 131, 161, 236
broadband see internet

Catalan 88, 142, 231
Catherine wheel model 84
Celtic Tiger, the
– demographic change during and after 118–122
– growth and decline of 38–40
– language policy during 30–33
census
– economic data 123–124
– Irish speakers 5, 11–12, 20, 22, 82, 120–122, 127
– population change 2006–2016 118–120
civic engagement 55–56, 183, 186, 196, 198, 200, 202
civil service see public service
class 21, 34–35, 57, 107, 110, 122–124, 139, 142, 178, 210, 228
climate change see ecological crisis
Coimisinéir Teanga, An [Language Commissioner, the] 31, 49, 53, 88, 95–106, 184, 187, 235
committee
– Culture, Welsh Language and Communications 88, 231, 234
– for implementation of the 20-Year Strategy 50, 104
– for Public Accounts 81
– language planning 50–60
– local democracy in county council 201
– on Communications, Climate Action and Environment 84

– on the Future Funding of Public Service Broadcasting 81
– on the Irish language, the Gaeltacht and the Islands 82, 89
community power debate 109
commuting 134, 144, 149, 206
competition state 38, 133, 194, 203, 228
Comprehensive Linguistic Study of the Use of Irish in the Gaeltacht 32, 47–48, 50–51, 54, 75–77, 111, 219
Conradh na Gaeilge [The Gaelic League] 20, 74, 91, 95, 179, 186
Cork 209
county council 24, 47, 67–68, 102, 190, 201, 230
Covid 40, 102, 110, 128, 131, 135, 155, 161, 163, 169–170, 210, 231–236

democratic confederalism 237
democratic deficit 51, 67–68, 71, 74, 109, 190, 202
demography 118–122
Department
– of Agriculture 59
– of Communications, Energy and Natural Resources 80
– of Education 28, 45, 62, 193
– of Finance 23, 25, 52, 70, 100
– of Public Expenditure and Reform 103
– of the Environment 101
– of the Taoiseach 49
Department responsible for the Gaeltacht
– affects of austerity on 45–46, 52, 56, 69–71, 164, 169
– and island transport links 189
– and publication of the Nuashonrú ar an Staidéar Cuimsitheach Teangeolaíoch 75–76
– and use of Irish in the public service 49, 104
– changes to department portfolio 30, 69
– establishment of 24
– suppressing dissent 180

ecological crisis 157, 236–237
education 5, 21, 23, 28, 51, 62–63, 126, 138, 150–152, 167–170, 193
educational inequality 123, 125, 130, 151
European Central Bank, the *see* Troika, the
European Commission, the *see* Troika, the
European Union (EU) 12, 32, 49, 102, 129, 156, 160, 179, 233
evidence-based policy making 48, 54, 77
exogamy 133, 153, 207, 212

Fianna Fáil 44, 98
Fine Gael 44, 51, 67, 98
Foreign Direct Investment 38, 66, 109, 133–140, 195

Gaeltacht *see* also class; Department responsible for
– Act 2012 50–60
– borders 24
– categories A, B, C 11
– Commission 1926 23
– Commission 2002 31
– numbers of Irish speakers in 120–122
– origin of concept 21
Gaeltarra Éireann 24, 27, 129, 144
gender 15, 81, 126–127, 168, 205–207
globalisation 9, 35, 40, 88, 129, 144, 147
grants *see* also Foreign Direct Investment; Scéim Labhairt na Gaeilge; training and scholarships, funding for
– and control of dissent 201
– Corporate "Social Responsibility" 193
– dependence of Irish on 108
– for housing 46
– for print media 89–93
– for students studying in the Gaeltacht 87
– from ÚnaG for local businesses 139
– proposed by Gaeltacht Commission 1926 22
– ÚnaG expenditure on capital 127

Hayek, Friedrich 33–34, 106–107
housing 22, 38, 46, 51, 102, 125, 150, 153, 156–157, 231, 235

incrementalism 29, 60
industrial action 38, 178
Industrial Development Agency (IDA) 63–64, 137
International Monetary Fund (IMF) 37, 39, 61, 102, 127, 224, 232, 235
internet 91–92, 127–130, 147, 208–213

Kerry 29, 80, 159, 173

language attitudes *see* language ideologies
Language Commissioner, the *see* Coimisinéir Teanga, An
language ideologies 110–112, 160, 186, 217, 219
language management 112
language planning process 51–53, 55–60, 67, 185, 195 *see* also Gaeltacht Act 2012
literacy rates in Irish 170, 209
local authority *see* county council

Meitheal Forbartha na Gaeltachta [the Gaeltacht development working group] 200
Misneach 92, 178, 187
mortgage repayments 150

National Development Plan 2018–2027 65, 77, 191
National University of Ireland 8, 21, 45, 56, 86, 103
new speakers 8, 156, 176, 217, 233
North of Ireland 4, 71, 91, 180, 184, 186

Ó Cadhain, Máirtín 122, 159
OECD 99, 102, 147, 178, 235
Official Languages Act 31–32, 56, 95–106, 183, 233

path dependence 44, 47, 109
pay differentials 80–81, 83, 230
post-materialism 55, 95, 110–112, 123, 142, 182, 186, 194, 218, 234
precarity 55, 57, 88, 95, 110–112, 122–124, 149, 206, 210, 218, 234

public service
- and implementation of language policies 49, 53, 106
- Public Service Reform Plan 67
- suppressing dissent 76
punctuated equilibrium 5, 29, 43, 71, 113

Randox 135
recommendation fatigue 77

satisficing 54
Scéim Labhairt na Gaeilge [the Irish-speaking scheme] 23, 46, 71, 75
schools 19–23, 26, 44, 47, 51, 62–63, 150–152, 154, 167–170, 193, 199–200, 211–212, 218, 225 *see also* education
Scotland 79, 123, 153, 156, 165, 198, 216, 229–231
second face of power, the 28, 68, 109
social Darwinism 111
social media 208–213

social partnership 38, 45, 177–178
strike *see* industrial action

trade unions 38, 45, 47, 66, 81, 129, 133, 137, 178, 181
training and scholarships, funding for 56, 64, 86–87
Troika, the 39, 43–44, 48, 52–54, 100, 108–110
trust, levels of 100, 110–111

unemployment blackspots 124
Universal Basic Income & Services 234
urbanisation 130–131, 147–148

voluntarism *see* civic engagement

Wales 86, 142, 155–156, 198, 229–231, 234
wealth distribution 33, 36–37, 110–111, 156
World Bank, the 25, 37, 127, 130

www.ingramcontent.com/pod-product-compliance
Lightning Source LLC
Chambersburg PA
CBHW071736150426
43191CB00010B/1595